# Programming 3D Applications with HTML5 and WebGL

*Tony Parisi*

Beijing · Cambridge · Farnham · Köln · Sebastopol · Tokyo

**Programming 3D Applications with HTML5 and WebGL**

by Tony Parisi

Printed in the United States of America.

Published by O'Reilly Media, Inc., 1005 Gravenstein Highway North, Sebastopol, CA 95472.

O'Reilly books may be purchased for educational, business, or sales promotional use. Online editions are also available for most titles (*http://my.safaribooksonline.com*). For more information, contact our corporate/institutional sales department: 800-998-9938 or *corporate@oreilly.com*.

| | |
|---|---|
| **Editors:** Mary Treseler and Brian Anderson | **Indexer:** Lucie Haskins |
| **Production Editor:** Kristen Brown | **Cover Designer:** Karen Montgomery |
| **Copyeditor:** Rachel Monaghan | **Interior Designer:** David Futato |
| **Proofreader:** Charles Roumeliotis | **Illustrator:** Rebecca Demarest |

February 2014:     First Edition

**Revision History for the First Edition:**

2014-02-07:   First release

See *http://oreilly.com/catalog/errata.csp?isbn=9781449362966* for release details.

Nutshell Handbook, the Nutshell Handbook logo, and the O'Reilly logo are registered trademarks of O'Reilly Media, Inc. *Programming 3D Applications with HTML5 and WebGL*, the image of a MacQueen's bustard, and related trade dress are trademarks of O'Reilly Media, Inc.

Many of the designations used by manufacturers and sellers to distinguish their products are claimed as trademarks. Where those designations appear in this book, and O'Reilly Media, Inc. was aware of a trademark claim, the designations have been printed in caps or initial caps.

ISBN: 978-1-449-36296-6

[LSI]

# Table of Contents

## Part II.   Application Development Techniques

# Preface

In its roughly twenty years of existence, 3D on the Web has taken a tortuous journey. In 1994 it was a Next Big Thing called *VRML* that grabbed industry attention, only to ultimately become a bastard stepchild of mainstream web development during the first Internet boom. Around 2000, a new Next Big Thing called *Shockwave 3D* promised to democratize game development; by 2004, that offspring was also shipped off to the orphanage. In 2007, the virtual world system *Second Life* leapfrogged the technology media establishment, landing on the cover of *BusinessWeek*, and a new 3D land grab ensued—literally, as folks rented *Second Life* islands in droves attempting to colonize a cyberspace that never quite materialized. By 2010, virtual worlds were yesterday's news, as consumers latched on to social and mobile gaming to sate their appetite for distraction. Viewed through one lens, this is a litany of failure. Viewed through another, it is a crucible.

Good ideas may take a long time, but they never truly die. 3D on the Web is one such notion. Once you look past the well-meaning but naïve overreaches of those early attempts, you can see what some of us (in all humility) have known all along: 3D is just another media type. Whether you use it to build a massively multiplayer online game, an interactive chemistry lesson, or any of countless other applications, 3D is just another way to get pixels moving on a screen at the behest of the user. Thankfully, the latest generations of browser makers get this, and have been slowly and steadfastly turning the web browser into a rich media development platform that includes first-rate, hardware-accelerated graphics and an integrated compositing architecture. Put in less flowery words: 3D is here; get used to it.

This book is intended to provide you with the information you need to create production-quality 3D applications for desktop and mobile browsers using graphics technologies available in modern browsers: WebGL, Canvas, and CSS3. It covers related topics such as JavaScript performance, mobile development, and high-performance web design; and it goes deep into tools and libraries that will help make you productive:

Three.js, Tween.js, new application frameworks, and the many options for 3D content creation.

Readers of my first book, *WebGL Up and Running*, will see a fair amount of overlap between that book and the early chapters of this one. This is unavoidable. Much of the material in the early chapters is overview and introductory; as such, it must stand on its own without requiring readers to get the earlier book. Regardless, despite the superficial similarities in the early chapters, readers of the first book will find much additional information. Even the introductory chapters here go far deeper into the material than the first book could afford, given its mission. And once we get past the initial three chapters, the material is almost completely different. *WebGL Up and Running* was intended to provide readers with an approachable introduction to a new and daunting subject. I like to think that what it lacked in technical rigor, it made up for in enthusiasm; if you came away from reading it with nothing other than an appetite to learn more, I consider my job well done. On the other hand, this book aims to give readers a thorough grounding in both theory and practice, allowing them to emerge from the experience ready to build production 3D applications.

## Audience

This book was written for experienced web developers looking to move into 3D development. It assumes that you are an intermediate-level developer with a solid grounding in HTML, CSS, and JavaScript, and at least working familiarity with jQuery. You do not need 3D graphics or animation experience, though it will be helpful. The book provides a basic 3D primer, and explains additional concepts as needed throughout.

## How This Book Is Organized

This book is divided into two parts:

Part I, Foundations, explores the underlying HTML5 APIs and technologies for developing 3D graphics in a browser, including WebGL, Canvas, and CSS3.

- Chapter 1 provides an introduction to 3D application development and 3D graphics core concepts.
- Chapters 2 through 5 dive into WebGL-based programming, covering the core API as well as two popular open source libraries used to develop graphics and animations: Three.js and Tween.js.
- Chapter 6 looks at the new features in CSS3 for creating 3D page effects and user interfaces.
- Chapter 7 describes the 2D Canvas API, and how it can be used to emulate 3D effects on resource-challenged platforms.

Part II, Application Development Techniques, goes hands-on into practical development topics, including the 3D content creation pipeline, programming using application frameworks, and deploying on HTML5 mobile platforms.

- Chapter 8 covers the content creation pipeline—tools and file formats used by artists to create 3D models and animations.
- Chapter 9 looks at using frameworks to accelerate 3D development and introduces Vizi, an open source framework for creating reusable 3D components.
- Chapters 10 and 11 dig into developing specific types of 3D applications: simple applications, oriented toward presenting a single interactive object with animations and interaction; and complex 3D environments with sophisticated navigation and multiple interacting objects.
- Chapter 12 explores issues related to programming 3D applications for the new generation of HTML5-enabled mobile devices and operating systems.

## Conventions Used in This Book

The following typographical conventions are used in this book:

*Italic*
>Indicates new terms, URLs, email addresses, filenames, and file extensions

`Constant width`
>Used for program listings, as well as within paragraphs to refer to program elements such as variable or function names, databases, data types, environment variables, statements, and keywords

**`Constant width bold`**
>Shows commands or other text that should be typed literally by the user

*`Constant width italic`*
>Shows text that should be replaced with user-supplied values or by values determined by context

 This element signifies a general note.

# This Book's Example Files

You can download all of the code examples for this book from GitHub at the following location:

*https://github.com/tparisi/Programming3DApplications*

Note that you must load most of the examples in this book from a web server rather than opening them from the desktop using *file://* URLs. This is because the JavaScript code loads additional content assets, such as image files in JPEG or PNG format; because of cross-origin security restrictions in WebGL's security model, those files must be delivered to the browser from a web server via HTTP.

I run a local version of a standard LAMP stack on my MacBook, but all you really need is the *A* part of LAMP—that is, a web server such as Apache. Or, if you have Python installed, another option is the SimpleHTTPServer module, which you can run by going to the root of the *examples* directory and typing:

```
python -m SimpleHTTPServer
```

and then pointing your web browser at *http://localhost:8000/*. There is a great tech tip on this feature at the *Linux Journal* website (*http://bit.ly/linuxjournal-http-python*).

In the example files you will find the completed versions of the applications built in the book, which will contain all the code required to run them. In a few cases you will need to download additional content files, such as 3D models, from their original sites before running the application; consult the *README* file in the top-level folder for details.

 Note that many of the content assets used in this book are subject to copyright. Their creators have kindly granted me permission to redistribute them for use with the book for the *sole* purpose of supporting the programming examples included. For any other purpose, including and especially use in your applications, you must obtain your own copies of those assets, which may include purchasing a license.

# Using Code Examples

This book is here to help you get your job done. In general, you may use the code in this book in your programs and documentation. You do not need to contact us for permission unless you're reproducing a significant portion of the code. For example, writing a program that uses several chunks of code from this book does not require permission. Selling or distributing a CD-ROM of examples from O'Reilly books does require permission. Answering a question by citing this book and quoting example code does not require permission. Incorporating a significant amount of example code from this book into your product's documentation does require permission.

We appreciate, but do not require, attribution. An attribution usually includes the title, author, publisher, and ISBN. For example: "*Programming 3D Applications with HTML and WebGL*, by Tony Parisi (O'Reilly). Copyright 2014 Tony Parisi, 978-1-449-36296-6."

If you feel your use of code examples falls outside fair use or the permission given here, feel free to contact us at *permissions@oreilly.com*.

## Safari® Books Online

 Safari Books Online (*http://my.safaribooksonline.com*) is an on-demand digital library that delivers expert content in both book and video form from the world's leading authors in technology and business. Technology professionals, software developers, web designers, and business and creative professionals use Safari Books Online as their primary resource for research, problem solving, learning, and certification training.

Safari Books Online offers a range of product mixes and pricing programs for organizations, government agencies, and individuals. Subscribers have access to thousands of books, training videos, and prepublication manuscripts in one fully searchable database from publishers like O'Reilly Media, Prentice Hall Professional, Addison-Wesley Professional, Microsoft Press, Sams, Que, Peachpit Press, Focal Press, Cisco Press, John Wiley & Sons, Syngress, Morgan Kaufmann, IBM Redbooks, Packt, Adobe Press, FT Press, Apress, Manning, New Riders, McGraw-Hill, Jones & Bartlett, Course Technology, and dozens more. For more information about Safari Books Online, please visit us online.

## How to Contact Us

Please address comments and questions concerning this book to the publisher:

O'Reilly Media, Inc.
1005 Gravenstein Highway North
Sebastopol, CA 95472
800-998-9938 (in the United States or Canada)
707-829-0515 (international or local)
707-829-0104 (fax)

We have a web page for this book, where we list errata, examples, and any additional information. You can access this page at:

*http://oreil.ly/program-3d-apps-html5-webGL*

To comment or ask technical questions about this book, send email to:

*bookquestions@oreilly.com*

For more information about our books, courses, conferences, and news, see our website at *http://www.oreilly.com*.

Find us on Facebook: *http://facebook.com/oreilly*

Follow us on Twitter: *http://twitter.com/oreillymedia*

Watch us on YouTube: *http://www.youtube.com/oreillymedia*

# Acknowledgments

This book is the result of a collaborative effort and would not exist without the help and support of many great people. First, I would like to thank the team at O'Reilly. My editor, Mary Treseler, is an amazing coach who helped me rise to meet the many challenges that come with a sophomore book effort. This book took almost a year to write—an eternity in Internet time—and as a result, I restructured the work several times as technologies evolved and audience needs changed. Mary was extremely patient and supportive throughout. Development editor Brian Anderson provided timely and useful feedback on chapter structure and flow, and editorial assistant Meghan Connolly displayed Herculean production skills in moving my raw Word files through O'Reilly's production pipeline.

I am grateful for the excellent technical reviews done by Ray Camden, Raffaele Cecco, Mike Korcynski, and Daniel Smith. Their detailed comments helped me clarify many concepts and strengthen the programming examples. Equally important, their overwhelmingly positive reactions to the book reinforced that I was on the right track with the material.

A lot of 3D content goes into crafting a graphically oriented programming book. My eternal gratitude goes to art director TC Chang for working so closely with me on the *Futurgo* concept car featured in Chapters 10 through 12. This is arguably the showpiece of the book, and it couldn't have come out better. I would also like to thank the artists who granted me permission to redistribute their work with the book samples. You can find detailed art credits in the *README* as well as the HTML and JavaScript files that go with each example. I would like to give special thanks to Christell Gause, head of support at TurboSquid, for his diligent efforts in helping me obtain permission from the TurboSquid artists whose content is featured here.

We are fortunate to have a strong community of 3D web developers pushing the envelope. I would like to thank the Three.js team, especially creator Ricardo Cabello ("Mr.doob"), for their pioneering work. Ken Russell and Brandon Jones of Google are among the folks building world-class WebGL implementations, but they are never too busy to answer questions, provide insights into why the API was designed in a certain way, and share thoughts on where the technology is going in the future. Outside of WebGL, there is a vibrant world of 3D in CSS and the 2D canvas. David DeSandro, Keith Clark, and Kevin Roast have done breakthrough development in these domains and kindly allowed me to reference their work. Also, I would be remiss if I didn't give a big shout-out to my friend Don Olmstead, whose design sessions with me a few years back resulted in what has ultimately become *Vizi*, my new framework for 3D development that is heavily featured in this book.

Finally, I would like to thank my family. They were patient beyond expectation as I wrote this book while working full time and juggling several other commitments. Marina and Lucian, I owe you a vacation—or three.

# Foundations

# CHAPTER 1

# Introduction

We live in a 3D world. People move, think, and experience in three dimensions.

Much of our media is also 3D—though it is usually presented on flat screens. Animated films are created from computer-generated 3D images. Online map services allow us to explore our destination, virtually, in a 3D environment. Most video games, whether running on dedicated consoles or mobile phones, are rendered in 3D. Even the news has gone 3D: the sight of a CNN analyst meandering through a virtual set, comically awkward a few years ago, has become an accepted part of the broadcast milieu as cable channels vie for increasing attention in a 24-hour news cycle.

3D graphics is nearly as old as the computer itself, tracing its roots back to the 1960s. It has been used in applications spanning engineering, education, training, architecture, finance, sales and marketing, gaming, and entertainment. Historically, 3D applications have relied on high-end computer systems and expensive software. But that has changed in the last decade. 3D processing hardware is now shipped in every computer and mobile device, with the consumer smartphone of today possessing more graphics power than the professional workstation of 15 years ago. More importantly, the software required to render 3D is now not only universally accessible, it's also free. It's called a web browser.

Figure 1-1 shows an excerpt from 100,000 Stars, a browser-based 3D flythrough simulation of our stellar neighbors in the Milky Way. Using the mouse, you can rotate about the galactic plane and zoom in on a star of interest. Stars are represented with renderings that approximate their apparent magnitude and color. Each star is labeled with its common name; when you mouse over the label, it highlights. Click on the label, and an overlay appears displaying the Wikipedia entry for that star. Click on a hyperlink in the overlay text, and the browser will launch that link in a new tab. 100,000 Stars is a stunningly produced interactive experience featuring beautiful renderings, pulsing animations, a majestic soundtrack, and an artfully integrated 2D user interface.

*Figure 1-1. The 100,000 Stars project by Google (http://workshop.chromeexperi ments.com/stars/); image courtesy Google, Inc.*

100,000 Stars was created as an experiment by Google's Data Arts team to demonstrate the rich capabilities of the Chrome browser. While the application is experimental, the technologies underlying it are not: it was built with HTML5 features available today in most browsers. The galaxy and stars are rendered in real time via WebGL, the new standard for hardware-accelerated 3D web graphics; the labels are placed relative to their stars through 3D transforms now available in CSS3; and the overlays blend seamlessly with the 3D content because browsers combine, or *composite*, all page elements into a unified presentation.

Just a few years ago, an experience like 100,000 Stars could only have been achieved in a native client application requiring a large download and installation, produced by developers using complex tools in a time-consuming and expensive development process. Today, it can be built with a browser, free and open source tools, and a standard web technology stack. What's more, you can instantly access updates by simply reloading the page, load information from anywhere on the Web via URL, and click hyperlinks from the 3D to access more information.

This book is about taking advantage of the awesome power of the modern browser to create a new breed of connected, visual application. Some of this breed will look a lot like its ancestors, essentially ports of traditional 3D products, refactored to reach new customers and reduce costs. But far more exciting are the possibilities for novel consumer applications in advertising, product marketing, customer support, education, training, tourism, gaming, and entertainment—to name a few. 3D brings a new dimension to the interactive experience; combined with web technology, the third dimension is now accessible to everyone on the planet.

100,000 Stars is a tour de force in interactive media development. Michael Chang, one of the creators, wrote a great case study of the project. To see what went into its development, go to *http:// www.html5rocks.com/en/tutorials/casestudies/100000stars/*.

# HTML5: A New Visual Medium

HTML has come a long way since the days of static pages, forms, and the Submit button. In the early 2000s, browsers introduced rich interaction by allowing portions of a page to be changed dynamically via Ajax techniques. Still, the ways in which pages could be changed with Ajax were constrained by the graphical features of HTML and CSS. If a developer wished to go beyond those limits, he had to use media plugins such as Flash and QuickTime.

This was pretty much the status quo during the 2000s, but things have changed over the last few years. Several browser advances under development during this period came together into HTML5. With HTML5, the web browser has become a platform capable of running sophisticated applications that rival native code in features and performance. HTML5 represents a massive overhaul to the HTML standard, including syntax clean-ups, new JavaScript language features and application programming interfaces (APIs), mobile capabilities, and breakthrough multimedia support. Central to the HTML5 platform is a set of advanced graphics technologies that are the focus of this book:

- **WebGL** for hardware-accelerated 3D rendering with JavaScript. Based on the time-tested graphics API OpenGL, WebGL is a standard supported by nearly all web browsers on the desktop as well as a growing number of mobile browsers.

- **CSS3 3D** transforms, transitions, and custom filters for advanced page effects. CSS has evolved over the past several years to include hardware-accelerated 3D rendering and animation features accessible through style sheet language.

- **The Canvas element** and its 2D drawing context API. Universally supported in browsers, this JavaScript API allows developers to draw arbitrary graphics to the surface of a DOM element. Though Canvas is a 2D API, with the help of additional JavaScript libraries it can be used to render 3D effects—providing an alternative for platforms where WebGL or CSS3 3D are not supported.

Each of these features has its strengths, weaknesses, and technical tradeoffs, and each has a role to play in delivering interactive and visually compelling 3D experiences. Which ones you use can depend on several factors—what you are trying to build, which platforms you have to support, performance concerns, and so on. Let's say, for example, that you are creating a first-person shooter game and you need the highest-quality graphics. This will be hard to pull off without using WebGL's extensive access to the rendering hardware. On the other hand, maybe you are developing a fancy channel tuner interface for a video website, including live video thumbnails, rotation effects on rollovers, and dissolve transitions between clips; in that case, CSS3 might have everything you need to deliver a killer experience.

 *And one standard to rule them all...*

What most web developers think of informally as HTML5 is actually a collection of technologies and standards. Some of these are already fully ratified by the World Wide Web Consortium (W3C) and implemented in all browsers. Others are less mature as standards, but nevertheless widely supported. Still others, such as WebGL, are mature and stable standards, but not controlled by the W3C.

## The Browser as Platform

HTML5 brings rich graphics to the Web; this would not amount to much without the presence of other essential browser improvements. In particular, a handful of advances have paved the way for true, rich Internet application development with HTML5:

*JavaScript Virtual Machine (VM) performance*
WebGL and Canvas 2D are JavaScript APIs; animation and interaction will run only as fast as the JavaScript code behind them. A few years ago, virtual machine performance would have made 3D development a nonstarter for practical use. Thankfully, today's VMs scream.

*Accelerated compositing*
The browser is responsible for combining, or compositing, the various elements on the page quickly and without unwanted visual artifacts. As content has become more dynamic, browsers have made huge improvements in compositing, including using the 3D hardware-rendering pipeline for all visual elements, both 2D and 3D.

*Animation support*
The function `requestAnimationFrame()` was introduced as an improvement to using `setInterval()` and `setTimeout()` to drive animations. This new method can greatly enhance performance and eliminate visual artifacts by allowing the developer to redraw the contents of canvas elements in the same pass that the browser redraws built-in page elements.

HTML5 browsers also include features for multithreaded programming (*Web Workers*), full-duplex TCP/IP networking (*WebSockets*), local data storage, and more that developers can use to deliver world-class application functionality. These features—taken together with WebGL, CSS3 3D, and the Canvas element—represent a revolutionary new *platform* for delivering connected visual applications on any computer or device.

Figure 1-2 shows a demonstration version of Epic Games' *Epic Citadel* running (as of this writing) in a development build of Firefox. *Epic Citadel* uses WebGL to render the graphics, but what really sets this work apart is the breakthrough in game engine performance. The game uses a version of Epic's *Unreal* engine that has been ported from its native C++/operating system–dependent code to a browser-based implementation, using the *Emscripten* compiler (*https://github.com/kripken/emscripten/wiki*) and asm.js, a new optimized low-level subset of JavaScript. By simply entering a URL, web browser users can access a beautifully rendered, full-screen console game experience running at 60 frames per second (fps), with very little download time and no installation required.

*Figure 1-2. Epic Citadel demonstration running in Firefox: 60 fps browser gaming powered by WebGL and asm.js (http://www.unrealengine.com/html5/); image courtesy Epic Games*

## Browser Realities

As of this writing, 3D feature coverage is not complete across the various browsers. Also, each browser supports a slightly different subset. We will explore these issues in detail in subsequent chapters, but here are the highlights:

- WebGL is supported in all desktop browsers. Microsoft introduced WebGL support in Internet Explorer version 11 in late 2013. While the implementation lags behind the other desktop browsers, Microsoft will likely catch up quickly.

- WebGL is supported in nearly all mobile browsers: mobile Chrome (Android), mobile Firefox (Android and Firefox OS), Amazon Silk (Kindle Fire HDX), Intel's new Tizen operating system, and BlackBerry 10. WebGL is supported in a limited fashion in mobile Safari (in the iAds framework only).

- CSS 3D transforms are supported in all browsers and mobile platforms. CSS Custom Filters are supported only experimentally in desktop Chrome, Safari, mobile Safari, and BlackBerry 10—not in IE or Firefox.

Clearly, this is not an optimal situation, but it's the sort of thing that comes with the web application development territory. Cross-browser support has always been notoriously difficult; with the explosion of features in HTML5 and the proliferation of devices and operating systems, it hasn't gotten any better. The only consolation is that the alternative is far worse: native applications are even harder to build, test, deploy, and port. Oh well… such is the life of a web developer in the 21st century.

 With all these standards, we should be approaching a state where we have to write our code only once. However, as we have become painfully aware, the mantra "write once—run anywhere" has been replaced by the lament "write once—debug everywhere."

# 3D Graphics Basics

This section provides a basic introduction to 3D graphics core concepts and terminology. Developers experienced with 2D Canvas drawing and animation may find some of the ideas new. If so, please take time to become familiar with them, as we will use them throughout the book. If you already have experience with 3D and/or OpenGL development, feel free to skip to the next chapter.

## What Is 3D?

Given that you picked up this book, chances are you have at least an informal idea about what I am talking about when I use the term *3D graphics*. But to make sure you are clear, we are going to get formal and examine a definition. Here is the Wikipedia entry (*http://en.wikipedia.org/wiki/3D_computer_graphics*):

> 3D computer graphics (in contrast to 2D computer graphics) are graphics that use a three-dimensional representation of geometric data (often Cartesian) that is stored in the computer for the purposes of performing calculations and rendering 2D images. Such images may be stored for viewing later or displayed in real-time.

Let's break this down into its components: 1) the data is represented in a 3D coordinate system; 2) it is ultimately drawn (*rendered*) as a 2D image (for example, on your computer monitor); and 3) it can be displayed in real time: when the 3D data changes as it is being animated or manipulated by the user, the rendered image is updated without a perceivable delay. This last part is key for creating interactive applications. In fact, it is so important that it has spawned a multibillion-dollar industry dedicated to specialized graphics hardware supporting real-time 3D rendering, with several companies you have probably heard of such as NVIDIA, ATI, and Qualcomm leading the charge.

As important as what this definition says is what it *doesn't* say: 3D graphics does not require special input hardware like trackballs and joysticks—though those can greatly enhance a 3D experience. Nor does it require custom display hardware: no stereo glasses required, no OmniMax theater tickets as the price of entry. 3D graphics are most commonly rendered on a flat, 2D display. This is not to say that 3D *can't* be displayed in stereo and seen with glasses or on a stereo TV—simply that it's not a requirement.

3D programming requires new skills and knowledge beyond that of the typical web developer. However, armed with a little starter knowledge and the right tools, we can get going fairly quickly. The remainder of this chapter is devoted to understanding basic 3D programming concepts that will be used throughout the book. It is by no means exhaustive—entire books are devoted to learning the subject in detail—but it should be enough to get started. If you already have experience with 3D programming, feel free to move on to Chapter 2.

## 3D Coordinate Systems

If you are familiar with 2D Cartesian coordinate systems such as the window coordinates of an HTML document, you know about $x$ and $y$ values. These 2D coordinates define where <div> tags are located on a page, or where the virtual pen or brush draws in the HTML Canvas element. Similarly, 3D drawing takes place (not surprisingly) in a 3D coordinate system, where the additional coordinate, $z$, describes depth (i.e., how far into or out of the screen an object is drawn). The coordinate systems we will work with in this book are arranged as depicted in Figure 1-3, with $x$ running horizontally (left to right), $y$ running vertically, and positive $z$ coming out of the screen. If you are already comfortable with the concept of the 2D coordinate system, the transition to a 3D coordinate system should be straightforward.

 Note that WebGL defines positive $y$ as going from the bottom to the top of the window, while the 2D Canvas API and CSS transforms define positive $y$ as going down. This is unfortunate, but it reflects the different heritages of the two technologies: WebGL is based on long-lived graphics standards that use the $y$-up convention, while Canvas and CSS are based on the HTML coordinate $y$-down convention—itself a descendant of time-worn, window-system coordinate schemes. If you end up working in both technologies on a project, you will have to keep this distinction straight. But it could be worse: $z$ could also be reversed! Fortunately, it's not.

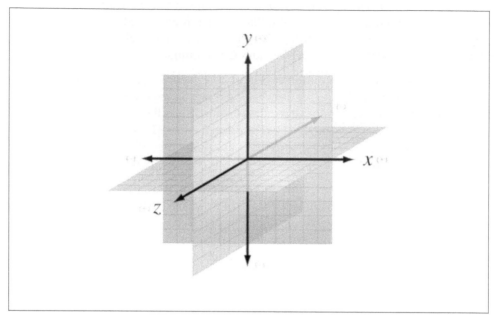

*Figure 1-3. A 3D coordinate system (http://bit.ly/wikimedia-3d-coordinate); Creative Commons Attribution-Share Alike 3.0 unported license*

## Meshes, Polygons, and Vertices

While there are several ways to draw 3D graphics, by far the most common is to use a *mesh*. A mesh is an object composed of one or more polygonal shapes, constructed out of *vertices* (*x*, *y*, *z* triples) defining coordinate positions in 3D space. The polygons most typically used in meshes are triangles (groups of three vertices) and quads (groups of four vertices). 3D meshes are often referred to as *models*.

Figure 1-4 illustrates a 3D mesh. The dark lines outline the quads that compose the mesh, defining the shape of the face. (You would not see these lines in the final rendered image; they are included for reference.) The *x*, *y*, and *z* components of the mesh's vertices define the shape *only*; surface properties of the mesh, such as the color and shading, are defined through additional attributes, as we will discuss shortly.

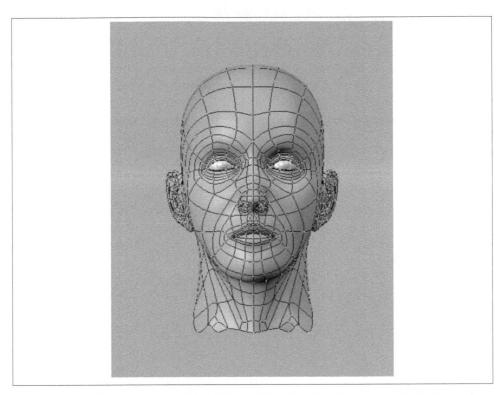

*Figure 1-4. A 3D mesh (http://bit.ly/1dnAjAG); Creative Commons Attribution-Share Alike 3.0 unported license*

## Materials, Textures, and Lights

You define the surface of a mesh using additional attributes beyond the $x$, $y$, and $z$ vertex positions. Surface attributes can be as simple as a single solid color, or they can be complex, comprising several pieces of information that define, for example, how light reflects off the object or how shiny the object looks. You can also represent surface information using one or more bitmaps, known as *texture maps* (or simply *textures*). Textures can define the literal surface look (such as an image printed on a T-shirt), or they can be combined with other textures to achieve sophisticated effects such as bumpiness or iridescence. In most graphics systems, the surface properties of a mesh are referred to collectively as *materials*. Materials typically rely on the presence of one or more *lights*, which (as you may have guessed) define how a scene is illuminated.

The head in Figure 1-4 has a material with a purple color and shading defined by a light source emanating from the left of the model. Note the shadows on the right side of the face.

## Transforms and Matrices

3D meshes are defined by the positions of their vertices. It would get really tedious to change a mesh's vertex positions every time you want to move it to a different part of the view, especially if the mesh were continually animating. For this reason, most 3D systems support *transforms*, operations that allow you to move the mesh by a relative amount without having to loop through every vertex, explicitly changing its position. Transforms allow you to scale, rotate, and translate (move) a rendered mesh without actually changing any values in its vertices.

Figure 1-5 depicts 3D transforms in action. In this scene we see three cubes. Each of these objects is a cube mesh that contains the same values for its vertices. To move, rotate, or scale the mesh, we do not modify the vertices; rather, we apply transforms. The red cube on the left has been translated 4 units to the left (−4 on the x-axis), and rotated about its x- and y-axes. (Note that rotation values are specified in *radians*—units that will be discussed in more detail in Chapter 4.) The blue cube on the right has been translated 4 units to the right, and scaled to be 1.5 times larger in all three dimensions. The green cube in the center has not been transformed.

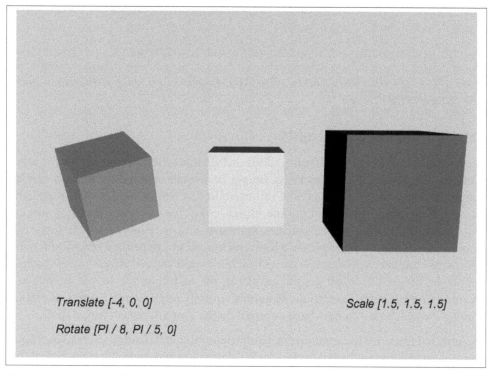

Translate [-4, 0, 0]

Rotate [PI / 8, PI / 5, 0]

Scale [1.5, 1.5, 1.5]

*Figure 1-5. 3D transforms: translation, rotation, and scale*

A 3D transform is typically represented by a *transformation matrix*, a mathematical entity containing an array of values used to compute the transformed positions of vertices. Most WebGL transforms use a *4×4 matrix*—that is, an array of 16 numbers organized into 4 rows and 4 columns. Figure 1-6 shows the layout of a 4×4 matrix. The translation is stored in elements m12, m13, and m14, corresponding to the x, y, and z translation values. x, y, and z scale values are stored in elements m0, m5, and m10 (known as the *diagonal* of the matrix). Rotation values are stored in the elements m1 and m2 (x-axis), m4 and m6 (y-axis), and m8 and m9 (z-axis). Multiplying a 3D vector by this matrix results in the transformed value.

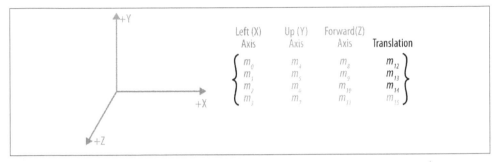

*Figure 1-6. A 4×4 transformation matrix (http://www.songho.ca/opengl/gl_trans form.html); adapted with permission*

If you are a linear algebra geek like I am, you probably feel comfortable with this idea. If not, please don't break into a cold sweat. The toolkits used to develop the examples in this book allow us to treat matrices like black boxes: we just say translate, rotate, or scale, and the right thing happens.

## Cameras, Perspective, Viewports, and Projections

Every rendered scene requires a point of view from which the user will be viewing it. 3D systems typically use a *camera*, an object that defines where (relative to the scene) the user is positioned and oriented, as well as other real-world camera properties such as the size of the *field of view*, which defines *perspective* (i.e., objects farther away appearing smaller). The camera's properties combine to deliver the final rendered image of a 3D scene into a 2D *viewport* defined by the window or canvas.

Cameras are almost always represented via a couple of matrices. The first matrix defines the position and orientation of the camera, much like the matrix used for transforms (as just discussed). The second matrix is a specialized one that represents the translation from the 3D coordinates of the camera into the 2D drawing space of the viewport. It is called the *projection matrix*. I know: more math. But the details of camera matrices are nicely hidden in most tools, so you usually can just point, shoot, and render.

Figure 1-7 depicts the core concepts of the camera, viewport, and projection. At the lower left we see an icon of an eye; this represents the location of the camera. The red vector pointing to the right (in this diagram, labeled as the x-axis) represents the direction in which the camera is pointing. The blue cubes are the objects in the 3D scene. The green and red rectangles are, respectively, the *near* and *far clipping planes*. These two planes define the boundaries of a subset of the 3D space, known as the *view volume* or *view frustum*. Only objects within the view volume are actually rendered to the screen. The near clipping plane is equivalent to the viewport, where we will see the final rendered image.

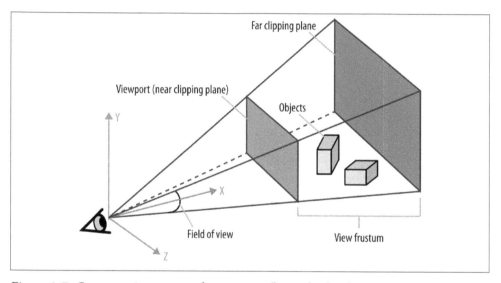

*Figure 1-7. Camera, viewport, and projection (http://bit.ly/obviam-perspective); adapted with permission*

Cameras are extremely powerful, as they ultimately define the viewer's relationship to a 3D scene and provide a sense of realism. They also provide another weapon in the animator's arsenal: by dynamically moving around the camera, you can create cinematic effects and control the narrative experience.

## Shaders

In order to render the final image for a mesh, a developer must define exactly how vertices, transforms, materials, lights, and the camera interact with one another to create that image. The developer does this using shaders. A *shader* (also known as a *programmable shader*) is a chunk of program code that implements algorithms to get the pixels for a mesh onto the screen. The graphics hardware understands vertices, textures, and little else; it has no concept of material, light, transform, or camera. Those high-level structures are interpreted by the shader program. Shaders are typically defined in a high-level C-like language and compiled into code that can be used by the graphics-processing unit (GPU).

 All modern computers and devices come equipped with a graphics-processing unit, a separate processor from the CPU that is dedicated to rendering 3D graphics. The majority of the 3D programming techniques discussed in this book assume the presence of a GPU.

Shaders put amazing power at the programmer's fingertips: full control over every pixel, each time the image is rendered. Shaders power the incredible visuals we see in Hollywood special effects, "CG" animated films, and real-time rendering in today's video games. With shader support now in web browsers, we can get the same production value as a top video game in our WebGL applications, as well as fine control over how CSS elements are presented and animated on a page.

Figure 1-8 shows a WebGL water simulation rendered by a programmable shader. The rippling water and dancing lights are incredibly realistic, and you can interact with the scene while it is simulating, all in real time. Reminder: this is running in a web browser!

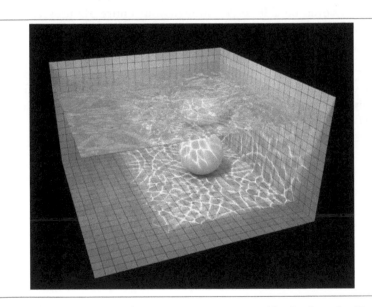

*Figure 1-8. WebGL water simulation using programmable shaders, by Evan Wallace (http://madebyevan.com/webgl-water/); reproduced with permission*

Shader-based effects aren't limited to WebGL; they can also be applied to DOM elements through an experimental technology called *CSS Custom Filters*. We will discuss this feature in Chapter 6.

Here are a few subtle things to note about shaders relative to the technologies we will cover in the book:

- WebGL and CSS Custom Filters both use shaders defined in the OpenGL ES Shader Language (called *GLSL ES*). There are some differences between the shaders you write for WebGL versus CSS, but the base languages are identical.

- WebGL *requires* the developer to supply shaders in order for objects to be drawn. If no shader is supplied, or there is an error in compiling or loading the shader, nothing will render on the screen.

- With CSS3 Filters, shaders are *optional*. When shaders are used with a CSS3 Filter, it is referred to as a *custom filter*.

- The 2D Canvas API *does not* support programmable shaders. If you plan to employ 2D Canvas drawing as a fallback to WebGL rendering, you will need to accommodate for this in your rendering code. More on this in Chapter 7.

Shaders represent a bit of a learning curve, with new concepts, another programming language, and great care required. If you find this daunting, don't worry. There are many popular open source libraries and tools to choose from that hide the gory details of shaders. You may even be able to get through your entire 3D programming career without ever writing a line of GLSL code—though I recommend you try it anyway, just to be able to say you did.

Those are the basics of 3D graphics. Each of the technologies in the book treats the details a little differently, but the concepts translate fairly well across each technology. In the next several chapters we are going to dive deep into the details of creating and animating 3D content with WebGL, CSS3, and Canvas 2D.

# CHAPTER 2

# WebGL: Real-Time 3D Rendering

WebGL is the standard 3D graphics API for the Web. It allows developers to harness the full power of the computer's 3D rendering hardware from within the browser using JavaScript. Before WebGL, developers had to rely on plugins or native applications and ask their users to download and install custom software in order to deliver a hardware-accelerated 3D experience.

While WebGL is not in the official HTML5 specification, it is shipped with most browsers that support HTML5. Like Web Workers, WebSockets, and other technologies outside the official W3C recommendations, WebGL comes with the package; the developers at Google, Apple, Mozilla, Microsoft, Amazon, Opera, Intel, and BlackBerry consider 3D an essential component for making the browser into a first-class application platform.

WebGL works on the majority of desktops, and almost all mobile browsers.[1] There are millions of WebGL-enabled seats already installed, most likely including the machines you run at home and in your office. There are numerous sites under development, with applications including games, data visualization, computer-aided design, 3D printing, and consumer retail.

WebGL is a low-level drawing API: you supply it with arrays of data and a shader, and tell it to draw. Anyone used to a graphics API like the 2D Canvas will find the lack of high-level constructs mystifying at first. However, there are several open source Java-Script toolkits that provider higher-level access to the API to make it look more like a traditional drawing library. Even with a toolkit, 3D is still hard work, but these tools at least make it approachable for folks with limited 3D development experience; and for experienced 3D developers, they are big time savers.

---

1. As of this writing, the sole holdout in supporting mobile WebGL is Mobile Safari on iOS. This is kind of a big deal; thankfully, there are adapter toolkits that allow us to create HTML5 and WebGL-based iOS native applications to work around the issue. This topic is covered in detail in Chapter 12.

In this chapter we will take a quick tour of the low-level underpinnings of WebGL to give you a foundation. For the majority of the book we will be using toolkit software that hides most of the API details. But it is important to know what these tools are built upon, so let's start by exploring WebGL's core concepts and API.

 As with many of the newer HTML5 features, WebGL may not be supported on your computer. WebGL is supported in all major desktop browsers, but for some browsers this is only in newer versions (such as version 11 of Internet Explorer). Also, there are certain older machine configurations that do not have the requisite graphics processor to perform hardware-accelerated 3D, and for those, the browsers "blacklist" WebGL (i.e., turn it off). If you want to get an idea if your target machines, devices, and/or browsers support WebGL, try the reference site *http://caniuse.com/* and type in the search term "WebGL," or hit the WebGL test directly via *http://caniuse.com/#search=WebGL*.

# WebGL Basics

WebGL grew out of experiments in 2006 by Mozilla engineer Vladimir Vukićević. Vukićević wanted to create a 3D drawing API for the Canvas element, to parallel the existing 2D Canvas API. He wisely based his design, called *Canvas 3D*, on OpenGL ES, the API standard that had been steadily gaining popularity for mobile graphics development. By 2007, there were independent implementations of Canvas 3D in both the Mozilla and Opera browsers.

In 2009, Vukićević was joined by participants from Opera, Apple, and Google to create the WebGL Working Group within the Khronos Group, the standards body that also governs OpenGL, COLLADA, and other specifications you may have heard of. Khronos continues to maintain the WebGL specification to this day. Vukićević served as the original chair of the working group, until 2010, when Kenneth Russell of Google assumed the role.

Here is the official description of WebGL, from the Khronos website:

> WebGL is a royalty-free, cross-platform API that brings OpenGL ES 2.0 to the web as a 3D drawing context within HTML, exposed as low-level Document Object Model interfaces. It uses the OpenGL shading language, GLSL ES, and can be cleanly combined with other web content that is layered on top or underneath the 3D content. It is ideally suited for dynamic 3D web applications in the JavaScript programming language, and will be fully integrated in leading web browsers.

This definition comprises several core ideas. Let's deconstruct them here.

- **WebGL is an API**. WebGL is accessed exclusively through a set of JavaScript programming interfaces; there are no accompanying tags like there are with HTML. 3D rendering in WebGL is analogous to 2D drawing using the Canvas element, in that it is all done through JavaScript API calls. In fact, access to WebGL is provided via the existing Canvas element and through a special drawing context specific to WebGL.

- **WebGL is based on OpenGL ES 2.0**. OpenGL ES is an adaptation of the long-established 3D rendering standard OpenGL. The *ES* stands for "embedded systems," meaning that it has been tailored for use in small computing devices, most notably phones and tablets. OpenGL ES is the API that powers 3D graphics for iPhone, iPad, Android phones, and Android tablets. WebGL's designers felt that basing the API on OpenGL ES's small footprint would make it easier to deliver a consistent, cross-platform, cross-browser 3D API for the Web.

- **WebGL combines with other web content**. WebGL layers on top of or underneath other page content. The 3D canvas can take up just a portion of the page, or the whole page. It can reside inside <div> tags that are *z*-ordered. This means that you develop your 3D graphics using WebGL, but you build all your other elements using familiar old HTML. The browser composites (combines) all of the graphics on the page into a seamless experience for the user.

- **WebGL is built for dynamic web applications**. WebGL has been designed with web delivery in mind. WebGL starts with OpenGL ES, but it has been adapted with specific features that integrate well with web browsers, work with the JavaScript language, and are friendly for web delivery.

- **WebGL is cross-platform**. WebGL is capable of running on any operating system, on devices ranging from phones and tablets to desktop computers.

- **WebGL is royalty-free**. Like all open web specifications, WebGL is free to use. Nobody will be asking you to pay royalties for the privilege.

The makers of Chrome, Firefox, Safari, and Opera have committed significant resources to developing and supporting WebGL, and engineers from these teams are also key members of the working group that develops the specification. The WebGL specification process is open to all Khronos members, and there are also mailing lists open to the public. See the Appendix for a list of mailing lists and other specification resources.

# The WebGL API

WebGL is based on the long-established graphics API known as OpenGL. Originally developed in the late 1980s, OpenGL has been an industry-standard API for a very long time, having endured competitive threats from Microsoft DirectX to emerge as the undisputed standard for programming 3D graphics.

But not all OpenGLs are the same. The characteristics of various platforms—including desktop computers, set-top televisions, smartphones, and tablets—are so divergent that different editions of OpenGL had to be developed. OpenGL ES is the version of OpenGL developed to run on small devices such as set-top TVs and smartphones. Perhaps unforeseen at the time of its development, it turns out the OpenGL ES forms the ideal core for WebGL. It is small and lean, which means that not only is it (relatively) straightforward to implement in a browser, but it also makes it much more likely that the developers of the different browsers implement it consistently, and that a WebGL application written for one browser will work identically in another browser.

The lean nature of WebGL puts the onus on application developers to do a lot of work. There is no DOM representation of the 3D scene; there are no natively supported 3D file formats for loading geometry and animations; and with the exception of a few low-level system events, there is no built-in event model to report the goings-on within the 3D canvas (e.g., no mouse-click events telling you what object was clicked on). To the average web developer, WebGL represents a steep learning curve full of truly alien concepts.

The good news here is that there are several open source code libraries out there that make WebGL development approachable. Think of them as existing at the level of jQuery or Prototype.js, though the analogy is rough at best. We will be talking about these libraries in the next few chapters. But right now, we are going to take a quick tour of the underpinnings, the drivetrain if you will, of WebGL. Even if you never write low-level WebGL for your projects, it's good to know what's happening under the hood.

# The Anatomy of a WebGL Application

At the end of the day, WebGL is just a drawing library—another kind of canvas, akin to the 2D Canvas supported in all HTML5 browsers. In fact, WebGL actually uses the HTML5 Canvas element to get 3D graphics into the browser page.

In order to render WebGL into a page, an application must, at a minimum, perform the following steps:

1. Create a Canvas element.
2. Obtain a drawing context for the canvas.
3. Initialize the viewport.

---

4. Create one or more buffers containing the data to be rendered (typically vertices).

5. Create one or more matrices to define the transformation from vertex buffers to screen space.

6. Create one or more shaders to implement the drawing algorithm.

7. Initialize the shaders with parameters.

8. Draw.

Let's look at a few examples to illustrate this flow.

## A Simple WebGL Example

To illustrate the basic workings of the WebGL API, we are going to write very simple code that draws a single white square on the canvas. See the file *Chapter 2/ example2-1.html* for a full code listing. The result is shown in Figure 2-1.

*Figure 2-1. A square drawn with WebGL*

The samples in this section are heavily inspired by the lessons at Learning WebGL (*http://www.learningwebgl.com/*), a wonderful site that was originally developed by Giles Thomas (*http://www.gilestho mas.com/*). Learning WebGL is a fantastic resource for getting to know the WebGL API through tutorials. The site also features a weekly roundup of new WebGL applications, so it is a good place to keep abreast of the latest developments.

## The Canvas Element and WebGL Drawing Context

All WebGL rendering takes place in a *context*, a browser DOM object that provides the complete WebGL API. This structure mirrors the 2D drawing context provided in the HTML5 Canvas element. To get WebGL into your web page, create a <canvas> tag somewhere on the page, get the DOM object associated with it (say, using docu ment.getElementById()), and then get a WebGL context for it.

Example 2-1 shows how to get the WebGL context from a canvas DOM element. The getContext() method can take one of the following context id strings: "2d" for a 2D Canvas context (covered in Chapter 7), "webgl" for a WebGL context, or "experimental-webgl" to get a WebGL context for earlier-version browsers. The "experimental-webgl" style is still supported in newer browsers, even if they also sup port "webgl", so we will use that to make sure we can get a context for all WebGL-capable browsers.

*Example 2-1. Obtaining a WebGL context from a canvas*

```
function initWebGL(canvas) {

    var gl = null;
    var msg = "Your browser does not support WebGL, " +
        "or it is not enabled by default.";
    try
    {
        gl = canvas.getContext("experimental-webgl");
    }
    catch (e)
    {
        msg = "Error creating WebGL Context!: " + e.toString();
    }

    if (!gl)
    {
        alert(msg);
        throw new Error(msg);
    }

    return gl;
}
```

Note the `try`/`catch` block in the example. This is very important, because some browsers still do not support WebGL, or even if they do, the user may not have the most recent version of that browser that includes WebGL support. Further, even browsers that do support WebGL may be running on old hardware, and may not be able to give you a valid WebGL rendering context. So, detection code like the preceding will help you with deploying a fallback such as a rendering based on a 2D canvas—or, at the very least, provide you with a graceful exit.

## The Viewport

Once you have obtained a valid WebGL drawing context from your canvas, you need to tell it the rectangular bounds of where to draw. In WebGL this is called a *viewport*. Setting the viewport in WebGL is simple; just call the context's `viewport()` method, as shown in Example 2-2.

*Example 2-2. Setting the WebGL viewport*

```
function initViewport(gl, canvas)
{
    gl.viewport(0, 0, canvas.width, canvas.height);
}
```

Recall that the `gl` object used here was created by our helper function `initWebGL()`. In this case we have initialized the WebGL viewport to take up the entire contents of the canvas's display area.

## Buffers, ArrayBuffer, and Typed Arrays

Now, we have a context ready for drawing. This is pretty much where the similarities to 2D Canvas end.

WebGL drawing is done with *primitives*—different types of objects to draw. WebGL primitive types include triangles, points, and lines. Triangles, the most commonly used primitive, are actually accessible in two different forms: as triangle sets (arrays of triangles) and triangle strips (described shortly). Primitives use arrays of data, called *buffers*, which define the positions of the vertices to be drawn.

Example 2-3 shows how to create the vertex buffer data for a unit (1×1) square. The results are returned in a JavaScript object containing the vertex buffer data, the size of a vertex structure (in this case, three floating-point numbers to store *x*, *y*, and *z*), the number of vertices to be drawn, and the type of primitive that will be used to draw the square—in this example, a triangle strip. A triangle strip is a rendering primitive that defines a sequence of triangles using the first three vertices for the first triangle, and each subsequent vertex in combination with the previous two for subsequent triangles.

*Example 2-3. Creating vertex buffer data*

```
// Create the vertex data for a square to be drawn
function createSquare(gl) {
    var vertexBuffer;
    vertexBuffer = gl.createBuffer();
    gl.bindBuffer(gl.ARRAY_BUFFER, vertexBuffer);
    var verts = [
        .5,  .5,  0.0,
       -.5,  .5,  0.0,
        .5, -.5,  0.0,
       -.5, -.5,  0.0
    ];
    gl.bufferData(gl.ARRAY_BUFFER, new Float32Array(verts), gl.STATIC_DRAW);
    var square = {buffer:vertexBuffer, vertSize:3, nVerts:4,
        primtype:gl.TRIANGLE_STRIP};
    return square;
}
```

Note the use of the type `Float32Array`. This is a new data type introduced into web browsers for use with WebGL. `Float32Array` is a type of *ArrayBuffer*, also known as a *typed array*. This is a JavaScript type that stores compact binary data. You can access typed arrays from JavaScript using the same syntax as ordinary arrays, but they are much faster and consume less memory. They are ideal for use with binary data where performance is critical. Typed arrays can be put to general use, but their introduction into web browsers was pioneered by the WebGL effort. The latest typed array specification can be found on the Khronos website (*http://www.khronos.org/registry/typedarray/specs/latest/*).

## Matrices

Before we can draw the square, we must create a couple of matrices. First, we need a matrix to define where the square is positioned in our 3D coordinate system, relative to the camera. This is known as a *ModelView matrix*, because it combines transformations of the model (3D mesh) and the camera. In our example, we are transforming the square by translating it along the negative z-axis (i.e., moving it away from the camera by −3.333 units). The second matrix we need is the *projection matrix*, which will be required by our shader to convert the 3D space coordinates of the model in camera space into 2D coordinates drawn in the space of the viewport. In this example, the projection matrix defines a 45-degree field-of-view perspective camera. (For a refresher on perspective projections, see the discussion in Chapter 1.)

In WebGL, matrices are represented simply as typed arrays of numbers; for example, a 4×4 matrix has a `Float32Array` of 16 elements. To help us with setting up and manipulating our matrices, we are using a great open source library called *glMatrix* (*https://github.com/toji/gl-matrix*), written by Brandon Jones, now an engineer at Google. The matrix setup code is shown in Example 2-4. *glMatrix* matrices are of type `mat4`, created via the factory function `mat4.create()`. The function `initMatrices()` creates the model view and projection matrices and stores them in the global variables `modelView Matrix` and `projectionMatrix`, respectively.

*Example 2-4. Setting up the projection and ModelView matrices*

```
var projectionMatrix, modelViewMatrix;

function initMatrices(canvas)
{
    // Create a model view matrix with camera at 0, 0, -3.333
    modelViewMatrix = mat4.create();
    mat4.translate(modelViewMatrix, modelViewMatrix, [0, 0, -3.333]);

    // Create a project matrix with 45 degree field of view
    projectionMatrix = mat4.create();
    mat4.perspective(projectionMatrix, Math.PI / 4,
        canvas.width / canvas.height, 1, 10000);
}
```

## The Shader

We are almost ready to draw our scene. There is one more important piece of setup: the shader. As described earlier, shaders are small programs written in GLSL (a high-level C-like language) that define how the pixels for 3D objects actually get drawn on the screen. WebGL requires the developer to supply a shader for each object that gets drawn. The shader can be used for multiple objects, so in practice it is often sufficient to supply one shader for the whole application, reusing it with different geometry and parameter values each time.

A shader is typically composed of two parts: the *vertex shader* and the *fragment shader* (also known as the *pixel shader*). The vertex shader is responsible for transforming the coordinates of the object into 2D display space; the fragment shader is responsible for generating the final color output of each pixel for the transformed vertices, based on inputs such as color, texture, lighting, and material values. In our simple example, the vertex shader combines the `vertexPos`, `modelViewMatrix`, and `projectionMa trix` values to create the final, transformed vertex for each input, and the fragment shader simply outputs a hardcoded white color.

In WebGL, shader setup requires a sequence of steps, including compiling the individual pieces from GLSL source code, then linking them together. Example 2-5 lists the shader code. Let's walk through it. First, we define a helper function, `createShader()`, that uses WebGL methods to compile the vertex and fragment shaders from source code.

*Example 2-5. The shader code*

```
function createShader(gl, str, type) {
var shader;
```

```
    if (type == "fragment") {
        shader = gl.createShader(gl.FRAGMENT_SHADER);
    } else if (type == "vertex") {
        shader = gl.createShader(gl.VERTEX_SHADER);
    } else {
        return null;
    }

    gl.shaderSource(shader, str);
    gl.compileShader(shader);

    if (!gl.getShaderParameter(shader, gl.COMPILE_STATUS)) {
        alert(gl.getShaderInfoLog(shader));
        return null;
    }

    return shader;
}
```

The GLSL source code is supplied as JavaScript strings that we define as the global variables `vertexShaderSource` and `fragmentShaderSource`:

```
var vertexShaderSource =
    "    attribute vec3 vertexPos;\n" +
    "    uniform mat4 modelViewMatrix;\n" +
    "    uniform mat4 projectionMatrix;\n" +
    "    void main(void) {\n" +
    "        // Return the transformed and projected vertex value\n" +
    "        gl_Position = projectionMatrix * modelViewMatrix * \n" +
    "            vec4(vertexPos, 1.0);\n" +
    "    }\n";

var fragmentShaderSource =
    "    void main(void) {\n" +
    "        // Return the pixel color: always output white\n" +
    "        gl_FragColor = vec4(1.0, 1.0, 1.0, 1.0);\n" +
    "}\n";
```

 The GLSL source code is supplied as JavaScript strings stored in global variables. This is a bit ugly, as we have to concatenate strings separated by newlines to construct the source. As an alternative, we could have defined the shader in external text files and loaded them via Ajax; or we could have created hidden DOM elements and tucked the source into their textContent. We did it this way for the example so that we could keep things simple for now. In your code you might consider using one of the other, more elegant schemes.

Once the parts of the shader have been compiled, we need to link them together into a working program using the WebGL methods gl.createProgram(), gl.attachShad er(), and gl.linkProgram(). Once linking is successful, we have to do one more thing before we are ready to use the shader program: obtain a handle to each of the variables defined in the GLSL shader code so that they can be initialized with values from the JavaScript code. We do this using the WebGL methods gl.getAttribLocation() and gl.getUniformLocation(). The initShader() function is defined in the following code:

```
var shaderProgram, shaderVertexPositionAttribute,
    shaderProjectionMatrixUniform,
    shaderModelViewMatrixUniform;

function initShader(gl) {

    // load and compile the fragment and vertex shader
    var fragmentShader = createShader(gl, fragmentShaderSource,
        "fragment");
    var vertexShader = createShader(gl, vertexShaderSource,
        "vertex");

    // link them together into a new program
    shaderProgram = gl.createProgram();
    gl.attachShader(shaderProgram, vertexShader);
    gl.attachShader(shaderProgram, fragmentShader);
    gl.linkProgram(shaderProgram);

    // get pointers to the shader params
    shaderVertexPositionAttribute =
        gl.getAttribLocation(shaderProgram, "vertexPos");
    gl.enableVertexAttribArray(shaderVertexPositionAttribute);

    shaderProjectionMatrixUniform =
        gl.getUniformLocation(shaderProgram, "projectionMatrix");
    shaderModelViewMatrixUniform =
        gl.getUniformLocation(shaderProgram, "modelViewMatrix");


    if (!gl.getProgramParameter(shaderProgram,
        gl.LINK_STATUS)) {
        alert("Could not initialise shaders");
    }
}
```

## Drawing Primitives

Now, we are ready to draw our square. Our context has been created; our viewport has been set; our vertex buffer, matrices, and shaders have been created and initialized. We define a function, draw(), which takes the WebGL context and our previously created square object. Let's walk through this function.

First, draw() clears the canvas with a black background color. The method gl.clear Color() sets the current clear color to black. This method takes a four-component RGBA (red, green, blue, alpha). Note that WebGL's RGBA values are floating-point numbers in the range 0.0 to 1.0 (in contrast to the integer range 0 to 255 used for web color values, e.g., in CSS). Then, gl.clear() uses the clear color to clear the WebGL *color buffer*; that is, the area in GPU memory used to render the bits on the screen. (WebGL uses several types of *buffers* for drawing, including the color buffer and a *depth buffer* for depth testing, which we will look at in the next section.)

Next, our draw() function sets (*binds*) the vertex buffer for the square to be drawn, sets (*uses*) the shader that will be executed to draw the primitive, and connects the vertex buffer and matrices to the shader as inputs. Finally, we call the WebGL drawArrays() method to draw the square. We simply tell it which type of primitive and how many vertices in the primitive; WebGL knows everything else already because we have previously set those other items (vertices, matrices, shaders) as state in the context. See the listing in Example 2-6.

*Example 2-6. The drawing code*

```
function draw(gl, obj) {

    // clear the background (with black)
    gl.clearColor(0.0, 0.0, 0.0, 1.0);
    gl.clear(gl.COLOR_BUFFER_BIT);

    // set the vertex buffer to be drawn
    gl.bindBuffer(gl.ARRAY_BUFFER, obj.buffer);

    // set the shader to use
    gl.useProgram(shaderProgram);

    // connect up the shader parameters: vertex position
    // and projection/model matrices
    gl.vertexAttribPointer(shaderVertexPositionAttribute,
        obj.vertSize, gl.FLOAT, false, 0, 0);
    gl.uniformMatrix4fv(shaderProjectionMatrixUniform, false,
        projectionMatrix);
    gl.uniformMatrix4fv(shaderModelViewMatrixUniform, false,
        modelViewMatrix);

    // draw the object
    gl.drawArrays(obj.primtype, 0, obj.nVerts);
}
```

And that—at long last—is it. The result is a white square drawn against a black background, depicted back in Figure 2-1.

# Creating 3D Geometry

The square was about as simple a WebGL example as we can contrive. Obviously, it's not very interesting—it's not even 3D—yet it clocks in at nearly 200 lines of code. The corresponding 2D Canvas drawing code would be around 30 lines at most. At this point it's clearly not a win over using other drawing APIs. But here is where it gets interesting. Now we are going to use WebGL to do true 3D drawing. We'll need a few extra lines of code to create the geometry for a 3D cube with multiple colors, and we will have to make a few small changes to the shader and the drawing function. We are also going to throw in a simple animation so that we can see the cube from all sides. Figure 2-2 shows a screenshot of the cube in mid-rotation.

*Figure 2-2. A multicolored cube*

To create and render the cube, we need to adapt the previous example in a few places. First, we must change the code that creates the buffers to create cube geometry instead of square geometry. We also need to change the drawing code to use a different WebGL drawing method. The *Chapter 2/example2-2.html* file contains the code.

Example 2-7 shows the buffer setup for our cube. It is a bit more involved than the code to draw a square, not only because there are more vertices, but because we also want to supply different colors for each face of the cube. We first create the vertex buffer data and store it our variable `vertexBuffer`.

*Example 2-7. Code to set up cube geometry, color, and index buffers*

```
// Create the vertex, color, and index data for a multicolored cube
function createCube(gl) {

    // Vertex Data
    var vertexBuffer;
    vertexBuffer = gl.createBuffer();
    gl.bindBuffer(gl.ARRAY_BUFFER, vertexBuffer);
    var verts = [
      // Front face
      -1.0, -1.0,  1.0,
       1.0, -1.0,  1.0,
       1.0,  1.0,  1.0,
      -1.0,  1.0,  1.0,

      // Back face
      -1.0, -1.0, -1.0,
      -1.0,  1.0, -1.0,
       1.0,  1.0, -1.0,
       1.0, -1.0, -1.0,

      // Top face
      -1.0,  1.0, -1.0,
      -1.0,  1.0,  1.0,
       1.0,  1.0,  1.0,
       1.0,  1.0, -1.0,

      // Bottom face
      -1.0, -1.0, -1.0,
       1.0, -1.0, -1.0,
       1.0, -1.0,  1.0,
      -1.0, -1.0,  1.0,

      // Right face
       1.0, -1.0, -1.0,
       1.0,  1.0, -1.0,
       1.0,  1.0,  1.0,
       1.0, -1.0,  1.0,

      // Left face
      -1.0, -1.0, -1.0,
      -1.0, -1.0,  1.0,
      -1.0,  1.0,  1.0,
      -1.0,  1.0, -1.0
      ];
    gl.bufferData(gl.ARRAY_BUFFER, new Float32Array(verts), gl.STATIC_DRAW);
```

Next, we create color data, one four-element color per vertex, and store it in `colorBuff`
`er`. The color values stored in the array `faceColors` are four-component RGBA.

```
// Color data
var colorBuffer = gl.createBuffer();
gl.bindBuffer(gl.ARRAY_BUFFER, colorBuffer);
var faceColors = [
    [1.0, 0.0, 0.0, 1.0], // Front face
    [0.0, 1.0, 0.0, 1.0], // Back face
    [0.0, 0.0, 1.0, 1.0], // Top face
    [1.0, 1.0, 0.0, 1.0], // Bottom face
    [1.0, 0.0, 1.0, 1.0], // Right face
    [0.0, 1.0, 1.0, 1.0]  // Left face
];
var vertexColors = [];
for (var i in faceColors) {
    var color = faceColors[i];
    for (var j=0; j < 4; j++) {
        vertexColors = vertexColors.concat(color);
    }
}
gl.bufferData(gl.ARRAY_BUFFER, new Float32Array(vertexColors),
    gl.STATIC_DRAW);
```

Finally, we create a new kind of buffer, called an *index buffer*, to hold a set of indices
into the vertex buffer data. We store this in the variable `cubeIndexBuffer`. We do this
because the drawing primitive we will use in our updated `draw()` function requires
indices into the set of vertices, instead of the vertices themselves, in order to define the
triangles. Why? Because 3D geometry often represents contiguous, closed regions where
vertex positions are shared among multiple triangles; indexed buffers allow the data to
be stored more compactly by avoiding repetition of data.

```
// Index data (defines the triangles to be drawn)
var cubeIndexBuffer = gl.createBuffer();
gl.bindBuffer(gl.ELEMENT_ARRAY_BUFFER, cubeIndexBuffer);
var cubeIndices = [
    0, 1, 2,     0, 2, 3,     // Front face
    4, 5, 6,     4, 6, 7,     // Back face
    8, 9, 10,    8, 10, 11,   // Top face
    12, 13, 14,  12, 14, 15,  // Bottom face
    16, 17, 18,  16, 18, 19,  // Right face
    20, 21, 22,  20, 22, 23   // Left face
];
gl.bufferData(gl.ELEMENT_ARRAY_BUFFER, new Uint16Array(cubeIndices),
    gl.STATIC_DRAW);

var cube = {buffer:vertexBuffer, colorBuffer:colorBuffer,
    indices:cubeIndexBuffer,
        vertSize:3, nVerts:24, colorSize:4, nColors: 24, nIndices:36,
        primtype:gl.TRIANGLES};
```

```
        return cube;
    }
```

In order for the cube colors to be drawn, they must be passed to the shader. Example 2-8 shows the updated shader code. Note the lines in boldface: we declare a new vertex attribute to represent the color. We also need to declare a GLSL `varying` variable, vColor, which is used to pass per-vertex color information from the vertex shader to the fragment shader. Unlike `uniform` types such as the matrices discussed earlier, which do not change values from vertex to vertex, `varying` types represent information for which the shader can output a different value for each vertex. In this case, we are going to pull the color input from the color buffer data stored in memory in the vertexColor attribute. The fragment shader uses vColor unchanged to output the final pixel color value.

*Example 2-8. Shader code to render the cube with colors*

```
var vertexShaderSource =

"    attribute vec3 vertexPos;\n" +
"    attribute vec4 vertexColor;\n" +
"    uniform mat4 modelViewMatrix;\n" +
"    uniform mat4 projectionMatrix;\n" +
"    varying vec4 vColor;\n" +
"    void main(void) {\n" +
"        // Return the transformed and projected vertex value\n" +
"        gl_Position = projectionMatrix * modelViewMatrix * \n" +
"            vec4(vertexPos, 1.0);\n" +
"        // Output the vertexColor in vColor\n" +
"        vColor = vertexColor;\n" +
"    }\n";

var fragmentShaderSource =
"    precision mediump float;\n" +
"    varying vec4 vColor;\n" +
"    void main(void) {\n" +
"        // Return the pixel color: always output white\n" +
"        gl_FragColor = vColor;\n" +
"}\n";
```

 This code may seem a bit complicated just to set a single color value. But a less trivial shader—such as one that implements a lighting model, or a shader that animates a procedural texture for grass, water, or other effects—would perform many additional calculations on vColor before outputting the final color. There's no doubt that shaders provide a lot of visual power, but with that great power comes—as Ben Parker famously observed—great responsibility.

Now for the drawing code, shown in Example 2-9. We have to do a few things differently for the more complex cube geometry. The lines in boldface show the changes. First, we make sure WebGL knows we are drawing depth-sorted 3D objects, by enabling depth testing. If we don't do this, there is no guarantee that WebGL will draw the faces we consider to be "in front" of other faces in such a way that they obscure the faces "in back." (To see what happens without depth testing enabled, comment out that line and have a look. You will still see some of the cube's faces, but not all of them.)

Next, we have to bind the color and index buffers created previously in the create Cube() function. Finally, we use the WebGL method gl.drawElements() instead of gl.drawArray(). gl.drawElements() draws a set of primitives using indexed buffer information.

*Example 2-9. Revised cube-drawing code*

```
function draw(gl, obj) {

    // clear the background (with black)
    gl.clearColor(0.0, 0.0, 0.0, 1.0);
    gl.enable(gl.DEPTH_TEST);
    gl.clear(gl.COLOR_BUFFER_BIT | gl.DEPTH_BUFFER_BIT);

    // set the shader to use
    gl.useProgram(shaderProgram);

     // connect up the shader parameters: vertex position,
     // color, and projection/model matrices
     // set up the buffers
    gl.bindBuffer(gl.ARRAY_BUFFER, obj.buffer);
    gl.vertexAttribPointer(shaderVertexPositionAttribute,
        obj.vertSize, gl.FLOAT, false, 0, 0);
    gl.bindBuffer(gl.ARRAY_BUFFER, obj.colorBuffer);
    gl.vertexAttribPointer(shaderVertexColorAttribute,
        obj.colorSize, gl.FLOAT, false, 0, 0);
    gl.bindBuffer(gl.ELEMENT_ARRAY_BUFFER, obj.indices);

    gl.uniformMatrix4fv(shaderProjectionMatrixUniform, false,
        projectionMatrix);
    gl.uniformMatrix4fv(shaderModelViewMatrixUniform, false,
        modelViewMatrix);

    // draw the object
    gl.drawElements(obj.primtype, obj.nIndices, gl.UNSIGNED_SHORT, 0);
}
```

# Adding Animation

If we want to see the cube as a 3D object instead of a static 2D drawing, we need to animate it. For now we will use a very simple animation technique to tumble the cube around one axis. The animation code is shown in Example 2-10. The function ani mate() rotates the cube around the previously defined rotationAxis over a period of five seconds.

animate() is called repeatedly by another function, run(), which drives continuous animation of the 3D scene using a new browser function called requestAnimation Frame(). This function asks the browser to call a callback function when it is time to redraw the contents of the page. (We will explore requestAnimationFrame() and various animation techniques in detail in later chapters.) Each time animate() is called, it stores the difference between the current time and the previous time it was called into the variable deltat, and uses that to derive an angle for rotating modelViewMatrix. The result is a full rotation around rotationAxis every five seconds.

*Example 2-10. Animating the cube*

```
var duration = 5000; // ms
var currentTime = Date.now();
function animate() {
    var now = Date.now();
    var deltat = now - currentTime;
    currentTime = now;
    var fract = deltat / duration;
    var angle = Math.PI * 2 * fract;
    mat4.rotate(modelViewMatrix, modelViewMatrix, angle, rotationAxis);
}

function run(gl, cube) {

    requestAnimationFrame(function() { run(gl, cube); });
    draw(gl, cube);
    animate();
}
```

## Using Texture Maps

The final WebGL API feature to explore in this chapter is texture mapping. *Texture maps*, or simply *textures*, are bitmap images displayed across the surface of geometry. You create image data for textures using the Image DOM element, which means that you can supply standard web image formats, such as JPEG and PNG, to WebGL as textures by simply setting the Image element's src property.

 WebGL textures don't need to be created from image files. You can also create them using 2D Canvas elements, allowing us to draw on the surface of an object using the 2D Canvas drawing API; they can even be created from Video elements, enabling video playback on the surface of an object. These dynamic texturing capabilities will be explored in Chapter 11.

We have adapted the previous rotating cube example to use a texture map instead of face colors. The texture-mapped cube is depicted in Figure 2-3.

*Figure 2-3. A texture-mapped cube*

I want to clarify one thing about this sample, in case you have been running it by opening the HTML file from your operating system's file explorer. This one needs to be loaded from a web server, because we are loading a texture map from a JPEG file, which, because of cross-origin security restrictions in WebGL's security model, requires web server operation rather than access via *file://* URLs. In general, most of the examples in this book must be loaded from a web server.

I run a local version of a standard LAMP stack on my MacBook, but all you really need is the *A* part of LAMP—that is, a web server such as Apache. Or if you have Python installed, another option is the SimpleHTTPServer module, which you can run by going to the root of the *examples* directory and typing:

```
python -m SimpleHTTPServer
```

and then pointing your web browser at *http://localhost:8000/*. There is a great tech tip on this feature at the *Linux Journal* website (*http://bit.ly/linuxjournal-http-python*).

The full code for this example is in the file *Chapter 2/example2-3.html*. Example 2-11 shows the code for loading the texture. First, we call gl.createTexture() to create a new WebGL texture object. Then we set the image property of the texture to a newly created Image object. Finally, we set the src property of the image to load a JPEG file—in this case, a 256-pixel square version of the official WebGL logo—but first we register an event handler for the image's onload event. We do that because we will need to do a few more things with the WebGL texture object once the image is loaded.

*Example 2-11. Creating a texture map from an image*

```
var okToRun = false;

function handleTextureLoaded(gl, texture) {
    gl.bindTexture(gl.TEXTURE_2D, texture);
    gl.pixelStorei(gl.UNPACK_FLIP_Y_WEBGL, true);
    gl.texImage2D(gl.TEXTURE_2D, 0, gl.RGBA, gl.RGBA, gl.UNSIGNED_BYTE,
        texture.image);
    gl.texParameteri(gl.TEXTURE_2D, gl.TEXTURE_MAG_FILTER, gl.NEAREST);
    gl.texParameteri(gl.TEXTURE_2D, gl.TEXTURE_MIN_FILTER, gl.NEAREST);
    gl.bindTexture(gl.TEXTURE_2D, null);
    okToRun = true;
}

var webGLTexture;

function initTexture(gl) {
    webGLTexture = gl.createTexture();
    webGLTexture.image = new Image();
    webGLTexture.image.onload = function () {
        handleTextureLoaded(gl, webGLTexture)
    }

    webGLTexture.image.src = "../images/webgl-logo-256.jpg";
}
```

In the callback, handleTextureLoaded(), we do several things. First, we tell WebGL which texture we are going to use for subsequent texture API calls, by calling gl.bind Texture(). All texture-related API calls will operate on this particular texture until we call gl.bindTexture() again—which we do, at the end of the function, setting it to null so that we don't accidentally change bits in the texture later on.

Next, we call gl.pixelStorei() to flip the *y* values of all of the pixels in the texture, because in WebGL, texture coordinates increase as *y* goes up the screen, whereas web image formats natively store pixel *y* values going downward.

The *i* in gl.pixelStorei() stands for *integer*. WebGL method names follow OpenGL naming conventions, which often include a letter suffix denoting the data type of the function's parameters. Image data is stored as an array of integer values (RGB or RGBA colors)—hence the *i*.

Now we are ready to copy the bits from the loaded image into the WebGL texture object. The texImage2D() method does this for us. This method's signature comes in a few variants; consult the WebGL specification for the different ways it can be used to create textures. In this case, we specify that we are creating a 2D texture at level zero—multiple levels can be created for a texture, for use with a technique known as *mip-mapping*, which we will cover later in the book—with an RGBA color format, and the source data as an array of unsigned bytes.

We also must set certain texture filter options, which are parameters that govern how WebGL computes the pixel colors in a texture map as the texture scales up or down in size when the image gets closer or farther away. In our example, we use the simplest and easiest-to-compute filtering option, gl.NEAREST, which essentially tells WebGL to compute the pixel color based on scaling the original image up or down. With this option, textures look fine as long as they are not scaled up or down too much, but look blocky and pixelated when too close (scaled up) and jaggy and aliased when too far away (scaled down). WebGL provides two other texture filtering possibilities: gl.LINEAR, which linearly interpolates pixels to provide a smoother look for textures that scale up, and gl.LINEAR_MIPMAP_NEAREST, which adds mip-map filtering for smoothing out far away textures.

To see the shortcomings of gl.NEAREST filtering, try playing with the location of the cube. Edit line 47 of the source file *Chapter 2/example2-3.html*, changing the *z* coordinate of the cube's position, –8, to make the cube appear either closer or farther away.

```
mat4.translate(modelViewMatrix, modelViewMatrix, [0, 0, -8]);
```

Try substituting –4 for –8. When the cube is closer, you can see how pixelated the texture becomes (Figure 2-4).

*Figure 2-4. gl.NEAREST filtering: textures are pixelated in close-up objects*

Now, try substituting −32 for −8. When the cube is farther away, you can see how jaggy (aliased) the pixels become on the texture (Figure 2-5).

Now that we have set our texture options, we null out the current texture using gl.bind Texture(). Finally, we set our okToRun global to true, which will tell the run() function that we now have a valid texture and therefore it is OK to call the drawing code.

As usual, we also have to adapt a few other sections of the code: the buffer creation, the shader, and the part of the drawing code that populates the shader values. First, we replace the code that created a buffer of color information with code that creates a buffer of *texture coordinates*. Texture coordinates are floating-point pairs defined at each vertex, with values typical ranging from 0 to 1. These values represent $x$, $y$ offsets into the bitmap image data; the shader will use these values to get pixel information from the bitmap, as we will see in the shader code momentarily. Texture coordinate values for our cube are pretty easy: each face uses the entire texture, so the values for any corner of the cube face are at a corner of the texture—for example, [0, 0], [0, 1], [1, 0], or [1, 1]. Note that the order of these values must correspond to the order of the vertices in the vertex buffer. Example 2-12 shows the code to create the texture coordinate buffer.

*Example 2-12. Buffer creation code for texture-mapped cube*

```
var texCoordBuffer = gl.createBuffer();
 gl.bindBuffer(gl.ARRAY_BUFFER, texCoordBuffer);
```

*Figure 2-5. gl.NEAREST filtering: textures are aliased in faraway objects*

```
var textureCoords = [
  // Front face
  0.0, 0.0,
  1.0, 0.0,
  1.0, 1.0,
  0.0, 1.0,

  // Back face
  1.0, 0.0,
  1.0, 1.0,
  0.0, 1.0,
  0.0, 0.0,

  // Top face
  0.0, 1.0,
  0.0, 0.0,
  1.0, 0.0,
  1.0, 1.0,

  // Bottom face
  1.0, 1.0,
  0.0, 1.0,
  0.0, 0.0,
  1.0, 0.0,
```

```
    // Right face
    1.0, 0.0,
    1.0, 1.0,
    0.0, 1.0,
    0.0, 0.0,

    // Left face
    0.0, 0.0,
    1.0, 0.0,
    1.0, 1.0,
    0.0, 1.0,
];
gl.bufferData(gl.ARRAY_BUFFER, new Float32Array(textureCoords),
    gl.STATIC_DRAW);
```

We must modify the shader code to use texture information instead of colors. The vertex shader defines a texCoord vertex attribute that is passed with the vertex data, and a varying output, vTexCoord, which will be sent to the fragment shader for each vertex. The fragment shader then uses this texture coordinate as an index into the texture map data, which is passed as a uniform to the fragment shader in the variable uSampler. We retrieve the pixel data from the texture using a GLSL function called texture2D(), which takes a sampler and a 2D vector *x*, *y* position. The updated shader code is shown in Example 2-13.

*Example 2-13. Shader code for texture-mapped cube*

```
var vertexShaderSource =

    "    attribute vec3 vertexPos;\n" +
    "    attribute vec2 texCoord;\n" +
    "    uniform mat4 modelViewMatrix;\n" +
    "    uniform mat4 projectionMatrix;\n" +
    "    varying vec2 vTexCoord;\n" +
    "    void main(void) {\n" +
    "        // Return the transformed and projected vertex value\n" +
    "        gl_Position = projectionMatrix * modelViewMatrix * \n" +
    "            vec4(vertexPos, 1.0);\n" +
    "        // Output the texture coordinate in vTexCoord\n" +
    "        vTexCoord = texCoord;\n" +
    "    }\n";

var fragmentShaderSource =
    "    precision mediump float;\n" +
    "    varying vec2 vTexCoord;\n" +
    "    uniform sampler2D uSampler;\n" +
    "    void main(void) {\n" +
    "    // Return the pixel color: always output white\n" +
    "        gl_FragColor = texture2D(uSampler, vec2(vTexCoord.s, vTexCoord.t));\n" +
    "}\n";
```

As our final step in getting textures onto our cube, we have to modify the drawing function a little. Example 2-14 shows the modified code. We replace the color buffer setup code with code that sets up the texture coordinate buffer. We also set the texture to be used and connect it to the shader inputs. (As with shaders and other state in the WebGL API, there is a notion of the current, or *active*, texture.) At long last, our cube is ready to draw with `gl.drawElements()`.

*Example 2-14. Setting up texture map data for drawing*

```
gl.vertexAttribPointer(shaderTexCoordAttribute, obj.texCoordSize, gl.FLOAT,
    false, 0, 0);
gl.bindBuffer(gl.ELEMENT_ARRAY_BUFFER, obj.indices);

gl.uniformMatrix4fv(shaderProjectionMatrixUniform, false, projectionMatrix);
gl.uniformMatrix4fv(shaderModelViewMatrixUniform, false, modelViewMatrix);

gl.activeTexture(gl.TEXTURE0);
gl.bindTexture(gl.TEXTURE_2D, webGLTexture);
gl.uniform1i(shaderSamplerUniform, 0);
```

# Chapter Summary

This chapter showed us how to use the WebGL API to render graphics. We went through the basics of setting up a WebGL application, including creating a context, viewports, buffers, matrices, shaders, and drawing primitives. We explored how to create 2D and 3D geometry and paint it with colors and bitmap textures. We even got a little help from the open source libraries *glMatrix* and *RequestAnimationFrame.js*, two staples of WebGL development.

It should be apparent by now that WebGL programming, at its lowest level, is a lot of work. We were able to get somewhat complex geometry with colors and textures moving around on the page; however, it took hundreds of lines of code. There is huge power in there—you can do practically anything you can imagine to every vertex and pixel on the screen, at blinding, hardware-accelerated speeds. But it requires heavy lifting. The designers of the standard made a conscious decision to trade size for power. The API is small and simple, at the cost of requiring a lot of coding on the application side.

If you're an experienced game or graphics programmer and you want to have fine control over the performance and feature set of your application, working directly with the WebGL API might be right for you. If you are building an application with very specific rendering requirements—say, an image-processing application or 3D modeling tool—staying close to the WebGL metal is probably your best option. You will still probably want to build some abstractions on top—nobody wants to write the same 40 lines of code over and over again to create a cube, for example—but that layer will be all your own and you will know and control every line of code.

However, if you are a mere mortal like most of us, you will want to work at a higher level than WebGL, hopefully by using tools that have already been developed. The good news is that several already exist: there are some great open source libraries built on top of WebGL. We will be exploring them in the next several chapters. Let's get to it.

# Three.js—A JavaScript 3D Engine

The previous chapter demonstrated both the power and complexity of programming in WebGL. WebGL allows access to the full capabilities of the GPU to create beautiful real-time 3D renderings and animations in web pages. But to do anything more than the most basic tasks using the API out of the box requires serious effort and literally hundreds of lines of code. This is not a recipe for rapidly building applications on web time. Depending on the kind of project you are contemplating, most developers are faced with a choice: build your own helper library to ease the pain, or use any one of several libraries already out there.

While there are many choices for getting started with your WebGL development, the undisputed leader in this category is Three.js (*http://threejs.org/*). Three.js provides an easy, intuitive set of objects that are commonly found in 3D graphics. It is fast, using many best-practice graphics engine techniques. It is powerful, with several built-in object types and handy utilities. It is open source, hosted on GitHub, and well maintained, with several authors contributing to it.

Three.js has become something of a de facto choice for WebGL development. Most of the great WebGL content you can view online has been built with it, including Google's 100,000 Stars (see Chapter 1), and several rich and highly innovative works live on the Web today.

## Three.js Flagship Projects

Perhaps the most well-known WebGL project to date is RO.ME "3 Dreams of Black" (*http://www.ro.me/*), an interactive piece created in 2011 by filmmaker Chris Milk with help from engineers at Google. The film is a companion to the song "Black" from ROME, a music project by Danger Mouse and Daniele Luppi, featuring Jack White and Norah Jones. See Figure 3-1.

RO.ME is a sweeping virtual world that allows the user to interactively control the camera, add items to the experience, and see items that other users have added. The project was developed with Three.js and features breakthrough WebGL effects for its time, including a depth-of-field shader that makes close objects appear crisp and far away objects blurry; a cel ("toon") shader to create a cel-animation-style look; flocking behaviors; and rendering of geometry using point clouds. For more on the technology behind RO.ME, see the team's project page (*http://www.ro.me/tech/*).

*Figure 3-1. RO.ME "3 Dreams of Black," an interactive video experience inspired by the song "Black" from the album ROME (http://www.ro.me/)*

Moving from the cinematic to the prosaic, we see a completely different but equally important use of WebGL built with Three.js: product visualization. The award-winning car configurator demo shown in Figure 3-2, created by the German team Plus 360 Degrees, allows the user to interactively rotate the scene, select from a set of highly detailed car models, and change the paint colors and the tires to create a customized car. Car configurator applications like this have been around for years, even running in web browsers using Flash; however, the production value of this demonstration is far above anything seen in the past on the Web. The high polygon count for the car detail, the environment maps to simulate reflection, and the use of lighting and shadows all contribute to a very realistic look, and as a result, a truly compelling interactive application.

As good as Three.js may be for rendering *real* things, it can also be used to display the completely abstract. Figure 3-3 shows an incredible example of this, a visualization of the global small-arms trade created as a Google Experiment. Small Arms Imports/Exports shows over 1 million data points of individual exports and imports to map the transfer of small arms, light weapons, and ammunition across 250 states and territories across the world between 1992 and 2010, using colors, lines, and glow effects mapped onto a virtual globe. The net effect is informative and visually stunning.

*Figure 3-2. A car configurator and visualizer, by Plus 360 Degrees (http://carvisualiz er.plus360degrees.com/threejs/)*

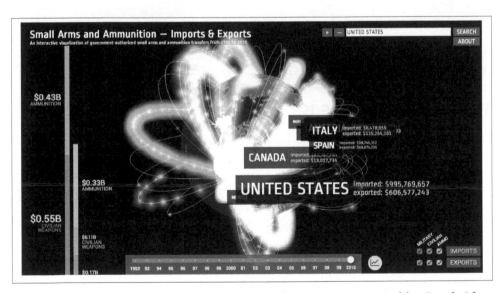

*Figure 3-3. Small Arms Imports/Exports, a Google Experiment created by Google Ideas (http://www.chromeexperiments.com/detail/arms-globe/)*

Three.js isn't a game engine in the traditional sense (more on this later); however, it can be used as a foundation upon which to build a game engine and decent games. In a tribute to the original *Wipeout* and *F-Zero* game series, Thibaut Despoulain created *HexGL*, a futuristic space racing game. *HexGL* features high production values that include glow effects, particle systems, realistic rendering of the buildings and ships, visual post-processing to create the hex lens effect, and a beautifully integrated heads-up display. *HexGL* is depicted in Figure 3-4.

*Figure 3-4. HexGL, a futuristic, fast-paced racing game built by Thibaut Despoulain using HTML5, JavaScript, and WebGL (http://hexgl.bkcore.com/)*

# An Overview of Three.js

Three.js was created by Barcelona-based Ricardo Cabello Miguel, more famously known as *Mr.doob* (I have never dared to ask why). Three.js grew out of Mr.doob's early participation developing 3D presentations for *demoparties*—today we would call them *hackathons*—nearly a decade ago. After being frustrated with the available tools and engines, Mr.doob began building his own, originally in ActionScript for Adobe Flash. When Google Chrome, fast JavaScript, and HTML5 hit the scene a few years later, Mr.doob applied his learning to this new platform, and in 2010 Three.js was born. The first version rendered to SVG and Canvas. A few short months later, when WebGL was released, Three.js was ported to use it—a feat Mr.doob characterizes as "easy to implement," presumably because he had already built two other renderers with it. Since that time, Three.js has grown in power and sophistication, and has become the most popular choice for building 3D applications in WebGL.

I chose Three.js as the basis for the examples in this book for reasons other than its popularity—though I admit that did play a part. First, I use it for my own development projects and really like it. Second, I believe it is the most complete WebGL library from a features standpoint. Third, I like the fact that it has several core contributors maintaining the code base in the context of creating real-world projects. Finally, it is easy to get started with; in fact, ease of use may be its single biggest selling point. That said, remember that Three.js is just one of many choices, including rolling your own if your project (or temperament) requires it. Throughout the book you will get to know Three.js in detail. For now, here is a summary of what it has to offer.

- **Three.js hides the low-level details of WebGL rendering**. Three.js abstracts out the details of the WebGL API, representing the 3D scene as meshes, materials, and lights (i.e., the object types graphics programmers typically work with).

- **Three.js is powerful**. More than just a wrapper around WebGL, Three.js contains many prebuilt objects useful for developing games, animations, presentations, data visualization, modeling applications, and post-processing special effects. In addition to the capabilities of the core package, there are numerous samples and extras that you can use in your projects.

- **Three.js is easy to use**. The Three.js API has been designed to be friendly and easy to learn. The library comes with many examples that you can use as a starting point.

- **Three.js is fast**. Three.js employs 3D graphics best practices to maintain high performance without sacrificing usability.

- **Three.js is robust**. There are extensive error checks, exceptions, and console warnings to keep the developer informed and out of trouble.

- **Three.js supports interaction**. WebGL provides no native support for *picking*—that is, knowing when the mouse pointer is over an object. Three.js helps with picking, making it easy to add interactivity to your applications.

- **Three.js does the math**. Three.js has powerful, easy-to-use objects for 3D math, such as matrices, projections, and vectors.

- **Three.js has built-in file format support**. You can load files in text formats exported by popular 3D modeling packages; there are also Three.js-specific JSON and binary formats.

- **Three.js is object-oriented**. Programmers work with first-class JavaScript objects instead of just making JavaScript function calls.

- **Three.js is extensible**. It is fairly easy to add features and customize Three.js. If you don't see a data type you need, write it and plug it in.

- **Three.js also renders to 2D Canvas, SVG, and CSS**. As popular as WebGL has become, it is still not running everywhere, or it may not be the best choice for some applications. The good news is that Three.js can also render most content into a 2D Canvas or a SVG element. This can be particularly helpful should the 3D Canvas context not be available, allowing your code to gracefully fall back to another solution. Three.js can also be used to render and transform CSS elements, as we will see in Chapter 6.

It is important to note a few things Three.js *doesn't* do. Three.js is not a game engine. It lacks some of the commonly used features you would find in game engines, such as billboards, avatars, finite state machines, and physics. Nor does Three.js have the built-in network support you would expect if you were writing a multiplayer game. If you need this functionality, you will have to build it yourself on top of Three.js or integrate other special-purpose libraries. Three.js is also not an application framework: it does not supply commonly required features such as setup, teardown, event handling, and the run loop. In later chapters we will see how you can use frameworks to save time and avoid implementing those ideas over and over again for each project. Finally, Three.js is not a development environment. You won't find an integrated set of tools for building your 3D applications end to end.

That said, for all the things Three.js is not, we can appreciate it for what it is: a high-performance, full-featured, easy-to-use 3D rendering engine for web browsers. That's huge. Let's have a look.

## Setting Up Three.js

To develop with Three.js, first you need to get the latest package from GitHub. As of this writing, the Three.js repository URL is *https://github.com/mrdoob/three.js/*. Once you have cloned the Git repository, you will want to use the nonminified version of the JavaScript located in *build/three.js*. (There is also a minified version of the library located in *build/three.min.js* that you can use when deploying finished projects; however, I suggest using the nonminified version while working with the samples in the book to make debugging easier.) Hang on to the full source located under the *src* folder, too. The API documentation is linked from the GitHub page, but it is pretty basic, so you will want to have the source handy for reference.

 The version of Three.js used for this book is revision 58 (r58). Mr.doob and company have a habit of changing versions fairly often, so if you are working with the book samples here but have downloaded the latest Three.js, you may find some inconsistency. All of the samples for the book are self-contained, with a copy of r58 stored in the folder *libs/three.js.r58/*.

## Three.js Project Structure

Take a little time with the source tree, documentation, and examples in order to familiarize yourself with Three.js. There is a lot going on in there. You are probably getting anxious to start writing code, but do yourself a favor and look it over; if nothing else, make sure to peruse the *examples* folder. You won't be sorry.

Here is a quick look at the main folders of interest in the project.

*build/*

> The output directory for the minified and nonminified builds of Three.js. Three.js is built with the Google Closure compiler: one build output file contains the entire Three.js library compiled from several separate source files. If you are not familiar with Closure and want to know more, go to *http://code.google.com/closure/compiler/*. Note that there is no need to rebuild Three.js from source, so if you don't want to deal with this, you can ignore the build process and just use *three.js* or *three.min.js* as is.

*docs/*

> This folder contains a full set of API documentation in HTML. It is sparse on details, but at least it provides a nicely laid out overview for getting acquainted with the library.

*editor/*

> The Three.js team has begun developing an editing system for creating 3D scenes. As of this writing, it is still very much a work in progress and not particularly useful for production. But you have to give Mr.doob credit: there is nothing he won't try taking his hand to, given a web browser and a text editor!

*examples/*

> This folder contains literally hundreds of samples covering a range of features and effects, rendered via various methods including Canvas, CSS, and WebGL. Some of these examples are simple "tech demos" that show off a particular feature; others are mind-blowing art pieces that combine several features to create something unique and beautiful. Take your time going through each and every one, and have a look at the source. This will be your best way to get familiar with the vast capabilities the come with Three.js.

*src/*

> The source files for the library. This is a rather complex tree roughly organized into two parts: *core* and *extras*. *core* comprises the main feature set. Think of it as the *minimum viable product* for Three.js; without it you wouldn't be able to use Three.js to render scenes. *extras* contains a host of useful features, including built-in geometric shapes such as cubes, spheres, and cylinders; animation utilities; and image loading classes. You can build all of these yourself on top of Three.js, but you may not want to. In any case, even though they are organized under *extras*, these classes are all included in the build.

*utils/*

This folder contains various tools, including Google Closure scripts to compile the minified and nonminified build, file converters from various 3D formats to the Three.js JSON and binary file formats (more on these later), and file exporters from popular modeling packages such as Blender and Maya.

# A Simple Three.js Program

Now that you know your way around Three.js, it's time to write a program. Our first example should make it abundantly clear how much value this library provides over developing to the bare-bones WebGL API.

Recall the texture-mapped cube from the previous chapter; here it is again, this time written with Three.js. The Three.js code is shown in Example 3-1, with a full listing in the file *Chapter 3/threejscube.html*.

*Example 3-1. Creating a texture-mapped cube with Three.js*

```
<script type="text/javascript">

    var renderer = null,
    scene = null,
    camera = null,
    cube = null;

    var duration = 5000; // ms
    var currentTime = Date.now();
    function animate() {

        var now = Date.now();
        var deltat = now - currentTime;
        currentTime = now;
        var fract = deltat / duration;
        var angle = Math.PI * 2 * fract;
        cube.rotation.y += angle;
    }

    function run() {
        requestAnimationFrame(function() { run(); });

            // Render the scene
            renderer.render( scene, camera );

            // Spin the cube for next frame
            animate();

    }

    $(document).ready(
            function() {
```

```
var canvas = document.getElementById("webglcanvas");

// Create the Three.js renderer and attach it to our canvas
renderer = new THREE.WebGLRenderer(
  { canvas: canvas, antialias: true } );

// Set the viewport size
renderer.setSize(canvas.width, canvas.height);

// Create a new Three.js scene
scene = new THREE.Scene();

// Add  a camera so we can view the scene
camera = new THREE.PerspectiveCamera( 45,
  canvas.width / canvas.height, 1, 4000 );
scene.add(camera);

// Create a texture-mapped cube and add it to the scene
// First, create the texture map
var mapUrl = "../images/webgl-logo-256.jpg";
var map = THREE.ImageUtils.loadTexture(mapUrl);

// Now, create a Basic material; pass in the map
var material = new THREE.MeshBasicMaterial({ map: map });

// Create the cube geometry
var geometry = new THREE.CubeGeometry(2, 2, 2);

// And put the geometry and material together into a mesh
cube = new THREE.Mesh(geometry, material);

// Move the mesh back from the camera and tilt it toward
// the viewer
cube.position.z = -8;
cube.rotation.x = Math.PI / 5;
cube.rotation.y = Math.PI / 5;

// Finally, add the mesh to our scene
scene.add( cube );

// Run the run loop
run();
      }
  );

</script>
```

The animation and run loop functions are similar to those in Chapter 2, with a few small changes that I'll explain in a bit. But what is significant about this version is the code to create the cube scene: what took us nearly 300 lines of WebGL code using the raw API now requires only 40 lines using Three.js. Our jQuery `ready()` callback fits on one page. Now that's more like it. Admittedly, this is a trivially simple example, but we can at least begin to imagine how to create a full-scale application like those surveyed at the beginning of this chapter. Let's take a look at this example in detail.

## Creating the Renderer

First, we need to create the renderer. Three.js uses a plug-in rendering system. We can render the same scene using different drawing APIs—for example, either WebGL or the 2D Canvas API. Here we create a new `THREE.WebGLRenderer` object with two initialization parameters: `canvas`, which is literally the `<canvas>` element we created in the HTML file, and the `antialias` flag, which tells Three.js to use hardware-based multisample *antialiasing* (MSAA). Antialiasing avoids nasty artifacts that would make some drawn edges look jagged. Three.js uses these parameters to create a WebGL drawing context attached to its renderer object.

After we create the renderer, we initialize its size to be the entire width and height of the canvas. This is equivalent to calling `gl.viewport()` to set the viewport size as we did in Chapter 2. The entirety of the renderer setup takes place in just two lines of code:

```
// Create the Three.js renderer and attach it to our canvas
renderer = new THREE.WebGLRenderer(
  { canvas: canvas, antialias: true } );

// Set the viewport size
renderer.setSize(canvas.width, canvas.height);
```

## Creating the Scene

Next, we create a *scene* by creating a new `THREE.Scene` object. The scene is the top-level object in the Three.js graphics hierarchy. It contains all other graphical objects. (In Three.js, objects exist in a parent-child hierarchy. More on this shortly.)

Once we have a scene, we are going to add a couple of objects to it: a *camera* and a *mesh*. The camera defines where we are viewing the scene from: in this example we will keep the camera at its default position, the origin. Our camera is of type `THREE.PerspectiveCamera`, which we initialize with a 45-degree field of view, the viewport dimensions, and front and back clipping plane values. Under the covers, Three.js will use these values to create a perspective projection matrix used to render the 3D scene to the 2D drawing surface. (Refer to the 3D graphics primer in Chapter 1 if you need a refresher on cameras, viewports, and projections.)

The code to create the scene and add the camera is quite concise:

```
// Create a new Three.js scene
scene = new THREE.Scene();
```

```
// Add  a camera so we can view the scene
camera = new THREE.PerspectiveCamera( 45,
  canvas.width / canvas.height, 1, 4000 );
scene.add(camera);
```

Now it's time to add the mesh to the scene. In Three.js, a mesh comprises a geometry object and a *material*. For geometry we are using a 2×2×2 cube we created using the built-in Three.js object CubeGeometry. The material tells Three.js how to paint the surface of the object. In this example our material is of type MeshBasicMaterial—that is, just a simple material with no lighting effects. We do, however, want to put the WebGL logo on the cube as a *texture map*. Texture maps, also known as *textures*, are bitmaps used to represent surface attributes of 3D meshes. They can be used in simple ways to define just the color of a surface, or they can be combined to create complex effects such as bumps or highlights.

WebGL provides several API calls for working with textures, and the standard provides important security features, such as limiting cross-domain texture use. Happily, Three.js gives us a simple API for loading textures and associating them with materials without too much fuss. We call THREE.ImageUtils.loadTexture() to load the texture from an image file, and then associate the resulting texture with our material by setting the map parameter of the material's constructor:

```
// Create a texture-mapped cube and add it to the scene
// First, create the texture map
var mapUrl = "../images/webgl-logo-256.jpg";
var map = THREE.ImageUtils.loadTexture(mapUrl);

// Now, create a Basic material; pass in the map
var material = new THREE.MeshBasicMaterial({ map: map });
```

Three.js is doing a lot of work under the covers here. It maps the bits of the JPEG image onto the correct parts of each cube face; the image isn't stretched around the cube or upside-down or backward on any of the faces. This might not seem like a big deal, but as we saw in the previous chapter, it is. Using WebGL by itself, we have a lot of details to get right; using Three.js, we need only a few lines of code.

Finally, we create the cube mesh. We have constructed the geometry, the material, and the texture; now we put them all together into a THREE.Mesh that we save into a variable named cube. Before adding it to the scene, we position the cube eight units back from the camera, just as we did in the example in Chapter 2, only this time we don't have to fuss with matrix math; we simply set the cube's position.z property. We also tilt the cube toward the viewer so that we can see the top face, by setting its rotation.x property. We then add the cube to our scene and—voilà!—we are ready to render.

```
// Move the mesh back from the camera and tilt it toward
// the viewer
cube.position.z = -8;
cube.rotation.x = Math.PI / 5;
```

```
cube.rotation.y = Math.PI / 5;

// Finally, add the mesh to our scene
scene.add( cube );
```

## Implementing the Run Loop

As with the example from the previous chapter, we have to implement a run loop using `requestAnimationFrame()`. But the details are quite a bit different. In the previous version, our `draw()` function had to set up buffers, set render states, clear viewports, set up shaders and textures, and much more. Using Three.js, we simply say:

```
renderer.render( scene, camera );
```

and the library does the rest. In my opinion, that alone is worth the price of admission.

The finishing touch in our presentation is to rotate the cube so we see its 3D-ness in full glory. Three.js also makes this a snap: set the `rotation.y` property to the new angle value and, under the covers, the library will do the matrix math, so we don't have to. Next time through the run loop, `render()` will use the new y rotation value and the cube will rotate. Here, again, are the `animate()` and `render()` functions:

```
var duration = 5000; // ms
var currentTime = Date.now();
function animate() {

    var now = Date.now();
    var deltat = now - currentTime;
    currentTime = now;
    var fract = deltat / duration;
    var angle = Math.PI * 2 * fract;
    cube.rotation.y += angle;
}

function run() {
    requestAnimationFrame(function() { run(); });

        // Render the scene
        renderer.render( scene, camera );

        // Spin the cube for next frame
        animate();

}
```

The end result, depicted in Figure 3-5, should look familiar.

*Figure 3-5. Texture-mapped cube using Three.js*

## Lighting the Scene

Example 3-1 illustrated one of the simplest Three.js 3D scenes we could create. But you may have noticed that this example, while depicting a 3D cube, doesn't really look very 3D. Sure, as the cube spins we can see its rough shape suggested by the texture map on each face. But still, there is a key element missing: shading. One of the amazing things about real-time 3D rendering is the ability to create a sense of lighter and darker areas on objects by using *lights*. Take a look at Figure 3-6. Now the faces of the cube have hard edges, as you would expect from an object in the real world. We did this by adding a light to the scene.

I had wanted to add this light to the cube example in Chapter 2, but the additional dozens of lines of code to update the vertex buffer data and rewrite the vertex and fragment shaders didn't seem worth it; by then, I think had hammered the point home that you could spend your life cranking out WebGL code to do simple things like this. With Three.js it isn't nearly that laborious. We need only a few extra lines of code. Take a look at Example 3-2. The source code for this version is in *Chapter 3/threejscubelit.html*.

*Figure 3-6. Three.js cube with lighting and Phong shading*

*Example 3-2. Lighting the cube with Three.js*

```
// Add a directional light to show off the object
var light = new THREE.DirectionalLight( 0xffffff, 1.5);

// Position the light out from the scene, pointing
// at the origin
light.position.set(0, 0, 1);
scene.add( light );

// Create a shaded, texture-mapped cube and add it to the scene
// First, create the texture map
var mapUrl = "../images/webgl-logo-256.jpg";
var map = THREE.ImageUtils.loadTexture(mapUrl);

// Now, create a Phong material to show shading; pass in the map
var material = new THREE.MeshPhongMaterial({ map: map });
```

The lines highlighted in boldface tell the story. First, we add a light to the scene. Lights are just another type of scene object: once you create them, you add them to the scene and their values will be used to render the other objects. In this example, we use a *directional light*; that is, a light that shines with parallel rays in a particular direction. The Three.js syntax for directional lights is (in my opinion) a little counterintuitive: you specify a position for the light, and a target position (by default located at the origin, so omitted here). Three.js then computes the direction by subtracting the target position from the light's position. In our example that means the light points into the screen from (0, 0, 1) to (0, 0, 0)—that is, directly at the cube, which is positioned at the origin.

Before we can see the effect of the light, we need to do one more thing. Instead of using a basic material with the cube, as in the previous example, we will use a *Phong* material. In Three.js, objects are lit based not only on the lights we add to the scene, but also on their material types. The Phong material type implements a simple, fairly realistic-looking shading model, called *Phong shading*, with high performance. We can now see the edges of the cube: faces that point more toward our light source are brightly lit, those that point away are less brightly lit, and the edges are visible where any two faces meet. There is much more to lighting than this, but those are the basics; we will explore the concept in more detail in the next chapter. But for now at least, we have created what passes for a real-looking 3D object in just one page of JavaScript code.

 Phong shading was developed at the University of Utah by Bui Tuong Phong. Phong's algorithms, considered radical at the time of their introduction, are now a standard shading method for many rendering applications, especially real-time rendering, because of their efficient computation of realistic shading. For more information on Phong shading, refer to the Wikipedia entry (*http://en.wikipedia.org/wiki/Phong_shading*).

# Chapter Summary

This chapter introduced us to Three.js, the most popular open source toolkit for creating 3D web applications in WebGL. We saw some of the amazing projects being built with it, from interactive cinematic experiments to promising e-commerce visualizations. We grabbed the latest source code from GitHub and took a quick tour of the project source. Finally, we built a few simple programs that show how much value the library adds: a program written in raw WebGL style using hundreds of lines of code can be expressed in just a few dozen lines of code with Three.js. Moreover, Three.js allows us to work with well-established 3D graphics concepts in familiar object-oriented style.

This chapter gave us a glimpse of how quickly Three.js can get us going. In the next few chapters, we will see how far it can take us.

# CHAPTER 4

# Graphics and Rendering in Three.js

In this chapter, we will tour the extensive set of features Three.js provides for drawing graphics and rendering scenes. If you are new to 3D programming, don't expect to comprehend all of the topics in this chapter right away. But if you take them one at a time and work through the code samples, you could be well on your way to building great WebGL sites using the power of Three.js.

Three.js has a rich graphics system, inspired by many 3D libraries that have come before and informed by the collective experience of its authors. Three.js provides the features one comes to expect from 3D libraries, and then some: 2D and 3D geometry built from polygonal meshes; a scene graph with hierarchal objects and transformations; materials, textures, and lights; real-time shadows; user-defined programmable shaders; and a flexible rendering system that enables multipass and deferred techniques for advanced special effects.

## Geometry and Meshes

One of the major benefits of using Three.js over coding straight to the WebGL API is the work it saves us in creating and drawing geometric shapes. Recall from Chapter 2 the pages of code it took to create the shape and texture map data for a simple cube using WebGL buffers, and then it required yet more code at drawing time in order for WebGL to move that data into its memory and actually draw with it. Three.js saves as all this grief by providing several ready-made geometry objects, including prebuilt shapes like cubes and cylinders, path-drawn shapes, extruded 2D geometry, and a user-extensible base class so that we can create our own. Let's explore these now.

## Prebuilt Geometry Types

Three.js comes with many prebuilt geometry types that represent common shapes. This includes simple solids such as cubes, spheres, and cylinders; more complex parametric shapes like extrusions and path-based shapes, toruses, and knots; flat 2D shapes rendered in 3D space, such as circles, squares, and rings; and even 3D extruded text generated from text strings. Three.js also supports drawing 3D points and lines. You can easily create most of these objects using a one-line constructor, though some require slightly more complex parameters and a little more code.

To see Three.js prebuilt geometry in action, run the sample located in the Three.js project at *examples/webgl_geometries.html*, depicted in Figure 4-1. Each mesh object contains a different geometry type, with a reference texture map displaying how texture coordinates are generated for each. The texture comes courtesy of PixelCG Tips and Tricks, a great computer graphics how-to site (*http://www.pixelcg.com/blog/*). The scene is lit with a directional light to show the shading for each object.

*Figure 4-1. Three.js built-in geometry demo. Pictured left to right and front to back: sphere, icosahedron, octahedron, tetrahedron; plane, cube, circle, ring, cylinder; lathe, torus, and torus knot; line drawing of x, y, z axes and up orientation vector*

## Paths, Shapes, and Extrusions

The Three.js Path, Shape, and ExtrudeGeometry classes provide many flexible ways to generate geometry—for example, to create extruded objects from curves. Figure 4-2 shows an extrusion generated from a spline-based curve. To see it in action, run the sample under the Three.js project at *examples/webgl_geometry_extrude_shapes.html*. Another sample, *examples/webgl_geometry_extrude_splines.html*, allows you to interactively select from a variety of spline generation algorithms and even follow the spline curve using an animated camera. Combining splines with extrusions is a great technique for generating organic-looking shapes. Spline curves are described in detail in Chapter 5.

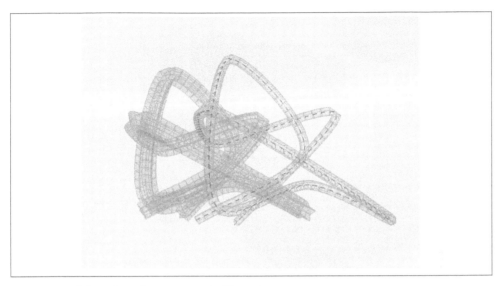

*Figure 4-2. Spline-based extrusions in Three.js*

The Shape classes can also be used to create flat 2D shapes or 3D extrusions of those shapes. Let's say you have an existing library of 2D polygon data (for example, geopolitical boundaries or vector clip art). You can fairly easily import that data into Three.js by using the Path class, which includes path-generation methods, such as moveTo() and lineTo(), that should be familiar to people with 2D drawing experience. (Essentially this is a 2D drawing API embedded in a 3D drawing library.) Why do this? Well, once you have your 2D shape, you can use it to create a flat mesh that lives in 3D space: it can be transformed like any other 3D object (translated, rotated, scaled); it can be painted with materials and lit and shaded like anything else in your scene. You can also extrude it to create a true 3D shape based on the 2D outline.

The demo in the file *examples/webgl_geometry_shapes.html*, depicted in Figure 4-3, shows an excellent example of this capability. We can see the outline of the state of California, some simple polygons, and whimsical hearts and smiley faces rendered in several forms, including flat 2D meshes, extruded and beveled 3D meshes, and lines— all derived from path-based data.

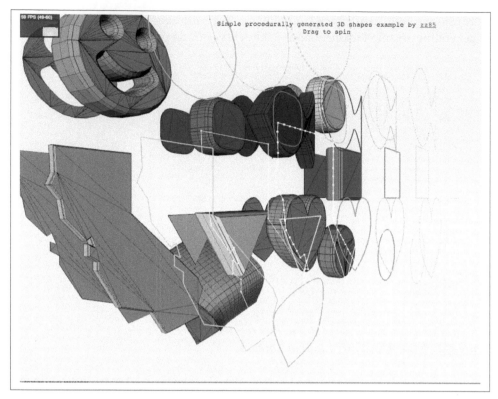

Figure 4-3. Path-based extruded shapes in Three.js

## The Geometry Base Class

The Three.js prebuilt geometry types are derived from the base class `THREE.Geometry` (*src/core/Geometry.js*). You can also use this class by itself to programmatically generate your own geometry. Have a look at the source code for the prebuilt types, located in the Three.js project under the folder *src/extras/geometries/*, to get a feel for how those classes implement geometry generation. To illustrate, let's take a quick look at one of the simpler objects, `THREE.CircleGeometry`. Example 4-1 lists the code for this object, in its entirety, which fits on a single page.

*Example 4-1. Three.js circle geometry code*

```
/**
 * @author hughes
 */

THREE.CircleGeometry = function ( radius, segments, thetaStart, thetaLength ) {

    THREE.Geometry.call( this );
```

```javascript
    radius = radius || 50;

    thetaStart = thetaStart !== undefined ? thetaStart : 0;
    thetaLength = thetaLength !== undefined ? thetaLength : Math.PI * 2;
    segments = segments !== undefined ? Math.max( 3, segments ) : 8;

    var i, uvs = [],
    center = new THREE.Vector3(), centerUV = new THREE.Vector2( 0.5, 0.5 );

    this.vertices.push(center);
    uvs.push( centerUV );

    for ( i = 0; i <= segments; i ++ ) {

        var vertex = new THREE.Vector3();
        var segment = thetaStart + i / segments * thetaLength;

        vertex.x = radius * Math.cos( segment );
        vertex.y = radius * Math.sin( segment );

        this.vertices.push( vertex );
        uvs.push( new THREE.Vector2( ( vertex.x / radius + 1 ) / 2,
            ( vertex.y / radius + 1 ) / 2 ) );

    }

    var n = new THREE.Vector3( 0, 0, 1 );

    for ( i = 1; i <= segments; i ++ ) {

        var v1 = i;
        var v2 = i + 1 ;
        var v3 = 0;

        this.faces.push( new THREE.Face3( v1, v2, v3, [ n, n, n ] ) );
        this.faceVertexUvs[ 0 ].push( [ uvs[ i ], uvs[ i + 1 ], centerUV ] );

    }

    this.computeCentroids();
    this.computeFaceNormals();

    this.boundingSphere = new THREE.Sphere( new THREE.Vector3(), radius );

};

THREE.CircleGeometry.prototype = Object.create( THREE.Geometry.prototype );
```

The constructor for THREE.CircleGeometry generates a flat, circular shape in the *XY* plane; that is, all *z* values are set to zero. At the heart of this algorithm is the code to generate the vertex data for such a shape, located within the first for loop:

```
vertex.x = radius * Math.cos( segment );
vertex.y = radius * Math.sin( segment );
```

In reality, the 3D circle is just a fan of triangles radiating from the center. By supplying enough triangles, we can create the illusion of a smooth edge around the perimeter. See Figure 4-4.

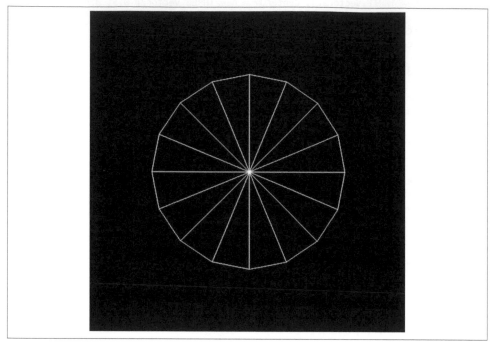

*Figure 4-4. Triangles making up THREE.CircleGeometry*

The first loop just took care of calculating the *x* and *y* vertex positions for the circumference of the circle. Now we have to create a *face* (polygonal shape) to represent each triangle, constructed of three vertices: the center, located at the origin; and two additional vertices positioned at the perimeter. The second for loop does that by creating and populating the array this.faces. Each face contains the indices for three vertices from the array this.vertices, indexed by indices v1, v2, and v3. Note that v3 is always equal to zero; that vertex corresponds to the origin. (You may recall the WebGL details from Chapter 2, where gl.drawElements() is used to render triangles using an indexed array. The same thing is going on here, being handled under the covers by Three.js.)

We glossed over one detail in each of the loops: texture coordinate generation. WebGL doesn't know how to map the pixels of a texture map onto the triangles it draws without us telling it how. In a similar way to how we created the vertex values, the two for loops generate texture coordinates, also known as *UV coordinates*, and store them in `this.faceVertexUVs`.

Recall that texture coordinates are floating-point pairs defined for each vertex, with values typically ranging from 0 to 1. These values represent *x, y* offsets into the bitmap image data; the shader will use these values to get pixel information from the bitmap. We calculate the texture coordinate for the first two vertices in each triangle in a similar manner to the vertex data, by using the cosine of the angle for the *x* value and the sin for the *y* value, but generating values in the range `[0..1]` by dividing the vertex values by the radius of the circle. The texture coordinate for the third vertex of each triangle, corresponding to the vertex at the origin, is simply the 2D center of the image (0.5, 0.5).

 Why *UV*? The letters *U* and *V* are used to denote the horizontal and vertical axes of a 2D texture map because *X*, *Y*, and *Z* are already used to denote the 3D axes of the object's coordinate system. For a complete exploration of the topic of UV coordinates and UV mapping, you can refer to the Wikipedia entry (*http://en.wikipedia.org/wiki/ UV_mapping*).

Once the vertex and UV data has been generated, Three.js has all it needs to render the geometry. The final lines of code in the `THREE.Circle` constructor are essentially doing bookkeeping, using helper functions supplied by the base geometry class. `computeCentroids()` determines the geometric center of the object by looping through all its vertices, averaging positions.

`computeFaceNormals()` is very important, because the object's normal vectors, or *normals*, determine how it is shaded. For a flat circle, the normals for each face are perpendicular to the geometry. `computeFaceNormals()` easily determines this by computing a vector perpendicular to the plane defined by the three vector positions making up each triangle of the circle. The face normal for a flat-shaded triangle is depicted in Figure 4-5.

Finally, the constructor initializes a bounding volume for the object, in this case a sphere, which is useful for picking, culling, and performing a number of optimizations.

## BufferGeometry for Optimized Mesh Rendering

Three.js recently introduced an optimized version of geometry called `THREE.BufferGeometry`. `THREE.BufferGeometry` stores its data as typed arrays, avoiding the extra overhead of dealing with arrays of JavaScript numbers. This class is also handy for static geometry, such as scene backgrounds and props, where you know the vertex values never change and the objects are never animated to move around the scene. If you know that to be true, you can create a `THREE.BufferGeometry` object, and Three.js will do a series of optimizations that render these objects really fast.

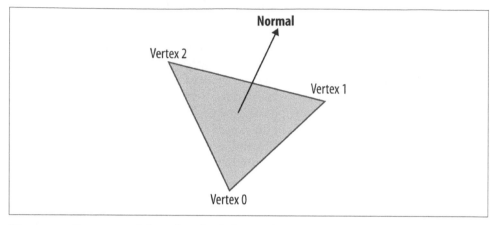

*Figure 4-5. Face normal for a flat-shaded triangle*

## Importing Meshes from Modeling Packages

So far we have looked at creating geometry in code. But many, if not most, applications will not be creating geometry programmatically; instead, they will be loading 3D models created by professional modeling packages such as 3ds Max, Maya, and Blender.

Three.js has several utilities to convert and/or load model files. Let's look at one example of loading a mesh, including its geometry and materials. Run the file *examples/webgl_loader_obj_mtl.html* under the Three.js project. You will see the model shown in Figure 4-6.

The male figure depicted here was imported via the Wavefront OBJ format *(.OBJ* file extension). This is a popular text-based format exported by many modeling packages. OBJ files are simple and limited, containing only geometry data: vertices, normals, and texture coordinates. Wavefront developed a companion file format for materials, MTL, which can be used to associate materials with the objects in the OBJ file.

The source code for the Three.js OBJ format loader (with materials) is located in *exam ples/js/loaders/OBJMTLLoader.js*. Take a look at how it works and you will see that, as with the prebuilt geometry and shape classes, Three.js file loaders create THREE.Geome try objects to represent the geometry. The MTL parser translates text options in the MTL file into materials Three.js understands. The two are then combined into a THREE.Mesh object suitable for adding to the scene.

Three.js has sample loaders for many different file formats. While most formats include support for defining objects with geometry and materials, many go beyond that, representing entire scenes, cameras, lights, and animations. We will cover those formats (and the tools to author them) in detail in Chapter 8, which is devoted to the content creation pipeline.

*Figure 4-6. Mesh loaded from a file in Wavefront OBJ format*

Most of the file loading code that comes with Three.js is not in the core library, but rather included with the examples. You will have to include them separately in your projects. Unless otherwise indicated, these file loader utilities are covered under the same licensing as the library and you can feel free to use them in your work.

# The Scene Graph and Transform Hierarchy

WebGL has no built-in notion of 3D scene structure; it is simply an API for drawing to the canvas. It is up to the application to provide scene structure. Three.js defines a model for structuring scenes based on the well-established concept of a *scene graph*. A scene graph is a set of 3D objects stored in a hierarchical parent/child relationship, with the base of the scene graph often referred to as the *root*. The application renders the scene graph by rendering the root and then, recursively, its descendants.

## Using Scene Graphs to Manage Scene Complexity

Scene graphs are particularly useful for representing complex objects in a hierarchy. Think of a robot, a vehicle, or a solar system: each of these has several individual parts — limbs, wheels, satellites—with their own behaviors. The scene graph allows these objects to be treated as either individual parts or as entire groups, as needed. This is not only for organizational convenience: it can also provide a very important capability known as *transform hierarchy*, where an object's descendants inherit its 3D transformation information (translation, rotation, scale). For example, say you are animating a car driving along a path. The car body moves along the path, but the wheels also rotate independently. By making the wheels *children* of the car body, your code can dynamically move the car along the path, and the wheels will move through 3D space with it; there is no need to separately animate the movement of the wheels, only their rotation.

 The use of the word *graph* in the Three.js scene graph is somewhat loose technically. In 3D rendering, the scene graph usually refers to a *directed acyclic graph* (DAG), which is a mathematical term that denotes a set of nodes in a parent/child relationship in which any object can have multiple parents. In the Three.js scene graph, objects can have only one parent. While it is technically correct to call the Three.js hierarchy a graph, it would more precisely be called a *tree*. For more information on graphs in mathematics, refer to the Wikipedia entry (*http://en.wikipedia.org/wiki/Directed_acyclic_graph*).

## Scene Graphs in Three.js

The foundation object of the Three.js scene graph is THREE.Object3D (see *src/core/Object3D.js* under the Three.js project sources). It is used both as the base class for visual types such as meshes, lines, and particle systems, as well as on its own to group other objects into a scene graph hierarchy.

Each Object3D carries its own transform information, represented in the properties position (translation), rotation, and scale. By setting these, you can move, rotate, and scale the object. If the object has descendants (children and their children), those will inherit these transformations. If those descendants' transform properties have been changed, those changes will combine with those of the ancestors all the way down the hierarchy. Let's look at an example. The page depicted in Figure 4-7 shows a very simple transform hierarchy. cube is a direct descendant of cubeGroup; sphereGroup is also a direct descendant of cubeGroup (and therefore a sibling of cube); and sphere and cone are descendants of sphereGroup.

Run this sample by loading the example file *Chapter 4/threejsscene.html*. You will see the cube, sphere, and cone each rotating in place. You can interact with this scene: clicking and dragging the mouse in the content area rotates the entire scene; dragging the slider below the content area scales the scene.

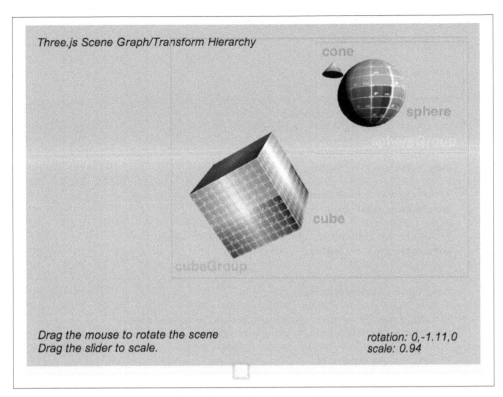

*Figure 4-7. Three.js scene graph and transform hierarchy*

Example 4-2 shows the relevant code for creating and manipulating the scene graph with transform hierarchy. The really important lines are highlighted in bold. First, to construct the scene: we create a new `Object3D`, cubeGroup, that will act as the root of the scene graph. We then add the cube mesh directly to it, as well as another `Object3D`: sphereGroup. The sphere and cone are added to sphereGroup. We also move the cone a bit up and away from the sphere by setting its `position` property.

Now for the animations: we see in function `animate()` that when sphereGroup rotates, the sphere rotates, and the cone seems to orbit around the sphere and traverse through space. Note that we did not write any code to individually rotate the sphere mesh or move the cone through space every animation frame; because those objects inherit their transform information from sphereGroup, those operations are taken care of for us automatically. In a similar way, interacting with the scene to rotate and scale it is trivially simple: we just set the `rotation` and `scale` properties, respectively, of cubeGroup, and these changes are propagated to its descendants automatically by Three.js.

*Example 4-2. A scene with transform hierarchy*

```
function animate() {

        var now = Date.now();
        var deltat = now - currentTime;
        currentTime = now;
        var fract = deltat / duration;
        var angle = Math.PI * 2 * fract;

        // Rotate the cube about its Y axis
        cube.rotation.y += angle;

        // Rotate the sphere group about its Y axis
        sphereGroup.rotation.y -= angle / 2;

        // Rotate the cone about its X axis (tumble forward)
        cone.rotation.x += angle;
}

        function createScene(canvas) {

        // Create the Three.js renderer and attach it to our canvas
        renderer = new THREE.WebGLRenderer( { canvas: canvas, antialias: true } );

        // Set the viewport size
        renderer.setSize(canvas.width, canvas.height);

        // Create a new Three.js scene
        scene = new THREE.Scene();

        // Add a camera so we can view the scene
        camera = new THREE.PerspectiveCamera( 45, canvas.width / canvas.height,
            1, 4000 );
        camera.position.z = 10;
        scene.add(camera);

        // Create a group to hold all the objects
        cubeGroup = new THREE.Object3D;

        // Add a directional light to show off the objects
        var light = new THREE.DirectionalLight( 0xffffff, 1.5);
        // Position the light out from the scene, pointing at the origin
        light.position.set(.5, .2, 1);
        cubeGroup.add(light);

        // Create a textured phong material for the cube
        // First, create the texture map
        var mapUrl = "../images/ash_uvgrid01.jpg";
        var map = THREE.ImageUtils.loadTexture(mapUrl);
        var material = new THREE.MeshPhongMaterial({ map: map });

        // Create the cube geometry
```

```
    var geometry = new THREE.CubeGeometry(2, 2, 2);

    // And put the geometry and material together into a mesh
    cube = new THREE.Mesh(geometry, material);

    // Tilt the mesh toward the viewer
    cube.rotation.x = Math.PI / 5;
    cube.rotation.y = Math.PI / 5;

    // Add the cube mesh to our group
    cubeGroup.add( cube );

    // Create a group for the sphere
    sphereGroup = new THREE.Object3D;
    cubeGroup.add(sphereGroup);

    // Move the sphere group up and back from the cube
    sphereGroup.position.set(0, 3, -4);

    // Create the sphere geometry
    geometry = new THREE.SphereGeometry(1, 20, 20);

    // And put the geometry and material together into a mesh
    sphere = new THREE.Mesh(geometry, material);

    // Add the sphere mesh to our group
    sphereGroup.add( sphere );

    // Create the cone geometry
    geometry = new THREE.CylinderGeometry(0, .333, .444, 20, 5);

    // And put the geometry and material together into a mesh
    cone = new THREE.Mesh(geometry, material);

    // Move the cone up and out from the sphere
    cone.position.set(1, 1, -.667);

    // Add the cone mesh to our group
    sphereGroup.add( cone );

    // Now add the group to our scene
    scene.add( cubeGroup );
}

function rotateScene(deltax)
{
    cubeGroup.rotation.y += deltax / 100;
    $("#rotation").html("rotation: 0," + cubeGroup.rotation.y.toFixed(2) + ",0");
}

function scaleScene(scale)
{
```

```
        cubeGroup.scale.set(scale, scale, scale);
        $("#scale").html("scale: " + scale);
    }
```

## Representing Translation, Rotation, and Scale

In Three.js, transformations are done via 3D matrix math, so not surprisingly, the components of `Object3D`'s transform are 3D vectors: `position`, `rotation`, and `scale`. `position` should be fairly self-explanatory: its $x$, $y$, and $z$ components define a vector offset from the object's origin. `scale` is also straightforward: $x$, $y$, and $z$ values are used to multiply the transformation matrix's scale by that amount in each of the three dimensions.

The components of `rotation` require a little more explanation: each of $x$, $y$, and $z$ defines a rotation around that axis; for example, a value of (`0, Math.PI / 2, 0`) is equivalent to a 90-degree rotation around the object's y-axis. (Note that degrees are specified in radians, where 2 * pi radians is equivalent to 360 degrees). This type of rotation—a combination of angles about the x, y, and z-axes—is known as a *Euler angle*. I assume Mr.doob chose Eulers as the base representation because they are so intuitive and easy to work with; however, they are not without their mathematical problems in practice. For that reason, Three.js also allows you to use *quaternions*, another form of specifying angles that is free from Euler issues, but requires more programming work. Quaternions are accurate, but not intuitive to work with.

Under the hood, Three.js is using the transform properties of each `Object3D` to construct a matrix. Objects that have multiple ancestors have their matrices multiplied by those of their ancestors in recursive fashion; that is, Three.js traverses all the way down to each leaf in its scene graph tree to calculate the transform matrix for each object every time the scene is rendered. This can get expensive for deep and complex scene graphs. Three.js defines a `matrixAutoUpdate` property for `Object3D`, which can be set to `false` to avoid this performance overhead. However, this feature has the potential to cause subtle bugs ("Why isn't my animation updating?"), so it should be used with great care.

# Materials

The visual shapes we see in WebGL applications have surface properties such as color, shading, and textures (bitmaps). Creating those properties using the low-level WebGL API entails writing GLSL shader code, which requires advanced programming skills, even for the simplest visual effects. Lucky for us, Three.js comes with ready-to-go GLSL code, packaged into objects called *materials*.

# Standard Mesh Materials

Recall that WebGL requires the developer to supply a programmable shader in order to draw each object. You may have noticed the absence of GLSL shader source code thus far in this chapter. That is for a very good reason: Three.js does the shader coding for us, with a library of predefined GLSL code suitable for a variety of uses out of the box.

Traditional scene graph libraries and popular modeling packages typically represent shaders via the concept of *materials*. A material is an object that defines the surface properties of a 3D mesh, point, or line primitive, including color, transparency, and shininess. Materials may or may not also include texture maps—that is, bitmaps wrapped onto the surface of the object. Material properties combine with the vertex data of the mesh, lighting information in the scene, and potentially the camera position and other global properties to determine the final rendered appearance of each object.

Three.js supports common material types in the prebuilt classes `MeshBasicMaterial`, `MeshPhongMaterial`, and `MeshLambertMaterial`. (The `Mesh` prefix denotes that these material types should be used in combination with the mesh object, as opposed to lines or particles; there are additional material types suitable for use with other object types. See the Three.js objects that live in the project source under *src/materials* for a complete and up-to-date set.) These material types implement, respectively, three well-known material techniques:

*Unlit (also known as prelit)*
> With this material type, only the textures, colors, and transparency values are used to render the surface of the object. There is no contribution from lights in the scene. This is a great material type to use for flat-looking renderings and/or for drawing simple geometric objects with no shading. It is also valuable if the lighting for objects has been precomputed into the textures prior to runtime (for example, by a 3D modeling tool with a light "baking" utility), and thus does not have to be computed by the renderer.

*Phong shading*
> This material type implements a simple, fairly realistic-looking shading model with high performance. It has become the go-to material type for achieving a classic shaded look quickly and easily and is still used in many games and applications. Phong-shaded objects will show brightly lit areas (*specular reflections*) where light hits directly, will light well along any edges that mostly face the light source, and will darkly shade areas where the edge of the object faces away from the light source.

*Lambertian reflectance*
> In Lambert shading, the apparent brightness of the surface to an observer is the same regardless of the observer's angle of view. This works really well for clouds, which broadly diffuse the light that strikes them, or satellites such as moons that have high *albedo* (reflect light brightly off the surface).

To get a feel for the Three.js material types, open the lab in the book example code, located in the file *Chapter 4/threejsmaterials.html*. The page, shown in Figure 4-8, displays a brightly lit sphere with a texture map of the moon. The moon is a good object to use here to illustrate differences between the various material types. Use the radio buttons to switch between Phong and Lambert, for example, to see how much more appropriate Lambert shading looks than Phong for this object. Now use the Basic (unlit) shader to see how the sphere appears rendered with just the texture and no lighting applied.

Try changing the diffuse and specular colors to see those effects. The material's *diffuse color* specifies how much the object reflects lighting sources that cast rays in a direction —that is, directional, point, and spotlights (see the discussion on lighting later in this chapter). The *specular color* combines with scene lights to create reflected highlights from any of the object's vertices facing toward light sources. (Note that specular highlights will be visible only when the Phong material is used; the other material types do not support specular color.) Also, try turning the texture map off with the checkbox so that you can see the effects of the material on simple sphere geometry. Finally, check the wireframe box to see how various changes affect the wireframe rendering.

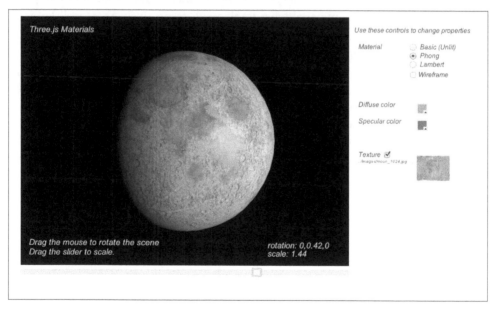

*Figure 4-8. Three.js standard mesh material types: Basic (Unlit), Phong, and Lambert*

## Adding Realism with Multiple Textures

The previous example shows how a texture map can be used to define the surface look for an object. Most Three.js material types actually support applying multiple textures to the object to create more realistic effects. The idea behind using multiple textures in a single material, or *multitexturing*, is to provide a computationally inexpensive way to add realism—versus using more polygons or rendering the object with multiple render passes. Here are a few examples to illustrate the more common multitexturing techniques supported in Three.js.

**Bump maps.** A *bump map* is a bitmap used to displace the surface normal vectors of a mesh to, as the name suggests, create an apparently bumpy surface. The pixel values of the bitmap are treated as heights rather than color values. For example, a pixel value of zero can mean no displacement from the surface, and nonzero values can mean positive displacement away from the surface. Typically, single-channel black and white bitmaps are used for efficiency, though full RGB bitmaps can be used to provide greater detail, since they can store much larger values. The reason that bitmaps are used instead of 3D vectors is that they are more compact and provide a fast way to calculate normal displacement within the shader code. To see bump maps in action, open the example *Chapter 4/threejsbumpmap.html*, depicted in Figure 4-9. Turn the main moon texture on and off, and play with the diffuse and specular color values to see different results. You will probably notice that, while the effect can be really cool, it can also yield unpleasant artifacts. Still, bump maps provide a cheap way to add realistic detail.

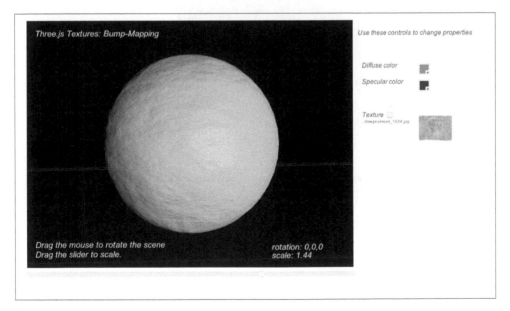

*Figure 4-9. Bump mapping*

Bump maps are trivially easy to use in Three.js. Simply provide a valid texture in the bumpMap property of the parameter object you pass to the THREE.MeshPhongMaterial constructor:

```
material= new THREE.MeshPhongMaterial({map: map,
    bumpMap: bumpMap });
```

**Normal maps.** *Normal maps* provide a way to get even more surface detail than bump maps, still without using extra polygons. Normal maps tend to be larger and require more processing power than bump maps, but the extra detail can be worth it. Normal maps work by encoding actual vertex normal vector values into bitmaps as RGB data, typically at a much higher resolution than the associated mesh vertex data. The shader incorporates the normal information into its lighting calculations (along with current camera and light source values) to provide apparent surface detail. Open the example *Chapter 4/threejsnormalmap.html* file to see the effect of a normal map. The normal map is depicted in the swatch on the bottom right (see Figure 4-10). Note the outlines of the Earth's elevation features. Now toggle the normal map on and off to see how much detail it is providing; it is quite astonishing how much detail a bitmap can add to a simple object like a sphere.

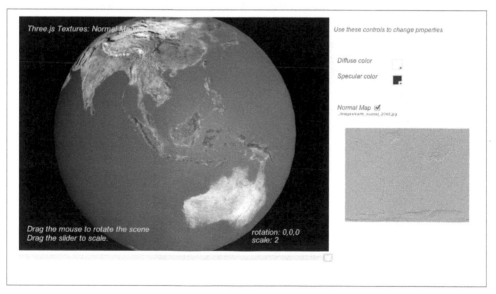

*Figure 4-10. Normal-mapped Earth*

Normal maps are also easy to use in Three.js. Simply provide a valid texture in the normalMap property of the parameter object you pass to the THREE.MeshPhongMaterial constructor:

```
Material = new THREE.MeshPhongMaterial({ map: map,
    normalMap: normalMap });
```

**Environment maps.** Environment maps provide another way to use extra textures to increase realism. Instead of adding surface detail through apparent changes to the geometry, as with bump maps and normal maps, environment maps simulate reflection of objects in the surrounding environment.

Open *Chapter 4/threejsenvmap.html* to see a demonstration of environment mapping. Drag the mouse in the content area to rotate the scene, or use the mouse wheel to zoom in and out. Notice how the image on the surface of the sphere appears to reflect the sky background surrounding it (see Figure 4-11). In fact, it does no such thing; it is simply rendering pixels from the same texture that is mapped onto the inside of the cube used for the scene's background. The trick here is that the texture being used on the sphere's material is a *cube texture*: a texture map made up of six individual bitmaps stitched together to form a contiguous image on the inside of a cube. This particular cube texture has been created to form a sky background panorama. Have a look at the individual files that make up this skybox in the folder *images/cubemap/skybox/* to see how it is constructed. This type of environment mapping is called *cubic environment mapping*, because it employs cube textures.

*Figure 4-11. Cubic environment maps for realistic scene backgrounds and reflection effects*

Using cube textures in Three.js is slightly more involved than using bump or normal maps. First, we need to create a cube texture instead of a regular texture. We do this with the Three.js utility `ImageUtils.loadTextureCube()`, passing it URLs for the six individual image files. Then, we set this as the value of the envMap parameter of the MeshPhongMaterial when calling the constructor. We also specify a reflectivity value defining how much of the cube texture will be "reflected" on the material when the object is rendered. In this case, we supply a value slightly higher than the default of 1, to make sure the environment map really stands out.

```
var path = "../images/cubemap/skybox/";

var urls = [ path + "px.jpg", path + "nx.jpg",
             path + "py.jpg", path + "ny.jpg",
             path + "pz.jpg", path + "nz.jpg" ];

envMap = THREE.ImageUtils.loadTextureCube( urls );
materials["phong-envmapped"] = new THREE.MeshBasicMaterial(
    { color: 0xffffff,
      envMap : envMap,
      reflectivity:1.3} );
```

There is more to be done. In order for this to be a realistic effect, the reflected bitmap needs to correspond to the surrounding environment. To make that happen, we create a *skybox*—that is, a large background cube textured from the inside with the same bitmap images representing a panoramic sky. This in itself could be a lot of work but, thankfully, Three.js has a built-in helper that does it for us. In addition to its prebuilt standard materials Basic, Phong, and Lambert, Three.js includes a library of utility shaders, contained in the global THREE.ShaderLib. We simply create a mesh with cube geometry, and as the material we use the Three.js "cube" shader defined in the library. It takes care of rendering the inside of the cube using the same texture as we used for the environment map.

```
// Create the skybox
var shader = THREE.ShaderLib[ "cube" ];
shader.uniforms[ "tCube" ].value = envMap;

var material = new THREE.ShaderMaterial( {

    fragmentShader: shader.fragmentShader,
    vertexShader: shader.vertexShader,
    uniforms: shader.uniforms,
    side: THREE.BackSide

} ),

mesh = new THREE.Mesh(new THREE.CubeGeometry( 500, 500, 500 ), material);
scene.add( mesh );
```

# Lights

Lights illuminate objects in the 3D scene. Three.js defines several built-in light classes that correspond to those typically found in modeling tools and other scene graph libraries. The most commonly used light types are *directional lights*, *point lights*, *spotlights*, and *ambient lights*.

*Directional lights*

> Represent a light source that casts parallel rays in a particular direction. They have no position, only a direction, color, and intensity. (In fact, in Three.js, directional lights *do* have a position, but it is used only to calculate the light's direction based on the position and a second vector, the target position. This is a clumsy and counterintuitive syntax that I hope Mr.doob someday fixes.)

*Point lights*

> Have a position but no direction; they cast their light in all directions from their position, over a given distance.

*Spotlights*

> Have a position and a direction. They also have parameters defining the size (angle) of the spotlight's inner and outer cones, and a distance over which they illuminate.

*Ambient lights*

> Have no position or direction. They illuminate a scene equally throughout.

All Three.js light types support the common properties `intensity`, which defines the light's strength, and `color`, an RGB value.

Lights do not do their job on their own; their values combine with certain properties of materials to define an object's ultimate surface appearance. `MeshPhongMaterial` and `MeshLambertMaterial` define the following properties:

`color`

> Also known as the *diffuse* color, this specifies how much the object reflects lighting sources that cast rays in a direction (i.e., directional, point, and spotlights).

`ambient`

> The amount of ambient scene lighting reflected by the object.

`emissive`

> This material property defines the color an object emits on its own, irrespective of light sources in the scene.

`MeshPhongMaterial` also supports a `specular` color, which combines with scene lights to create reflected highlights from the object's vertices that are facing toward light sources.

Recall that `MeshBasicMaterial` ignores lights completely.

Figure 4-12 depicts a lighting experiment built with the basic Three.js light types. Open the file *Chapter 4/threejslights.html* to run it. The scene contains four lights, one of each type, and displays a simple black-and-white textured ground plane and three plain white geometry objects to illustrate the effects of the various lights. The color picker controls on the page allow you to interactively change the color of each light. Set a light's color to black, and it will turn the light off completely. Drag the mouse within the content area to rotate around the scene and see the effects of the lights on various parts of the model.

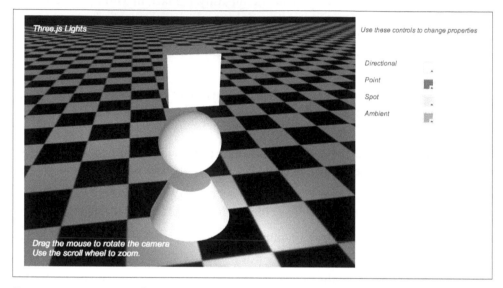

*Figure 4-12. Directional, point, spot, and ambient lights*

The following code listing shows the light setup code. The white directional light positioned in front of the scene lights bright white areas on the front of the geometry objects. The blue point light illuminates from behind the model; note the blue areas on the floor to the back of the object. The green spotlight casts its cone toward the floor near the front of the scene, as defined by `spotLight.target.position`. Finally, the ambient light provides a small amount of illumination to all objects in the scene equally. Play with the controls and inspect the model from all sides to see the individual and combined effects of the lights.

```
// Create and add all the lights
directionalLight.position.set(.5, 0, 3);
root.add(directionalLight);

pointLight = new THREE.PointLight (0x0000ff, 1, 20);
pointLight.position.set(-5, 2, -10);
root.add(pointLight);

spotLight = new THREE.SpotLight (0x00ff00);
spotLight.position.set(2, 2, 5);
spotLight.target.position.set(2, 0, 4);
root.add(spotLight);

ambientLight = new THREE.AmbientLight ( 0x888888 );
root.add(ambientLight);
```

At this juncture, here is a friendly reminder about what is going on. As with nearly everything else in WebGL, lights are an artificially created construct. WebGL knows only about buffers and shaders; developers need to synthesize lighting effects by writing shader code. Three.js offers an astounding set of material and lighting capabilities...all the more incredible when you realize that it was written in JavaScript. Of course, none of this would be possible if WebGL didn't give us access to the GPU to create these amazing effects in the first place.

# Shadows

For years, designers have used shadows to add an extra visual cue that enhances realism. Typically these are faked, prerendered affairs, and moving the light source or any of the shadowed objects destroys the illusion. However, Three.js allows us to render shadows in real time based the current positions of the lights and objects.

The example in the file *Chapter 4/threejsshadows.html* demonstrates how to add real-time shadows to a scene. Refer to Figure 4-13: the geometry casts shadows onto the ground plane based on a spotlight positioned above the ground and in front of the scene. Note how the shadow follows the shape of the rotating cube. Also, as the floor rotates, the shadow does not move along with it. If the shadows were faked with prerendering, the shadow would stay "glued" to the floor and it would not rotate along with the cube. Play with the light controls, in particular the spotlight, to see how the shadow changes dynamically.

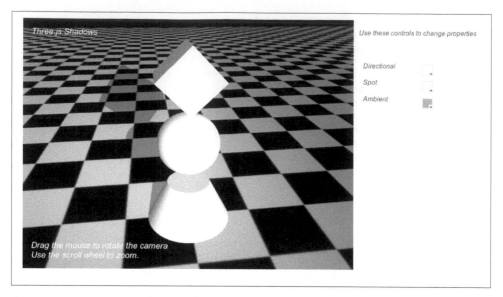

*Figure 4-13. Using a spotlight and shadow map to cast real-time shadows*

Three.js supports shadows using a technique called *shadow mapping*. With shadow mapping, the renderer maintains an additional texture map, to which it renders the shadowed areas and combines with the final image in its fragment shaders. So, enabling shadows in Three.js requires a few steps:

1. Enable shadow mapping in the renderer.
2. Enable shadows and set shadow parameters for the lights that cast shadows. Both the THREE.DirectionalLight type and the THREE.SpotLight type support shadows.
3. Indicate which geometry objects cast and receive shadows.

Let's take a look at how this is done in code. Example 4-3 shows the code added to createScene() to render shadows, highlighted in boldface.

*Example 4-3. Shadow mapping in Three.js*

```
var SHADOW_MAP_WIDTH = 2048, SHADOW_MAP_HEIGHT = 2048;

function createScene(canvas) {

    // Create the Three.js renderer and attach it to our canvas
    renderer = new THREE.WebGLRenderer( { canvas: canvas, antialias: true } );

    // Set the viewport size
    renderer.setSize(canvas.width, canvas.height);
```

```
// Turn on shadows
renderer.shadowMapEnabled = true;
renderer.shadowMapType = THREE.PCFSoftShadowMap;

// Create a new Three.js scene
scene = new THREE.Scene();

// Add a camera so we can view the scene
camera = new THREE.PerspectiveCamera( 45, canvas.width / canvas.height,
    1, 4000 );
camera.position.set(-2, 6, 12);
scene.add(camera);

// Create a group to hold all the objects
root = new THREE.Object3D;

// Add a directional light to show off the object
directionalLight = new THREE.DirectionalLight( 0xffffff, 1);

// Create and add all the lights
directionalLight.position.set(.5, 0, 3);
root.add(directionalLight);

spotLight = new THREE.SpotLight (0xffffff);
spotLight.position.set(2, 8, 15);
spotLight.target.position.set(-2, 0, -2);
root.add(spotLight);

spotLight.castShadow = true;

spotLight.shadowCameraNear = 1;
spotLight.shadowCameraFar = 200;
spotLight.shadowCameraFov = 45;

spotLight.shadowDarkness = 0.5;

spotLight.shadowMapWidth = SHADOW_MAP_WIDTH;
spotLight.shadowMapHeight = SHADOW_MAP_HEIGHT;

ambientLight = new THREE.AmbientLight ( 0x888888 );
root.add(ambientLight);

// Create a group to hold the spheres
group = new THREE.Object3D;
root.add(group);

// Create a texture map
var map = THREE.ImageUtils.loadTexture(mapUrl);
map.wrapS = map.wrapT = THREE.RepeatWrapping;
map.repeat.set(8, 8);

var color = 0xffffff;
```

```
var ambient = 0x888888;
// Put in a ground plane to show off the lighting
geometry = new THREE.PlaneGeometry(200, 200, 50, 50);
var mesh = new THREE.Mesh(geometry, new THREE.MeshPhongMaterial({color:color,
    ambient:ambient, map:map, side:THREE.DoubleSide}));
mesh.rotation.x = -Math.PI / 2;
mesh.position.y = -4.02;

// Add the mesh to our group
group.add( mesh );
mesh.castShadow = false;
mesh.receiveShadow = true;

// Create the cube geometry
geometry = new THREE.CubeGeometry(2, 2, 2);

// And put the geometry and material together into a mesh
mesh = new THREE.Mesh(geometry, new THREE.MeshPhongMaterial({color:color,
    ambient:ambient}));
mesh.position.y = 3;
mesh.castShadow = true;
mesh.receiveShadow = false;

// Add the mesh to our group
group.add( mesh );

// Save this one away so we can rotate it
cube = mesh;

// Create the sphere geometry
geometry = new THREE.SphereGeometry(Math.sqrt(2), 50, 50);

// And put the geometry and material together into a mesh
mesh = new THREE.Mesh(geometry, new THREE.MeshPhongMaterial({color:color,
    ambient:ambient}));
mesh.position.y = 0;
mesh.castShadow = true;
mesh.receiveShadow = false;

// Add the mesh to our group
group.add( mesh );

// Create the cylinder geometry
geometry = new THREE.CylinderGeometry(1, 2, 2, 50, 10);

// And put the geometry and material together into a mesh
mesh = new THREE.Mesh(geometry, new THREE.MeshPhongMaterial({color:color,
    ambient:ambient}));
mesh.position.y = -3;

mesh.castShadow = true;
mesh.receiveShadow = false;
```

```
    // Add the  mesh to our group
    group.add( mesh );

    // Now add the group to our scene
    scene.add( root );
}
```

First, we enable shadows in the renderer by setting `renderer.shadowMapEnabled` to `true` and setting its `shadowMapType` property to `THREE.PCFSoftShadowMap`. Three.js supports three different types of shadow mapping algorithms: basic, PCF (for "percentage close filtering"), and PCF soft shadows. Each algorithm provides increasing realism, at the expense of higher complexity and slower performance. Try experimenting with this sample by changing the `shadowMapType` to `THREE.BasicShadowMap` and `THREE.PCFShadowMap` and have a look at the results; shadow quality degrades noticeably with the lower-quality settings. But you may need to go that route for performance if your scenes are complex.

Next, we need to enable shadow casting for the spotlight. We set its `castShadow` property to `true`. We also set several parameters required by Three.js. Three.js renders shadows by casting a ray from the position of the light toward its target object. Essentially, it treats the spotlight as another "camera" for rendering the scene from the position. So we must set camera-like parameters, including near and far clipping planes and field of view. The near and far values are very much dependent on the size of the scene and objects, so we chose fairly small values for both. The field of view was determined empirically. We also provide a darkness value for the shadow; the Three.js default of 0.5 is suitable for this application. Then, we set properties that determine the size of the Three.js-generated shadow map. The shadow map is an additional bitmap created by Three.js into which it will render the shadow dark areas and ultimately blend with the final rendered image of each object. Our values for `SHADOW_MAP_WIDTH` and `SHADOW_MAP_HEIGHT` are 2,048, which is much higher than the Three.js default of 512. This produces very smooth shadows; lower values will yield more jagged results. Experiment with this value in the example to see how lower-resolution shadow maps affect shadow quality.

Finally, we must tell Three.js which objects cast and receive shadows. By default, Three.js meshes do not cast or receive shadows, so we must set this explicitly. In this example, we want the solid geometries to cast shadows onto the floor, and the floor to receive the shadows. So, for the floor we set `mesh.castShadow` to `false` and `mesh.receiveShadow` to `true`; for the cube, sphere, and cone we set `mesh.castShadow` to `true` and `mesh.receiveShadow` to `false`.

As a finishing touch, we would like the intensity of the shadow to correspond to the brightness of the spotlight casting it. However, Three.js shadow mapping does not automatically take into account the brightness of the light sources when rendering shadows. Rather, it uses the light's `shadowDarkness` property. So, as the color of the spotlight is updated via the user interface, we need to update `shadowDarkness` ourselves. The following fragment shows the code for the helper function `setShadowDark ness()`, which calculates a new value for the shadow darkness based on the average brightness of the light color's red, green, and blue components. As you change the spotlight's color in the demo to a darker value, you will see the shadow fade away.

```
function setShadowDarkness(light, r, g, b)
{
    r /= 255;
    g /= 255;
    b /= 255;
    var avg = (r + g + b) / 3;

    light.shadowDarkness = avg * 0.5;
}
```

 Real-time shadows are a fantastic enhancement to the WebGL visual experience, and Three.js makes them fairly easy to work with. However, they come at a cost. First, the shadow map, which is just another texture map, requires additional graphics memory; for a 2,048 × 2,048 map, that amounts to an additional 4 MB. See if you can get away with smaller shadow map sizes and still get the desired visual effect. Also, depending on the graphics hardware being used, rendering off-screen to the shadow map can introduce extra processing overhead that slows down frame rate considerably. So, you must take care when using this feature. Be ready to profile and, potentially, fall back to another solution that doesn't require real-time shadows.

# Shaders

Three.js provides a powerful set of materials out of the box, implemented via predefined GLSL shaders included with the library. These shaders were developed to support commonly used shading styles, such as unlit, Phong, and Lambert. But there are many other possibilities. In the general case, materials can implement a limitless variety of effects, can use many and variegate properties, and can get arbitrarily complex. For example, a shader simulating grass blowing in the wind might have parameters that determine the height and thickness of the grass and the wind speed and direction.

As computer graphics evolved, and production values rose over the last two decades—originally for film special effects and later for real-time video games—shading started looking more like a general-purpose programming problem than an art production exercise. Instead of trying to predict every potential combination of material properties and code them into a runtime engine, the industry banded together to create programmable pipeline technology, known as *programmable shaders*, or simply *shaders*. Shaders allow developers to write code that implements complex effects on a per-vertex and per-pixel basis in a C-style language compiled for execution on the GPU. Using programmable shaders, developers can create highly realistic visuals with high performance, freed from the constraints of predefined material and lighting models.

## The ShaderMaterial Class: Roll Your Own

GL Shading Language (GLSL) is the shading language developed for use with Open GL and OpenGL ES (the basis for the WebGL API). GLSL source code is compiled and executed for use with WebGL via methods of the WebGL context object. Three.js hides GLSL under the covers for us, allowing us to completely bypass shader programming if we so choose. For many applications, the prebuilt material types suffice. But if our application needs a visual effect that is not supplied out of the box, Three.js also allows us to write custom GLSL shaders using the class THREE.ShaderMaterial.

Figure 4-14 shows an example of ShaderMaterial in action. This example, which can be found under the Three.js project tree at *examples/webgl_materials_shaders_fres nel.html*, demonstrates a Fresnel shader. Fresnel shading is used to simulate the reflection and refraction of light through transparent media such as water and glass.

*Figure 4-14. Fresnel shader provides high realism via reflection and refraction*

Fresnel shaders (pronounced "fre-nel") are named after the Fresnel Effect, first documented by the French physicist Augustin-Jean Fresnel (1788–1827). Fresnel advanced the wave theory of light through a study of how light was transmitted and propagated by different objects. For more information, consult the online 3D rendering glossary (*http://www.3drender.com/glossary/fresneleffect.htm*).

The setup code in this example creates a `ShaderMaterial` as follows: it clones the *uniform* (parameter) values of the `FresnelShader` template object—each instance of a shader needs its own copy of these—and passes the GLSL source code for the vertex and fragment shaders. Once these are set up, Three.js will automatically handle compiling and linking the shaders, and binding JavaScript properties to the uniform values.

```
var shader = THREE.FresnelShader;
var uniforms = THREE.UniformsUtils.clone( shader.uniforms );

uniforms[ "tCube" ].value = textureCube;

var parameters = {
    fragmentShader: shader.fragmentShader,
    vertexShader: shader.vertexShader,
    uniforms: uniforms };

var material = new THREE.ShaderMaterial( parameters );
```

The GLSL code for the Fresnel shader is shown in Example 4-4. The source can also be found under the Three.js project tree in the file *examples/js/shaders/FresnelShader.js*. This shader code was written by frequent Three.js contributor Branislav Ulicny, better known by his "nom de code," *AlteredQualia*. Let's walk through the listing to see how it is done.

*Example 4-4. Fresnel shader for Three.js*

```
/**
 * @author alteredq / http://alteredqualia.com/
 * Based on Nvidia Cg tutorial
 */

THREE.FresnelShader = {

    uniforms: {

        "mRefractionRatio": { type: "f", value: 1.02 },
        "mFresnelBias": { type: "f", value: 0.1 },
        "mFresnelPower": { type: "f", value: 2.0 },
        "mFresnelScale": { type: "f", value: 1.0 },
        "tCube": { type: "t", value: null }

    },
```

The uniforms property of THREE.ShaderMaterial specifies the values Three.js will pass to WebGL when the shader is used. Recall that the shader program is executed for each vertex and each pixel (fragment). Shader *uniforms* are values that, as the name implies, do not change from vertex to vertex; they are essentially global variables whose value is the same for all vertices and pixels. The Fresnel shader in this example defines uniforms controlling the amount of reflection and refraction (e.g., mRefractionRatio and mFres nelScale). It also defines a uniform for the cube texture used as the scene background. In a similar fashion to the cubic environment-mapping sample we saw in a previous section, this shader simulates reflection by rendering the pixels from the cube map. However, with this shader, we will see not only pixels reflected from the cube map, but refracted ones as well.

## Using GLSL Shader Code with Three.js

Now it's time to set up the vertex and fragment shaders. First, the vertex shader:

```
vertexShader: [

    "uniform float mRefractionRatio;",
    "uniform float mFresnelBias;",
    "uniform float mFresnelScale;",
    "uniform float mFresnelPower;",

    "varying vec3 vReflect;",
    "varying vec3 vRefract[3];",
    "varying float vReflectionFactor;",

    "void main() {",

        "vec4 mvPosition = modelViewMatrix * vec4( position, 1.0 );",
        "vec4 worldPosition = modelMatrix * vec4( position, 1.0 );",

        "vec3 worldNormal = normalize( mat3( modelMatrix[0].xyz, ",
        "    modelMatrix[1].xyz, modelMatrix[2].xyz ) * normal );",

        "vec3 I = worldPosition.xyz - cameraPosition;",

        "vReflect = reflect( I, worldNormal );",
        "vRefract[0] = refract( normalize( I ), worldNormal, ",
        "    mRefractionRatio );",
        "vRefract[1] = refract( normalize( I ), worldNormal, ",
        "    mRefractionRatio * 0.99 );",
        "vRefract[2] = refract( normalize( I ), worldNormal, ",
        "    mRefractionRatio * 0.98 );",
        "vReflectionFactor = mFresnelBias + mFresnelScale * ",
        "    pow( 1.0 + dot( normalize( I ), worldNormal ), ",
        "    mFresnelPower );",

        "gl_Position = projectionMatrix * mvPosition;",
```

```
    "}"
  ].join("\n"),
```

The vertex shader program is the workhorse for this particular material. It uses the camera position and the position of each vertex of the model—in this example, the sphere geometry used for the bubble shape—to calculate a direction vector, which is then used to compute reflection and refraction coefficients for each vertex. Note the varying declarations in the vertex and fragment shader programs. Unlike uniform variables, varying variables are computed for each vertex and are passed along from the vertex to the fragment shader. In this way, the vertex shader can output values in addition to the built-in gl_Position that is its primary job to compute. For the Fresnel shader, the varying outputs are the reflection and refraction coefficients.

The Fresnel vertex shader also makes use of several varying and uniform variables that we do not see here because they are predefined by Three.js, and passed to the GLSL compiler automatically: modelMatrix, modelViewMatrix, projectionMatrix, and cameraPosition. These values do not need to be—in fact, should not be—explicitly declared by the shader programmer.

modelMatrix *(uniform)*
: The world transformation matrix for the model (mesh). As discussed in the section "The Scene Graph and Transform Hierarchy" on page 67, this matrix is computed by Three.js every frame to determine the *world space position* of an object. Within the shader, it is used to calculate the world space position of each vertex.

modelViewMatrix *(uniform)*
: The transformation representing each object's position in camera space—that is, in coordinates relative to the position and orientation of the camera. This is particularly handy for computing camera-relative values (e.g., to determine reflection and refraction, which is exactly what is being done in this shader).

projectionMatrix *(uniform)*
: Used to calculate the familiar 3D-to-2D projection from camera space into screen space.

cameraPosition *(uniform)*
: The world space position of the camera maintained by Three.js and passed in automatically.

position *(varying)*
: The vertex position, in model space.

normal *(varying)*
: The vertex normal, in model space.

The vertex shader also makes use of built-in GLSL functions, `reflect()` and `refract()`, to compute reflection and refraction vectors based on the camera direction, normal, and refraction ratio. (These functions were built into the GLSL language because they are so generally useful for lighting computations like the Fresnel equations.)

Finally, note the use of `Array.join()` to set up the vertex shader. This illustrates yet another useful technique for putting together the long text strings that implement shaders in the GLSL language. Rather than escaping newlines at the end of each line of code and using string concatenation, we use `join()` to insert newlines between each line of code.

From here, the fragment shader's job is straightforward. It uses the reflection and refraction values computed by the vertex shader to index into the cube texture passed in the uniform variable `tCube`. This variable is of type `samplerCube`, a GLSL type designed to handle cube textures. We blend these two colors using the GLSL function `mix()`, to produce the final pixel output by storing it in the built-in `gl_FragColor`.

```
fragmentShader: [

    "uniform samplerCube tCube;",

    "varying vec3 vReflect;",
    "varying vec3 vRefract[3];",
    "varying float vReflectionFactor;",

    "void main() {",

        "vec4 reflectedColor = textureCube( tCube, ",
        "    vec3( -vReflect.x, vReflect.yz ) );",
        "vec4 refractedColor = vec4( 1.0 );",

        "refractedColor.r = textureCube( tCube, ",
        "    vec3( -vRefract[0].x, vRefract[0].yz ) ).r;",
        "refractedColor.g = textureCube( tCube, ",
        "    vec3( -vRefract[1].x, vRefract[1].yz ) ).g;",
        "refractedColor.b = textureCube( tCube, ",
        "    vec3( -vRefract[2].x, vRefract[2].yz ) ).b;",

        "gl_FragColor = mix( refractedColor, ",
        "    reflectedColor, clamp( vReflectionFactor, ",
        "    0.0, 1.0 ) );",

    "}"

].join("\n")

};
```

Creating a custom shader may seem like a lot of work, but the final result is worth it, as it produces a very convincing simulation of real-world optics. And the extra machinery

Three.js puts in place for us—keeping world matrices up to date per object, tracking the camera, predeclaring dozens of GLSL variables, compiling and linking the shader code —saves us literally days of development and debugging effort and makes the thought of developing our own custom shaders not only conceivable, but inviting. With this framework in place, you should feel free to experiment writing your own shaders. I suggest starting with the Fresnel and other shaders that come with the Three.js samples. There are many different kinds of effects and a lot to learn in there.

# Rendering

This chapter has climbed a Three.js ladder of sorts, an ascent of increasing realism that began with the drawing of simple geometric shapes, up through materials, textures, lights, and shadows, and eventually to writing our own shaders in GLSL. We have climbed high, creating more realistic graphics at each step, but we are not quite at the top. Believe it or not, there is one more rung: rendering.

The ultimate output of manipulating the Three.js 3D scene graph is a 2D image rendered onto a browser Canvas element. Whether we achieve this by using WebGL, using the 2D Canvas drawing API, or fiddling with CSS to move elements around on the page is almost irrelevant; the end goal is painting pixels. We choose to use WebGL because it can get the job done fast. Using the other technologies we might—*might*—be able to achieve many of these visual effects, but not an acceptable frame rate. So we often choose WebGL.

This being said, even with WebGL we have several choices about exactly how to have it render images. For example, the API allows us to use *Z-buffered* rendering—where the hardware uses additional memory to paint only those pixels frontmost in the scene— or not. It's our choice. If we don't use Z-buffering, our application will have to sort objects itself, potentially down to the triangle level. That sounds like a big hassle, but depending on the use case, we may want to do exactly that. This is but one such choice we can make regarding rendering.

Three.js was designed to make it easy to do basic graphics. The built-in WebGL renderer is ready to go with game-quality graphics without causing too much developer grief. As we have seen in the examples thus far, it's as easy as 1) creating the renderer, 2) setting the viewport dimensions, and 3) calling `render()`. But the library also allows us to do much more, providing the ability to control the WebGL rendering process at a fine-grained level. When this capability is combined with advanced rendering techniques such as post-processing, multipass rendering, and deferred rendering, we can create some truly realistic effects.

# Post-Processing and Multipass Rendering

Sometimes, one render isn't enough. It often takes several renderings of a scene with different parameters to create a high-quality, realistic-looking image. These separate renderings, or *passes*, are ultimately combined together to produce the final image in a process known as *multipass rendering*. Many multipass rendering approaches involve using *post-processing*, or improving an image's quality via image-processing techniques.

Post-processing and multipass rendering have become increasingly popular in real-time 3D rendering, so the authors of Three.js have taken great pains to support it. Figure 4-15 shows a subtle yet dramatic example of Three.js post-processing written by Altered-Qualia. Load the file *examples/webgl_terrain_dynamic.html*. Birds flock majestically over an otherworldly landscape in the foggy dawn light. As if the simplex noise-based, procedurally generated terrain weren't impressive enough, this piece also features multiple render passes, including bloom shading to emphasize the bright sunlight diffusing through the morning fog, and a Gaussian filter to softly blur the scene, further enhancing the scene's serene qualities.

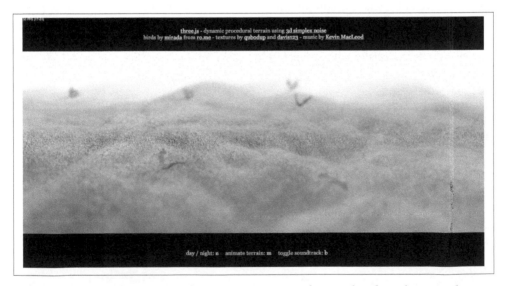

*Figure 4-15. Dynamic procedural terrain example, rendered with several post-processing passes—programming by AlteredQualia; birds by Mirada (of RO.ME fame)*

Three.js post-processing relies on the following features:

- Support for *multiple render targets* via the THREE.WebGLRenderTarget object. With multiple render targets, a scene can be rendered more than once to off-screen bitmaps and then combined later in a final image. (Source file: *src/renderers/WebGLRenderTarget.js*.)

- A multipass rendering loop implemented in class `THREE.EffectComposer`. This object contains one or more *render pass* objects that it will call in succession to render the scene. Each pass has access to the entire scene as well as the image data produced by the previous pass, allowing it to further refine the image.

`THREE.EffectComposer`, and the sample multipass techniques that use it, are located in the Three.js project folder examples, under *examples/js/postprocessing/* and *examples/js/shaders/*. A scan of these folders will unearth a treasure trove of post-processing special effects.

## Deferred Rendering

We have one more rendering approach to explore: *deferred rendering*. As the name implies, this approach delays rendering to the WebGL canvas until a final image is computed from multiple sources. Unlike multipass rendering, which successively renders a scene and refines the image before finally copying it to the WebGL canvas, deferred rendering employs multiple *buffers* (actually just texture maps) into which the data required for the shading computations is gathered in an initial pass. In a subsequent pass, the pixel values are calculated with the values gathered from the first pass. This approach can be memory- and computationally expensive, but it can produce highly realistic effects, especially with respect to lighting and shadows. See Figure 4-16 for an example (*http://localhost/three.js/examples/webgldeferred_arealights.html*).

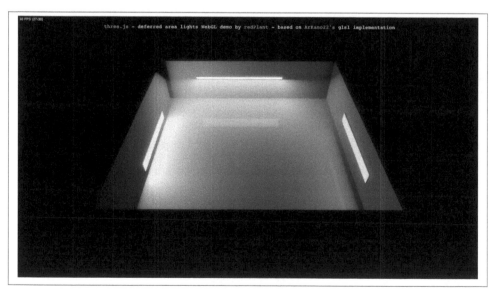

*Figure 4-16. Per-pixel lighting using deferred rendering*

# Chapter Summary

This chapter covered broad ground, touching on most of the graphics drawing and rendering capabilities present in Three.js. We saw how to use the prebuilt geometry classes to easily create 3D solids, meshes, and parameterized and extruded shapes. We discussed the Three.js scene graph and transform hierarchy for constructing complex scenes. We got hands-on experience with materials, textures, and lighting. Finally, we explored how programmable shaders and advanced rendering techniques such as post-processing and deferred rendering can increase visual realism. The graphics features in Three.js represent a massive arsenal, packaged up in an accessible and easy-to-use library. These facilities, combined with the raw power of WebGL, allow us to create nearly any 3D visuals we can imagine.

# CHAPTER 5

# 3D Animation

Animation means making changes to the image on the screen over time. With animation, an otherwise static 3D scene comes to life. While there are many techniques for animating, and many ways to model the problem conceptually, at the end of the day, animation is all about one thing: making the pixels move.

WebGL doesn't have built-in animation capability per se. However, the power and speed of the API allow us to render amazing graphics and change them at up to 60 frames per second, providing us with several options for animating 3D content. Combined with improvements to the runtime architecture of modern browsers, this enables animations that blend seamlessly with the other elements on the page, without tearing or other unwanted artifacts.

Animation can be used to change anything in a WebGL scene: transforms, geometry, textures, materials, lights, and cameras. Objects can move, rotate, and scale, or follow paths; geometry can bend, twist, and change into other shapes; textures can be moved, scaled, rotated, and scrolled, and have their pixels modified every frame; material colors, specular highlights, transparency values, and more can change over time; lights can blink, move, and change color; and cameras can be moved and rotated to create cinematic effects. The possibilities are essentially limitless.

In this chapter, we will look at a variety of animation techniques, and the tools and libraries to implement them. These techniques are grounded in years of film and video game industry practice, backed by rigorous mathematics. Animation with WebGL is an evolving area, so our exploration involves cobbling together various solutions. Three.js comes with animation utilities that handle certain situations well. We will also look at another open source library, Tween.js. Tween.js is a small, easy-to-use library for creating simple transitions. But these are far from complete packages. If your application is sufficiently complex, you may need to create your own animation engine.

Animating WebGL content involves employing one or more of the following concepts, which will be covered in detail in this chapter:

- Using `requestAnimationFrame()` to drive the run loop.

- Programmatically *updating properties* of visual objects each time through the run loop. This is good for creating simple animations, such as spinning an object about a single axis. This technique can also be useful when an object's position, orientation, or other property is best expressed as a function of a variable such as time. Overall, this is the simplest animation technique to implement, but it is limited to very specific use cases.

- Using *tweens* to transition properties smoothly from one value to another. Tweens are perfect for simple, one-shot effects (e.g., moving an object from one position to another along a straight path).

- Using *key frames*, where data structures represent individual values along a timeline, and an engine calculates (*interpolates*) intermediate values to produce a smooth result. Key frames work well for basic animation of translation, rotation, and scale, and simple properties such as material colors. Unlike tweens, which support a single transition from one value to another, key frames allow us to create a series of transitions within one animation.

- Animating objects along *paths*—user-generated curves and line segments—to create complex and organic-looking motion based on formulas or preauthored path data.

- Using *morph targets* to deform geometry by blending among a set of distinct shapes. This is an excellent technique for facial expressions and for very simple character animation.

- Using *skinning* to deform geometry based on animating an underlying skeleton. This is the preferred way to animate characters and other complex shapes.

- Using *shaders* to deform vertices and/or change pixel values over time. Sometimes, a desired animated effect is best calculated on a per-vertex or per-pixel basis, suggesting the use of GLSL to implement it. Shaders can also be used to accelerate the performance of the other techniques—in particular, morphs and skinning, which can be computationally expensive if done on the CPU.

Often an application will make use of more than one, or sometimes all, of these approaches. There are no hard and fast rules about which techniques apply in which situations, though some are better suited for implementing particular effects. Often the choice of technique is driven by production concerns; for example, if you don't have a needed artist on staff, it may be easier to have a programmer generate the animations in code. Other times, it may simply come down to personal preference. 3D animation is equal parts art and science, a mix of production and engineering.

# Driving Animation with requestAnimationFrame()

In previous chapters we saw how to power our application's run loop using `request AnimationFrame()`, a relatively recent arrival to web browser APIs.

`requestAnimationFrame()` was designed to allow web applications to provide consistent, reliable presentation of visual content driven by JavaScript code. The content might be changing the page DOM, adjusting layouts, modifying styles using CSS, or creating arbitrary graphics with one of the drawing APIs such as WebGL and Canvas. The feature was first introduced in Firefox version 4 and eventually adopted by all the other browsers. Robert O'Callahan of Mozilla was looking for a way to ensure that animations handled by the browser for built-in features like CSS Transitions and SVG could be synchronized with user code written in JavaScript.

Historically, web applications used timers to animate page content, via either `setTime out()` or `setInterval()`. As applications began to incorporate more complex animations and interactivity, it became clear that this approach suffered from several key problems:

- The timer functions call callbacks at a specific interval (or as close to it as possible), regardless of whether it is a good time to draw or not.
- JavaScript executed in a timer callback has no reliable way to synchronize with the timing of other browser-generated animation on the page (e.g., SVG or CSS Transitions).
- Timers execute regardless of whether a page or tab is visible or the browser window has been minimized, potentially resulting in wasted drawing calls.
- JavaScript application code has no idea of the display's refresh rate and so has to make an arbitrary choice for the interval value: make it 1/24 of a second, and you deprive the user of resolution on a 60 Hz display; make it 1/60 of a second and on slow-refresh displays, you waste CPU cycles drawing content that is never seen.

`requestAnimationFrame()` was designed to solve all of the preceding problems. Recalling examples from previous chapters, our run loop takes a form similar to the following:

```
function run() {

    // Request the next animation frame
     requestAnimationFrame(run);

    // Run animations
    animate();

    // Render the scene
    renderer.render( scene, camera );
```

Note the absence of a time value in the call to requestAnimationFrame(). We are not asking the browser to call our animation and drawing code at any specific time or interval; rather, we are asking it to call it *when it is ready to present the page again*. This is a key distinction. With this scheme in place, the browser can call user drawing code during its internal repaint cycle. This has several benefits. First, the browser can do this as frequently—or equally important, as *infrequently*—as needed. When the browser has sufficient idle cycles, it can try to ensure the highest frame rate possible to match the display refresh rate. Conversely, if a page or tab is hidden, or the entire browser is minimized, it can throttle the amount of times it calls such callbacks, optimizing use of the computer or device's resources. Second, the browser can invoke batch user drawing, which ultimately results in fewer repaints of the screen, also a resource saver. Third, any user drawing code executed from requestAnimationFrame() will be blended, or *composited*, with all other drawing calls, including internal ones. The net result of all this is smoother, faster, more efficient page drawing and animation.

## Using requestAnimationFrame() in Your Application

Like many recent developments in the HTML5 suite of features, requestAnimation Frame() is not necessarily supported in all versions of all browsers—though that is rapidly changing. Also, given its evolution from an experimental feature in one browser through to W3C recommendations, the function has been implemented with different, prefixed names in each of the browsers. Thankfully, we can make use of a great polyfill created by Paul Irish at Google. The code for it, listed in Example 5-1, can be found in the book example file *libs/requestAnimationFrame/RequestAnimationFrame.js*. It attempts to find the correctly named version of the function for the current browser or, failing that, falls back to setTimeout(), going for it with a 60 frames-per-second interval.

*Example 5-1. RequestAnimationFrame polyfill by Paul Irish*

```
/**
 * Provides requestAnimationFrame in a cross browser way.
 * http://paulirish.com/2011/requestanimationframe-for-smart-animating/
 */

if ( !window.requestAnimationFrame ) {

    window.requestAnimationFrame = ( function() {

        return window.webkitRequestAnimationFrame ||
        window.mozRequestAnimationFrame ||
        window.oRequestAnimationFrame ||
        window.msRequestAnimationFrame ||
        function( /* function FrameRequestCallback */ callback,
            /* DOMElement Element */ element ) {

            window.setTimeout( callback, 1000 / 60 );
```

```
    };

  } )();

}
```

For those not familiar with the term, a *polyfill* is code (usually Java-Script) that provides facilities not built into a web browser. Polyfills are routinely used with older browser versions that do not support new or experimental features. The term was coined by UK-based engineer Remy Sharp. For more on the background and etymology of the polyfill, consult Sharp's blog posting (*http://remysharp.com/2010/10/08/what-is-a-polyfill/*).

One key to successful use of `requestAnimationFrame()` is to make sure you request the next frame *before* calling any other user code, as was done in the run loop fragment shown earlier. This is important for dealing with exceptions. If you are driving your entire 3D application from the animation callback, and code somewhere generates an exception before requesting the next frame, your application is dead. However, if you request the next frame before doing anything else, at least you are guaranteed to continue running. This allows parts of your application to function and repaint elements, even if something is wrong elsewhere.

## requestAnimationFrame() and Performance

While `requestAnimationFrame()` is a boon for animation performance, it comes with a certain responsibility. If the browser is calling your callback every 60th of a second, the onus is on you to write callbacks that take 16 milliseconds or less. If you don't, your application may appear unresponsive to the user. Because 16 milliseconds is not a lot of time, you must take care to do the minimum amount of work required to make the necessary drawing changes and no more. Industrial-strength 3D applications might consider using timers, workers, and other animation techniques like CSS Transforms and Transitions in conjunction with `requestAnimationFrame()` to deliver the most responsive, powerful, resource-efficient experiences possible.

`requestAnimationFrame()` is arguably one of the most important features introduced for HTML5. This section merely scratched the surface on the topic. There are several excellent online resources for learning more about it. Do a web search on the name and you will discover a trove of articles, backgrounders, how-tos, tips and tricks, and explanations of what is under the hood.

## Frame-Based Versus Time-Based Animation

Early computer animation systems emulated predecessor film animation techniques by presenting a succession of still images on the display, or, in vector-based graphics, a series of vector-based images generated by the program. Each such image is known as a *frame*. Historically, film was shot and played back at a rate of 24 images every second, known as a *frame rate* of 24 frames per second (fps). This speed was adequate for large projection screens in low light settings. However, in the world of computer-generated animation and 3D games, our senses are actually able to perceive and appreciate changes that occur at higher frame rates, upward of 30 and up to 60 or more fps. Despite this, many animation systems, such as Adobe Flash, originally adopted the 24 fps convention due to its familiarity for traditional animators. These days, the frame rates have changed —Flash supports 60 fps if the developer requests it—but the concept of discrete frames remains. This technique of organizing animation into a series of discrete frames is known as *frame-based animation*.

Frame-based animation has one serious drawback: by tying it to a specific frame rate, the animator has ensured that animation will never be able to be presented at a higher frame rate, even if the computer can support it. This was not an issue for film, where the hardware was fairly uniform throughout the industry. However, in computer animation, performance can vary wildly from device to device. If you create your animations at 24 fps, but your computer can refresh the screen at 60 Hz, you effectively deprive the user of additional detail and smoothness during playback.

A different technique, known as *time-based animation*, solves this problem. In time-based animation, a series of vector graphics images is connected to particular points in time, not specific frames in a sequence with known frame rates. In this way, the computer can present those images, and the interpolated frames between them, as frequently as possible and deliver the best images and smoothest transitions. In the examples in the previous chapters, we used time-based animation. Each time through the run loop, the `animate()` function calculated a time delta between the current and previous frame and used that to compute an angular rotation. All of the examples developed for this and subsequent chapters use time-based animation. So, even though the word *frame* is right in the name `requestAnimationFrame()`, rest assured that it can be used equally well for time-based animations.

# Animating by Programmatically Updating Properties

By far, the simplest way to get started animating a WebGL scene is to write code that updates an object's properties each time through the run loop. We have seen examples of this already in previous chapters. To rotate the Three.js cube in Chapter 3, we simply updated the cube's `rotation.y` property—that is, the angle of its rotation about the y-axis, each frame. Here is the code again:

```
var duration = 5000; // ms
var currentTime = Date.now();
function animate() {

    var now = Date.now();
    var deltat = now - currentTime;
    currentTime = now;
    var fract = deltat / duration;
    var angle = Math.PI * 2 * fract;
    cube.rotation.y += angle;
}
```

The variables `duration`, `currentTime`, `now`, and `deltat` are used to compute a time-based animation value for the rotation. In this example, we want a full rotation about the y-axis over the course of five seconds. The computed `angle` is a fraction of one complete rotation, the amount that must be added to the cube's current `rotation.y` property. Recall that rotations are represented in Three.js as *radians*, the distance around a unit circle; that is, `Math.PI * 2` is equal to a full (360 degree) rotation.

This concept can be applied to animate anything in a scene: position, rotation, scale, material colors and transparency, and so on. Moreover, it is completely general: by using JavaScript code to update properties, we can apply arbitrary computation. Animations can be driven by mathematical formulae, Boolean logic, statistical values, data streams, real-time sensor input, and so on. So this is a great technique for scientific illustration and data visualization: depicting solar systems, physical processes, and natural phenomena; or presenting time series information, statistical analyses, geographic data, website traffic, and other dynamic, database-driven information. It is also excellent for creating really lively and entertaining applications like music visualizers.

Figure 5-1 depicts the wild world of Ellie Goulding's Lights, a WebGL music visualization developed by UK-based interactive agency Hello Enjoy (*http://helloenjoy.com/*). This piece has been around for a while, but it still packs a punch. Glowing globes blink on and off, comet trails wind a curvy path through the scene, colored balls fade in and out and change color, spotlights twirl madly, and teardrop-shaped balloons blossom out of the multicolored, undulating terrain—all in time to the music of the hit song. This is eye candy at its best, with all effects being generated programmatically.

Example 5-2 shows a portion of the code that animates the visuals. The application's `update()` method is called each time through the run loop. It in turn calls `update()` on all the objects in the scene. The following excerpt is from `LIGHTS.StarManager.up date()`, which animates the background stars. The stars are rendered as Three.js particles belonging to a `THREE.ParticleSystem` object. The lines highlighted in bold show how the RGB color for each star is updated based on elapsed time, a decay factor, and the mod operator (%) to create a blink effect.

*Figure 5-1. Ellie Goulding's Lights (http://lights.elliegoulding.com/): A music visualizer built with programmatic animation; image courtesy Hello Enjoy, Inc.*

*Example 5-2. Animating to the beat: Code fragment from Ellie Goulding's Lights*

```
update: function() {

    var stars = this.stars,
        deltaTime = LIGHTS.deltaTime,
        star, brightness, i, il;

    for( i = 0, il = stars.length; i < il; i++ ) {

        star = this.stars[ i ];

        star.life += deltaTime;

        brightness = (star.life * 2) % 2;

        if( brightness > 1 )
            brightness = 1 - (brightness - 1);

        star.color.r =
        star.color.g =
        star.color.b = (Math.sin( brightness * rad90 - rad90 ) + 1) * 4;
    }

    this.particles.__dirtyColors = true;
},
```

As flexible and powerful as programmatic animation is, it has its limitations. It requires handcoding for each effect; as a consequence, it's hard to scale up to animate many different kinds of objects. It also tends to be more verbose than other data-driven methods such as tweening and key frames, which we will cover shortly. Finally, it puts the programmer at the center of the action, instead of the artist, who may be much better suited to creating the desired visual effect. Still, programmatic animation is an excellent way to quickly and easily add some life to a scene, and the effects can be truly stunning, as in the case of Ellie Goulding's Lights.

# Animating Transitions Using Tweens

Many animation effects are better represented as data structures, rather than values that are programmatically generated each time through the run loop. The application supplies a set of values and a time series, and a general-purpose engine calculates the per-frame values used to update properties. One such data-driven approach is known as *tweening*.

Tweening is the process of generating values that lie between a pair of other values. With tweening, the animator supplies only the values at the beginning and end points of the animation, and the engine calculates the intermediate values (*tweens*) for the intervening times. Tweening is perfect for simple one-time transitions from one state to another, such as moving an object in reaction to a mouse click.

## Interpolation

Tweening is accomplished through a mathematical technique called *interpolation*. Interpolation refers to the generation of a value that lies between two values, based on a scalar input such as a time or fraction value. Interpolation is illustrated in Figure 5-2. For any values A and B, and a fraction u between 0 and 1, the interpolated value P can be calculated by the formula A + u * (B − A). For the example depicted in Figure 5-2, we can see the interpolated value P(u) = 0.4. This is the simplest form of interpolation, known as *linear interpolation* because the mathematical function used to calculate the result could be graphed with a straight line. Other, more complex interpolation functions, such as splines (a type of curve) and polynomials, are also commonly used in animation systems. We will look at spline-based animation shortly.

Interpolation is used to calculate tweens of 3D positions, rotations, colors, scalar values (such as transparency), and more. With a multicomponent value such as a 3D vector, a linearly interpolated tween simply interpolates each component piecewise. For example, the interpolated value P at u = 0.5 for the 3D vector AB from (0, 0, 0) to (1, 2, 3) would be (0.5, 1, 1.5).

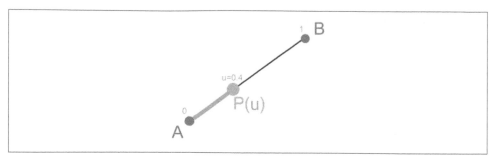

*Figure 5-2. Linear interpolation (http://bit.ly/gpwiki-linear-interlopation); reproduced with permission*

## The Tween.js Library

It is pretty straightforward to implement simple tweening on your own. However, if you want to have nonlinear interpolation functions, and other bells and whistles such as ease in/ease out (where the animation appears to accelerate to its main speed and decelerate out of it), then the problem becomes more complex. Rather than build your own tweening system, you may want to use an existing library. Tween.js (*https:// github.com/sole/tween.js*) is a popular open source tweening utility created by Soledad Penadés. It has been used in conjunction with Three.js on popular WebGL projects, including RO.ME (*http://www.ro.me/*), the WebGL Globe (*http://workshop.chromeex periments.com/globe/*), and Mine3D (*http://egraether.com/mine3d/*), a web version of the classic single-player game *Minesweeper*.

The example in the file *Chapter 5/tweenjstweens.html* contains a sandbox for testing out various Tween.js options. See Figure 5-3 for a screenshot. The sandbox uses Tween.js to apply various transitions to a textured cube: position, rotation, material color, and opacity. There are sliders for adjusting the tween duration and delay time (time before the tween starts), checkboxes to enable and disable the specific tweens, and an option to *loop* the tween (repeat it continuously). There is also an option to control easing functions, but we will talk about that in the next section. Play with the different options to see how they modify the effect.

Tween.js is very easy to work with. The syntax is simple, and thanks to the polymorphism of JavaScript, we can target any property using the exact same method calls. It also uses chained method syntax similar to jQuery, allowing for a very concise expression. Let's have a look. Example 5-3 shows a portion of the function `playAnimations()`, called to trigger the tweens each time a property is changed.

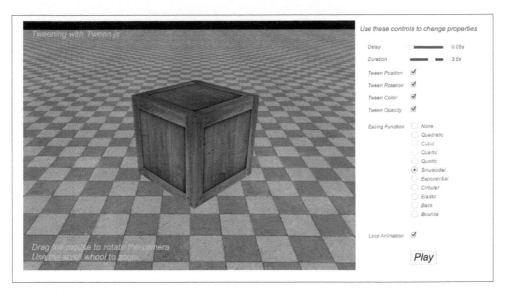

*Figure 5-3. Animating transitions with Tween.js*

*Example 5-3. Tween.js code to animate position*

```
positionTween =

    new TWEEN.Tween( group.position )
     .to({ x: 2, y: 2, z:-3 }, duration * 1000)
     .interpolation(interpolationType)
     .delay( delayTime * 1000 )
     .easing(easingFunction)
     .repeat(repeatCount)
     .start();
```

The position tween is set up with a single chained set of methods:

- The constructor, new TWEEN.Tween. It takes a single argument, the target object whose properties it will tween.

- to(), which takes a JavaScript object defining the properties to tween, and a duration in milliseconds.

- interpolation(), an optional method that specifies the type of interpolation. This can be omitted for linear interpolation, as this is the default (TWEEN.Interpolation.Linear).

- delay(), an optional method for inserting a delay before the tween starts.

- easing(), an optional method for applying an easing function (covered in the next section).

- `repeat()`, an optional method for specifying the number of times the tween repeats (default is zero).
- `start()`, which starts the tween.

Note that these methods can also be called separately. Each of the tweens—position, rotation, material color, and opacity—is set up in a similar fashion. A great thing about Tween.js is that you do not have to supply all values of the object to the `to()` method, only those that will be changed. For example, the rotation tween changes only the rotation about the y-axis, so it is created as follows:

```
rotationTween =

    new TWEEN.Tween( group.rotation )
    .to( { y: Math.PI * 2 }, duration * 1000)
    .interpolation(interpolationType)
    .delay( delayTime * 1000 )
    .easing(easingFunction)
    .repeat(repeatCount)
    .start();
```

Once the tween is set up and started, it is now a matter of making sure that Tween.js updates it every animation frame. It is up to the application to do this, so we add the following line to our `run()` function:

```
TWEEN.update();
```

Under the hood, Tween.js keeps a list of all its running tween objects and calls their `update()` methods in turn. `update()` calculates how much time has elapsed, applies easing functions and delay and repeat options, and ultimately sets the properties of the target object as specified in the `to()` method. This is a beautifully elegant yet simple scheme for making object properties change over time without having to handcode the changes each frame.

## Easing

Basic tweens with linear interpolation can result in a stiff, unnatural effect, because the objects change at a constant rate. This is unlike objects in the real world, which behave with inertia, momentum, acceleration, and so on. With Tween.js, we can create more natural-feeling tweens by incorporating *easing*—nonlinear functions applied to the start and end of the tween. Easing is a great tool for adding more realism to your tweens. It can even do a fair job approximating physics without requiring the hard work of integrating a physics engine into your application.

Try out the various easing functions in the tweening sandbox and note their effects. Some simply create a gradual speedup and slowdown of the tween; others provide bouncy and springy effects. The polynomial easing functions `Quadratic`, `Cubic`, `Quartic`, and `Quintic` ease the tween just as their names imply: via second-, third-, fourth-, and fifth-degree functions. Other easing functions provide sine wave, bounce, and spring effects. Each easing function can be used to ease in (at the beginning of the tween), ease out (at the end of the tween), or do both.

What the easing functions are actually doing is modifying *time*. Example 5-4 shows the code for the easing function TWEEN.Easing.Cubic. Inputs to the easing functions are in the range [0..1] (i.e., a fraction of the tween's full duration). The input, k, is cubed by the easing function; therefore, small input values of k return even smaller output values; however, as k approaches 1, so does the return value.

*Example 5-4. The Tween.js cubic easing function*

```
Cubic: {

    In: function ( k ) {

        return k * k * k;

    },

    Out: function ( k ) {

        return --k * k * k + 1;

    },

    InOut: function ( k ) {

        if ( ( k *= 2 ) < 1 ) return 0.5 * k * k * k;
        return 0.5 * ( ( k -= 2 ) * k * k + 2 );

    }

},
```

 The Tween.js easing functions are based on the seminal animation work of Robert Penner (*http://www.robertpenner.com/index2.html*). They offer a wide range of powerful easing equations, including linear, quadratic, quartic, sinusoidal, and exponential. Penner's work has been ported from the original ActionScript to several languages, including JavaScript, Java, CSS, C++, and C#, and has been incorporated into jQuery's animation utilities.

As we have just seen, tweens are great for easily creating simple, natural-looking effects. Tween.js even lets you chain animations together into a sequence so that you can compose simple effects into more powerful ones. However, as you begin building complex animation sequences you are going to want a more general solution. That's where key frames come in.

# Using Key Frames for Complex Animations

Tweens are perfect for simple transition effects. More complex animations take the tween concept to the next level by using *key frames*. Rather than specifying a single pair of values to tween, a key frame animation consists of a list of values, with potentially different durations in between each successive value. Note that the term *key frame animation* is used in both frame-based and time-based systems—a holdover from frame-based nomenclature.

Key frame data consists of two components: a list of time values (*keys*) and a list of values. The listed values represent the property values to be applied at the time of the corresponding key; the animation system computes tweens for time values lying between any pair of keys.

The following code fragment (from a hypothetical animation engine) shows sample key frame values for an animation that moves an object from the origin up and away from the camera. Over the course of a second, the object moves upward in the first quarter of a second, then up some more and away from the camera in the remaining three-quarters of a second. The animation system will calculate tweens for the points (0, 0, 0) to (0, 1, 0) over the first quarter-second, then tweens for (0, 1, 0) to (0, 2, 5) over the remaining three-quarters of a second.

```
var keys = [0, 0.25, 1];
var values = [[0, 0, 0],
              [0, 1, 0),
         [0, 2, 5]
              ];
```

Key frame animations can work with linear interpolation, or more complex interpolation such as spline-based; in other words, the data points representing the keys can be thought of as points in a line graph or as the graph of a more complicated function such as a cubic spline. While both tweening and key framing employ interpolation, there are two main aspects that differentiate key frame animations from simple tweens: 1) key frame animations can contain more than two values, and 2) the time interval can vary between successive keys. This enables more powerful effects and gives the animator more control.

## Keyframe.js—A Simple Key Frame Animation Utility

Before we can look at a key-framing example, we need to identify an animation library that supports the technique. Tween.js has taken baby steps toward supporting key framing, by allowing lists of property values instead of just pairs. However, in my opinion the syntax for these is a bit cumbersome. Also, there is no way to vary the interval between successive keys. Three.js actually provides built-in animation classes for animating with key frames, but these are not easy to use for handcoding quick and dirty effects; they were built primarily to support the file loading utilities for loading JSON,

---

COLLADA, and other formats. Fair enough: in general, key frame content is meant to be generated by authoring tools such as 3ds Max, Maya, or Blender, not written by hand. Still, it would nice to have an easy way for programmers to put together simple key frames. My frustration with the lack of an easy key framing solution for WebGL led me to write my own utility, Keyframe.js.

Keyframe.js is very simple. It implements two classes, a `KeyFrameAnimator` class that controls the animation state (start, stop, looping logic, and so on), and an `Interpola tor` class that calculates the tweens for each key pair. At the moment, the library supports only linear interpolation. However, Keyframe.js does allow the programmer to supply easing functions, and for those we can borrow the excellent Penner equations implemented in Tween.js—no need to reinvent the wheel. To see Keyframe.js in action, open the file *Chapter 5/keyframeanimation.html*. You will see a page that looks like the screenshot in Figure 5-4. Here we see a high seas adventure in progress: a wooden crate bobs in turbulent water, while the sky occasionally brightens and darkens, signaling an impending storm. The controls on the right allow you to play with the duration, turn individual animations on and off, and toggle looping.

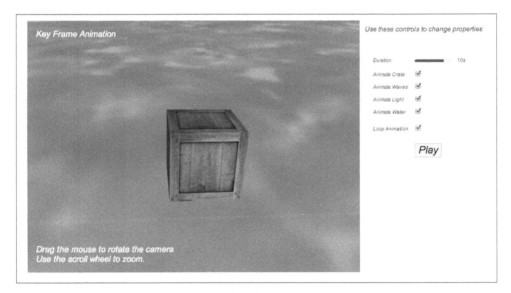

*Figure 5-4. Complex animations using key frames*

Example 5-5 shows the code to animate the wooden crate. First, we create a new `KF.Key FrameAnimator` and initialize it with parameters: looping, a time duration (in milliseconds), an easing function (borrowed from Tween.js), and a set of key frame interpolation data in the parameter `interps`. Most notably in contrast with Tween.js, the keys and values are lists, not just pairs; moreover, the intervals between successive keys are different. Following the details of the position interpolator (`target:group.position`), the crate moves left and forward from time t = 0 to t = 0.2, then back to the origin quickly (t = 0.2 to 0.25), after which it quickly dips into the water (t = 0.25 to 0.375). It then moves back up to the surface at t = 0.5, slowly sinks (t = 0.5 to 0.9), and finally bobs back up at t = 1.0. Note that in Keyframe.js, keys are specified as a fraction of the duration; that is, they always range from 0 to 1, so the actual time of a frame is equal to:

```
time = t × duration
```

There is a second interpolator for rotation, to tilt the crate about the x-axis. Note that this interpolator has a different number of keys; that is valid, and in fact a feature. The position and rotation animations were created intentionally to be a little out of sync, to make the effect more chaotic. The final flourish is the incorporation of the easing function TWEEN.Easing.Bounce.InOut. The combination of independent, uncoordinated translation and rotation with the bouncy math of the easing function does the trick: the crate does a fair job of appearing to bounce around in the water. The only thing left to do is play the animation, by calling its start() method.

*Example 5-5. Key frame animation for the crate*

```
if (animateCrate)
{
    crateAnimator = new KF.KeyFrameAnimator;
    crateAnimator.init({
        interps:
            [
                {
                    keys:[0, .2, .25, .375, .5, .9, 1],
                    values:[
                            { x : 0, y:0, z: 0 },
                            { x : .5, y:0, z: .5 },
                            { x : 0, y:0, z: 0 },
                            { x : .5, y:-.25, z: .5 },
                            { x : 0, y:0, z: 0 },
                            { x : .5, y:-.25, z: .5 },
                            { x : 0, y:0, z: 0 },
                            ],
                    target:group.position
                },
                {
                    keys:[0, .25, .5, .75, 1],
                    values:[
                            { x : 0, z : 0 },
                            { x : Math.PI / 12, z : Math.PI / 12 },
                            { x : 0, z : Math.PI / 12 },
                            { x : -Math.PI / 12, z : -Math.PI / 12 },
                            { x : 0, z : 0 },
                            ],
                    target:group.rotation
                },
            ],
```

```
        loop: loopAnimation,
        duration:duration * 1000,
        easing:TWEEN.Easing.Bounce.InOut,
    });
    crateAnimator.start();

}
```

The animations for the water and storm are handled similarly, though none of the other animations use an easing function. There is an animation to make the water surface move up and down (simple rotation of the water plane about the x-axis); one for creating the appearance of waves, essentially "scrolling" the texture map by interpolating its offset property; and one to make the light flash by interpolating its RGB color values.

This example is a simple illustration of how key frames can create more interesting effects than the basic transitions supported in Tween.js. Key frames can be expressed easily as arrays of keys and values, allowing the animator to sequence tweens of different durations. In practice, programmers rarely create these kinds of animations by hand; rather, artists do it using professional tools. This is the preferred way to go for developing complex effects, especially those involving multiple objects—the subject of the next section.

## Articulated Animation with Key Frames

The animation strategies we have discussed so far can be used to move single objects in place (i.e., with rotation) or around and within the scene, but they can also be used to create complex motions in composite objects using a transform hierarchy.

Let's say we want to create a robot that walks and waves its arms. We would model the robot as a hierarchical structure: the robot body contains an upper body and lower body, the upper body contains arms and a torso, the arms contain upper arms and lower arms, and so on. By properly constructing the hierarchy and animating the right parts, we can get the robot to move its arms and legs. The technique of constructing bodies by combining a hierarchy of discrete parts and animating them in combinations is known as *articulated animation*.

The Three.js examples come with a nice demonstration of articulated animation. Load the Three.js example file *examples/webgl_loader_collada_keyframe.html*. You will see an animated model of a pump that shows its inner workings. As the pump rotates, it opens up to assemble and disassemble itself, exposing various parts such as valves, gaskets, gears, housings, and the bolts that hold the pump together. Each of the parts animates individually; however, thanks to the Three.js transform hierarchy, each part also moves with its ancestors as they go through their paces, opening and closing, inserting one part into another, and so on. Figure 5-5 depicts the pump in action.

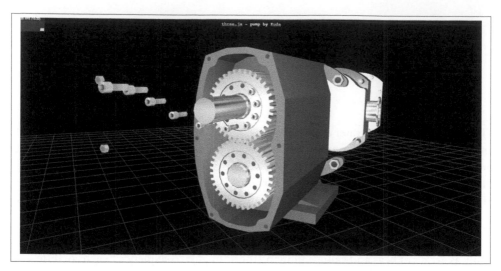

*Figure 5-5. Articulated animation: the inner workings of a pump using key frames with a transform hierarchy (COLLADA model created with the Kuda open source authoring system (https://code.google.com/p/kuda/))*

This pump model is loaded via the COLLADA file format (.*dae* file extension), an XML-based text format for describing 3D content. COLLADA can represent individual models or entire scenes, and supports materials, lights, cameras, and animations. We won't get too deep into the details, but key frame data in COLLADA looks similar to the following excerpt from the pump model (file *examples/models/collada/pump/pump.dae*):

```
<animation id="camTrick_G.translate_camTrick_G">
  <source id="camTrick_G..." name="camTrick_G...">
    <float_array id="camTrick_G..." count="3">0.04166662 ... </float_array>
    <source id="camTrick_G..." name="camTrick_G...">
    <float_array id="camTrick_G..." count="3">8.637086 ... </float_array>
```

The COLLADA <animation> element defines an animation. The two <float_array> child elements shown here define the keys and values, respectively, required to animate the *x* component of the transform for an object named camTrick_G. The keys are specified in seconds. Over the course of 7.08333 seconds, camTrick_G will translate in *x* from 8.637086 to 0. There is an additional key in between at 6.5 seconds that specifies an *x* translation of 7.794443. So, for this animation, there is a rather slow *x* translation over the first 6.5 seconds, followed by a rapid one over the remaining 0.58333 seconds. There are dozens of such animation elements defined in this COLLADA file (74 in all) for the various objects that compose the pump model.

Example 5-6 shows an excerpt from the code that sets up the animations for this example. The example makes use of the built-in Three.js classes THREE.KeyFrameAnimation and THREE.AnimationHandler. THREE.KeyFrameAnimation implements general-purpose key frame animation for use with COLLADA and other animation-capable formats. THREE.AnimationHandler is a singleton that manages a list of the animations in the scene and maintains responsibility for updating them each time through the application's run loop. (The code for these classes can be found in the Three.js project in the folder *src/extras/animation.*)

*Example 5-6. Initializing Three.js key frame animations*

```
var animHandler = THREE.AnimationHandler;

for ( var i = 0; i < kfAnimationsLength; ++i ) {

    var animation = animations[ i ];
    animHandler.add( animation );

    var kfAnimation = new THREE.KeyFrameAnimation(
            animation.node, animation.name );
    kfAnimation.timeScale = 1;
    kfAnimations.push( kfAnimation );

}
```

The example does a little more setup before eventually calling each animation's play() method to get it running. play() takes two arguments: a loop flag and an optional start time (with zero, the default, meaning play immediately):

```
animation.play( false, 0 );
```

This example shows how key frame animation can combine with a transform hierarchy to create complex, articulated effects. Articulated animation is typically used as the basis for animating mechanical objects; however, as we will see later in this chapter, it is also essential for driving the skeletons underlying skinned animation.

 As is the case with many of the file format loaders that come with Three.js, the COLLADA loader is not part of the core package but rather included with the samples. The source code for the Three.js COLLADA loader can be found in *examples/js/loaders/ColladaLoader.js.* The COLLADA format will be discussed in detail in Chapter 8.

# Using Curves and Path Following to Create Smooth, Natural Motion

Key frames are the perfect way to specify a sequence of transitions with varying time intervals. By combining articulated animation with hierarchy, we can create complex interactions. However, the samples we have looked at so far look mechanical and artificial because they use linear functions to interpolate. The real world has curves: cars hug curved roads, planes travel in curved paths, projectiles fall in an arc, and so on. Attempting to simulate those effects using linear interpolation produces unsettling, unnatural results. We could use a physics engine, but for many uses that is overkill. Sometimes we just want to create a predefined animation that looks natural, without having to pay the costs of computing a physics simulation.

Key frame data is not just limited to describing linear animations. It can be treated as points on a curve, too. The most common type of curve used in animation is a *spline* curve—a smooth, continuous curve. Certain types of splines, called *B-splines*, are common in computer graphics because they are relatively fast to compute. We define a B-spline using a set of data points to define the basic shape of the curve, plus additional *control points* that modulate the shape of the curve. The simple B-spline depicted in Figure 5-6 shows the control points in black. If you have ever used a professional drawing program such as Adobe Illustrator, you will be familiar with control points used to modify the shape of a spline curve.

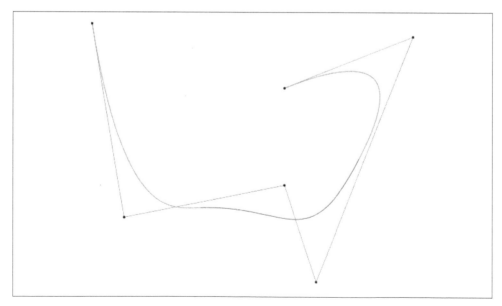

*Figure 5-6. A B-spline curve, by Wojciech mula (licensed under Creative Commons CC0 1.0 Universal Public Domain Dedication)*

Spline interpolation is more complex than simple linear interpolation, incorporating polynomial formulas akin to those found in the Tween.js easing functions, and an additional value on either side of the key values to compute the smooth curve. A full explanation of spline interpolation mathematics is beyond the scope of this book. However, Figure 5-7 shows an intuitive view of how it works: to compute an interpolated value along the curve between points P1 and P2, we also use control points P0 and P3 in order to generate a value that lies on the spline curve.

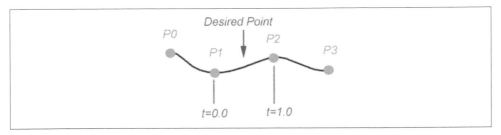

*Figure 5-7. Spline interpolation (http://www.mvps.org/directx/articles/catmull/); reproduced with permission*

 Splines come in several varieties, including *B-splines*, *cubic Bézier splines*, and *Catmull-Rom splines*, named after animation genius and Pixar founder Ed Catmull. Catmull-Rom has become popular because it is easier to construct and compute than Bézier curves. Three.js comes with a built-in animation class that uses Catmull-Rom interpolation. See the Three.js source file *src/extras/animations/animation.js*.

There are several good online Catmull-Rom tutorials, including *http://flashcove.net/795/cubic-spline-generation-in-as3-catmull-rom-curves/* and *http://www.mvps.org/directx/articles/catmull/*.

Spline animation often needs to take into account orientation as well as position. If, for example, you want to animate an object following a curved path, you need to have it turn, tilt, and roll in order to make it appear natural. That involves computing a new orientation at each point. Figure 5-8 depicts that process. At each point on the curve, a *tangent*, *normal*, and *binormal* are computed. Informally, the tangent is the straight line following the direction of the curve, intersecting it at one point only. The normal is the line perpendicular to the direction of the curve (and to the tangent). The binormal is the cross product of the other two lines. Together, these three vectors define a frame of reference known as the *TNB frame*, which defines the orientation for an object following the path.

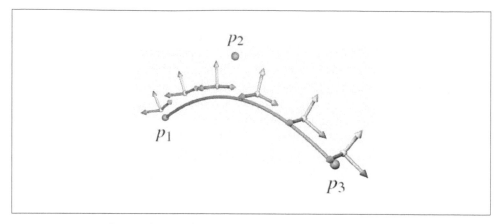

*Figure 5-8. Coordinate frames for spline animation (http://circecharacterworks.word press.com/tag/skinning/); tangents, normals, and binormals are represented by blue (forward), green (up), and red (right) arrows, respectively; image courtesy Cedric Bazillou, reproduced with permission*

There is a nice example of path-following animation in the Three.js samples. Open the file *examples/webgl_geometry_extrude_splines.html*. Be sure to press the button labeled Camera Spline Animation View to see the animation depicted in Figure 5-9. The camera follows the spline curve from a short distance away, continually adjusting its position and orientation. This particular example was animated programmatically, computing the spline interpolation and TNB frame in code. But it could conceivably be packaged into a reusable path-following animation class.

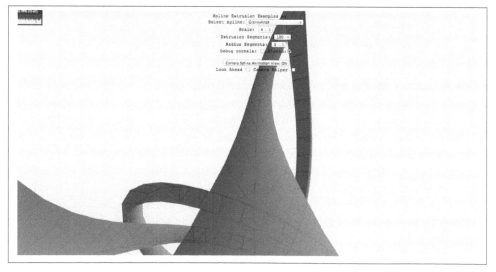

*Figure 5-9. A camera animating along a path*

# Using Morph Targets for Character and Facial Animation

Key frames and articulated animation are great for moving objects around within the scene, but many animation effects require changing the geometry of the object itself. A common way to do this is via *morph target animation*, or simply, *morphing*. Morphing uses vertex-based interpolations to change the vertices of a mesh. Typically, a subset of the vertices of a mesh is stored, along with their indices, as a set of *morph targets* to be used in a tween. The tween interpolates between each of the vertex values in the morph targets, and the animation uses the interpolated values to deform the vertices in the mesh.

Morph targets are excellent for facial expressions and other fine details that are not so easy to implement in a skinned animation (see next section); they are compact and don't require a highly detailed skeleton with numerous facial bones. In addition, they allow the animator to create very specific expressions by tweaking the mesh right down the vertex level. Figure 5-10 illustrates the use of morphing to create facial expressions. Each different expression, such as the pursed lips or the smile, is represented by a set of vertices including the mouth and surrounding areas.

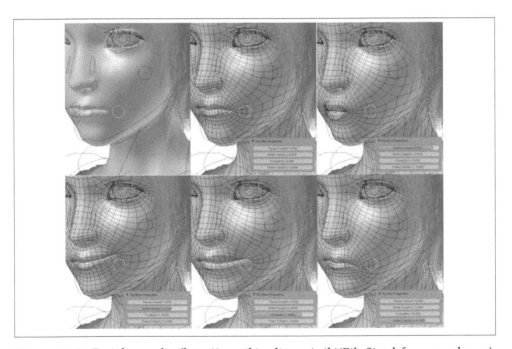

*Figure 5-10. Facial morphs (http://en.wikipedia.org/wiki/File:Sintel-face-morph.png); Creative Commons Attribution-Share Alike 3.0 unported license*

Morphs can be used for more than just faces. Several examples in the Three.js project use morph targets to animate entire characters. Figure 5-11 depicts characters animated using morphs. These characters were originally modeled in the id Software MD2 file format, a popular morph-based format used for animating player characters in id games such as *Quake II*. The MD2 file was then converted to the Three.js JSON file format (see Chapter 8).

*Figure 5-11. Animating characters with morph targets; models converted from MD2 format to Three.js JSON ("Ogro" character by Magarnigal (http://bit.ly/L0ppGl))*

To see these animations, load the file *examples/webgl_morphtargets_md2_control.htm*. You will see several ogre characters lumbering, turning, and looking over their shoulders. The arrow and WASD keys on the keyboard will make the characters move around the scene, transitioning from their idle animations to walking and turning animation sequences. The effect is quite convincing.

To get a feel for what morph target data looks like, open the converted MD2 file located in *examples/models/animated/ogro/ogro-light.js*. At around line 18, you will see a JSON property that begins as follows:

```
"morphTargets": [
{ "name": "stand001", "vertices": [0.6,-2.7,1.5,-5.5,-3.3,-0.6 ...
```

This continues for several lines. Each element of the morphTargets array is a single morph target; each morph target contains the complete set of vertices for the ogre mesh, but with different position values. Three.js animates the morph by cycling through the set of targets for the model, interpolating vertex values to blend from one target to the next. You can find the code for loading, setting up, and animating MD2 characters implemented in the class THREE.MD2CharacterComplex, in the Three.js example source file *examples/js/MD2CharacterComplex.js*.

 The MD2 file for this example was converted to the Three.js JSON file format using a wonderful online utility written by Klas, aka OutsideOfSociety (*https://twitter.com/oosmoxiecode*), a team member at Swedish-based interactive developer North Kingdom. For details on how to use the converter, see Klas's blog entry (*http://oos.moxie code.com/blog/index.php/2012/01/md2-to-json-converter*).

# Animating Characters with Skinning

Articulated animation works very well for inorganic objects—robots, cars, machines, and so on. It breaks down badly for organic objects. Plants swaying in the breeze, animals bounding, and people dancing all involve changes to the geometry of a mesh: branches twist, skin ripples, muscles bulge. It is nearly impossible to do this well with the tinker-toy approach that is articulated animation. So we turn to another technique called *skinned animation*, also known as *skinning, skeletal animation*, or *single mesh animation*.

Skinned animation involves deforming the actual vertices of a mesh, or *skin*, over time. Animation is driven by an articulated object hierarchy known as a *skeleton* (sometimes called a *rig*). The skeleton is used only as the underlying mechanism for animating; we don't see it on the screen. Changes to the skeleton, combined with additional data describing how the skeleton influences changes to the skin in various regions of the mesh, drive the skinned animation. Figure 5-12 depicts a simple skeleton and its associated skin.

A skeleton is composed, not surprisingly, of *bones*. Bones are organized in a hierarchy, in the intuitive way you would expect. Like the old song goes: foot bone connected to the leg bone, leg bone connected to the knee bone…and so on. Just as with articulated animation, transforming a bone moves all its child bones. However, unlike with articulated animation, the skeleton is not visible.

Each bone in the skeleton is associated with a set of vertices of the mesh, along with a *blend weight* (also known as a *vertex weight*) for each associated vertex. The blend weight specifies how much that particular bone influences its associated vertices. Vertices can be associated with multiple bones, so the ultimate position and orientation of a vertex is determined by the combined transformations of all associated bones, scaled by the respective weights. If this sounds complicated, it is. Skinned animations are almost always produced by authoring tools rather than created by hand. They are also algorithmically complex; these days, most runtime engines animate skins using the GPU if possible. This includes Three.js.

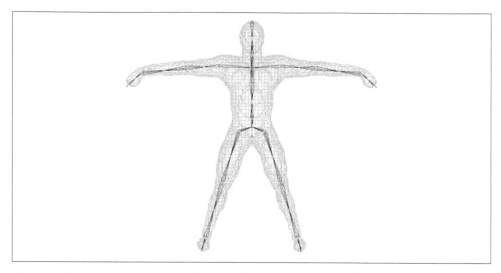

*Figure 5-12. A character mesh with underlying skeleton, suitable for skinned animation —from a tutorial on skinning by Frank A. Rivera (http://www.animationartist.com/ 2000/Tutorials/trueSpaceBones/Bones.html)*

To see an example of skinned animation in action, open the file under the Three.js project located in *examples/webgl_animation_skinning.html*. You will see many instances of a buffalo model. Click to start the animation; the buffalo will run in place with natural-looking movement. See Figure 5-13.

Let's walk through a portion of the code for this sample to see how Three.js implements skinning. First, we load the buffalo model by creating a new THREE.JSONLoader object and calling its load() method. This class loads files in the Three.js JSON file format. The format contains skinning information as well as the geometry.

```
var loader = new THREE.JSONLoader();
loader.load( "obj/buffalo/buffalo.js", createScene );
```

load() takes as its second argument a callback function that will be invoked once the file has been downloaded and parsed. Example 5-7 shows an excerpt from the callback function createScene(), with the relevant lines highlighted in bold.

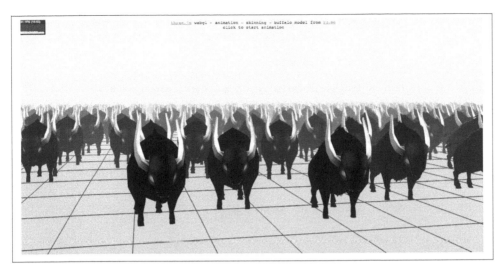

*Figure 5-13. Meshes animated using skinning in Three.js; buffalo model from RO.ME*

*Example 5-7. Callback to set up skinned animation after file load*

```
function createScene( geometry, materials ) {

    buffalos = [];
    animations = [];

    var x, y,
        buffalo, animation,
        gridx = 25, gridz = 15,
        sepx  = 150, sepz = 300;

    var material = new THREE.MeshFaceMaterial( materials );

    var originalMaterial = materials[ 0 ];

    originalMaterial.skinning = true;
    originalMaterial.transparent = true;
    originalMaterial.alphaTest = 0.75;

    THREE.AnimationHandler.add( geometry.animation );

    for( x = 0; x < gridx; x ++ ) {

        for( z = 0; z < gridz; z ++ ) {

            buffalo = new THREE.SkinnedMesh( geometry,
                    material, false );

            buffalo.position.x = - ( gridx - 1 ) * sepx * 0.5 +
                x * sepx + Math.random() * 0.5 * sepx;
```

```
buffalo.position.z = - ( gridz - 1 ) * sepz * 0.5 +
    z * sepz + Math.random() * 0.5 * sepz - 500;

buffalo.position.y =
    buffalo.geometry.boundingSphere.radius * 0.5;
buffalo.rotation.y = 0.2 - Math.random() * 0.4;

scene.add( buffalo );

buffalos.push( buffalo );

animation = new THREE.Animation( buffalo, "take_001" );
animations.push( animation );

offset.push( Math.random() );

}
```

createScene() runs a loop to create many instances of a buffalo mesh from the one loaded geometry. Note the type of mesh created: instead of the THREE.Mesh type we are familiar with from previous examples, this uses a different kind of mesh: THREE.Skin nedMesh. This particular Three.js type will be rendered via a special vertex shader that performs skinned animation on the GPU for performance.

createScene() also uses the built-in Three.js animation classes THREE.Animation and THREE.AnimationHandler. THREE.Animation is a class that implements general-purpose key frame animation, which in the case of skinning, is used to drive the skeleton animation. THREE.AnimationHandler is a singleton object that stores all animations for a scene, and maintains responsibility for updating them each time through the application's run loop. Our callback first adds the animation data to the animation handler's list by calling THREE.AnimationHandler.add(), passing it the geometry's animation data, which was loaded automatically by the Three.js JSON loader. A little later, the code creates a new THREE.Animation for each buffalo instance, associating the instance stored in variable buffalo with the animation named "take_001" from the JSON file.

After the animations are set up, we are ready to play them. The application does this by calling the function startAnimation() when the mouse is clicked. See Example 5-8. startAnimation() loops through the array of animations, calling play() on each. Each animation is also given a different, random time offset, to keep the animals from being perfectly synchronized.

*Example 5-8. Playing the skinned animations*

```
function startAnimation() {

    for( var i = 0; i < animations.length; i ++ ) {

        animations[ i ].offset = 0.05 * Math.random();
        animations[ i ].play();
```

```
        }

        dz = dstep;
        playback = true;

    }
```

If you are interested in the details of the JSON animation format, look at the file *exam ples/obj/buffalo.js*. Search through the file for the properties bones, skinWeights, and skinIndices to see how the skeleton data is laid out; also look for the property anima tion, which contains the hierarchy of key frames used to animate the skeleton. There is a lot going on under the covers, and Three.js adds a lot of value, not the least of which is a shader-based implementation of skinning that relies on the GPU for computation.

# Animating Using Shaders

The techniques we have explored thus far in this chapter, such as key frames, tweens, and skinning, can be implemented in JavaScript, but you can also develop them using GLSL programmable shaders to obtain hardware-accelerated performance. The ani mation support in the Three.js library uses both strategies: the key frame system is pure JavaScript, while the morphing and skinning are implemented as part of the built-in shader code for Three.js built-in material types such as Phong and Lambert. If skinning or morphing data is present in the mesh (using THREE.SkinnedMesh, described earlier, or THREE.MorphAnimMesh), then the Three.js shader will use that information to calcu late new vertex positions.

 If you are interested in the details of Three.js's GLSL skinning and morphing code, open the Three.js source file *src/renderers/WebGL Shaders.js* and search for "skin" and "morph"—but be advised that this gets deep into both the GLSL language and the specifics of the Three.js implementation. If you do manage to get around in there, it will be worth it, as there is a wealth of information.

Beyond using the GPU to optimize performance of common techniques like skinning, we can also write GLSL code to create arbitrary effects. Perhaps we want make the surface of an ocean shimmer, to simulate light reflecting and refracting as the waves undulate; or maybe we want to create grass that sways in the breeze. We could code these effects purely in JavaScript, but GLSL is much better suited to manipulating the large amounts of vertex and image data involved. The Three.js project comes with an excellent example of shader-based animation. Open the example file *examples/webgl_shader_lava.html*. You will see a torus shape, slowly rotating, with a flowing lava surface. See Figure 5-14.

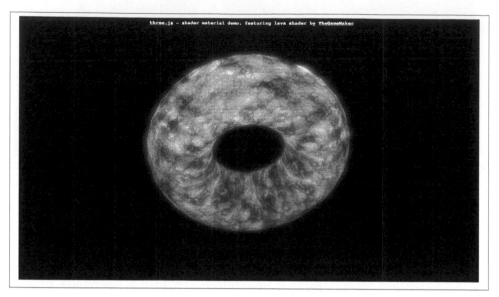

*Figure 5-14. Animated lava effect using a GLSL shader; shader code by TheGameMaker (http://irrlicht.sourceforge.net/forum//viewtopic.php?t=21057)*

The lava flow is animated via a THREE.ShaderMaterial with custom GLSL code. Let's have a look. Example 5-9 shows the code to set up the ShaderMaterial. There are several uniform values passed to the shader. The important ones for our purposes are time and the two texture maps, texture1 and texture2. As we will see momentarily, those three parameters, plus a little magic with numbers, are all we need to create realistic-looking, flowing lava.

*Example 5-9. Creating the torus mesh and ShaderMaterial*

```
uniforms = {

    fogDensity: { type: "f", value: 0.45 },
    fogColor: { type: "v3",
      value: new THREE.Vector3( 0, 0, 0 ) },
    time: { type: "f", value: 1.0 },
    resolution: { type: "v2",
      value: new THREE.Vector2() },
    uvScale: { type: "v2",
      value: new THREE.Vector2( 3.0, 1.0 ) },
    texture1: { type: "t",
      value: THREE.ImageUtils.loadTexture(
        "textures/lava/cloud.png" ) },
    texture2: { type: "t",
      value: THREE.ImageUtils.loadTexture(
        "textures/lava/lavatile.jpg" ) }

};
```

```
uniforms.texture1.value.wrapS =
  uniforms.texture1.value.wrapT = THREE.RepeatWrapping;
uniforms.texture2.value.wrapS =
  uniforms.texture2.value.wrapT = THREE.RepeatWrapping;
```

Now that the uniforms are set up, we can create the shader material. We need to supply vertex and fragment shader GLSL code to the constructor. Note the following technique for doing this: we use <script> elements in the HTML to hold the GLSL source code, and retrieve the textContent property of the script to get the GLSL text. Contrast this with previous shader examples we have seen. Rather than having to construct multiline text strings with escaped newlines, we can write the shader code in a straightforward manner. We will look at the GLSL source code in a moment.

```
var size = 0.65;

material = new THREE.ShaderMaterial( {

    uniforms: uniforms,
    vertexShader: document.getElementById(
      'vertexShader' ).textContent,
    fragmentShader: document.getElementById(
      'fragmentShader' ).textContent

} );
```

We then create the torus mesh with the new THREE.ShaderMaterial and add it to the scene:

```
mesh = new THREE.Mesh(
  new THREE.TorusGeometry( size, 0.3, 30, 30 ),
    material );
mesh.rotation.x = 0.3;
scene.add( mesh );
```

The shader algorithm is quite clever. It combines two texture maps, one for the base lava color and visual pattern, and a cloud texture as a source of "noise" that perturbs the base texture over time to create the flowing effect. The two textures are depicted in Figure 5-15.

The GLSL code for the vertex shader is simple; see Example 5-10. As with most shaders, it does the transformation math to multiply vertices by the model, view, and projection matrices to get them into screen space and outputs this value in the built-in GLSL variable gl_Position. Beyond that, we declare a varying parameter, vUv. This is the texture coordinate at each vertex, which the vertex shader outputs for use in the fragment shader, as we will see shortly. This particular shader also allows a scale parameter to be passed in, which it uses to scale the texture coordinates.

*Figure 5-15. Texture maps for lava and noise*

As noted, the GLSL source is embedded in a `<script>` element, so we can easily read the code without all the clutter of quotation marks, newline characters, and the like. The trick here is to use a different script `type` property, in this case `x-shader/x-vertex`. The browser has no idea what this type is; we just use it to indicate that this is *not* a JavaScript language script.

*Example 5-10. Vertex shader code embedded in an HTML <script> element*

```
<script id="vertexShader" type="x-shader/x-vertex">

    uniform vec2 uvScale;
    varying vec2 vUv;

    void main()
    {

        vUv = uvScale * uv;
        vec4 mvPosition = modelViewMatrix * vec4( position, 1.0 );
        gl_Position = projectionMatrix * mvPosition;

    }

</script>
```

The GLSL code for the fragment shader does most of the work. Example 5-11 shows the code. After declaring uniform parameters to match those in the JavaScript, we declare a varying parameter, vUv, to match the output of the vertex shader.

*Example 5-11. Fragment shader code for the shader-based animation*

```
<script id="fragmentShader" type="x-shader/x-fragment">

    uniform float time;
    uniform vec2 resolution;

    uniform float fogDensity;
```

```
uniform vec3 fogColor;

uniform sampler2D texture1;
uniform sampler2D texture2;

varying vec2 vUv;
```

Now for the main fragment shader program. The gist of it is that `texture1`, the cloud texture, is used as a source of noise to slightly displace the texture coordinate value used to get color values from `texture2`, the lava texture. (The GLSL function `texture2D()` fetches color data from a texture, given a 2D texture coordinate.) By multiplying the noise texture coordinate by the current `time` value, and adding some empirically determined offsets (e.g., 1.5, −1.5), we get the flowing effect. The color value for the pixel is then saved to the built-in GLSL variable `gl_FragColor`.

```
void main( void ) {

        vec2 position = -1.0 + 2.0 * vUv;

        vec4 noise = texture2D( texture1, vUv );
        vec2 T1 = vUv + vec2( 1.5, -1.5 ) * time  *0.02;
        vec2 T2 = vUv + vec2( -0.5, 2.0 ) * time * 0.01;

        T1.x += noise.x * 2.0;
        T1.y += noise.y * 2.0;
        T2.x -= noise.y * 0.2;
        T2.y += noise.z * 0.2;

        float p = texture2D( texture1, T1 * 2.0 ).a;

        vec4 color = texture2D( texture2, T2 * 2.0 );
        vec4 temp = color * ( vec4( p, p, p, p ) * 2.0 ) +
            ( color * color - 0.1 );

        if( temp.r > 1.0 ){ temp.bg += clamp( temp.r - 2.0, 0.0, 100.0 ); }
        if( temp.g > 1.0 ){ temp.rb += temp.g - 1.0; }
        if( temp.b > 1.0 ){ temp.rg += temp.b - 1.0; }

        gl_FragColor = temp;
```

At this point, the flowing lava effect is complete. However, this shader also adds a fog effect. The value stored in `gl_FragColor` is then mixed with a fog value calculated from fog parameters passed to the shader. The final color value for the pixel is output in the built-in GLSL variable `gl_FragColor`, and we are finished.

```
        float depth = gl_FragCoord.z / gl_FragCoord.w;
        const float LOG2 = 1.442695;
        float fogFactor = exp2( - fogDensity * fogDensity * depth *
            depth * LOG2 );
        fogFactor = 1.0 - clamp( fogFactor, 0.0, 1.0 );
```

```
        gl_FragColor = mix( gl_FragColor,
            vec4( fogColor, gl_FragColor.w ), fogFactor );

    }

</script>
```

The only piece remaining is to drive the animation during our run loop by updating the value of time each time through. Three.js makes this trivial; it automatically passes all uniform values to the GLSL shaders each time the renderer updates. All we need to do is set a property in the JavaScript. In this example, the function render() is called each animation frame. See the line of code in bold.

```
function render() {

    var delta = 5 * clock.getDelta();

    uniforms.time.value += 0.2 * delta;

    mesh.rotation.y += 0.0125 * delta;
    mesh.rotation.x += 0.05 * delta;

    renderer.clear();
    composer.render( 0.01 );

}
```

Admittedly, coding an animation like this requires a certain level of artistry. Not only must we learn the details of GLSL syntax and built-in functions, but we must also master some esoteric computer graphics algorithms. But if you have the appetite, it can be really rewarding. And the Internet is full of information and readily usable code examples to get started.

## Chapter Summary

As we have seen, there are many ways to animate 3D content in WebGL. At its core, animation is driven by the new browser function requestAnimationFrame(), the workhorse that ensures user drawing happens in a timely and consistent manner throughout the page. Beyond that, we have several choices for animating, ranging from simple to complex, depending on the desired effect. Content can be animated programmatically each frame, or we can use data-driven methods that include tweening, key framing, morphs, and skinning. We can achieve naturalistic motion by combining key frames with path following. We can also use shaders to animate content in the GPU, enabling even more possibilities. The tools and libraries for animating WebGL are still evolving, with no one clear choice. But there are many possibilities and, thanks to JavaScript and open source, few barriers to getting going.

# CHAPTER 6

# CSS3: Advanced Page Effects

The last several chapters showed you how to use WebGL to create stunning content featuring hardware-accelerated rendering of 3D objects, scenes, and animations. As powerful as WebGL is, as of this writing it has a fundamental limitation in that arbitrary HTML content cannot be mapped as a texture on the surface of a 3D object. If we want to apply the 3D techniques we have seen in previous chapters to elements on a page, we have to turn to another HTML5 innovation: CSS3.

With CSS3, single elements or entire pages can be brought to life with animation, image filtering, and 2D or 3D transformations. These features enable the creation of a variety of 3D effects for use in simple games, engaging banner ads, and intuitive user interfaces. In contrast with WebGL, which requires at least rudimentary 3D programming knowledge plus mastery of a library such as Three.js, using CSS3 requires knowing only markup, CSS, and basic JavaScript, perhaps with an assist from a framework like jQuery. This makes CSS3 development much easier than WebGL; however, developers have access only to the features built into the browser. Put another way, 3D CSS trades simplicity and ease of use for power and flexibility.

The 3D features of CSS3 trace their roots back to 3D transitions initially developed by Apple for its Core Animation framework, powering now-familiar user interface effects such as the screen transitions in the iOS Weather application, depicted in Figure 6-1. The 3D advances in CSS3 were originally proposed by the WebKit development team in 2009 and 2010, and first taken to market by Apple's Safari teams for Mac OS and iOS. They were later adopted in Chrome and, ultimately, by all browser makers.

*Figure 6-1. Screen transitions in the iOS Weather app*

The ability to apply 3D effects to HTML elements opens up similar possibilities for web page content. Figure 6-2 shows Snowstack (*http://www.satine.org/research/webkit/ snowleopard/snowstack.html*), a showcase developed by the Safari team. Snowstack is a photo-viewing visual effects library that uses pure HTML, 3D CSS, and JavaScript to render a Flickr feed in perspective. With Snowstack, the user can navigate through an apparently infinite set of photo tiles using the arrow keys on the keyboard. The application works in all browsers and devices. While Snowstack is really a technology demo, it points to the potential for using 3D CSS to visualize and explore vast amounts of information.

*Figure 6-2. Snowstack, a CSS-based 3D photo viewer (http://www.satine.org/research/ webkit/snowleopard/snowstack.html)*

Many developers are exploring 3D CSS to create innovative web content. Beyond simply transforming flat tiles, some programmers have figured out how to simulate rendering of full 3D objects, and as we will see later in the chapter, one enterprising soul has even used 3D CSS to build prototypes of a first-person shooter game! 3D CSS can also be used in conjunction with WebGL, with the latter handling true 3D rendering tasks and the former used to overlay and/or integrate HTML elements for the user interface.

CSS3 is a collection of specifications that allow dynamic effects to be applied to the elements on a page. This chapter covers the various CSS technologies used to build 3D effects:

*CSS Transforms*
> 3D operations (translate, rotate, scale) applied to an entire element.

*CSS Transitions*
> Simple changes applied to CSS properties over time. Like tweens (discussed in the previous chapter), CSS Transitions are excellent for one-time effects.

*CSS Animations*
> Complex changes applied to CSS properties over time, using key frame data.

# CSS Transforms

Core to 3D CSS development is the ability to manipulate page elements using CSS Transforms. The CSS Transforms specification (*http://www.w3.org/TR/css3-transforms/*) represents the convergence of earlier 2D and 3D work on using CSS to modify the position, orientation, scale, and other layout properties of page elements using transformation operations rather than simple left/top and width/height properties.

As a refresher, 3D graphics use a three-dimensional coordinate system that employs a third axis, *z*, to represent positions in and out of the screen, creating a sense of depth. Figure 6-3 depicts the 3D coordinate system used for CSS. Note that, in contrast with traditional 3D systems, the positive y-axis points down instead of up, to be consistent with the 2D *xy* system used for the web browser's page and window coordinates.

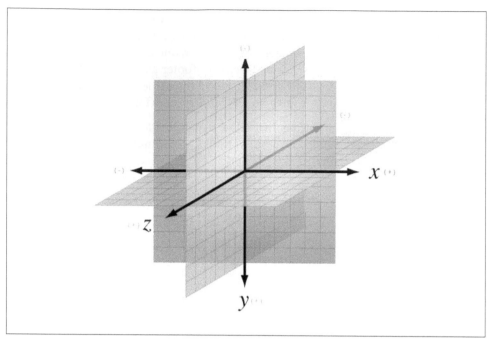

*Figure 6-3. The 3D coordinate system for CSS, with positive y-axis pointing down (adapted from http://bit.ly/wikimedia-3d-coordinate; Creative Commons Attribution-Share Alike 3.0 unported license)*

## Using 3D Transforms

You specify CSS 3D transforms like any other CSS: using properties. The CSS3 specification defines several properties for transforming elements. Let's start with an example. Figure 6-4 depicts three elements with different transforms applied: translation, rotation, and scale.

The source code for this example can be found in the file *Chapter 6/css3dtransforms.html* and the corresponding CSS file, *css/css3dtransforms.css*. The fragment in Example 6-1 shows the HTML that defines the first DIV element, applying a 3D translation.

*Example 6-1. Element with CSS 3D transforms applied*

```
<div id="card1" class="container perspective">
    <div class="legend">
    Translate
    </div>
    <div class="code">{translateX(20px) translateY(20px) translateZ(-100px);}</div>
    <div class="cardBorder">
        <div class="card translate">
          <p>This element is translated.</p>
```

```
            <img width=96 height=96 src="../images/HTML5rawkes.png"></img>
            <p>Transformed elements can contain anything: text, images,
                divs, tables...</p>
        </div>
    </div>
</div>
```

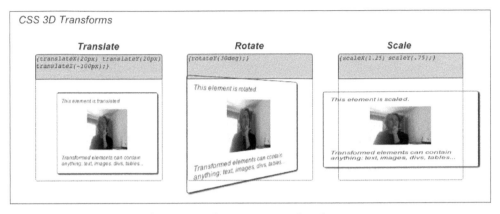

*Figure 6-4. CSS 3D transforms: translate, rotate, and scale*

The text in bold specifies two classes for the innermost DIV element: `card` and `trans
late`. `card` defines the properties common to all three of the "card" elements on the
page—for example, the solid border, drop shadow, and rounded corners. The `trans
late` class defines the 3D translation. Example 6-2 shows the CSS definitions for these
two classes, as well as `cardBorder`, which is used on the parent element of the card to
display a dotted-line border indicating where the card would be if it had no transforms
applied to it. For now, ignore the `-moz-transform-style` property in these declarations.
They are required for proper functioning in Firefox, as I will describe in the next section
on perspective.

*Example 6-2. CSS to define a translation transform*

```
.cardBorder {
    position: absolute;
    width: 100%;
    height: 80%;
    top:30%;
    border:1px dotted;
    border-radius:0 0 4px 4px;
    -moz-transform-style: preserve-3d;
}

.card {
    position: absolute;
    width: 99%;
    height: 99%;
```

```
    border:1px solid;
    border-radius: 4px;
    box-shadow: 2px 2px 2px;
    -moz-transform-style: preserve-3d;
}

.translate {
    -webkit-transform: translateX(20px) translateY(20px) translateZ(-100px);
       -moz-transform: translateX(20px) translateY(20px) translateZ(-100px);
         -o-transform: translateX(20px) translateY(20px) translateZ(-100px);
            transform: translateX(20px) translateY(20px) translateZ(-100px);
}
```

The translate class specifies a CSS 3D transform by setting its transform property. In this example, the element is translated 20 pixels in *x* and *y*, respectively, and 100 pixels along negative *z* (into the screen). In general, you can use transform to create transforms by applying one or more *transform methods* to the element. In addition to translation, CSS supports methods for rotation and scale, arbitrary matrix transformation, and perspective projection. The CSS 3D transform methods are summarized in Table 6-1.

*Table 6-1. CSS 3D transform methods*

| Method | Description |
|---|---|
| translateX(x) | Translation along the x-axis |
| translateY(y) | Translation along the y-axis |
| translateZ(z) | Translation along the z-axis |
| translate3d(x, y, z) | Translation along the x-, y-, and z- axes |
| rotateX(angle) | Rotation about the x-axis |
| rotateY(angle) | Rotation about the y-axis |
| rotateY(angle) | Rotation about the z-axis |
| rotate3d(x, y, z, angle) | Rotation about an arbitrary axis |
| scaleX(x) | Scale along the x-axis |
| scaleY(y) | Scale along the y-axis |
| scaleZ(z) | Scale along the z-axis |
| scale3d(x, y, z) | Scale along the x-, y-, and z- axes |
| matrix3d(...) | Define arbitrary 4×4 transformation matrix with 16 values |
| perspective(depth) | Define perspective projection of depth pixels |

The second and third cards are transformed in a similar manner, by using the classes rotate and scale defined in the CSS:

```
.rotate {
    -webkit-transform: rotateY(30deg);
       -moz-transform: rotateY(30deg);
         -o-transform: rotateY(30deg);
            transform: rotateY(30deg);
}

.scale {
    -webkit-transform: scaleX(1.25) scaleY(.75);
       -moz-transform: scaleX(1.25) scaleY(.75);
         -o-transform: scaleX(1.25) scaleY(.75);
            transform: scaleX(1.25) scaleY(.75);
}
```

Rotation values can be specified in degrees, radians, or *gradians* (1/400 of a circle)—for example, 90deg, 1.57rad, or 100grad. Scale values are scalars that multiply along each axis (i.e., an unscaled element has a scale of 1 along each axis).

 Note the use of browser-specific prefixes in the CSS (e.g., -webkit-transform). This is required to ensure cross-browser support because CSS Transforms were experimental among browsers for several years. This is cumbersome, but it is among many such CSS features that require use of browser prefixes, and developers have grown accustomed to dealing with it. If you find all the duplication annoying, you may want to look into using a style sheet–generation tool such as LESS (*http://lesscss.org/*) to ease the pain. From time to time I will omit the browser-specific prefixes in our examples, for brevity. Always make sure to use them in your code.

CSS supports an additional property, transform-origin, which allows the developer to specify the origin of transformations. This property defaults to 50% 50% 0—that is, the center of the coordinate system. By changing it, you can have objects rotate about a different point than the center. transform-origin can be specified in any CSS offset unit, such as left, center, right, %, or a CSS distance value (pixels, inches, em spaces, etc.).

## Applying Perspective

You may have noticed the use of the class perspective for each of the top-level DIV elements in the previous example. You can apply CSS 3D transforms with or without using a perspective projection, though it is more useful when using a perspective projection.

Perspective projections are very simple to define in CSS3. Example 6-3 shows the CSS for defining perspective.

*Example 6-3. CSS perspective property*

```
.perspective {
    -webkit-perspective: 400px;
      -moz-perspective: 400px;
        -o-perspective: 400px;
           perspective: 400px;
}

.noperspective {
    -webkit-perspective: 0px;
      -moz-perspective: 0px;
        -o-perspective: 0px;
           perspective: 0px;
}
```

We define a CSS class, `perspective`, for use with elements to which we want to apply perspective projection. The value we supply represents the distance from the view plane to the $xy$ plane ($z=0$). Perspective can be specified in any CSS distance unit: pixels, points, inches, em spaces, and so on. The CSS file also defines a second class, `noperspective`, which is handy for ensuring an element is not rendered with perspective. The values in this class are set to zero, which is the default.

> While the details of CSS perspective are different from those of WebGL, the concepts are the same. If you need a refresher on the topic, there is a detailed discussion in Chapter 1.

To illustrate the contrast between elements rendered with and without perspective, let's look at an example. Open the example file *Chapter 6/css3dperspective.html*. You will see two cards. The left one is rendered with perspective, the right one without. The only difference between the two elements is the use of the CSS `perspective` property; each card is rotated by 30 degrees about the y-axis; however, without the use of perspective, the element on the right appears squished horizontally instead of rotated. See Figure 6-5.

You can also apply perspective to elements using the `perspective()` transform function described in Table 6-1. However, in practice it is usually better to keep the perspective value separate from the transform value using the two distinct properties. Otherwise, you will need to resupply the perspective value every time you want to change the other transform function values.

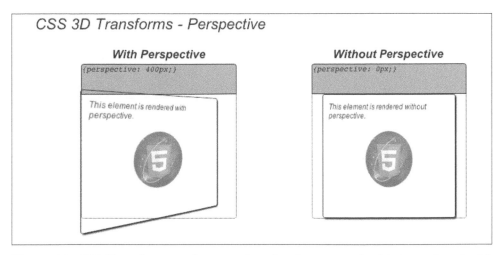

*Figure 6-5. CSS Transforms and perspective: the element on the left is rendered with perspective, the element on the right without (HTML5 Rawkes Logo by Phil Banks (https://twitter.com/emirpprime))*

## Creating a Transform Hierarchy

CSS3 allows 3D transforms to be inherited throughout the DOM object hierarchy. An element with 3D transforms defined for it can either inherit those of its ancestors or ignore them, based on the value of the `transform-style` property.

Figure 6-6 illustrates how `transform-style` can be used to create a transform hierarchy. Each of the `card` elements is transformed with a 30-degree rotation about *y*. Each card also has a `childCard` with its own 30-degree rotation about *y*. Note that the left card's child appears to be rotated 30 degrees away from the plane of its parent; however, the right card's child appears to be in the same plane as its parent.

The code for this example can be found in the files *Chapter 6/css3dhierarchy.html* and *css/css3dhierarchy.css*. The HTML defines two DOM element hierarchies that are nearly identical, except that the first card uses a class `hierarchy`, while the second uses one called `nohierarchy`.

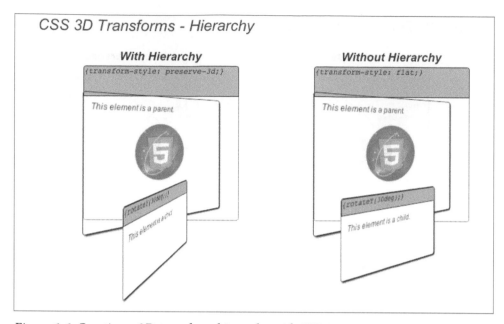

*Figure 6-6. Creating a 3D transform hierarchy with CSS*

```
<div id="hierarchy1" class="container perspective">
    <div class="legend">
    With Hierarchy
    </div>
    <div class="code">{transform-style: preserve-3d;}</div>
    <div class="cardBorder">
        <div class="card hierarchy rotate">
          <p>This element is a parent.</p>
          <img width=96 height=96 src="../images/HTML5rawkes.png"></img>
          <p></p>
            <div class="childCard rotate">
            <div class="code">{rotateY(30deg);}</div>
                <p>This element is a child.</p>
            </div>
        </div>
    </div>
</div>

<div id="hierarchy2" class="container perspective">
    <div class="legend">
    Without Hierarchy
    </div>
    <div class="code">{transform-style: flat;}</div>
    <div class="cardBorder">
        <div class="card nohierarchy rotate">
          <p>This element is a parent.</p>
          <img width=96 height=96 src="../images/HTML5rawkes.png"></img>
```

```
      <p></p>
      <div class="childCard rotate">
        <div class="code">{rotateY(30deg);}</div>
        <p>This element is a child.</p>
      </div>
    </div>
  </div>
</div>
```

The CSS definitions for the classes `hierarchy` and `nohierarchy` are as follows:

```
.hierarchy {
    -webkit-transform-style: preserve-3d;
       -moz-transform-style: preserve-3d;
         -o-transform-style: preserve-3d;
            transform-style: preserve-3d;
}

.nohierarchy {
    -webkit-transform-style: flat;
       -moz-transform-style: flat;
         -o-transform-style: flat;
            transform-style: flat;
}
```

The `transform-style` property accepts two values: `flat` (the default), which specifies that transforms in descendant DOM elements not be applied; and `preserve-3d`, which tells the browser to apply transforms in descendants. By using `preserve-3D` throughout, an application can create a deep hierarchy of 3D objects, especially in combination with the other techniques described in this chapter.

*Browser compatibility alert:* In the first example in this section, we glossed over one detail in the definitions of the `card` and `cardBor der` CSS classes. They contained the statement:

```
-moz-transform-style: preserve-3d;
```

Apparently the Firefox browser, unlike WebKit-based browsers, does not propagate the value of `transform-style` to its descendants. Without our explicitly setting it in each descendant, not only will child transforms not work, but perspective rendering is also disabled. The workaround is to set `transform-style` to `preserve-3d` for every descendant in the DOM hierarchy. This is unfortunate but necessary.

The worst part of this situation is that the interpretation varies across browsers. Apparently Internet Explorer version 10 doesn't support the feature at all, but the plan is to add it for IE 11.

# Controlling Backface Rendering

In classic 3D rendering, when a polygon faces away from the viewer, the rendering system can either display the back of the polygon, known as the *backface*, or not display it, depending on settings controlled by the programmer. CSS3 transforms also provide this capability. If an element is rotated such that it faces away from the viewer, it will be displayed or not based on the `backface-visibility` transform property.

CSS3 backface rendering is important for creating the illusion of double-sided objects. Let's say we want to create a screen flip transition like those in the iOS Weather app depicted in Figure 6-1. Creating this effect requires careful construction of our markup, and correct use of `backface-visibility`. Figure 6-7 illustrates how to use the technique in practice.

Open the file *Chapter 6/css3dbackfaces.html* to see backface rendering in action. There are four cards. On the top row, there are two single-sided cards, rendered with backface visibility on and off, respectively. The card on the top left is rotated to face away from the viewer and rendered with backfaces visible; the one on the top right is rotated away from the viewer and rendered with backfaces hidden. Note that we can see the card on the top left, but the text "FRONT" is rendered in reverse, while the card on the top right is not visible.

On the bottom row we see two double-sided cards, rendered with backface visibility on and off, respectively. Again, the objects have been rotated such that their front faces are away from the viewer. However, these cards define an additional element, with the text "BACK," that is rotated toward the viewer to simulate a double-sided object. The bottom-left card has backface visibility on, and because it also has a 0.8 opacity value, we can see through the front face to the reversed text "FRONT." Conversely, the bottom-right card turns backface visibility off and so hides the front side of the card. The bottom-right card demonstrates the proper technique for using CSS to simulate a double-sided object. Let's look at the code.

Example 6-4 shows the HTML code for this page. Elements with backfaces visible are defined through the class `backface`; elements with backfaces hidden are defined through the class `nobackface`. In order to create the double-sided cards on the bottom row, we actually need to create *two* card elements: one for the front and another for the back, as defined in the CSS classes `frontside` and `backside`, respectively. The card on the bottom right of the page combines those classes with the `nobackface` class to create a card that displays correctly no matter which side is facing the viewer.

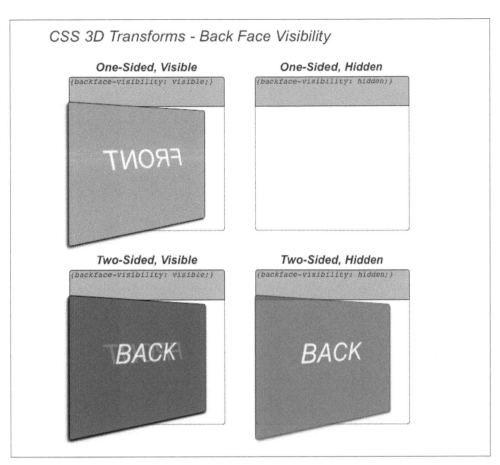

*Figure 6-7. Using backface visibility to create double-sided objects*

*Example 6-4. Constructing a double-sided HTML element*

```
<div id="backface1" class="container perspective ">
    <div class="legend">
    One-Sided, Visible
    </div>
    <div class="code">{backface-visibility: visible;}</div>
    <div class="cardBorder">
        <div class="card backface frontside">
        FRONT
        </div>
    </div>
</div>

<div id="backface2" class="container perspective ">
    <div class="legend">
    One-Sided, Hidden
```

```
        </div>
        <div class="code">{backface-visibility: hidden;}</div>
        <div class="cardBorder">
            <div class="card nobackface frontside">
            FRONT
            </div>
        </div>
    </div>

    <div id="backface3" class="container perspective ">
        <div class="legend">
        Two-Sided, Visible
        </div>
        <div class="code">{backface-visibility: visible;}</div>
        <div class="cardBorder">
            <div class="card backface frontside">
            FRONT
            </div>
            <div class="card backface backside">
            BACK
            </div>
        </div>
    </div>

    <div id="backface4" class="container perspective ">
        <div class="legend">
        Two-Sided, Hidden
        </div>
        <div class="code">{backface-visibility: hidden;}</div>
        <div class="cardBorder">
            <div class="card nobackface frontside">
            FRONT
            </div>
            <div class="card nobackface backside">
            BACK
            </div>
        </div>
    </div>
```

Example 6-5 shows the style declarations from the file *css/css3dbackfaces.css*. First, we define the frontside and backside classes somewhat counterintuitively. frontside is intended for the front of the card, but because our example is intended to illustrate backface rendering, we are going to rotate the card away from the viewer by applying a 210-degree rotation about the y-axis. Conversely, the back of the card is rotated toward the viewer by 30 degrees. The two sides of the card line up because their rotations are 180 degrees apart. When combined with hiding the backface using the nobackface class, we get a perfect two-sided card like the card on the bottom right. The class noback face sets the property backface-visibility to hidden to produce the desired result.

*Example 6-5. CSS declarations for creating double-sided objects*

```
.frontside {
    -webkit-transform: rotateY(210deg);
      -moz-transform: rotateY(210deg);
        -o-transform: rotateY(210deg);
           transform: rotateY(210deg);
           line-height:160px;
           font-size:40px;
           color:White;
           background-color:DarkCyan;
           border-color:Black;
           box-shadow:2px 2px 2px Black;
}

.backside {
    -webkit-transform: rotateY(30deg);
      -moz-transform: rotateY(30deg);
        -o-transform: rotateY(30deg);
           transform: rotateY(30deg);
           line-height:160px;
           font-size:40px;
           color:White;
           background-color:DarkRed;
           border-color:Black;
           box-shadow:2px 2px 2px Black;
           opacity:0.8;
}

.backface {
    -webkit-backface-visibility: visible;
      -moz-backface-visibility: visible;
        -o-backface-visibility: visible;
           backface-visibility: visible;
}

.nobackface {
    -webkit-backface-visibility: hidden;
      -moz-backface-visibility: hidden;
        -o-backface-visibility: hidden;
           backface-visibility: hidden;
}
```

# A Summary of CSS Transform Properties

This section covered the transform properties CSS provides for adding 3D effects to HTML elements. These properties are summarized in Table 6-2.

*Table 6-2. CSS transform properties*

| Property | Description |
| --- | --- |
| transform | Applies a transformation using one or more transform methods (see Table 6-1) |
| transform-origin | Defines the origin of all transformations (default: 50%, 50%, 0) |
| perspective | Specifies perspective depth in CSS distance units (default: 0 = no perspective) |
| perspective-origin | Specifies the perspective vanishing point in *xy* coordinates |
| transform-style | Specifies whether descendants of a 3D element are rendered flat or in 3D |
| backface-visibility | Specifies whether or not elements facing away from the screen are rendered |

As we have seen, CSS Transforms provide a powerful way to add 3D effects to page elements. CSS Transforms become even more powerful when we create dynamic effects, by combining them with transitions and animations.

 The examples in this section were heavily inspired by David DeSandro's great blog site "24 Ways" (as in, 24 ways to impress your friends). David was kind enough to grant me permission to liberally adapt his work. Refer to the examples on his site (*http://24ways.org/2010/intro-to-css-3d-transforms/*) and other postings for a wealth of CSS 3D information.

# CSS Transitions

CSS Transitions allow gradual changes to properties over time. CSS Transitions are a lot like the Tween.js tweens we explored in the previous chapter. However, these effects are built into the browser; there is no need for a helper JavaScript library. While our focus in this chapter is on animating 3D properties, it is worth noting that CSS Transitions can be used to animate most (though not all) CSS properties: width, position, color, z-index, opacity, and so on.

The basic syntax for a CSS Transition is as follows:

```
transition : property-name duration timing-function delay-time;
```

where:

property-name
: Is the name of an individual property, the keyword all to specify that this transition applies to all properties being changed, or the keyword none to specify that it applies to none of the properties.

duration
: Is a time value, in seconds or milliseconds, that specifies the length of time the transition will take.

`timing-function`

> Is the name of a timing function for animating the transition. It can be one of `linear`, `ease`, `ease-in`, `ease-out`, `ease-in-out`, or `cubic-bezier`.

`delay-time`

> Specifies an amount of time to wait (in seconds or milliseconds) before beginning the transition.

`transition` is actually a shorthand CSS property for the four individual CSS properties `transition-property`, `transition-duration`, `transition-timing-function`, and `transition-delay`. Let's see how this works with an example. Open the file *Chapter 6/css3dtransitions.html*, depicted in Figure 6-8. There are two cards. Clicking on either causes it to flip to the other side, using the double-sided technique described in the previous section. The flip transition takes two seconds, with a slight ease in and out. The cards also change color, from their original `DarkCyan` to `Goldenrod`. However, the card on the left changes color as it flips, while the card on the right changes color *after* it flips.

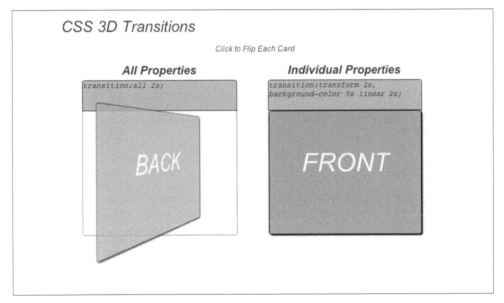

*Figure 6-8. Using CSS Transitions to animate properties*

The HTML defines the front and back of each card similarly. The primary difference between the two cards is the use of class `easeAll2sec` for the card on the left and class `easeTransform2secColor5secDelay` for the card on the right. We will look at those classes in a moment.

```
<div id="transition1" class="container perspective ">
    <div class="legend">
    All Properties
    </div>
    <div class="code">transition:all 2s;</div>
    <div class="cardBorder">
        <div id="front1"
          class="card nobackface frontside clickable easeAll2sec">
        FRONT
        </div>
        <div id="back1"
          class="card nobackface backside clickable easeAll2sec">
        BACK
        </div>
    </div>
</div>

<div id="transition2" class="container perspective ">
    <div class="legend">
    Individual Properties
    </div>
    <div class="code">transition:transform 2s,
        background-color 5s linear 2s;</div>
    <div class="cardBorder">
        <div id="front2"
class="card nobackface frontside clickable easeTransform2secColor5secDelay">
        FRONT
        </div>
        <div id="back2"
class="card nobackface backside clickable easeTransform2secColor5secDelay">
        BACK
        </div>
    </div>
</div>
```

The effect is triggered on a mouse click. We make this happen with a little jQuery magic that adds click handlers to the front and back of each card. It uses a Boolean for each to keep track of which side is showing, and adds or removes the flip and goGold classes as needed. flip rotates the card 180 degrees; goGold sets the color to Goldenrod. Without CSS Transitions, these changes would take effect immediately, but with Transitions, they animate smoothly from one state to the other over time.

```
<script type="text/javascript">

    var front1 = true;
    var front2 = true;
    $(document).ready(
            function() {
                $('#transition1 .clickable').click(function(){
                    // alert("Clicked");
                    if (front1)
                    {
```

```
                    $('#front1').addClass('flip');
                    $('#back1').addClass('flip');
                    $('#front1').addClass('goGold');
                    $('#back1').addClass('goGold');
                }
                else
                {
                    $('#front1').removeClass('flip');
                    $('#back1').removeClass('flip');
                    $('#front1').removeClass('goGold');
                    $('#back1').removeClass('goGold');
                }

                front1 = !front1;
            });

            $('#transition2 .clickable').click(function(){
                if (front2)
                {
                    $('#front2').addClass('flip');
                    $('#back2').addClass('flip');
                    $('#front2').addClass('goGold');
                    $('#back2').addClass('goGold');
                }
                else
                {
                    $('#front2').removeClass('flip');
                    $('#back2').removeClass('flip');
                    $('#front2').removeClass('goGold');
                    $('#back2').removeClass('goGold');
                }

                front2 = !front2;
            });

        }

    );

</script>
```

The CSS for this example can be found in the file *css/css3dtransitions.css*. See the listing in Example 6-6.

The front and back of the card are defined with the appropriate rotations defined in the classes `frontside` and `backside`; when combined with the class `flip`, they rotate by 180 degrees to flip the card over. `goGold` is the class used to change the element's background color to goldenrod. The classes in bold define the two different transitions. `easeAll2sec` is simple: it transitions all changed properties in two seconds with a subtle ease in/out (using the default value of `ease`).

easeTransform2secColor5secDelay is more involved. It actually contains two separate transitions, one for the transform and one for the background color, separated by commas. The transform transition is exactly like easeAll2Sec, a two-second transition with subtle easing. The background color transition is different: it is a five-second linear interpolation of the color that starts *after* two seconds, using the fourth argument to the transition property, delay time.

*Example 6-6. Specifying CSS Transitions*

```
.frontside {
    -webkit-transform: rotateY(0deg);
       -moz-transform: rotateY(0deg);
         -o-transform: rotateY(0deg);
            transform: rotateY(0deg);
...
}

.backside {
    -webkit-transform: rotateY(180deg);
       -moz-transform: rotateY(180deg);
         -o-transform: rotateY(180deg);
            transform: rotateY(180deg);
...
}

.frontside.flip {
    -webkit-transform: rotateY(-180deg);
       -moz-transform: rotateY(-180deg);
         -o-transform: rotateY(-180deg);
            transform: rotateY(-180deg);

}


.backside.flip {
    -webkit-transform: rotateY(0deg);
       -moz-transform: rotateY(0deg);
         -o-transform: rotateY(0deg);
            transform: rotateY(0deg);

}

.goGold {
    background-color:Goldenrod;
}

.easeAll2sec {
    -webkit-transition:all 2s;
       -moz-transition:all 2s;
         -o-transition:all 2s;
            transition:all 2s;
}
```

```
.easeTransform2secColor5secDelay {
    -webkit-transition:-webkit-transform 2s, background-color 5s linear 2s;
      -moz-transition:-moz-transform  2s, background-color 5s linear 2s;
        -o-transition:-o-transform 2s, background-color 5s linear 2s;
          transition:transform 2s, background-color 5s linear 2s;
}
```

 This section just scratches the surface of using CSS Transitions. There is an excellent article on the feature by Microsoft CSS development wizard Kirupa Chinnathambi on his blog (*http://www.kirupa.com/html5/all_about_css_transitions.htm*).

Transitions are a straightforward way to create effects. But their use is limited to simple, one-time effects. If we want to create complex sequences and loops, we need to turn to another CSS3 technology: CSS Animations.

# CSS Animations

CSS Animations provide a more general animation solution than CSS Transitions. Like the 3D key frame animations covered in the previous chapter, CSS Animations use a sequence of key frames, plus properties to control duration, timing function, delay time, and looping. Let's take a look at some examples.

Open the file *Chapter 6/css3danimations.html*. You will see three cards; click on each to trigger a different animation (Figure 6-9). The card on the top left does a simple one-time rotation about the y-axis. The card on the top right shakes left and right forever. The card on the bottom "flies" up and to the right, rotating about *y* as it moves.

The CSS for creating animations comprises two parts: an `@keyframe` rule, which creates a block of CSS in which you place the key frame data, and several properties you can define for an element:

animation-name
> The name of a set of key frames declared in an `@keyframe` rule, to be used as the source of key frame data.

animation-duration
> Specifies the length of the animation in seconds or milliseconds.

animation-timing-function
> The name of a timing function for animating the key frames. It can be one of `linear`, `ease`, `ease-in`, `ease-out`, `ease-in-out`, or `cubic-bezier`.

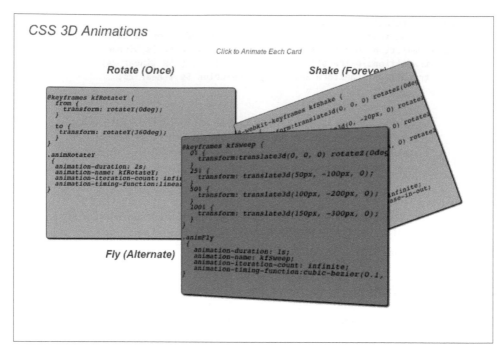

*Figure 6-9. CSS 3D Animations*

animation-delay
> Specifies an amount of time to wait (in seconds or milliseconds) before beginning the animation.

animation-iteration-count
> Specifies the number of times to play the animation. The default is 1. The keyword infinite may also be used to define a forever looping animation.

animation-direction
> Determines whether the animation plays forward, in reverse, or alternates forward and reverse playback for multiple iterations. Valid values are normal (forward), reverse, alternate (play forward and then reverse, alternating), and alternate-reverse (play in reverse and then forward, alternating).

We can combine all of the preceding properties using the CSS shorthand property animation as follows:

```
animation: name duration timing-function delay iteration-count direction;
```

The CSS for the example in Figure 6-9 can be found in the example file *css/css3danima tions.css*. The excerpt in Example 6-7 shows the important fragments. We have @keyframe rules that set up the key frames kfRotateY and kfRotateMinusY (for rotating the front and back sides of the card, respectively), kfShake for the shaking animation, and kfFly for the flying animation. We then define individual classes for each of the animations, with different parameters. The classes animRotateY and animRotate MinusY define infinitely looping linear interpolation animations to rotate the element about the y-axis. These are created with simple key frame data that goes from the initial frame to the end frame.

The kfShake class is more complicated: it uses key frame data with four frames at 0%, 25%, 50%, and 100%, respectively, to define translations in *x* and *y* and a rotation about *z*. Finally, the kfFly class is still more complex, defining a series of translations in the key frames, a custom cubic Bézier function for interpolating, and multiple iterations with the direction alternating from forward to reverse. kfFly defines only the flight path of the element; it also appears to "flap its wings" because the classes animRotateY and animRotateMinusY are added to the front/back of the element when clicked. So there are actually nested animations being applied to the card on the bottom.

*Example 6-7. CSS declarations to create key frame animations*

```
@-webkit-keyframes kfRotateY {
  from {
    -webkit-transform: rotateY(0deg);
  }

  to {
   -webkit-transform: rotateY(360deg);
  }
}

.animRotateY
 {
  -webkit-animation-duration: 2s;
  -webkit-animation-name: kfRotateY;
  -webkit-animation-iteration-count: infinite;
  -webkit-animation-timing-function:linear;
}

@-webkit-keyframes kfRotateMinusY {
  from {
    -webkit-transform: rotateY(-180deg);
  }

  to {
   -webkit-transform: rotateY(180deg);
  }
}

.animRotateMinusY
 {
  -webkit-animation-duration: 2s;
  -webkit-animation-name: kfRotateMinusY;
```

```
      -webkit-animation-iteration-count: infinite;
      -webkit-animation-timing-function:linear;
    }

@-webkit-keyframes kfShake {
  0% {
    -webkit-transform:translate3d(0, 0, 0) rotateZ(0deg);
  }
  25% {
    -webkit-transform: translate3d(0, -20px, 0) rotateZ(20deg);
  }
  50% {
    -webkit-transform: translate3d(0, 0, 0) rotateZ(-20deg);
  }
  100% {
    -webkit-transform: translate3d(0, -20px, 0) rotateZ(-20deg);
  }
}

.animShake
 {
  -webkit-animation-duration: .5s;
  -webkit-animation-name: kfShake;
  -webkit-animation-iteration-count: infinite;
  -webkit-animation-timing-function:ease-in-out;
}

@-webkit-keyframes kfFly {
  0% {
    -webkit-transform:translate3d(0, 0, 0);
  }
  25% {
    -webkit-transform: translate3d(100px, -100px, 20px0);
  }
  50% {
    -webkit-transform: translate3d(200px, -200px, 40px);
  }
  100% {
    -webkit-transform: translate3d(400px, -300px, 20px);
  }
}

.animFly
 {
  -webkit-animation-duration: 2s;
  -webkit-animation-name: kfFly;
  -webkit-animation-iteration-count: 2;
  -webkit-animation-timing-function:cubic-bezier(0.1, 0.2, 0.8, 1);
  -webkit-animation-direction:alternate;
}
```

You may have noticed that `animRotateY` and `animRotateMinusY` are defined with an `animation-iteration-count` of `infinite`, yet the top-left card rotates only once. This is because the jQuery code for click handling stops the animation after an iteration (see code in bold):

```
$('#front1').click(function(){
    $('#front1').addClass('animRotateY');
    $('#back1').addClass('animRotateMinusY');
    setTimeout(function(){
        $('#front1').removeClass('animRotateY');
        $('#back1').removeClass('animRotateMinusY');

    }, 2000);
    }
);
```

These classes were designed to infinitely loop so they could be reused in different animation effects, such as when they are combined with the class `animFly`. By defining them as infinitely looping, we can easily control start and stop within the JavaScript for specific uses.

# Pushing the Envelope of CSS

So far, the examples in this chapter largely consist of moving around flat tiles. These are excellent techniques for creating 3D user interface elements and transition effects, but fall a bit short of the 3D rendering we expect in today's games and other full 3D applications. That said, some developers are pushing the boundaries of what can be done with this technology. The rest of this chapter surveys just how far we can take CSS3 to create great 3D effects.

## Rendering 3D Objects

In previous sections, we saw that it took a bit of HTML and CSS work to make a two-sided flat object. It takes even more effort to create an object with depth, such as a cube. There are several sites dedicated to CSS3 that show great examples of how to do this. Figure 6-10 depicts a 3D virtual product box created by German-based Dirk Weber for his HTML5 development site *http://www.eleqtriq.com*. The box has front, back, sides, top, and bottom, and can be rotated. It even has simulated reflections!

Rotated packshot

*Figure 6-10. Rotatable 3D object built with CSS (http://www.eleqtriq.com/2010/11/ natural-object-rotation-with-css3-3d/)*

The team at Codrops (*http://tympanus.net/codrops/*), a web design and development blog, has taken the box concept a step further, creating a 3D virtual book. You can open the cover to look inside, and even turn the pages. See Figure 6-11.

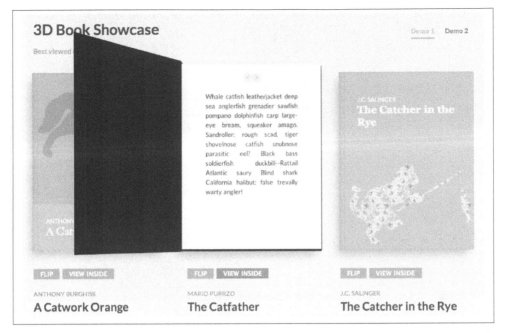

*Figure 6-11. 3D virtual book showcase (http://tympanus.net/codrops/2013/01/08/3d-book-showcase/)*

Creating full 3D objects like these involves making one or more HTML elements for each face, defining several CSS classes and typically some JavaScript for the logic. It is not exactly easy, but the results can be worth it. Check out the sites on CSS3 listed here and in the Appendix to see the groundbreaking work developers are doing with CSS 3D. Most of these sites share their code freely, so you will have a great starting point for your own CSS 3D work.

## Rendering 3D Environments

Given the foundations of CSS 3D—essentially a technology for manipulating rectangular objects—it may seem out of reach to attempt to build something like an immersive game environment. Incredibly, UK-based developer Keith Clark has done just that, creating a demo of a first-person shooter environment in the style of *Doom*, built entirely with JavaScript and CSS 3D transforms. The result is depicted in Figure 6-12.

*Figure 6-12. First-person shooter demo built with CSS 3D and JavaScript (http:// blog.keithclark.co.uk/creating-3d-worlds-with-html-and-css/)*

Clark's work demonstrates features that barely seem possible in CSS3, even with 3D transforms. These include:

*3D geometry*

CSS allows us to work only with rectangles. That appears limiting at first until we realize that even true 3D rendering systems typically work by composing many flat polygons—usually triangles or quads—into more complex shapes. Also, PNG images can make use of the alpha channel to create cutout shapes within a single quad. Working with those two components, Clark was able to build cylinders, guns, the shooter's hand, and other realistic 3D geometry.

*Camera, navigation, and collision*

CSS support for perspective is rudimentary, but Clark figured out how to move a virtual camera in real time based on keyboard input, and calculate collisions by projecting the player's position onto the 2D ground plane and comparing it to a hand-crafted 2D height map.

*Lighting and shadows*

CSS doesn't support lighting of elements. To create a realistic lighting model, Clark needed to construct normal vectors for each quad, create virtual light sources in JavaScript, and render off-screen texture maps to a `<canvas>` element that was then blended with the base texture map to create a lit surface.

Keith Clark's work goes beyond what most developers would venture to do. An environment like this would be much more straightforward to create using WebGL with a library like Three.js. However, the project represents a significant case study in what is possible with CSS3. For more information, see his description of the project (*http://blog.keithclark.co.uk/creating-3d-worlds-with-html-and-css/*).

## Using CSS Custom Filters for Advanced Shader Effects

Some browsers are experimenting with allowing developers to use the GLSL shading language to manipulate CSS elements by applying arbitrary 3D effects. This technology, pioneered by Adobe Systems, is known as CSS Custom Filters (formerly CSS Shaders). Figure 6-13 shows the before/after of a DOM element using a CSS Custom Filter to create a "crumple" effect. When the mouse is rolled over the element, a shader program distorts the vertices that compose the display rectangle for the element, animating the vertices over a short time interval until they appear like crumpled paper. What is most significant about animating with CSS Custom Filters is that the contents of the DOM element are standard HTML: a few bits of text with styles, plus an image. CSS Custom Filters allow web developers to leverage their existing knowledge of HTML while creating new eye-catching interactive effects.

*Figure 6-13. Crumple shader, a CSS3 Custom Filter by Altered Qualia (http://altered qualia.com/css-shaders/crumple.html)*

CSS Custom Filters use a subset of the GLSL shading language (GLSL ES). While it is nearly identical to the GLSL ES used in WebGL, there are a few very small differences. For security reasons, a CSS Custom Filter is not allowed to directly access the pixel color of any page element; rather, the filter must generate a blend color that is ultimately combined with the destination pixel of the element to produce a final color. In addition, the browsers supply a few predefined values as built-in uniform variables, such as the element's 3D transformation matrix as defined by its standard CSS 3D transform (see earlier discussion). One other important difference is that the use of a CSS Custom Filter is optional, whereas a shader is *required* in order to render with WebGL.

 Note that CSS Custom Filters are still an experimental feature, and supported only in some browsers. As of this writing, the feature is also in danger of being shelved in favor of integrating DOM elements into the WebGL specification by allowing their use as texture maps. This is all very much a work in progress. In the meantime, the feature is still supported in Chrome and can be accessed via a special command-line switch (`--enable-css-shaders`), or the user preference Enable CSS Shaders.

## Rendering CSS 3D Using Three.js

Even today, in 2014, there are some browsers that do not support WebGL. Mobile Safari for iOS comes to mind. So there may be occasions when it is necessary to use other web technologies as fallbacks for creating 3D. CSS3 is one, as we have seen. However, doing deep 3D development can get pretty labor-intensive, involving dozens of classes and HTML elements to create a small set of 3D objects.

Recently, Mr.doob got inspired to create a CSS-based rendering system for Three.js. One of the great things about this library is that it can render using various browser display technologies. Three.js has a plug-in rendering architecture, with renderers built for WebGL, 2D Canvas, SVG, and now, CSS.

The Three.js CSS renderer translates, rotates, and scales objects using CSS 3D transforms, which is ideal for mapping interactive page elements into a 3D space. Refer to Figure 6-14, which depicts an interactive periodic table. Each entry in the table is a fully functioning DIV tag, so it can be populated with HTML and styled using CSS. The CSS renderer is a great choice for creating innovate layouts of mostly rectangular, text-rich objects.

# Chapter Summary

This chapter explored the browser's built-in CSS3 features for creating 3D effects: CSS Transforms, CSS Transitions, and CSS Animations. You saw how to use CSS Transforms to apply 3D translation, rotation, and scale to elements; render them with and without perspective; propagate 3D transforms down through the DOM hierarchy; and control rendering of an element's backfaces. We created simple animation effects using CSS Transitions, and more complex ones using CSS Animations.

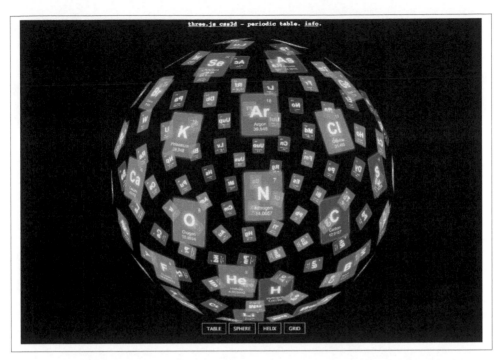

*Figure 6-14. An interactive periodic table, built with Three.js, rendered with CSS 3D transforms (http://mrdoob.github.io/three.js/examples/css3d_periodictable.html)*

CSS3 provides powerful capabilities for creating 3D user interface elements and transition effects, but it falls a bit short of the 3D rendering we expect in today's games and other graphically intensive 3D applications. On the other hand, the effects are easy to create; they can be done mostly in CSS with a little JavaScript; they run universally across browsers and devices; and, most significantly, they are built into the browsers and therefore require no additional libraries. In some rare cases, when we want to push the envelope on using CSS3, we can do serious JavaScript hacking or lean on a library like Three.js that renders to CSS3.

# CHAPTER 7

# Canvas: Universal 2D Drawing

At the end of the day, 3D graphics are rendered on a 2D surface such as the display of your computer, tablet, or phone. What makes them 3D is the appearance of depth and perspective: some objects appear closer, others farther away. If we also want our 3D to be interactive, then the rendering must happen quickly enough so that the changes are displayed without a perceptible delay—at least 30, and ideally, up to 60 times per second.

WebGL and CSS3 enable real-time 3D rendering using the GPU, the specialized graphics-processing unit present on today's computers and devices. While 3D hardware acceleration is extremely important to interactive 3D graphics, it is not a prerequisite. It is also possible to create compelling 3D experiences using software rendering. For web applications, software rendering means using the Canvas 2D context—the universal API for drawing 2D graphics in a browser.

There are a few situations in which we should consider using Canvas 2D over WebGL. First, while it is near ubiquitous, as of this writing WebGL is not supported in all mobile platforms, the most notable exception being Mobile Safari on iOS. For those platforms we can treat Canvas 2D as a fallback and deliver an experience that we know will work —albeit with potentially lower performance or less crisp graphics than its WebGL counterpart. Or we may be targeting power-challenged environments like certain smartphones where the GPU consumes battery quickly, and thus want to employ a software-only solution to extend battery life. Finally, we may want to create simple 3D effects for which WebGL is overkill but CSS3 is underpowered. Any of these are valid reasons to look into software-based rendering with the 2D Canvas API as an alternative to WebGL.

In this chapter, we will explore how the 2D Canvas API can be used to render 3D, and the performance and feature tradeoffs you should keep in mind when using Canvas 2D versus WebGL. We will also look at open source libraries that can be used to handle the 3D math and rendering, allowing us to focus on building the application.

# Canvas Basics

Apple first introduced Canvas in 2004 to support advanced interface development in its Dashboard widgets and Safari browsers. The idea was to provide a general-purpose surface for drawing graphics. Over the next few years it was adopted in Mozilla's Gecko engine, other WebKit-based browsers such as Google Chrome, and eventually in all HTML5 browsers and platforms.

Unlike DOM UI elements or SVG, the earlier standard for drawing 2D vector graphics, Canvas graphics are not constrained to a fixed set of shapes defined with markup tags; instead, an API is provided that allows JavaScript developers to draw and fill arbitrary shapes, including lines, curves, polygons, and text. Also unlike the DOM or SVG, Canvas employs a low-level procedural model akin to WebGL. The browser does not retain the visual content of Canvas-based elements in a scene graph; rather, the application must maintain its own objects and call drawing primitives each time the element needs to be redrawn (such as during an animation).

A full study of the Canvas API is beyond the scope of this book. But to understand Canvas drawing as it relates to 3D, we will go over the basics here.

## The Canvas Element and 2D Drawing Context

HTML5 defines a new DOM element, `<canvas>`, which specifies a drawable region of the page with a given `width` and `height`. The Canvas element is similar to an Image element: you can create it in markup, or using a DOM API like `document.createEle` `ment()`. Once you've created it, you can style the Canvas element with CSS to give it borders and margins, position it, and even animate it with transitions.

The Canvas element simply defines the region on the page for drawing. In order to draw graphics, you must obtain a *context*, which is an object that exposes the drawing API. For Canvas drawing, we obtain a 2D context—as opposed to the 3D drawing context used to render WebGL graphics we have seen in previous chapters.

Example 7-1 shows how to create a Canvas element and draw a white square. In the styles section, we specify a black background for the canvas. In the markup, we create the canvas using a `<canvas>` tag, and specify a width and a height in pixels. In our page load function, we fetch the Canvas element by its id and get a 2D drawing context for it by calling `canvas.getContext("2d")`. Once we have a context, we can draw. We set the context's `fillStyle` property to white using CSS color syntax; then we draw a filled rectangle by calling the `context.drawRectangle()`, passing the *x,y* coordinates of the top-left corner, and a width and height.

*Example 7-1. Basic Canvas drawing example*

```html
<html>
<head>
<meta http-equiv="Content-Type" content="text/html; charset=UTF-8">
<title>Programming 3D Applications in HTML5 and WebGL &mdash;
        Basic Canvas Example</title>

</head>

<style>
    #basicCanvas {
        background-color:Black;
    }
</style>
<body>

<canvas id="basicCanvas" width=500 height=500></canvas>

</body>
<script src="../libs/jquery-1.9.1/jquery-1.9.1.js"></script>
<script type="text/javascript">

    $(document).ready(
            function() {

                var canvas = document.getElementById("basicCanvas");
                var context = canvas.getContext("2d");
                context.fillStyle = '#ffffff';
                context.fillRect(125, 125, 250, 250);
            }
    );

</script>
</html>
```

The result should be quite familiar—see Figure 7-1.

Pretty simple stuff; this is a lot like the examples from Chapters 2 and 3; however, it took only about a half-dozen lines of JavaScript. (When I said there are easier ways to draw 2D on a page, I wasn't kidding.) The code for this example can be found in *Chapter 7/canvasbasic.html.*

*Figure 7-1. Drawing a square with the Canvas API*

## Canvas API Features

The Canvas 2D context provides a raster-based API; that is, drawing is done in pixels (versus the vectors found in some graphics systems, like SVG). If an application needs to scale graphics based on window size, it must do so manually. 2D Canvas API calls fall into the following rough categories:

*Shape drawing*
> Rectangular, polygonal, and curved shapes; either filled or stroke outlined.

*Line and path drawing*
> Line segments, arcs, and Bézier curves.

*Image drawing*
> Bitmap data from other sources such as Image elements or another canvas.

*Text drawing*
> Filled or stroked text, with text properties defined through CSS-style attributes.

*Fill and stroke styles*
> CSS styles and gradients for defining fill patterns and stroked line patterns.

*Transformations*
> 2D transformations, including translate, rotate, scale, and an arbitrary 3×3 matrix.

*Compositing*
Control over how newly drawn shapes are blended with the existing canvas contents.

Figure 7-2 shows a screenshot of a Canvas element drawn with various calls to illustrate the API's drawing features. We can see a filled rectangle; a rectangle drawn with a stroke outline; filled and stroked text; a filled polygon (triangle); a filled Bézier curve with a stroke outline; a bitmap image; a circle filled with a bitmap pattern; a polyline; and a gradient-filled rectangle.

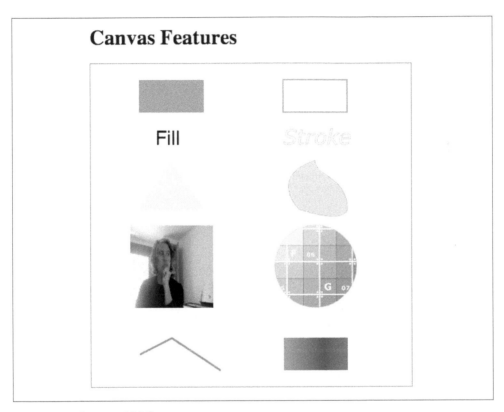

*Figure 7-2. Canvas API features*

Example 7-2 shows the JavaScript code for this example (source file *Chapter 7/canvas features.html*). The rest of the markup has been omitted for brevity.

*Example 7-2. Detailed Canvas drawing example*

```
function init()
{
    image1 = new Image;
    image1.src = '../images/parisi1.jpg';
```

```
        image2 = new Image;
        image2.onload = function()
        {
            imagepattern = context.createPattern(image2, "repeat");
        }

        image2.src = '../images/ash_uvgrid01.jpg';

        gradient = context.createLinearGradient(250,0,350,0);
        gradient.addColorStop(0,"green");
        gradient.addColorStop(1,"blue");
    }

    function run()
    {
        requestAnimationFrame(run);
        draw(canvas, context);
    }

    $(document).ready(
            function() {

                canvas = document.getElementById("features");
                context = canvas.getContext("2d");
                init();
                run();
            }
    );
```

First, our page load function finds the Canvas element and creates a 2D context. Then it calls init() and finally, run(), which implements a requestAnimationFrame()-based run loop. Unlike the previous example, which drew the canvas as a one-shot, this time we are going to paint it repeatedly. We do this for two reasons: 1) this is a more typical structure for a real Canvas-based application, where content is animated or reacting to user input in some way, so we may as well develop good practice now; and 2) we actually need it here for at least a few frames, because we need to test to see if our images have been loaded. We don't want to try to draw the images unless their contents are ready to be painted. We will get into the details of this in a moment.

The function init() creates two Image elements, one for the bitmap contents, and one for the gradient that will be used to fill the rectangle on the bottom right. It also creates a fill pattern based on the second bitmap by adding an onload event handler to the image before loading it. The onload handler uses the context's createPattern() method to create the fill pattern; this method requires valid bitmap data, so we must wait until the image is loaded.

The function run() implements the run loop. First, it requests a new animation frame so that it will get called again the next time through the browser's update cycle. Then, it calls draw(), which does the drawing. The code for this function is presented here in its entirety.

```
function draw(canvas, context)
{
    context.clearRect(0, 0, canvas.width, canvas.height);

    context.save();
    context.translate(50, 0);

    // Small red filled rectangle
    context.save();
    context.fillStyle = '#ff0000';
    context.fillRect(25, 25, 100, 50);
    context.restore();

    // Small dark blue filled rectangle
    context.save();
    context.strokeStyle = 'DarkBlue';
    context.strokeRect(250, 25, 100, 50);
    context.restore();

    // Filled text
    context.save();
    context.lineWidth = 1;
    context.fillStyle = 'Black';
    context.font = '30px sans-serif';
    context.fillText('Fill', 50, 125);
    context.restore();

    // Stroked text
    context.save();
    context.lineWidth = 1;
    context.strokeStyle = 'Orange';
    context.font = 'italic 2em Verdana';
    context.strokeText('Stroke', 250, 125);
    context.restore();


    // A triangle
    context.save();
    context.beginPath();
    context.fillStyle = 'Yellow';
    context.moveTo(75, 150);
    context.lineTo(25, 225);
    context.lineTo(125, 225);
    context.lineTo(75, 150);
    context.fill();
    context.closePath();
    context.restore();
```

```
// A filled Bezier curve
context.save();
context.beginPath();
context.strokeStyle = 'Green';
context.fillStyle = 'LightBlue';
context.moveTo(300,150);
context.bezierCurveTo(225,175,275,225,275,225);
context.bezierCurveTo(350,250,350,225,350,225);
context.bezierCurveTo(350,175,300,175,300,150);
context.stroke();
context.fill();
context.closePath();
context.restore();

// A bitmap
if (image1.width)
{
    context.save();
    context.drawImage(image1, 11, 250, 128, 128);
    context.restore();
}

// A bitmap-filled circle
if (image2.width)
{
    context.save();
    context.strokeStyle = 'DarkGray';
    context.fillStyle = imagepattern;
    context.beginPath();
    context.arc(300, 314, 64, 0, 2 * Math.PI, false);
    context.scale(.5, .5);
    context.fill();
    context.stroke();
    context.closePath();
    context.restore();
}

// A polyline
context.save();
context.strokeStyle = "rgb(128, 0, 255)";
context.beginPath();
context.lineWidth = 3;
context.moveTo(25, 450);
context.lineTo(75, 425);
context.lineTo(150, 475);
context.stroke();
context.closePath();
context.restore();

// A gradient fill
context.save();
```

```
context.fillStyle = gradient;
context.fillRect(250, 425, 100, 50);
context.restore();

context.restore();
}
```

draw() shows off many features of the 2D Canvas API. I will highlight a few of them here.

- context.clearRect() is called to clear the contents of the canvas. Without this, graphics will continually be added to the canvas on top of the ones drawn in previous frames.

- context.translate() is used to translate the position of all objects subsequently drawn; the values supplied are essentially added to the positions of any other drawing operations.

- Note the liberal use of context.save() and context.restore(). These methods allow the programmer to take a snapshot of the graphics state before making changes, and restore it to that state after drawing. The saved state includes transformations, stroke and fill styles, fonts, line widths, and more. The browser maintains state on a stack, so calls to these methods can be nested. This is really handy for drawing hierarchical objects. In general, you want to use these to keep state from "bleeding" from one drawing operation into another. However, understand that they incur some performance overhead, so you may need to put some thought into where and when to use them.

- The context methods beginPath() and closePath() allow us to create user-defined paths for polylines and curves. The canvas maintains a virtual "pen" position, which we manipulate using methods such as moveTo(), lineTo(), and bezierCurve To(). beginPath() resets the state of the pen; closePath() connects the current pen position to the initial positioned defined with the first moveTo() call.

- Image drawing is done via context.drawImage(). We need to wait until the image has been loaded before drawing it to the canvas; we do that by testing for a nonzero width. drawImage() can draw images at their natural size, or scale them if we pass a width and height in the fourth and fifth arguments. Images can also be used as a pattern to fill objects; we use that feature here by calling context.createPat tern() once image2 has been loaded. The resulting pattern is saved in the variable imagepattern and used as a fill for the circle.

This example just touches on drawing 2D graphics with the Canvas API. It is a rich system with many capabilities. Rendering with Canvas also comes with a unique set of performance concerns and best practices. This is outside of what we can cover here. For a list of resources on the Canvas API, refer to the Appendix.

# Rendering 3D with the Canvas API

Now that we have seen the basics of Canvas 2D drawing, we can discuss the issues involved in using it as a software rendering system for 3D. While there are many possible approaches, most software implementations mimic the operations of a hardware-based 3D rendering pipeline—namely, drawing shaded triangles, lines, and points in screen space after transforming them from model (object) space.

Using 3D hardware, we do most such calculations in GLSL shader code, with the help of very powerful built-in primitives compiled to low-level machine code on the GPU. Without 3D hardware, we need to do this in JavaScript before calling methods of the 2D Canvas API to render the final shaded, transformed objects on the screen. The calculations required to manipulate 3D geometry, transforms, lighting, and shading, as well as the math to project the 3D objects onto a 2D viewport, represent a lot of computation that can tax even the fastest machines—not to mention the brain power of the implementer.

A software renderer typically has to perform the following tasks:

- **Transform triangles** from object space to screen space. This involves multiplying several matrices, depending on the complexity of the scene graph. At a minimum, it requires transforming the triangles of an object from world space (assuming it has no additional transforms) to camera space, then to 2D screen space via perspective projection.

- **Shade triangles** based on materials. If lighting is involved, vertex normals and lighting have to be factored in. Using the 2D Canvas API requires dynamically generating textures or gradients to create the lighting effects; this can be very computationally expensive. If a material has textures, textures must also be filtered, perspective-corrected, and otherwise processed to look smooth and realistic. It is particularly difficult to perspective-correct and filter textures in real time. As you will discover in the examples to follow, texture mileage varies based on the application.

- **Sort triangles** based on distance from the viewport. In order for our scenes to look correct, triangles that are closer to the viewport should be rendered in front of triangles that are farther away; that is, they should obscure them. Hardware-based systems use a *depth buffer*, also known as a *z-buffer*, to track the distance of each drawn pixel to the camera. The depth buffer is a parallel array to the color buffer. At each coordinate corresponding to the color buffer, the depth buffer maintains a distance value, which the renderer tests before drawing a pixel to the color buffer. If a pixel is closer to the viewport than any previously drawn pixel recorded in the depth buffer, the pixel will be drawn; if it is farther away, it will be discarded. Software rendering systems almost never have a depth buffer, because it is too memory- and CPU-intensive to calculate the depth values. Instead, they sort by triangle, based on the location of a point on the triangle. Often, this is the geometric center of the triangle, though it can also be its closest or farthest away *z* value. There is no standard. Triangle sorting is one of the most performance-sensitive areas when it comes to software rendering, and you may find that overall triangle count represents one of your biggest performance bottlenecks.

Even a quality software rendering implementation that pulls out all the stops is facing certain obstacles. Antialiased rendering—the smoothing out of *aliased*, or jagged, lines at the edges of objects—is very difficult to do in real time in software, requiring multiple passes to render an object or the entire scene. Texture filtering with techniques like mipmapping and bilinear filtering can be computationally prohibitive, and as a consequence software-based texturing goes without and tends to look rough and grainy. See Figure 7-3 for an example. Also, bitmap fill rates (e.g., for sprites) are much slower in software than in hardware.

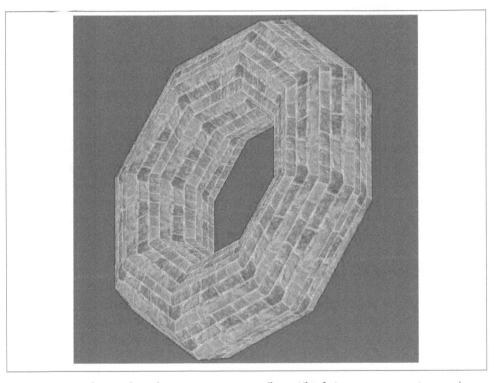

*Figure 7-3. Software-based texture mapping (http://bit.ly/nomone-mapping-test); reproduced with permission*

In addition, triangle sorting, while being a fair substitute for a depth buffer in some circumstances, breaks down completely in others. For example, when two triangles partially overlap, there is no good way to sort them. Refer to Figure 7-4: from the camera's point of view, triangle B is both behind and in front of triangle A. A software-sorting algorithm would have to choose either triangle A or B to draw in front, hence obscuring the other triangle completely. As a result, you will occasionally see triangles "popping" in and out of the scene as objects move relative to the camera. This never happens with a hardware depth buffer.

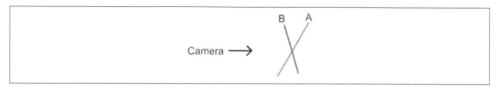

*Figure 7-4. Depth sorting triangles: a portion of triangle A is closer to the camera than triangle B, but a portion of triangle B is also closer to the camera than triangle A, so there is no good solution (image from MSDN article on depth sorting (http://bit.ly/ depth-sorting-alpha-blended-objects); reproduced with permission)*

As we can see, software rendering is not an optimal solution if hardware rendering is available. It is difficult, if not impossible, to get the same visual quality and performance. But despite the inherent limitations, there have been some amazing efforts to create high-performance 3D in software using the 2D Canvas API.

A few years ago, UK-based Jean dArc created a 2D Canvas-based viewer for exploring *Quake 3* level maps. Figure 7-5 shows a screenshot. Go to *http://www.zynaps.com/site/ experiments/quake.html* to try it out. Performance is reasonable on a recent laptop, and the textures, though grainy because they are not filtered, look pretty good. This was a Chrome experiment originally designed to show off 2D Canvas capabilities, built at a time when WebGL was far from pervasive. While its significance now is largely historical, it shows what is possible with the 2D Canvas API and good software techniques.

## Canvas-Based 3D Libraries

As discussed, there are intense technical problems to solve to render 3D in software using Canvas. Several libraries have cropped up to tackle the problem, including K3D (*https://launchpad.net/canvask3d*), Cango3D (*http://bit.ly/cango3d*), Nihilogic (*http:// www.nihilogic.dk/labs/canvas3d/*), and, of course, Three.js (*https://github.com/mrdoob/ three.js/*). In this section, we will take a look at two of these libraries, K3D and Three.js.

*Figure 7-5. Quake 3 map viewer rendered in software using the 2D Canvas API (http://www.zynaps.com/site/experiments/quake.html); reproduced with permission*

## K3D

K3D is the creation of UK-based Kevin Roast (*http://www.kevs3d.co.uk/dev/*; Twitter *@kevinroast*). Kevin is a UI developer and graphics enthusiast. While K3D is early in its development and not as feature-rich as Three.js, it is very impressive. In particular, it is fast and does a great job with shading and textures. Figure 7-6 shows a screenshot from *Asteroids [Reloaded]*, Kev's K3D-based implementation of the arcade classic. Note the smooth shading, lighting, and highly detailed textures on the rocks.

*Figure 7-6. Asteroids [Reloaded], a K3D-based 3D game rendered with the 2D Canvas API (http://www.kevs3d.co.uk/dev/asteroids/)*

Building upon his early work with K3D, Kev is now working on *Phoria (http://www.kevs3d.co.uk/dev/phoria/)*, a complete rewrite of K3D. *Phoria* promises to be more powerful and general purpose, but it is still in its early stages and, at the moment, the K3D demos are far more interesting.

## The Three.js Canvas Renderer

Since we have been using Three.js to develop the other examples in the book, it makes sense to consider it as a solution for software-rendered 3D, especially if the main goal is to develop a fallback for non-WebGL platforms. By using Three.js, we can render to WebGL where it is available, and Canvas 2D where it is not, with a minimum of code changes. While the switch between 3D and 2D renderers is not completely transparent —you will have to make a few code changes to take full advantage of Canvas rendering —it is fairly unobtrusive.

Three.js uses a plugin rendering architecture and comes with a ready-to-go renderer based on the 2D Canvas API. This is unsurprising, given its origin. Three.js was originally based on earlier work done by Mr.doob to render using Flash 2D graphics primitives, so the HTML5 Canvas renderer was a natural transition. In fact, the HTML5 Canvas renderer was implemented before the 3D WebGL renderer.

Three.js comes with a large number of Canvas-based samples. Unfortunately, most of them aren't very interesting. There are a few worth noting here. In the Three.js project sources, open up *examples/canvas_geometry_earth.html*, shown in Figure 7-7. You will see a rotating texture-mapped Earth. It's not as pretty as its WebGL counterpart, but it's still nice. The biggest thing you might notice is that the sphere isn't very highly tessellated; that is, there aren't that many triangles used to render it. You can see the triangular edges as it rotates. It's not quite a golf ball, but it's cruder than we'd like. This is because of triangle depth sorting. You must take care to keep triangle counts down because depth sorting the triangle is at best a *O(N log N)* operation, so higher triangle counts mean slower sorting.

*Figure 7-7. Texture-mapped Earth rendered with Three.js Canvas renderer*

The Canvas renderer is really good at simple 3D panoramas. Here we are talking about rendering 12 triangles (i.e., the faces on the inside of a cube), so triangle count is not an issue. Open the Three.js sample in *examples/canvas_geometry_panoramas.html* to see the 3D panorama depicted in Figure 7-8. Use the mouse to rotate the scene. The navigation is smooth and the panoramic textures look great.

*Figure 7-8. Canvas-rendered Three.js panorama*

The Three.js Canvas renderer also excels at drawing lots of simple shapes, such as flat 2D polygons, laid out in 3D space. This is a great way to create fancy page effects such as animated particles. Figure 7-9 shows an example (source file *examples/canvas_parti cles_random.html*) of 1,000 randomly placed particles animating as the mouse moves around on the screen. The shapes are flat, but they move around in 3D space. As an alternative, imagine doing this with CSS 3D transforms. A thousand individual moving elements would most certainly place undue burden on the browser's DOM. With a Canvas implementation, it's peppy, and Three.js makes it easy to create.

### Using the Three.js Canvas renderer

Getting going with Canvas and Three.js is as simple as creating a different type of renderer object. But there are subtleties involved. Let's take a look at a basic example to see it in operation. While we are at it, let's also explore some visual and performance differences between the Three.js Canvas and WebGL renderers. Finally, we will do this in a context of something approaching a real-world example. The examples presented thus far are totally contrived—little more than tech demos. Let's see what it would be like instead to try to build something tangible, like game graphics with polygonal models and textures.

*Figure 7-9. 1,000 animated particles using the Three.js Canvas renderer*

Figure 7-10 shows a screenshot of an experiment using the Three.js Canvas renderer to build a game. It is a simple viewer intended to assess visual quality and frame rate. Open the file *Chapter 7/threejscanvasmodel.html* in your browser. You will see a trio of slowly rotating spaceships against a simple star background. Use the mouse to rotate the scene, and the scroll wheel to zoom in/out. You can start/stop the animation by clicking on the Animate checkbox. As a bonus, the demo allows you to switch between Canvas- and WebGL-based renderers to compare. But before we do that, let's look at the Canvas version.

Note the frame rate counter at the top left. It stays in the range of 20–23 frames per second. If you stop the animation and zoom into the scene so that one of the ships is out of frame, you should see the frame rate bump up to around 30. Do it again, so that only one ship is visible; you will see around 50, perhaps up to 60, fps in the frame rate counter. This is a clear demonstration of the triangle-sorting issue discussed earlier. Because the Three.js Canvas renderer does not have a depth buffer, the library has to triangle sort. More triangles mean slower sorting. When we zoom in to see only one ship, Three.js is smart enough to ignore (*cull*) that object and thus not sort the triangles. These spaceship models are quite simple, around 1,200 triangles per model. This is not a very high number for modern games, so this example illustrates how thrifty we might need to be with our polygon budgets when rendering to the 2D Canvas. Now look at the materials. The ships are lit, and there is a directional light in the scene that should be highlighting various parts of the ships' geometry; however, we don't see that effect. Three.js is able to apply some lighting, but the effects are basic; we don't see smooth shading across the faces. Play with some of the other Canvas examples in the Three.js project tree, and you will see how far you can take materials and lighting.

*Figure 7-10. Rendering models with the Three.js Canvas renderer (spaceship models by gentlemenk (http://bit.ly/JYP2an), via Turbosquid (http://bit.ly/1cju38z))*

### Comparing the Canvas renderer to the WebGL renderer

It's time to switch renderers so that we can compare. Click the WebGL radio button to render the scene with WebGL. See Figure 7-11. The visual contrast is pretty stark. In the WebGL version, textures look smoother, especially as the object gets far away, whereas they are quite grainy in the Canvas version. Edge antialiasing is much smoother in WebGL, though it is also present in the Canvas rendering. Most dramatic is the lighting, where we can now clearly see highlights from the directional light that simply weren't there in the Canvas version. As to performance, look at the frame rate counter. It stays at a steady 60 fps, with no need to cull out objects. This is unsurprising given that Three.js has very little work to do in software. There are only a few objects in the scene, with modest polygon counts and simple textures. Nearly all of the computation is handled in hardware (i.e., in the GLSL shader code built into the Three.js WebGL renderer).

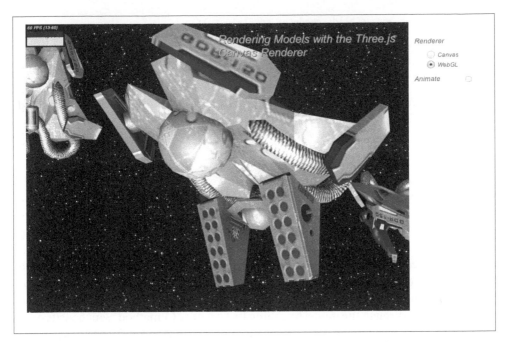

*Figure 7-11. Spaceship scene rendered with Three.js WebGL renderer*

All of this might seem to paint a discouraging picture of using Canvas for 3D game rendering. We topped out frame rate on a fairly simple scene, and we had to compromise visual quality. But that is the glass-half-empty point of view. If we look at this in another way, it's pretty impressive that we can push thousands of textured triangles around on a page using JavaScript. If we are developing simple games, and we can create an art direction style conducive to the limitations of the medium (e.g., low polygon and prelit), we can do some amazing things.

It takes only a few lines of code to use the Three.js Canvas renderer. The source for this example can be found in the file *Chapter 7/threejscanvasmodel.html*. The listing in Example 7-3 shows the code for creating the renderer. Note the line in bold. Instead of creating a WebGL renderer, we create an object of type THREE.CanvasRenderer.

*Example 7-3. Creating the Three.js Canvas renderer*

```
function createRenderer(container, useCanvas)
{
    if (useCanvas) {
        renderer = new THREE.CanvasRenderer( { } );
    }
    else {
        renderer = new THREE.WebGLRenderer( { antialias: true } );
    }
```

```
        container.appendChild( renderer.domElement );

        // Set the viewport size
        renderer.setSize(container.offsetWidth, container.offsetHeight);
    }
```

Once the Canvas renderer is created, we can render to it in the same way we would render to WebGL:

```
        // Render the scene
        renderer.render( scene.scene, scene.camera );
```

For simple uses, that is actually the only line of code we need to change. But for this example, we are going to do one other thing. Three.js gives us the option of doing a simple edge antialiasing by "overdrawing" our triangles; that is, drawing everything a pixel bigger than it should be to hide seams between triangles. Unfortunately, instead of simply setting an `antialias` creation flag in the renderer (the way we would with WebGL), we need to set this up on a per-material basis. That requires iterating through the materials in the model after it is loaded, and setting the `overdraw` property to true. See Example 7-4. We set up a load callback for when each model is loaded. That callback iterates through the model by calling its `traverse()` method, which visits each descendant in its scene graph. Our helper function `processNodes()` tests to see if the object is a mesh. If so, it sets the `overdraw` property on the mesh's material. This extra bit of work is a bit inconvenient, but overall the setup work required is still pretty trivial. These two changes are the only differences between the Canvas and WebGL-based versions of the code.

*Example 7-4. Iterating through materials in the scene*

```
    function processNodes(n)
    {
        if (n instanceof THREE.Mesh)
        {
            n.material.overdraw = true;
        }
    }

    function handleSceneLoaded(data, parent)
    {
        // Add the mesh to our group
        parent.add( data.scene );
        data.scene.traverse(function(n) { processNodes(n) });
    }
```

# Chapter Summary

This chapter took a detailed look at software-based 3D rendering using the 2D Canvas API supported in all HTML5 browsers. After taking a quick tour of the drawing features of the Canvas API, we examined issues inherent in software rendering, including transformations, shading, and depth sorting. We surveyed Canvas-based 3D libraries, in particular how to use the Three.js Canvas renderer as an alternative to WebGL. While there are many tradeoffs, especially in the areas of performance and visual fidelity, Canvas presents a viable alternative to WebGL for simple, limited use cases and as a fallback when WebGL is not present on the target platform.

# Application Development Techniques

# CHAPTER 8

# The 3D Content Pipeline

In the early days of the Web, if you knew how to write markup, you were a content creator. There was no Dreamweaver WYSIWYG editing; no Photoshop tool for slicing images. The task was left, largely, to programmers—and the Web looked like it. Eventually, the makers of professional authoring software developed tools for creating web-ready content. Once the tools were in place, artists and designers assumed the content responsibilities, and the Internet transformed into a consumer-grade experience.

WebGL development is going through an evolution similar to those early days of the Web. For the first few years of the technology's existence, content was created by hand by programmers typing into text editors, or cobbled from whatever 3D format they could find a converter for. If a converter didn't exist, you would write one to get the project done.

Fortunately, the situation is changing rapidly. Three.js and other WebGL libraries are getting better at importing content created by professional tools. The industry is also pulling together to create new 3D file format standards designed specifically for web use. The content creation landscape is still a bit rocky, but at least we have moved beyond the "stone tools" stage of a few years ago into more of a Bronze Age of 3D development.

This chapter covers the 3D content pipeline for web development. First, we will look at the overall content creation process. You may find this useful if you are new to 3D authoring. Then, we survey popular modeling and animation tools being used in today's WebGL projects, and dig into the details of the 3D file formats that are best suited to web deployment. Finally, we will learn how to load those files into applications using Three.js utilities, in preparation for projects to come in following chapters.

## The 3D Creation Process

3D content creation involves a set of highly specialized disciplines. Professional careers in 3D require extensive training and a deep understanding of complex authoring tools and workflows. Often, one 3D artist does everything, including modeling, texture mapping, and animating. But sometimes, especially on bigger projects, people specialize.

In many ways, 3D content creation is similar to making 2D art with Photoshop or Illustrator. But 3D authoring is also different from 2D art creation in a few fundamental respects. Even if you consider yourself a technical person, if you are planning on a developing a 3D project, it's good to know what it takes to make the content that goes into it. With that in mind, let's take a look at the basic steps involved in the 3D creation process.

## Modeling

3D model creation typically starts with a sketch by the artist. Before long, a modeling package is used to turn that sketch into a digital representation in 3D. Models are usually created as 3D polygonal meshes, drawn first as wireframes and then shaded with materials. This activity is known as *3D modeling*, and the person who does it for a living is called a *modeler*. Figure 8-1 depicts a basic model of a teapot, created with Autodesk 3ds Max. The model is seen from four different views: top, left, front, and perspective.

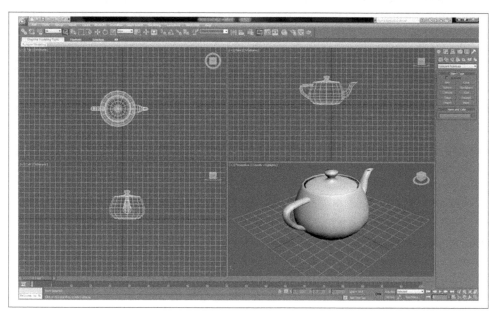

*Figure 8-1. 3D modeling in 3ds Max with top, front, left, and perspective views (image ©Autodesk, from the main Wikipedia entry on 3ds Max (http://en.wikipedia.org/wiki/ File:3dsmax_2010_800px.png))*

## Texture Mapping

*Texture mapping,* also known as *UV mapping,* is the process of creating 2D art to wrap onto the surface of a 3D object. Modelers often do their own texture mapping, though in larger projects the responsibilities may be divided, and specialized *texture artists* do the texturing. Texture mapping is usually done with assistance from a visual tool built directly into the modeling package. The tool allows the artist to associate vertices of the mesh with positions on the 2D texture map while providing visual feedback. Figure 8-2 depicts texture mapping, where we see the map on the left; the combined view is on the bottom right and overlays vertex positions with the image data; and the resulting preview is on the top right. Note the somewhat counterintuitive layout of the image data on the left. Only half the face is shown. This is because, in the case of this texture map, the left and right sides of the face are mirror images. This strategy allows the artist to pack more data into less space and/or use other parts of the image for additional detail.

*Figure 8-2. Texture mapping: a 2D image is wrapped and reflected onto the surface of a 3D object (image courtesy Simon Wottge (http://www.simonwottge.com/?cat=13))*

## Animation

The process of creating 3D animations ranges from easy to extremely difficult, depending on the task. Key frame animating tends to be simple, at least in concept. The interfaces can get tricky to use and cluttered visually. A key frame editor, like the one depicted in Figure 8-3 from Autodesk Maya, contains a set of timeline controls (highlighted in the red rectangle near the bottom of the Maya window) that allow the artist, also known as the *animator,* to move or otherwise changes the object in the view, and then identify and click on positions in the timeline to define the key frames. Key frames can be used to change translation, rotation, scale, and even light and material attributes. When an animator wants to key frame more than one attribute, he or she adds another track to the animation timeline. The animator lays out tracks in the interface by stacking them, which is what can lead to the visual clutter.

Animating characters with skinning is much more involved. Before the character can be animated, a set of bones, or *rig*, must be created. The rig determines various aspects of how the skin moves in response to movements of the bones. *Rigging*, or the process of creating the rig, is a very specialized skill. Often, different artists do the character animation and rigging.

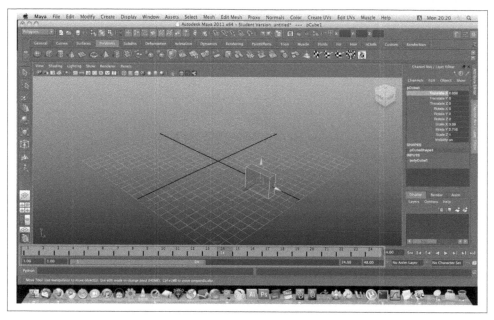

*Figure 8-3. Maya's animation timeline tool, with controls for key frames animating translation, rotation, scale, and other attributes (image courtesy UCBUGG Open Course Ware (http://ucbugg.github.io/learn.ucbugg/introduction-to-maya/))*

## Technical Art

We may not think of programming as a content creation activity, but in 3D development it often is. Complex special effects, such as certain shaders and post-processing techniques, can require the skills of an experienced programmer. In game and animation shops, this job falls to a *technical artist (TA)* or *technical director (TD)*. There is no formal definition of these job positions, or strict difference between the two positions; though as the name implies, the TD is usually a more senior and experienced person. TDs write scripts, rig characters, write converter programs to get art from one format into another, implement special effects, develop shaders—in other words, all the stuff that is too technical for a visual artist to handle. It is a highly valued set of skills, and to many producers, good TDs are worth their weight in gold.

Given that they program for a living, TDs' tool of choice is usually a text editor. However, there are now some interesting visual development tools for creating shaders and special effects. One example is ShaderFusion, a recently released visual tool for use with the *Unity* game engine. ShaderFusion allows the developer to develop shaders by defining data flows between one object's outputs (such as time or position) and another object's inputs (e.g., color and refraction). The interface is depicted in Figure 8-4.

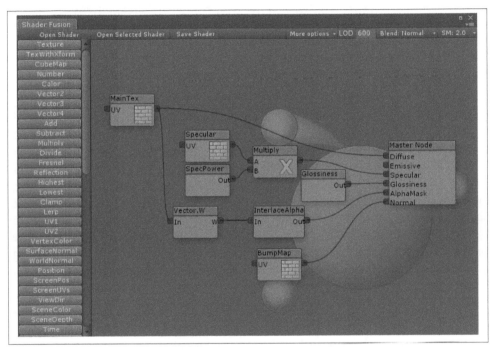

*Figure 8-4. ShaderFusion (http://www.shaderfusionblog.com/), a visual shader editor for the Unity3D engine*

# 3D Modeling and Animation Tools

This section explores the many tools 3D artists can use to create content. There are traditional packaged desktop software products, catering to a range of users and skill levels. There is also a new and promising class of authoring tool that runs as a cloud-based service with an HTML5 interface; some of these services are free, while others charge monthly subscription fees. Finally, artists can leverage their peers' work by downloading existing models and animations from any of several online sites.

# Traditional 3D Software Packages

For the most part, 3D art creation happens inside software applications known as *digital content creation tools*, or *DCC tools* for short. There is a long legacy of 3D DCC tools originating in film production and engineering, and now used widely in architecture, game development, still-rendered art, and more. Think of these packages as analogous to Adobe Photoshop, but for 3D development. They occupy a similar place in the web production pipeline—as sources of original art that needs to be further converted, optimized, and integrated into a web page.

3D DCC tools are typically packaged as native operation system applications, "boxed software" if you will (though of course these days they are usually downloaded from the creators' websites). 3D DCC tools tend to require professional-level skills, and feature complicated user interfaces with a steep learning curve. The good news is that there are a large and growing number of digital artists learning to use 3D DCC tools as part of their education and early professional training. Like a resident Photoshop expert, an experienced 3D artist will likely become part of the web team as you undertake 3D development projects going forward.

3D DCC tools are offered at a broad range of prices, from the completely free Blender to the Autodesk products 3ds Max and Maya, which cost a few thousand dollars per license. The tools tend to have a general set of features covering modeling, texturing, and animation; however, some products are specialized toward one or another of these capabilities. Most 3D DCC tools come with built-in importers from and exporters to the standard file formats we will look at later in this chapter. They also usually have some form of extensibility, such as a native (C++-based) SDK and/or a high-level scripting language for writing plugins that extend the user interface, provide custom rendering, export to new file types, and so on.

Here is a survey of widely used modeling and animation tools that you may encounter when working on WebGL projects. Later in the chapter, we will look into how a few of those can be integrated into a working WebGL content pipeline.

## Autodesk 3ds Max, Maya, and MotionBuilder

San Rafael, California–based Autodesk makes three of the most popular 3D modeling and animation products on the market: 3ds Max, Maya, and MotionBuilder. While the latter is focused primarily on character animation, 3ds Max and Maya are full-featured 3D suites. 3ds Max and Maya are quite similar in terms of feature coverage, and in that sense they can be hard for new users to choose between. Existing users of the products attribute the choice of one or the other to taste, preferences for workflow, and so on. One big difference is that Maya runs on Windows and Mac OS, while 3ds Max runs only on Windows. All three of the Autodesk tools publish to the company's common file format, FBX.

Why would Autodesk have so many similar products? About a decade ago, the company went on a bit of a spree and purchased competing products—Maya from Alias Systems Corporation, and MotionBuilder from Kaydara. While MotionBuilder is really focused on character animation, the other two products have similar feature sets. There is an informative article comparing 3ds Max and Maya on Tom's Hardware (*http://www.tomshardware.com/forum/247220-49-maya*).

The Autodesk tools have complicated user interfaces with lots of controls, views, property sheets, and pop-up windows. They are full "workbench"-style products for complete 3D development. The interface usually starts with a four-viewport view like the 3ds Max screenshot in Figure 8-1, which can be collapsed into single scene view as depicted in the Maya screenshot in Figure 8-5. Common features in these products include material editors, toolbars for creating new objects like geometry primitives (spheres, cubes, etc.), tools for drawing and editing free-form meshes, animation timeline tools, rendering plugins, shader editors—and the list goes on.

*Figure 8-5. Autodesk Maya, a complete 3D modeling and animation package (image ©Autodesk, from the main Wikipedia entry (http://bit.ly/1hndkGA))*

The Autodesk tools are priced for professionals: about US $3,000–4,000 for a single product. The company also offers annual subscription-based pricing, and student and learning editions.

## Blender

Blender (*http://www.blender.org/*) is a free, open source, cross-platform suite of tools for 3D creation. It runs on all major operating systems and is licensed under the GNU General Public License (GPL). Blender was created by Dutch software developer Ton Roosendaal, and is maintained by the Blender Foundation, a Netherlands-based non-profit organization. Blender is extremely popular, with the foundation estimating two million users. It used by artists and engineers from hobbyist/student level to professional.

Like 3ds Max and Maya, Blender has a complex user interface with multiple views, several toolbars and controls, and the associated steep learning curve. So, while the price may be right, it is not for the faint of heart. Still, Blender is an attractive choice for web developers for several reasons:

- It is free of charge.
- It is open source.
- It features an extensibility layer programmable in Python.
- It supports import and export for many different file formats, including 3ds Max, OBJ, COLLADA, and FBX. The Three.js team has also developed an exporter from Blender to the Three.js JSON format (described later in this chapter).

## Trimble SketchUp

Occupying an intermediate rung of the 3D DCC tools ladder is SketchUp (officially, Trimble SketchUp), an easy-to-use 3D modeling program used in architecture, engineering, and to a lesser degree, game development.

SketchUp has had an interesting history. First developed by @Last Software in 1999, the product eventually attracted the interest of the Google Earth team based on @Last's work building a plugin for that system, and Google purchased the company in 2006. For many years, SketchUp was promoted as a way to create user-generated 3D content to represent the world's buildings and architectural landmarks within Google Earth. SketchUp was accompanied by the 3D Warehouse, an online repository for casual creators to upload and share 3D models. In 2012, Google decided to exit the user-generated 3D content business and sold SketchUp to Trimble Navigation, a California-based maker of GPS systems. Trimble continues to distribute SketchUp and maintain the 3D Warehouse, though it is no longer being used to generate content for placing inside Google Earth.

SketchUp runs on all platforms. It has a reasonable price point, around US $500 for the Pro version. There is also a completely free version for casual use. SketchUp is known for its ease of use, with a line-drawing-based approach to modeling that is great for architecture and engineering. SketchUp features an excellent COLLADA exporter (see "COLLADA: The digital asset exchange format" on page 207), so it is potentially a great choice for WebGL development. SketchUp can be downloaded from the official website (*http://www.sketchup.com/*).

## Poser

Smith Micro's Poser is an intermediate 3D tool for character animation. Like SketchUp, it is priced attractively and targets a casual content creation audience. It has an intuitive user interface for posing and animating characters. Poser comes with a large library of modeled, rigged, and fully textured human and animal characters, as well as set background scenes and props, vehicles, cameras, and lighting setups. Poser is used to create both photorealistic still renderings and real-time animations. The Poser user interface is depicted in Figure 8-6.

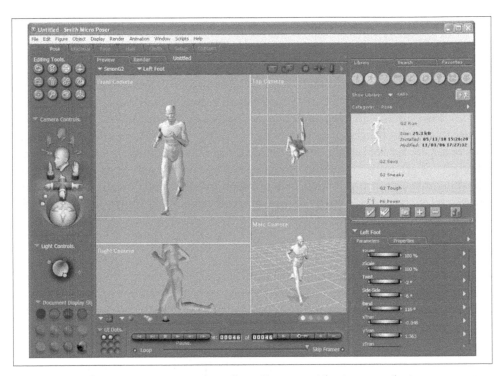

*Figure 8-6. The Poser user interface (http://poser.smithmicro.com/); image courtesy Smith Micro Software, Inc.*

Of the tools discussed so far, Poser is also notable because the development team has been very involved in the creation of the COLLADA file format since its inception, and is also active within the Khronos group in developing the new standard, glTF, which we will discuss later in this chapter. The Poser team strongly believes in standard formats as a way to democratize the adoption of 3D content, especially in a web context. Uli

Klumpp, senior director of engineering at Smith Micro, had this to say about using Poser with WebGL:

> WebGL-enabled applications are no different than other media; there is often a need to depict the human form (or a decidedly non-human form for that matter). Web designers have been using Poser for illustration purposes since the 90s. They have finally gained a ubiquitous 3rd dimension for their work, and Poser's vast world of content is already there.

## Browser-Based Integrated Environments

The emergence of HTML5 and cheap cloud computing has set the stage for a new breed of DCC tool: the in-browser 3D integrated development environment. Modeling and animation still generally happen in native tools such as the ones just mentioned, but scene layout, interaction programming, and web publishing take place in a browser-based interface.

Browser-based integrated environments offer unique capabilities over their native counterparts. First, obviously, there is nothing to download. Second, they are built in WebGL, so they provide a WYSIWYG display that matches the deployed application. Browser-based tools tend to be attractively priced, using "freemium" models that allow free use to start, and charge a fee only once the developer does something commercial —for example, developing a team project, or using file storage above a set limit. Some of these tools are restrictive about how the content can be used, requiring hosting or publishing through their servers in order to support a particular business model. This is a new and evolving space, so developers can expect a web-style flux in business models and pricing in the coming years.

### Verold

Verold Studio is a lightweight publishing platform for 3D interactive content developed by Toronto-based Verold, Inc. It is a no-plugin, extensible system with a simple Java-Script API, so that hobbyists, students, educators, visual communication specialists, and web marketers can integrate 3D animated content easily into their web properties.

A typical Verold workflow has a CG artist upload assets (3D models, animations, textures) to a Verold project. The collaboration tools can be used to provide feedback on iterations of the assets and the editing tools to set up materials and shaders, and to lay out scenes/levels. Once the team is satisfied with the way the assets are set up, the web designer can export boilerplate code and wire it up to the target web page. This workflow works whether the CG artist is located with the developer, or remotely—and likewise for scenarios where the assets are purchased rather than custom-developed. The Verold Studio user interface is depicted in Figure 8-7. Note the clean, browser-based design, in stark contrast to the busy, toolbar- and pop up–heavy look of traditional DCC tools.

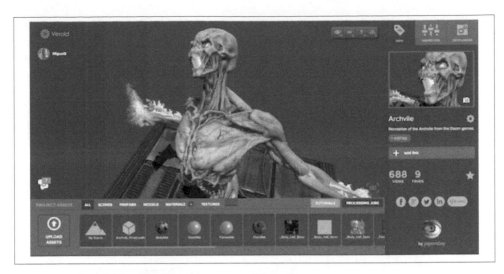

*Figure 8-7. Verold Studio (http://www.verold.com)*

Verold's capabilities to work together in real time, publish online, and share content are enabling novel ways of working on 3D development projects. According to founder and CTO Ross McKegney:

> A great case study of using Verold Studio is Swappz Interactive. Swappz is building toys for Teenage Mutant Ninja Turtles, Smurfs, Power Rangers, and other brands. These toys are special, in that they can be "scanned" into the associated mobile games. The child buys the toy, downloads the game, and now can "scan" their toy into the game. Swappz used Verold technology through the development process: as a means to give feedback between the offshore character artists and local animators, to show progress to the parent company, to get approval of assets from Nickelodeon, and finally, when the games were ready for launch, the game assets were used in the marketing websites for the games.

## Sketchfab

Another class of online 3D tool is the upload-and-share service. A 3D artist can upload creations in any of several formats, and preview and share the results online using WebGL. The most thoroughly developed of these to date is Sketchfab (*http://sketch fab.com/*), created by the Paris-based team of Cédric Pinson and partners Alban Denoyel and Pierre-Antoine Passet. Sketchfab is a web service to publish and share interactive 3D models online in real time without a plugin. With a few clicks, the artist can upload a 3D model to the website and get the HTML code for sharing an embedded view of the model hosted at Sketchfab.

Sketchfab supports several native 3D formats as well as most of the standard shaders: normal maps, specular, bump, diffuse, and so on. Sketchfab also provides a material editor, letting artists adjust shaders and renderings in real time in the browser. The company has also developed exporters for the major native DCC tools, so that models can be exported and uploaded directly from within the authoring environment (e.g., Maya), a potentially more convenient workflow. The Sketchfab home page is depicted in Figure 8-8. The graphic that takes up the majority of the page is actually a live view of one of the models from the Sketchfab gallery, rendered with WebGL.

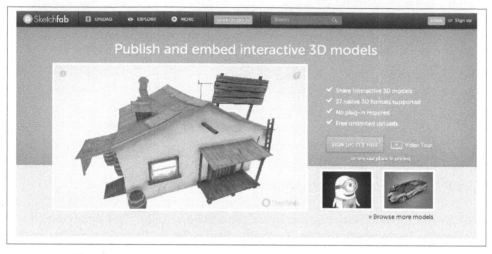

*Figure 8-8. The Sketchfab website (http://sketchfab.com/) allows content creators to upload and share real-time viewable 3D models*

## SculptGL

The limitations of 3D rendering and user interfaces would have made the idea of building an in-browser 3D modeling tool unthinkable a few years ago. Now, with HTML5 and WebGL, it's not such an outlandish idea. Stephane Ginier has created SculptGL, a web-based solid modeling tool with a very easy-to-use interface for creating simple, sculpture-style models. SculptGL is free and open source, available on GitHub at *https:// github.com/stephomi/sculptgl*. SculptGL features export to various formats and direct publishing to both Verold and Sketchfab. SculptGL is depicted in Figure 8-9.

*Figure 8-9. SculptGL (http://stephaneginier.com/sculptgl/), an open source, browser-based 3D modeling tool*

### Shadertoy

Given the rise in popularity of web "sandbox tools" like JSFiddle (*http://jsfiddle.net/*) that allow programmers to experiment with code using in-browser editing and live preview, it was inevitable that someone would develop sandbox tools for use with WebGL. Shadertoy (*https://www.shadertoy.com/*) is a browser-based code tool for writing and testing GLSL shaders. It is a combination sandbox and online community. Once a shader is written and tested, it can be submitted to the Shadertoy site for others to discover. This is a great way to learn GLSL shader coding—by emulating the work of others. After a shader has been developed, you can share it via the Shadertoy website, or simply copy and paste the GLSL code directly into your application source code. Figure 8-10 depicts the Shadertoy interface, which includes a live preview frame, a full code-editing frame, and interactive icons for selecting shader input sources.

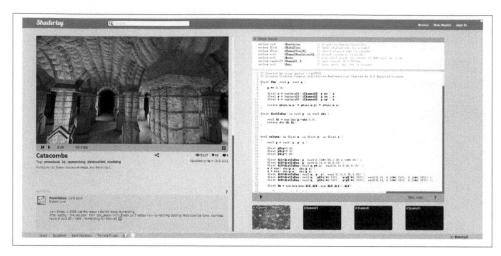

*Figure 8-10. Catacombs, a Shadertoy experiment featuring procedural texturing (https://www.shadertoy.com/view/lsf3zr)*

## 3D Repositories and Stock Art

Not all of us possess 3D modeling talent, and budget and time restrictions on our projects don't always allow us to hire the right people. So it's a good thing that there are great online sources of stock content—3D "clip art," if you will. Prices can range from free to hundreds, even thousands, of dollars for some models and content packs. The quality can also vary widely. Some creators offer their models for use without restriction; others limit use. Make sure to review the licensing terms carefully, especially when developing web applications that distribute the content over the wire.

To create 3D content for this book, I used models from various online sources, including:

*The Trimble 3D Warehouse (http://sketchup.google.com/3dwarehouse/)*
> The 3D Warehouse was originally created by Google as a way for amateurs and hobbyists to upload faithful SketchUp recreations of the world's buildings and architectural landmarks, and geolocate them within Google Earth. With the acquisition of SketchUp by Trimble, the service has transitioned away from use with Google Earth, but it still remains a vital source of nicely rendered buildings and other 3D data.

*Turbosquid (http://www.turbosquid.com/)*
> Founded in 2000, Turbosquid is a top site featuring thousands of models for use in animation, gaming, and architecture. Many of the models have been designed with low- to medium-polygon counts, appropriate for real-time and web use.

*Renderosity (http://renderosity.com/)*

> Renderosity is a diverse community of 2D and 3D creative professionals founded in 1998. The site features a large catalog of models and texture art. Its focus tends to be on high-polygon models for use in prerendered still images, over lower-polygon models for real-time use.

*3DRT.com*

> 3DRT is a no-nonsense online store with quality 3D art for real-time game and web use. The site is organized to make it easy for professionals to find characters, vehicles, props, and environment art. The models are not cheap, but they are of high quality.

# 3D File Formats

There have been many 3D file formats developed over the years—so many that an exhaustive list would not be possible here. Some 3D formats have been designed to store files for a single authoring package; others have been designed to exchange data between packages. Some formats are proprietary—that is, completely controlled by a single company or software vendor—whereas others are open standards defined by an industry group. Some 3D file formats are entirely text-based and, therefore, human-readable, while others use a binary representation to save space.

3D file formats fall into three general categories: model formats, used to represent single objects; animation formats for animating key frames and characters; and full-featured formats that support entire scenes, including multiple models, transform hierarchy, cameras, lights, and animations. We will look at each of these kinds of formats, with a special emphasis on the ones that are best suited for web-based applications.

## Model Formats

Single-model 3D formats are used extensively for interchange between different packages. Most modeling packages, for example, can import and export the OBJ format (see next section). Because they tend to have a simple syntax and only a few features, it is easy to implement support for them, and their use is prevalent. They do, however, tend to be quite limited in the features they support.

### Wavefront OBJ

The OBJ file format, originally developed by Wavefront Technologies, is one of the oldest and best-supported single-model formats in the industry. It is extremely simple, supporting only geometry (with the associated vertices, normals, and texture coordinates). Wavefront introduced the companion MTL (Material Template Library) format for applying materials to geometry.

Example 8-1 illustrates the basics of an OBJ file, an excerpt from the classic "ball chair" model that we will be loading with Three.js later in the chapter (and depicted in Figure 8-12 later in the chapter). The OBJ file is packaged with the code examples in the file *models/ball_chair/ball_chair.obj*. Let's have a look at the syntax. The # character is used as a comment delimiter. The file consists of a series of declarations. The first declaration is a reference to the material library stored in the associated MTL file. After that, several geometry objects are defined. This excerpt shows a partial listing of the definition for the object shell, the outer shell of the ball chair. We define the shell by specifying vertex position, normal, and texture coordinate data, one entry per line, followed by face data, also one per line. Each vertex of the face is specified by a triple in the form v/vt/vn, where v is the index of the previously supplied vertex position, vt the index of the texture coordinate, and vn the index of the vertex normal.

*Example 8-1. A model in Wavefront OBJ format*

```
# 3ds Max Wavefront OBJ Exporter v0.97b - (c)2007 guruware

# File Created: 20.08.2013 13:29:52

mtllib ball_chair.mtl
#
# object shell
#

v  -15.693047 49.273174 -15.297686
v  -8.895294 50.974277 -18.244076
v  -0.243294 51.662109 -19.435429
... more vertex positions here
vn -0.537169 0.350554 -0.767177
vn -0.462792 0.358374 -0.810797
vn -0.480322 0.274014 -0.833191
... more vertex normals here
vt 0.368635 0.102796 0.000000
vt 0.348531 0.101201 0.000000
vt 0.349342 0.122852 0.000000
... more texture coordinates here
g shell
usemtl shell
s 1
f 313/1/1 600/2/2 58/3/3 597/4/4
f 598/5/5 313/1/1 597/4/4 109/6/6
f 313/1/1 598/5/5 1/7/7 599/8/8
f 600/2/2 313/1/1 599/8/8 106/9/9
f 314/10/10 603/11/11 58/3/3 600/2/2
... more face definitions here
```

The material definitions that accompany the ball chair are in the MTL file *models/ball_chair/ball_chair.mtl*. The syntax is very simple; see Example 8-2. A material is declared with the newmtl statement, which contains a handful of parameters used to Phong shade the object: specular colors and coefficients (Ks, Ns, and Ni keywords), diffuse color (Kd), ambient color (Ka), emissive color (Ke), and texture maps (map_Ka and map_Kd). The texture map model for MTL has evolved over the years to include bump maps, displacement maps, environment maps, and other types of textures. In this example, only the diffuse and ambient texture maps are defined for the shell material.

*Example 8-2. Material definitions for Wavefront OBJ format*

```
newmtl shell
    Ns 77.000000
    Ni 1.500000
    Tf 1.000000 1.000000 1.000000
    illum 2
    Ka 0.000000 0.000000 0.000000
    Kd 0.588000 0.588000 0.588000
    Ks 0.720000 0.720000 0.720000
    Ke 0.000000 0.000000 0.000000
    map_Ka maps\shell_color.jpg
    map_Kd maps\shell_color.jpg
...
```

## STL

Another simple, text-based, single model format is STL (for StereoLithography), developed by 3D Systems for rapid prototyping, manufacturing, and 3D printing. STL files are even simpler than OBJ. The format supports only vertex geometry—no normals, texture coordinates, or materials. Example 8-3 shows a fragment from one of the Three.js example STL files (*examples/models/stl/pr2_head_pan.stl*). To see the file in action, open the Three.js example file *examples/webgl_loader_stl.html*. STL is an excellent candidate 3D format for building online 3D printing applications in WebGL, because the files can potentially be sent directly to 3D printing hardware. In addition, it loads easily and renders quickly.

*Example 8-3. The STL file format*

```
solid MYSOLID created by IVCON, original data in binary/pr2_head_pan.stl
  facet normal -0.761249 0.041314 -0.647143
    outer loop
      vertex -0.075633 -0.095256 -0.057711
      vertex -0.078756 -0.079398 -0.053025
      vertex -0.074338 -0.088143 -0.058780
    endloop
  endfacet
...
endsolid MYSOLID
```

STL is such an easy and popular format that GitHub has actually added STL viewing directly into its interface (*https://github.com/blog/1465-stl-file-viewing*). The viewer is built in WebGL, using our old friend Three.js.

For technical details on the STL format, visit the Wikipedia page (*http://en.wikipedia.org/wiki/STL_%28file_format%29*).

## Animation Formats

The formats described in the previous section represent static model data only. But much of the content in a 3D application is moving around on the screen (i.e., animated). A few specialty formats have evolved to deal with representing animated models. These include the text-based—and therefore web-friendly—formats MD2, MD5, and BVH.

### id Software animation formats: MD2 and MD5

A couple of 3D formats that you will see crop up in web use from time to time are the animation formats for id Software's popular *Doom* and *Quake* franchises. The MD2 format and its successor, MD5, are formats that define character animation. While the formats are essentially controlled by id, their specifications were released long ago, and many tools have been written to import them.

The MD2 format, created for *Quake II*, is a binary file format. It supports vertex-based character animation only via morph targets. MD5 (not to be confused with the Message Digest algorithm, a cryptographic hash function used widely on the Web) was developed for *Quake III* and introduced skinned animation and a text-based, human-readable format.

Excellent documentation on the MD2 (*http://tfc.duke.free.fr/coding/md2-specs-en.html*) and MD5 (*http://tfc.duke.free.fr/coding/md5-specs-en.html*) specifications can be found online.

To use these formats in WebGL applications, we could write a loader that reads them directly, or if using a library like Three.js, we can use a converter. When an MD2 file is converted to JSON, the format looks something like the example from Chapter 5, depicted in Figure 5-11. As a refresher, run the Three.js example located at *examples/webgl_morphtargets_md2_control.htm*, and have a look at the source code. There is a lot going on to load and interpret MD2 data.

Three.js does not come with an MD5 loader as part of the example set. However, there is a wonderful online converter from MD5 to Three.js JSON that was written by Klas (*OutsideOfSociety*) of the Swedish web agency North Kingdom (developers of Find Your Way to OZ). To see already-converted models in action, go to Klas's blog and open this link (*http://oos.moxiecode.com/js_webgl/md5_example/*). You should see a fairly detailed model of a monster, with controls for starting the various gesture animations.

To run the converter on your own MD5 files, you can open this link (*http://oos.moxie code.com/js_webgl/md5_converter/*), which lets you drag and drop MD5 files into the view window, and produces JSON code.

### BVH: The motion capture data format

*Motion capture*, the process of recording the movement of objects, has become a very popular way to create content, especially animations of people. It is used extensively in film, animation, military, and sports applications. Motion capture is widely supported in open formats, including the Biovision Hierarchical Data format, or BVH. BVH was developed by the motion capture company Biovision to represent movements in the animation of human characters. BVH is a very popular, text-based format supported as an import and export format by many tools.

Developer Aki Miyazaki has created an early experiment to import BVH data into WebGL applications. His BVH Motion Creator, a web-based BVH preview tool written using Three.js, is depicted in Figure 8-11. BVH can be uploaded, and its animations previewed on the simple character.

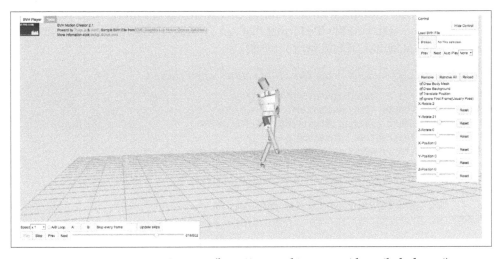

*Figure 8-11. BVH Motion Creator (http://www.akjava.com/demo/bvhplayer/), a previewer for motion capture files in BVH format*

# Full-Featured Scene Formats

Over the years, a few standard formats have been developed by the industry to support representing the entire contents of a 3D scene, including multiple objects, transform hierarchy, lights, cameras, and animations—essentially anything created by an artist in a full-featured tool like 3ds Max, Maya, or Blender. In general, this is a much harder technical problem to solve, and few formats have survived to enjoy widespread use. This situation may change, however, with WebGL driving new requirements for reuse of content and interoperability between applications. In this section, we look at a few potential full-scene formats for use with WebGL.

## VRML and X3D

Virtual Reality Markup Language (VRML) is the original text-based standard for 3D on the Web, created in 1994 by a group that includes inventor and theorist Mark Pesce, members of the Silicon Graphics Open Inventor software team, and myself. VRML went through a couple of iterations in the 1990s, enjoying broad industry backing and the support of a nonprofit standards consortium. A successor featuring XML-based text representation was developed in the early 2000s, and renamed as X3D. While these standards are no longer widely deployed in web applications, they are still supported by most modeling tools as import and export formats.

VRML and X3D define full scenes, animation (key frames, morphs, and skinning), materials, lights, and even scripted, interactive objects with behaviors. Example 8-4 shows the X3D syntax for creating a scene with a red cube that will make a full rotation about the y-axis in two seconds when clicked. The geometry, behavior, and animations are all in this single XML file with an intuitive, human-readable syntax. To this day, there is no other open-standard 3D file format that can express all this functionality in such a simple, elegant syntax (if I do say so myself).

*Example 8-4. X3D sample: A red cube that rotates when clicked*

```
 <?xml version="1.0" encoding="UTF-8"?>
<!DOCTYPE X3D PUBLIC "ISO//Web3D//DTD X3D 3.0//EN"
  "http://www.web3d.org/specifications/x3d-3.0.dtd">
<X3D profile='Interactive' version='3.0'
  xmlns:xsd='http://www.w3.org/2001/XMLSchema-instance'
    xsd:noNamespaceSchemaLocation =
    ' http://www.web3d.org/specifications/x3d-3.0.xsd '>
<head>
... <!-- XML meta information for X3D file goes here -->
</head>
<!--
Index for DEF nodes: Animation, Clicker, TimeSource, XForm
-->
<Scene>
<!-- XForm ROUTE:  [from Animation.value_changed to rotation ] -->
<Transform DEF='XForm'>
<Shape>
<Box/>
<Appearance>
<Material diffuseColor='1.0 0.0 0.0'/>
</Appearance>
</Shape>
<!-- Clicker ROUTE:  [from touchTime to TimeSource.startTime ] -->
<TouchSensor DEF='Clicker' description='click to animate'/>
```

```
<!-- TimeSource ROUTEs:
[from Clicker.touchTime to startTime ] [from fraction_changed to
Animation.set_fraction ] -->
<TimeSensor DEF='TimeSource' cycleInterval='2.0'/>
<!-- Animation ROUTEs:
[from TimeSource.fraction_changed to set_fraction ]
[from value_changed to XForm.rotation ] -->
<OrientationInterpolator DEF='Animation' key='0.0 0.33 0.66 1.0'
keyValue='0.0 1.0 0.0 0.0 0.0 1.0 0.0 2.1 0.0 1.0 0.0 4.2 0.0 1.0 0.0 0.0'/>
</Transform>
<ROUTE fromNode='Clicker' fromField='touchTime' toNode='TimeSource'
  toField='startTime'/>
<ROUTE fromNode='TimeSource' fromField='fraction_changed'
  toNode='Animation' toField='set_fraction'/>
<ROUTE fromNode='Animation' fromField='value_changed' toNode='XForm'
  toField='rotation'/>
</Scene>
</X3D>
```

The design of VRML embodies many key concepts of interactive 3D graphics, and for that reason, you might expect that it is well suited for WebGL use. However, the standard was developed in a pre-JavaScript, pre-DOM world, and also before the advent of many key hardware-accelerated graphics features in use today. At this point, in my humble opinion, VRML/X3D is too out of date to consider for practical use. At the same time, there are many ideas in there yet to be tapped for use in WebGL, so it is a great area for study and inspiration.

Over the years, a wealth of VRML and X3D content has been developed. The folks at the German-based Fraunhofer Institute continue to soldier down the X3D path and are now creating X3DOM, a library for viewing X3D content using WebGL, without the need for a plugin. For more information on X3DDOM, go to *http://www.x3dom.org/*.

The VRML (*http://bit.ly/web3d-vrml*) and X3D (*http://bit.ly/web3d-x3d*) specifications may be found online.

### COLLADA: The digital asset exchange format

In the mid-2000s, as VRML began showing signs of age, a group of companies, including Sony Computer Entertainment, Alias Systems Corporation, and Avid Technology, teamed up to develop a new format for exchanging 3D digital assets among games and interactive 3D applications. Rémi Arnaud and Mark C. Barnes of Sony led the design of the format, named COLLADA (for COLLAborative Design Activity). After the initial specification work and support from individual companies, development of the standard was turned over to the Khronos Group, the same nonprofit organization that develops WebGL, OpenGL, and other graphics hardware and software API standards.

COLLADA, like X3D, is a full-featured, XML-based format that can represent entire scenes, with a variety of geometry, material, animation, and lighting types. Unlike X3D, the goal of COLLADA is not to deliver an end-user experience complete with behaviors and runtime semantics. In fact, it is a stated *nongoal* of the technology. Rather, COLLADA is intended to preserve all of the information that could be exported from a 3D authoring tool so that it can be used downstream in another tool, or imported into a game engine or development environment before being deployed into the final application. The main idea was that, once COLLADA was widely accepted by the industry, the makers of various DCC tools would not have to worry about writing exporters to custom formats ever again; export to COLLADA, and, in theory, any package could import it.

Example 8-5 shows an excerpt from a COLLADA scene that we are going to load with Three.js later in this chapter. As we walk through it, there are several things to note about the structure of COLLADA files. First, all constructs are organized into *libraries* — collections of types such as images, shaders, and materials. These libraries usually come first in the XML definition, to be later referenced by constructs that need them (for example, images used in a material definition). Second, note that there are explicit declarations of what would normally be considered a built-in function, such as Blinn shading. COLLADA assumes nothing about shading and rendering models; it simply stores that data so that another tool can get the information and try to do something with it. Then, we see the vertex data for a mesh, expressed as a series of float_array elements. Finally, the mesh is assembled into a scene the user can see by referencing previously defined geometry and materials (using the instance_geometry, bind_material, and instance_material XML elements).

*Example 8-5. COLLADA file structure, sample libraries, geometry, and scene*

```
<?xml version="1.0"?>
<COLLADA xmlns="http://www.collada.org/2005/11/COLLADASchema"
  version="1.4.1">
    <asset>
        <contributor>
            <authoring_tool>CINEMA4D 12.043 COLLADA Exporter
            </authoring_tool>
        </contributor>
        <created>2012-04-25T16:44:59Z</created>
        <modified>2012-04-25T16:44:59Z</modified>
        <unit meter="0.01" name="centimeter"/>
        <up_axis>Y_UP</up_axis>
    </asset>
    <library_images>
        <image id="ID5">
            <init_from>tex/Buss.jpg</init_from>
        </image>
        ... <!-- more image definitions here -->
    </library_images>
    <library_effects>
        <effect id="ID2">
            <profile_COMMON>
```

```xml
<technique sid="COMMON">
    <blinn>
        <diffuse>
            <color>0.8 0.8 0.8 1</color>
        </diffuse>
        <specular>
            <color>0.2 0.2 0.2 1</color>
        </specular>
        <shininess>
            <float>0.5</float>
        </shininess>
    </blinn>
</technique>
</profile_COMMON>
</effect>
... <!-- more effect definitions here -->
<library_geometries>
<geometry id="ID56">
    <mesh>
        <source id="ID57">
            <float_array id="ID58" count="22812">36.2471
9.43441 -6.14603 36.2471 11.6191 -6.14603 36.2471 9.43441 -9.04828
36.2471 11.6191 -9.04828 33.356 9.43441 -9.04828 33.356 11.6191
-9.04828 33.356 9.43441
        ... <!-- remainder of mesh definition here -->
...
<!-- define the scene as a hierarchy of nodes -->
<library_visual_scenes>
<visual_scene id="ID53">
    <node id="ID55" name="Buss">
        <translate sid="translate">5.08833 -0.496439
-0.240191</translate>
        <rotate sid="rotateY">0 1 0 0</rotate>
        <rotate sid="rotateX">1 0 0 0</rotate>
        <rotate sid="rotateZ">0 0 1 0</rotate>
        <scale sid="scale">1 1 1</scale>
        <instance_geometry url="#ID56">
            <bind_material>
                <technique_common>
                    <instance_material
                    symbol="Material1" target="#ID3">
                        <bind_vertex_input
                            semantic="UVSET0"
                            input_semantic="TEXCOORD"
                            input_set="0"/>
                    </instance_material>
                </technique_common>
            </bind_material>
        </instance_geometry>
    </node>
... <!-- remainder of scene definition here -->
```

After an initial period of high enthusiasm and broad vendor adoption, COLLADA support began to wane. Beginning around 2010, active development on exporter plugins for the popular DCC tools all but stopped. Recently, interest in COLLADA has picked up again, primarily due to the surge of support for WebGL—and the lack of a built-in file format for WebGL (more in this in a moment). There is a new open source project called OpenCOLLADA (*http://bit.ly/open-collada*), with updated exporters for 3ds Max and Maya, from 2010 versions onward. It exports clean, standard-compliant COLLADA.

While improved COLLADA support is a boon to the 3D content pipeline, there is a problem. As we saw in the previous example, COLLADA is very verbose. The format was designed to preserve data, not to be fast to download and parse. That is why the Khronos Group has undertaken a new initiative that reimagines the best aspect of COLLADA—its full representation of rich, animated 3D scenes—into a new format designed for web delivery: glTF.

### glTF: A new format for WebGL, OpenGL ES, and OpenGL applications

The rise in popularity of WebGL created a problem for web developers: the need to deliver full-scene content from 3D DCC tools into a running WebGL application. Single-mesh text formats such as OBJ are adequate for representing one object, but do not contain scene graph structure, lighting, cameras, and animation. COLLADA is fairly full-featured; however, as we saw in the previous section, it is verbose. In addition, it is represented in XML, requiring intensive CPU cycles to process into data structures suitable for rendering in WebGL. What was needed was a compact, web-ready format that requires minimal extra processing before rendering, something akin to a "JPEG for 3D."

In the summer of 2012, Fabrice Robinet, an engineer at Motorola and chair of the Khronos COLLADA working group, began working on a 3D file format with the graphics features of COLLADA but with a more compact, WebGL-friendly representation. Originally, the project was dubbed COLLADA2JSON, the idea being that this would be a translation of the heftier XML syntax into lightweight JSON. Since then, the project has taken on a life of its own. Fabrice was joined by other contributors from the working group, including myself, COLLADA creator Remi Arnaud, and Patrick Cozzi, an engineer at defense software vendor AGI. Our mandate was expanded to broaden the scope beyond simple translation/optimization of COLLADA into a ground-up design of a new format for use with OpenGL-based applications for the Web and mobile, and glTF, the Graphics Library Transmission Format, was born.

glTF uses the full-featured nature of COLLADA as a jumping-off point, but it is a completely new format. The COLLADA feature set acts as a reference for the group to determine what sort of graphics features to support, but the details are completely different. glTF uses JSON files to describe scene graph structure and high-level information (such as cameras and lights), and binary files to describe rich data such as vertices, normals, colors, and animation. The binary format for glTF has been designed so that it can be loaded directly into WebGL buffers (typed arrays such as `Int32Array` and `FloatArray`). So, the process of loading a glTF file can be as simple as the following:

1. Read a small JSON wrapper file.

2. Load an external binary file via Ajax.

3. Create a handful of typed arrays.

4. Call WebGL drawing context methods to render.

Of course, in practice it is a bit more complicated. But this is far more efficient than downloading and parsing an XML file, and converting arrays of JavaScript `Number` types to typed arrays. glTF promises significant wins in both file size and speed of loading content—both critical factors in building high-performance web and mobile applications.

Example 8-6 shows the syntax of the JSON for a typical glTF scene, the famous COLLADA duck model. Note that there are structural similarities to COLLADA: libraries appear first, and we define a scene graph structure at the end by referencing elements in those libraries. But this is where the similarity ends. glTF dispenses with any information not absolutely required for runtime use, opting instead to define structures that will load quickly into WebGL and OpenGL ES. glTF defines in painstaking detail the attributes (vertex positions, normals, colors, texture coordinates, and so on) that are used to render objects with programmable shaders. Using this attribute information, a glTF application can faithfully render any meshes, even if it does not have its own sophisticated materials system.

In addition to the JSON file, glTF references one or more binary files (*.bin* extension) that store rich data (e.g., vertex data for meshes and animations) in structures called *buffers* and *buffer views*. Using this approach, we can stream, download incrementally, or load glTF content in one whack, as appropriate for the application.

*Example 8-6. glTF JSON file format example*

```
{
    "animations": {},
    "asset": {
        "generator": "collada2gltf 0.1.0"
    },
    "attributes": {
        "attribute_22": {
            "bufferView": "bufferView_28",
            "byteOffset": 0,
            "byteStride": 12,
            "count": 2399,
            "max": [
                96.1799,
```

```json
                        163.97,
                        53.9252
                    ],
                    "min": [
                        -69.2985,
                        9.92937,
                        -61.3282
                    ],
                    "type": "FLOAT_VEC3"
                },
... more vertex attributes here
    "bufferViews": {
        "bufferView_28": {
            "buffer": "duck.bin",
            "byteLength": 76768,
            "byteOffset": 0,
            "target": "ARRAY_BUFFER"
        },
        "bufferView_29": {
            "buffer": "duck.bin",
            "byteLength": 25272,
            "byteOffset": 76768,
            "target": "ELEMENT_ARRAY_BUFFER"
        }
    },
    "buffers": {
        "duck.bin": {
            "byteLength": 102040,
            "path": "duck.bin"
        }
    },
    "cameras": {
        "camera_0": {
            "aspect_ratio": 1.5,
            "projection": "perspective",
            "yfov": 37.8492,
            "zfar": 10000,
            "znear": 1
        }
    },
... other high-level objects here, e.g., materials and lights
... finally, the scene graph
    "nodes": {
        "LOD3sp": {
            "children": [],
            "matrix": [
                ... matrix data here
            ],
            "meshes": [
                "LOD3spShape-lib"
            ],
```

```
        "name": "LOD3sp"
    },
```

While the design focus of glTF is on compact and efficient representation of OpenGL data, the team has taken a balanced design approach that preserves other essential 3D data authored in DCC tools, such as animation, cameras, and lighting. The current version of glTF (version 1.0) supports the following features:

*Meshes*
>   Polygonal meshes made up of one or more geometry primitives. The mesh definition is in the JSON file, which references one or more binary data files that contain the vertex data.

*Materials and shaders*
>   Materials can be expressed as high-level common constructs (Blinn, Phong, Lambert), or implemented in GLSL vertex and fragment shaders that are included as external files referenced by the glTF JSON file.

*Lights*
>   Common light types (directional, point, spot, and ambient) are represented as high-level constructs in the JSON file.

*Cameras*
>   glTF defines common camera types such as perspective and orthographic.

*Scene graph structure*
>   The scene is represented as a hierarchical graph of nodes (i.e., meshes, cameras, and lights).

*Transform hierarchy*
>   Each node in the scene graph has an associated transformation matrix. Each node can contain children; child nodes inherit their parents' transformation information.

*Animations*
>   glTF defines data structures for key frame, skinned, and morph-based animations.

*External media*
>   Images and video used as texture maps are referenced via URL.

The glTF project, although executed under the auspices of the Khronos Group, is a completely open effort to which anyone can contribute. There is a source code repository on GitHub that includes working viewers and sample content, and the specification itself. Following a philosophy that we will standardize no features without first proving them in code, the team has already developed four independent glTF viewers, including one for use with Three.js (which we will look at shortly). For more information, see the main Khronos glTF page (*http://gltf.gl/*).

### Autodesk FBX

There is one more full-featured scene format worth mentioning, at least in passing. The FBX format from Autodesk is a file format originally developed by Kaydara for use with MotionBuilder. After Autodesk acquired Kaydara, it began to use the FBX format in several of its products. At this point, FBX has become a standard for interchanging data between the various Autodesk products (3ds Max, Maya, and MotionBuilder).

FBX is a rich format that supports many 3D and motion data types. Unlike the other formats covered in this chapter, FBX is proprietary, completely controlled by Autodesk. Autodesk has documented the format, and provided SDKs to read and write FBX in C++ and Python; however, the SDKs require product licenses, which can represent a prohibitive cost for some. There have been successful FBX imports and exports written without the SDKs, such as for Blender, but it is not clear whether these can be used legitimately, given the terms of the FBX license.

Given the proprietary nature of the format, and the ambiguities around licensing, it may be wise to steer clear of FBX. On the other hand, it is a very powerful technology used by the industry's top tools. So it may be worth a look. For more information, go to the main FBX page (*http://www.autodesk.com/products/fbx/overview*).

## Loading Content into WebGL Applications

Remember that WebGL is a drawing library. It has no inherent concept of a polygonal mesh, material, lights, or any of the high-level constructs developers use to conceptually model a 3D graphic. WebGL just knows triangles and math. So it may not come as a surprise that WebGL does not define its own file format, nor does it have built-in support for any of the formats discussed earlier in this chapter. In order to load 3D files into your web applications, you will need to write code, or use a library that knows how to load 3D files.

Happily, Three.js comes with sample code to load many popular formats: OBJ, STL, VRML, and COLLADA, to name a few. Not so happily, the loader code really is *sample* code and as such, mileage varies. Some of the Three.js file loaders are quite robust, but others are incomplete and buggy. Three.js also defines its own file formats designed specifically for the library. There is a clear-text, JSON-based format, and one that uses a binary representation for compact size and fast load speed, similar to glTF. There is even a JSON-based format that can handle complete scenes with multiple objects; however, that format is still experimental and, in my opinion, not ready for production use.

Long story short, we should think of the 3D content pipeline for WebGL as an ongoing adventure. While we will ultimately reach our destination, there are bound to be a few twists, turns, and surprises along the way. Let's embark, and for the remainder of the chapter, cruise through what it takes to load content into WebGL applications using Three.js.

## The Three.js JSON Format

The core Three.js package defines its own file format for loading meshes, comparable to the OBJ format. Unlike OBJ, the format is JSON-based, so once it is parsed it can pretty much be used as is by Three.js.

As of this writing, there aren't that many tools that export Three.js JSON format. The Three.js team wrote an exporter for Blender, so that is one viable path. In fact, the Blender-to-Three.js art path is something to consider if you need to import content from a variety of sources, because Blender is good at importing many other file formats. If Blender isn't your cup of tea, another option is to convert OBJ files. Three.js comes with an OBJ converter utility written in Python. We are going to use that to develop the next example.

Open the book example file *Chapter 8/pipelinethreejsmodel.html*. You should see a model of a classic "ball chair," one of those mid-century ovoid chairs with a large cushion in the middle. Use the left mouse button to rotate the model, and the scroll wheel or trackpad to zoom in and out. See Figure 8-12.

*Figure 8-12. A Wavefront OBJ file, converted to Three.js JSON format and loaded via THREE.JSONLoader; classic ball chair model from Turbosquid (http://bit.ly/1dNri0m) and created by Luxxeon (http://luxxeon.deviantart.com/)*

The shadows and lighting in this scene are handcoded to provide a nice backdrop, but the model is all OBJ. After downloading this wonderful model from Turbosquid, I ran the OBJ converter to create a JSON file loadable by Three.js.

The converter is located in the *utils* subfolder of the Three.js project. To convert the model, run the following command:

```
python <path-to-three.js>/utils/exporters/convert_obj_three.py -i ball_chair.obj
-o ball_chair.js
```

This will produce the file *ball_chair.js*. Let's have a look at the JSON syntax, excerpted in Example 8-7. After some metadata describing version numbers and other details, we get to the content. First, there are some material definitions. These should look quite familiar, as they are the converted material from the OBJ MTL file we saw in Example 8-2. After that comes the mesh definition, the bulk of the file. Unsurprisingly, this is just a set of JSON arrays defining vertex positions, normals, texture coordinates, and faces. Once Three.js has all this information in JSON, it makes light work of building the meshes we see rendered on the screen.

*Example 8-7. Three.js JSON format example*

```
{

    "metadata" :
    {
        "formatVersion" : 3.1,
        "sourceFile"    : "ball_chair(blender).obj",
        "generatedBy"   : "OBJConverter",
        "vertices"      : 12740,
        "faces"         : 12480,
        "normals"       : 13082,
        "colors"        : 0,
        "uvs"           : 15521,
        "materials"     : 4
    },

    "scale" : 1.000000,

    "materials": [    {
    "DbgColor" : 15658734,
    "DbgIndex" : 0,
    "DbgName" : "shell",
    "colorAmbient" : [0.0, 0.0, 0.0],
    "colorDiffuse" : [0.588, 0.588, 0.588],
    "colorSpecular" : [0.72, 0.72, 0.72],
    "illumination" : 2,
    "mapAmbient" : "shell_color.jpg",
    "mapDiffuse" : "shell_color.jpg",
    "opticalDensity" : 1.5,
    "specularCoef" : 77.0
    },

... more material definitions here

    "vertices": [-1.569305,4.927318,-1.529769,-0.889529,
```

```
... more vertex data here

    "morphTargets": [],

    "morphColors": [],

   "normals": [-0.53717,0.35055,-0.76718,-0.46279,0.35837,

... more normal, color, and texture coordinate data here

    "faces": [43,312,599,57,596,0,0,1,2,3,0,1,2,3,43,597

... more face data here

}
```

Now let's look at the code to actually load the model. Three.js doesn't come with a canned model viewer application—we need to build that. But it's quite easy, at least to create a simple one. We are going to split this example into two listings: one to create the scene and load the model, and a second listing to go through the details of setting up a nice viewing environment with lighting, backdrop art, and camera controls. The scene creation and loading code is shown in Example 8-8.

*Example 8-8. Code to load a Three.js JSON model*

```
function loadModel() {
    // Ball chair by Luxxeon
    // http://www.turbosquid.com/FullPreview/Index.cfm/ID/761919
    // http://www.turbosquid.com/Search/Artists/luxxeon
    // http://luxxeon.deviantart.com/

    var url = "../models/ball_chair/ball_chair.json";

    // Egg chair by Luxxeon
    // http://www.turbosquid.com/FullPreview/Index.cfm/ID/738230
    // http://www.turbosquid.com/Search/Artists/luxxeon
    // http://luxxeon.deviantart.com/
    // var url = "../models/egg_chair/eggchair.json";

    var loader = new THREE.JSONLoader();
    loader.load( url, function( geometry, materials ) {
        handleModelLoaded(geometry, materials) } );

}

function handleModelLoaded(geometry, materials) {

    // Create a new mesh with per-face materials
    var material = new THREE.MeshFaceMaterial(materials);
    var mesh = new THREE.Mesh( geometry, material  );
```

```
// Turn on shadows
mesh.castShadow = true;

// Translate the object to the origin if it's not modeled centered
geometry.computeBoundingBox();
center = new THREE.Vector3().addVectors(geometry.boundingBox.max,
    geometry.boundingBox.min).multiplyScalar(0.5);
mesh.position.set(-center.x, 0, -center.z);
scene.add( mesh );

// Find a good camera position based on the size of the geometry
var front = geometry.boundingBox.max.clone().sub(center);
//camera.position.set(0, geometry.boundingBox.max.y / 2,
    geometry.boundingBox.max.z * 8);
camera.position.set(0, front.y, front.z * 5);

if (orbitControls)
    orbitControls.center.copy(center);
}

function createScene(container) {

    // Create a new Three.js scene
    scene = new THREE.Scene();

    // Add a camera so we can view the scene
    camera = new THREE.PerspectiveCamera( 45, container.offsetWidth /
        container.offsetHeight, 1, 4000 );
    camera.position.z = 10;
    scene.add(camera);

    // Lights
    createLights();

    // Ground
    if (addEnvironment)
        createEnvironment();

    // The model
    loadModel();
}
```

First, the function createScene() sets up an empty Three.js scene; then it creates a camera and some lighting and backdrop art using helper functions that we will look at shortly. Remember, these single-model formats do not contain cameras and lights, so we must set those up ourselves.

Next, we call the function loadModel() to do the load. This uses the built-in Three.js class THREE.JSONLoader, which converts the parsed JSON into usable Threej.s geometry. We call the loader's load() method, supplying the URL to the model and a callback function. The callback, handleModelLoaded(), does a bit of work. Upon successful parsing of the JSON, Three.js creates a geometry object and calls our callback. It's up to us to create the materials (a bit strange, in my opinion), which we do by using a special material type, `THREE.MeshFaceMaterial`. This material is a container for a list of several materials: the JSON format supports geometry that can have a different material on each face of the object (hence the name). We create a new `MeshFaceMaterial` using the list of materials supplied in the second argument to the callback.

Now we have a mesh ready for rendering, so we add it to the scene. But we also add a few finishing touches. We want a shadow, so we set the mesh's `castShadow` property to `true`. We want the mesh to be nicely positioned for use with the orbit camera controller, so we center it at the origin. We can figure out where that center is by calling the Three.js method `getBoundingBox()`. We also use the bounding box to figure out a good position for the camera, placing it at the top of the bounding box and a bit out in front.

Example 8-9 shows some of the code for creating a general-purpose model viewing setup. First, our render loop contains a subtlety: rotating the headlight (just a white directional light) to always point from the camera's current position to the scene center. That way, we can see the geometry no matter which part of the model we are looking at.

We want nice shadows to add a finishing touch to the viewing experience, so we set up the necessary Three.js shadow properties when creating the renderer and scene lights. See the functions `createRenderer()` and `createLights()`, respectively. Finally, we need a ground upon which to cast the shadows, so we set that up in the function `createEnvironment()`.

The code shown to view the ball chair model is essentially boilerplate stuff: create a backdrop, create some default lights and a camera, load the model, and keep the highlight properly oriented when the camera moves. This could be used to view any basic model.

However, the way it is structured is not optimal for reuse across applications. We will fix this situation in the next chapter, when we develop a set of general-purpose model viewer classes. But for now, the point is clear: loading single model files originally in OBJ format isn't that hard to do with Three.js.

*Example 8-9. Backdrop and scene lighting for the JSON model viewer*

```
function run() {
    requestAnimationFrame(function() { run(); });

        // Update the camera controller
        orbitControls.update();

        // Reposition the headlight to point at the model
        headlight.position.copy(camera.position);

        // Render the scene
```

```
            renderer.render( scene, camera );

}

var shadows = true;
var addEnvironment = true;
var SHADOW_MAP_WIDTH = 2048, SHADOW_MAP_HEIGHT = 2048;

function createRenderer(container) {
    // Create the Three.js renderer and attach it to our canvas
    renderer = new THREE.WebGLRenderer( { antialias: true } );

    // Turn on shadows
    if (shadows) {
        renderer.shadowMapEnabled = true;
        renderer.shadowMapType = THREE.PCFSoftShadowMap;
    }

    // Set the viewport size
    renderer.setSize(container.offsetWidth, container.offsetHeight);

    container.appendChild(renderer.domElement);
}


function createLights() {

    // Lighting setup
    headlight = new THREE.DirectionalLight;
    headlight.position.set(0, 0, 1);
    scene.add(headlight);

    var ambient = new THREE.AmbientLight(0xffffff);
    scene.add(ambient);

    if (shadows) {
        var spot1 = new THREE.SpotLight(0xaaaaaa);
        spot1.position.set(0, 150, 200);
        scene.add(spot1);

        spot1.shadowCameraNear     = 1;
        spot1.shadowCameraFar      = 1024;
        spot1.castShadow           = true;
        spot1.shadowDarkness       = 0.3;
        spot1.shadowBias = 0.0001;
        spot1.shadowMapWidth = SHADOW_MAP_WIDTH;
        spot1.shadowMapHeight = SHADOW_MAP_HEIGHT;
    }
}

function createEnvironment() {
    // floor
```

```
    var floorMaterial = new THREE.MeshPhongMaterial({
        color: 0xffffff,
        ambient: 0x555555,
        shading: THREE.SmoothShading,
    });
    var floor = new THREE.Mesh( new THREE.PlaneGeometry(1024, 1024), floorMaterial);

    if (shadows) {
        floor.receiveShadow = true;
    }

    floor.rotation.x = -Math.PI / 2;
    scene.add(floor);
}
```

# The Three.js Binary Format

Three.js defines a more compact and optimized format for loading meshes, a binary equivalent to the JSON format. The binary format consists of two files: a small JSON wrapper describing the high-level aspects of the mesh (e.g., materials list), and a binary (*.bin*) file contain the vertex and face data.

We can use the Three.js OBJ converter to create Three.js binary files, simply by using the -t command-line switch:

```
python <path-to-three.js>/utils/exporters/convert_obj_three.py -i
ball_chair.obj -o ball_chair_bin.js -t binary
```

Run the preceding command to create the file *ball_chair_bin.js*. Take a look at the resulting file; the JSON looks more or less the same as the text version, except all mesh data has been moved to a binary file, which is referenced in the JSON in the buffers property:

```
    "buffers": "ball_chair_bin.bin"
```

Note the file size difference. The binary format (JSON plus *.bin* file) is about half as big as the pure JSON version. To see the binary format in action, open the example file *Chapter 8/pipelinethreejsmodelbinary.html*. The model looks the same as before, as in Figure 8-12. To load Three.js binary files, we only need to make a one-line change, replacing the class THREE.JSONLoader with THREE.BinaryLoader. See Example 8-10.

*Example 8-10. Loading models using the Three.js binary format*

```
function loadModel() {
    // Ball chair by Luxxeon
    // http://www.turbosquid.com/FullPreview/Index.cfm/ID/761919
    // http://www.turbosquid.com/Search/Artists/luxxeon
    // http://luxxeon.deviantart.com/

    var url = "../models/ball_chair/ball_chair_bin.json";
```

```
// Egg chair by Luxxeon
// http://www.turbosquid.com/FullPreview/Index.cfm/ID/738230
// http://www.turbosquid.com/Search/Artists/luxxeon
// http://luxxeon.deviantart.com/
// var url = "../models/egg_chair/eggchair.json";

var loader = new THREE.BinaryLoader();
loader.load( url, function( geometry, materials ) {
    handleModelLoaded(geometry, materials) } );

}
```

## Loading a COLLADA Scene with Three.js

Three.js has placed a lot of emphasis on loading quality models using single-model formats like OBJ and its own JSON. This is great as far as it goes, but it falls short for many uses. If we want to load scenes that contain multiple objects, and preserve the transform hierarchy and other goodies such as cameras, lights, and animations, then we need to move to a format that supports those features. Otherwise, we will be forced to import models one by one and arrange, light, and animate our scenes by hand. (Unfortunately, this scenario still happens far too often in WebGL development today. But it is changing, slowly, for the better.)

As discussed earlier, COLLADA is a great format for representing full-scene data. It supports the features we need, and several 3D packages already export it. With COLLADA, it is possible to have an artist model, texture, light, and animate a complex scene, and then export it for use with WebGL—*without* needing a programmer to hand-crank values. And that is a major goal: leave art creation to the artists. Granted, COLLADA does have the big shortcoming of a slow, bulky XML representation. Still, for our purposes here it is a good format for exploring issues related to loading and viewing full scenes.

Open the example file located in *Chapter 8/pipelinethreejsdaescene.html*. You should see some nice background game art, a set of ruins and abandoned cars. See Figure 8-13.

This example loads a COLLADA scene with several objects in a hierarchy. We load the COLLADA using a one-line load call. The Three.js COLLADA loader knows how to create the entire hierarchy of objects, including any cameras, animations, lights, and so on, without requiring us to get involved. The load callback does a little extra work, looking for cameras and lights, so that it can set up defaults if it doesn't find them in the scene. But that's it. Conspicuously absent from this picture are any hardcoded positions, orientations, and scales to lay out the individual objects. Contrast this with the typical sample scene included in the Three.js project—a goulash of hand-typed numbers. It's refreshing.

Let's walk through the code to load a COLLADA scene, listed in Example 8-11. This example shows only the code specific to loading the COLLADA scene, and the associated handler callback.

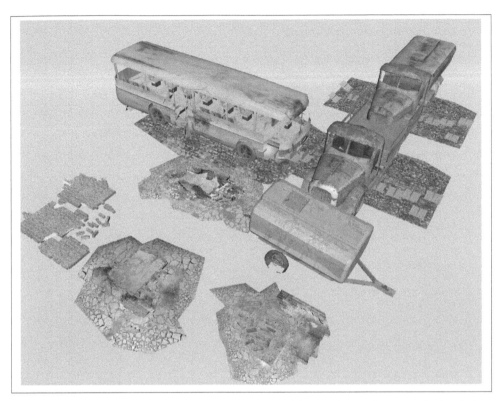

*Figure 8-13. Game scene background art, with full hierarchy and materials, loaded in COLLADA format via THREE.ColladaLoader; art from Turbosquid (http://bit.ly/ 1eQEq6V) and created by ERHLN (http://www.turbosquid.com/Search/Artists/ ERLHN)*

*Example 8-11. Loading a COLLADA scene using Three.js*

```
function loadScene() {
    // Ruins by ERLHN
    // http://www.turbosquid.com/FullPreview/Index.cfm/ID/668298
    // http://www.turbosquid.com/Search/Artists/ERLHN
    var url = "../models/ruins/Ruins_dae.dae";

    var loader = new THREE.ColladaLoader();

    loader.load( url, function( data ) {
        handleSceneLoaded(data) } );
```

```
}

function handleSceneLoaded(data) {
    // Add the objects to the scene
    scene.add(data.scene);

    // Look for a camera and lighting
    var result = {};
    data.scene.traverse(function (n) { traverseScene(n, result); });

    if (result.cameras && result.cameras.length)
        camera = result.cameras[0];
    else {
        // Find a good camera position based on the size of the scene
        createDefaultCamera();
        var boundingBox = computeBoundingBox(data.scene);
        var front = boundingBox.max;
        camera.position.set(front.x, front.y, front.z);
    }

    if (result.lights && result.lights.length) {
    }
    else
        createDefaultLights();

    // Create the controller
    initControls();
}

function traverseScene(n, result)
{
    // Look for cameras
    if (n instanceof THREE.Camera) {
        if (!result.cameras)
            result.cameras = [];

        result.cameras.push(n);
    }

    // Look for lights
    if (n instanceof THREE.Light) {
        if (!result.lights)
            result.lights = [];

        result.lights.push(n);
    }

}
```

The loadScene() function loads the ruins using the THREE.ColladaLoader class. The load callback function, handleSceneLoaded(), is passed a single argument, data, that contains a JSON object with several properties that were stored when the COLLADA file was parsed. We are interested in `data.scene`, which is a `THREE.Object` that contains the entire loaded scene hierarchy. We add that to our top-level scene, so that Three.js will render it.

We are now basically ready to view the scene, but we are going to add a few bits of polish to the user experience. First, we traverse the contents of the loaded scene looking for cameras and lights. If there are any cameras supplied, we will use the first one we find as our initial viewing camera; if not, we will create a default camera. If there are lights supplied with the scene, we will use those; if not, we will create a default lighting setup. We handle scene traversal using the object's `traverse()` method, which recursively visits that object and any descendants, calling the supplied callback function. Our callback function `traverseScene()` looks for camera and lights by testing their JavaScript object types against `THREE.Camera` and `THREE.Light`, using the `instanceof` operator, and pushes anything it finds onto the arrays `result.cameras` and `result.lights`.

In the case where the scene does not contain any cameras, we create our own default camera. We also want to position it appropriately, based on the size of the scene. To calculate the size of the scene we'll use a helper function, `computeBoundingBox()`. This function recursively walks the scene to calculate a containing bounding box. Whenever it finds a geometry object, it uses the Three.js built-in bounding-box method to find the geometry's bounding box, which it then merges into the bounding box for the whole scene. This function is a little lengthy, so the code is not shown here.

## Loading a glTF Scene with Three.js

glTF represents a new approach to 3D file formats. It is designed specifically for use in web and mobile OpenGL-based applications, with many graphics features represented "to the metal" as native buffers and other rendering-ready structures. At the same time, glTF contains many commonly used 3D constructs that have no direct representation in OpenGL ES, such as materials, cameras, and lights. The goal is to create a compact format that will load easily in web and mobile applications but still represent 3D data for practical production use.

There are already several development projects under way to implement glTF support in graphics libraries and applications. This includes a glTF loader that I am writing for use with Three.js. Open the example file *Chapter 8/pipelinethreejsgltfscene.html* in your browser to see it in action. You should see something that resembles the screenshot in Figure 8-14. Several spaceships cruise around a futuristic cityscape. The rendering in this scene is really nice, with environment maps and Blinn shading. There are several animations, including moving cameras. Use the drop-downs to change cameras and load different scenes, and toggle the animation checkbox to start and stop the animations. The scene depicted here was originally created in 3ds Max. Fabrice Robinet downloaded the 3ds Max file from 3DRT.com, exported it to COLLADA, and then ran a converter tool to convert it to glTF.

*Figure 8-14. Loading glTF scenes—including animation, scene graph hierarchy, materials, lights, and cameras—using the experimental THREE.glTFLoader class, still under development; source code for the loader is on the glTF GitHub project page (https:// github.com/KhronosGroup/glTF), and the virtual city scene is courtesy of 3DRT (http:// 3drt.com/store/free-downloads/33-sci-fi-skyscrapers-collection.html)*

I patterned the design of the Three.js glTF loader on the other file format loaders that come with the Three.js examples. The class `THREE.glTFLoader` inherits from the base loader class, `THREE.Loader`. Its `load()` method parses the glTF JSON file; loads external resources such as binary buffers, textures, and shaders; and returns the result via a callback function. The callback function has access to the Three.js object hierarchy created by the loader so that it can easily load it into a scene and start rendering.

The early returns on glTF loading are very promising, at least in comparison to the equivalent COLLADA. Files are generally about half the size of the COLLADA text format, and load times for some models are up to 80% faster. This is in part due to our using the new Three.js `BufferGeometry` type, which allows us to create geometry directly from already-loaded typed array data such as `Int32Array` and `FloatArray`, instead of using regular JavaScript `Number` arrays (which, under the covers, have to be converted back to typed arrays anyway, before WebGL can render them).

# Chapter Summary

This chapter explored the universe of 3D content creation for WebGL. After a brief look at the authoring process, we surveyed 3D content creation tools, ranging from amateur to professional, packaged as downloadable software applications or running in the browser.

We then took an extensive tour of 3D file formats used in today's applications, especially those suitable for online use with WebGL. This includes well-worn standards as well as a new format, glTF, designed explicitly for use in today's web and mobile applications. Finally, we looked at detailed examples of how to use the Three.js library to load various formats into our WebGL applications, including single-model formats and full scenes.

While there is no one preferred way to bring 3D content into a web application, and the content pipeline for WebGL is young and still evolving, at least there are several viable approaches to getting the job done.

# CHAPTER 9

# 3D Engines and Frameworks

Three.js is a fantastic library. It turns a Herculean task—rendering complex 3D content in WebGL—into one manageable by mere mortals. Without a library like Three.js, a WebGL developer would be facing months of programming to get all those pixels on the screen. But for all its graphics power, Three.js is limited. It takes care of the drawing, and that's about it. For everything else, you are on your own.

Let's say you want to build a shopping application that allows the user to configure a custom car before buying. A web page displays a 3D model of a car; the user can click on various parts of the car to change colors and styles; and at the touch of a button, the view animates smoothly from the exterior to the inside of the car. Using only Three.js, you would potentially have to write hundreds of lines of code to build this application. The raw toolbox is there, but it is not factored into a set of high-level reusable components. Three.js was designed to be a scene graph and rendering library, but there is more to 3D application development than drawing pictures.

The car configurator scenario involves common 3D programming chores: loading a model, accessing individual parts of the model by name or id, triggering a behavior when a part is clicked, and changing camera views. These design patterns are prevalent in games, virtual worlds, architectural walkthroughs, educational titles, and training simulations—basically most types of 3D applications. If you are developing professional-grade 3D applications, and don't want to spend your time inventing new ways to solve old problems, then you should consider using a high-level engine or framework.

This chapter explores 3D application framework concepts and looks at WebGL-based solutions. Many of these systems are built on top of Three.js, so if you have already made a large investment in learning graphics in Three.js, you won't have to master something entirely new. Later in the chapter I introduce Vizi, a framework of my own design, which we will use to create examples in the chapters that follow. The concepts embodied in these frameworks are general; most of them apply to whichever one you choose, or they may be helpful should you decide to develop one of your own.

# 3D Framework Concepts

Frameworks provide developers with prebuilt functionality and implement common design patterns in a reliable, repeatable way. They can help us save time and write better applications—at least in theory. A good framework can keep us from "reinventing the wheel" by leveraging the experience of seasoned developers, allowing us to focus on the application tasks at hand.

## What Is a Framework?

There is no hard and fast definition of a framework. In fact, it is often difficult to tell the difference between a framework and a library. Both are designed to save us time by providing reusable code, and both mask the details of the underlying operating system or platform, providing a high-level interface to lower-level services. There are, however, a few distinctions that suggest we are dealing with a framework versus a library:[1]

*Level of abstraction*
> Frameworks operate at a higher level of abstraction than libraries. For example, a 3D library might support skinned meshes for character animation, while a 3D framework would package the skinned mesh along with a set of animated gestures and call it an *avatar*. The framework would automatically move the avatar around the scene based on user input, and inform us after the fact via callbacks.

*Default behaviors*
> Frameworks supply default behaviors. For example, when a scene is created, a default camera is placed inside it at a known location and viewing direction. Good frameworks go to great lengths to also provide flexibility by letting developers override the defaults.

*Extensibility*
> Frameworks emphasize extensibility, allowing third-party add-on development and customization. The best frameworks strike an artful balance between the power of their prebuilt components, and ways to extend or completely replace parts of the system.

*Inverted control flow*
> Perhaps the most distinctive feature of a framework is that it, not the developer, owns the control flow. The developer simply supplies callback functions or over-

---

1. This is based on an extensive discussion of software frameworks in the Wikipedia entry (*http://en.wikipe dia.org/wiki/Software_framework*).

ridden methods to implement application-specific functionality. Think of the typical page setup for a WebGL application: the scene is created, the renderer is initialized, and the run loop is invoked. With a WebGL framework, the developer would supply only the scene creation code, while the framework would do the rest of the setup.

There is one more, nontechnical distinction between a framework and a library: frameworks tend to be more polarizing. They are often viewed as a double-edged sword, a Faustian bargain that grants us fast time to market, only to ultimately steal our souls before the project is over. A framework can provide 90% of the features we need quickly —giving us a false sense of confidence early in the development cycle—and then be frustratingly hard when it comes to implementing the last 10%. Frameworks can be difficult to debug and optimize, because we are using Other Peoples' Code. Anyone who has used a web development framework like Zend or Rails should be intimately familiar with such laments. For these reasons, many developers avoid using frameworks altogether. By contrast, a nonintrusive *library* like jQuery gets developer props for providing most of the power without the associated hassles.

 Developers are creatures of passion, just like everyone else, and nothing can incite developer passion like a good old-fashioned framework dust-up. If you see one in progress, it's probably best to walk the other way. I myself have strong opinions about using frameworks for my own projects, which can best be summed up in the following aphorism:

> *I love frameworks...as long as they're mine.*

Regardless of your feelings about frameworks, if you plan to build a 3D application of any scale you will face the issues discussed in this chapter. You will also be faced with a choice: develop your own framework, adopt an existing one, or be prepared to write a lot of extra code.

## WebGL Framework Requirements

We can think of the web browser as a 2D application framework. The DOM and CSS provide a predefined set of visual objects, which the browser renders. Application development consists of supplying callbacks for when something "interesting" happens based on user behavior: a button is clicked, a page is loaded, and so on. When the application wants to change the look or contents of a page, it sets one or more properties and the browser automatically updates the display.

Unfortunately for us, with the exception of CSS 3D transforms, the browser's predefined objects do not extend into the third dimension. With the introduction of HTML5, the emphasis of browser architecture has shifted from providing prebuilt visual objects (text, scrollbars, buttons, etc.) to allowing fine control over rendering and other system-level features. WebGL and Canvas let us *draw* whatever we want...but we have to make up the rest as we go. Once we enter the world of the Canvas element, it falls on us to build our own scene graph, event model, interactions, behaviors, animations, and transitions—or, preferably, use an existing framework that takes care of these tasks for us.

WebGL applications present unique issues in framework design. In addition to a host of classic 3D-specific problems, we have additional requirements that come with working on a browser-based platform. A WebGL framework should include many of the following capabilities:

*Environment setup*
> The framework checks for WebGL support, and creates the drawing context and any objects to support rendering. It also adds DOM event handlers for window resize, mouse and keyboard input, WebGL context loss, and other page events, and dispatches to the application as needed.

*Capability detection and fallbacks*
> The framework tests various browser capabilities and potentially polyfills or provides fallbacks, such as 2D Canvas drawing if WebGL is not available.

*Default scene creation*
> The framework creates an empty scene, perhaps with a default camera and default lighting.

*Simulation/run loop*
> The framework supplies the run loop, while the application provides callbacks for events and overrides methods to implement application-specific functionality. The framework may also define a strict notion of a clock or time model that the application must follow for consistent behavior.

*Graphics and rendering*
> The framework provides objects to render graphics. In the case of a Three.js-based framework, this may simply mean providing access to Three.js objects managed by the framework.

*Object and event models*
> The framework specifies a consistent model for the properties of objects, how objects relate to each other in a hierarchy or graph, and how objects interoperate via events, callbacks, and/or accessor methods.

*Interaction*
> The framework automatically maps mouse and other input to specific objects in the scene, and informs the application when an object has been clicked, dragged, etc.

*Navigation/viewing models*

The framework may supply one or more navigation models—that is, high-level modes of moving the camera within a scene (e.g., first-person shooter), handling collision and terrain following, or rotating the camera to look at a specific object. There may also be built-in logic for switching between cameras and transitioning from scene to scene. First-person navigation models may also often define the concept of an avatar for representing the user within multiuser environments.

*Behaviors and animation*

The framework comes with predefined behaviors, from simple rotations and translations applied to an object over time, to complex animation sequences triggered by an interaction.

*Physics*

Some frameworks offer rich physics models, animating bodies in a direction with velocity, applying gravity, detecting interobject collisions, and so on.

*Asset loading*

The framework loads models, textures, video, and sounds automatically for the programmer and communicates back to the application when assets are loaded. High-powered frameworks may even include client-server loading schemes that stream 3D data and animations, and/or provide progressive level of detail for high-resolution meshes.

*Scene utilities*

Frameworks often have extensive support for manipulating the scene graph. A query API will find all objects of a certain type, or with an id that matches a regular expression pattern or selector, and then allow various operations to be applied: changing material properties, applying 3D transformations, adding/removing children, and showing/hiding objects.

*Memory management*

Even though JavaScript-based applications are automatically garbage-collected, rich applications must take great care in how and when memory is allocated. Otherwise, garbage collection sweeps can happen at inopportune times, compromising the frame rate and, hence, the user experience. Some frameworks provide smart memory management services to help avoid these problems. (More on this subject in Chapter 12.)

*Performance support/graceful degradation*

The framework may auto-adjust resolution or rendering quality based on frame rate or resource consumption, with the goal of providing a consistent user experience.

*Extension mechanism*

Good frameworks don't trap programmers into using only the prebuilt components. They allow for extensibility. For a WebGL framework, that means providing ways to hook behaviors, override interactions, and, most importantly, provide custom rendering to change the visual appearance.

This is a long list. There is a lot that goes into creating a quality 3D application, and frameworks can go a long way in helping. There are already several good frameworks for use with WebGL. Let's take a look at a few in the next section.

# A Survey of WebGL Frameworks

WebGL frameworks fall into two general categories: game engines and presentation frameworks. Game engines are generally higher-powered but harder to use and master, while presentation frameworks are better suited to creating simpler applications, such as a model embedded in a page with basic interaction. This section surveys the many WebGL frameworks under development as of this writing.

## Game Engines

If your goal is to build a top-notch WebGL game, you might consider using any of a number of game engines that have appeared in the last few years. The difference between a game engine and a framework is subtle. Typically, game engines provide even more features than your average framework. On the flip side, they are usually designed for a more expert developer. Game development involves a combination of difficult technical disciplines, and the engines to support it tend to reflect that.

There are several WebGL game engines to choose from. Capabilities vary widely, as do the required level of expertise. Some engines are open source; others are not. Some are free to use, while others charge for a license, hosting fee, or other tithe such as encouraging you to publish games through their distribution network. None of the game engines listed next uses Three.js for rendering—opting instead to control the entire pipeline. These are some of the tradeoffs you should consider when evaluating game engines for your projects.

*playcanvas (http://www.playcanvas.com/)*

London-based playcanvas has developed a rich engine and cloud-based authoring tool. The authoring tool features real-time collaborative scene editing to support team development, GitHub and Bitbucket integration, and one-button publishing to social media networks. Figure 9-1 shows a playcanvas game in action.

*Figure 9-1. First-person shooter game created with playcanvas (http://www.play canvas.com/)*

*Turbulenz (http://biz.turbulenz.com/developers/)*

An extremely powerful, open source, royalty-free game engine, packaged as a downloadable SDK. The company charges royalties if you want to publish through its network (*http://biz.turbulenz.com/developers/*). Turbulenz is the most intense of the APIs, with a huge class set and steep learning curve. It is definitely for experienced game developers.

*Goo Engine (http://www.gootechnologies.com/)*

As of this writing, this engine is in alpha test. The website boasts a list of traditional game engine features, plus cross-platform portability via WebGL. The site is lean on technical and licensing information, but the featured demos are beautiful. See Figure 9-2.

*Babylon.js (http://www.babylonjs.com/)*

Microsoft recently jumped on the WebGL bandwagon, giving it a big push along the way. *Babylon.js* is an easy-to-use engine that lies somewhere on the spectrum between Three.js and a hardcore game engine in terms of feature set and ease of use. The demo site shows a range of applications, from space shooters to architectural walkthroughs.

*Figure 9-2. Image from Pearl Boy, an underwater adventure game developed with the Goo Engine (http://www.gootechnologies.com/)*

*KickJS (http://www.kickjs.org/)*

An open source game engine and rendering library created by Morten Nobel-Jørgensen. This project grew out of Nobel-Jørgensen's academic work. It appears to have less development and support behind it, so you may want to approach it with caution. I include it here because, of all of the engines mentioned, KickJS most closely follows established best practices in modern game engine design. (More on this topic when we discuss Vizi shortly.) If nothing else, it could be a great reference if you plan to design your own framework.

As you can see, there are many potential WebGL game engine choices. You may even consider using a game engine to build applications other than games. Just remember that game engines have a big learning curve, so make sure the solution fits the problem. For simpler visual applications, you may be able to use a more modest 3D framework like the ones described in the next section.

## Presentation Frameworks

Games represent a mere fraction of the potential 3D applications we can build with WebGL. For nongame applications such as page graphics, e-commerce product displays, or scientific visualization, game engines are overkill. A presentation application usually just needs to load a simple scene into a page, play a few animations, and react to user input by changing a few properties. As noted, even these basic activities require a lot of additional coding in Three.js, so we turn to frameworks for help. Here are a few general-purpose 3D presentation frameworks to consider.

## tQuery

tQuery (*http://jeromeetienne.github.io/tquery/*) is the creation of Jerome Etienne. Jerome operates the popular blog site Learning Three.js (*http://learningthreejs.com/*), which contains a trove of Three.js development tips and tricks.

Modeled after the jQuery library, the idea behind tQuery is to provide "Three.js Power + jQuery API Usability"—that is, a very simple API to the Three.js scene graph. It uses a chained-function programming style and supports high-level interactive behaviors via callbacks. Using tQuery can save many lines of Three.js handcoding. It is probably not accurate to call tQuery a framework, since it is more of a nonintrusive library in the spirit of jQuery. If you are a Three.js developer looking to save a few keystrokes, you should take a serious look at it.

Example 9-1 shows a brief listing that is the entire code to put a torus object on a page using tQuery. Contrast this with our Three.js examples from previous chapters, and you can begin to see how frameworks help make simple 3D development a snap.

*Example 9-1. Creating a simple scene with tQuery*

```
<!doctype html><title>Minimal tQuery Page</title>
<script src="tquery-bundle.js"></script>
<body><script>
    var world = tQuery.createWorld().boilerplate().start();
    var object = tQuery.createTorus().addTo(world);
</script></body>
```

Etienne's design philosophy can be summarized roughly as "make 3D development look as much like 2D development as possible." Web developers already know jQuery; give them a jQuery-like API to develop their 3D, and they will be immediately productive. It's hard to argue with that logic.

## Voodoo.js

Seattle-based Brent Gunning is on a mission to create 3D for everyone. Excited by the power of WebGL, but frustrated by how hard it is to program, he created Voodoo.js (*http://www.voodoojs.com/*). The goals of Voodoo.js are to make it easy to create 3D content, and easy to integrate it into web pages. Gunning sums this up in the blog manifesto that accompanied the initial launch:

> Today on the web, 3D is a toy. A gimmick. It takes exceptional work to create anything in 3D and almost nothing is easily reusable. Worse yet, we imprison our 3D scenes in walled-off canvases that are strictly segregated from 2D content, all because they have an extra D. It's a design nightmare, and an injustice. I want to do something about it. Therefore, I am pleased to announce the first public release of Voodoo, 0.8.0 beta.

Gunning's vision includes not only easy drag-and-drop development, but also an ecosystem of reusable objects, components, visual styles, and themes. The Voodoo.js framework consists of a small set of classes with prebuilt functionality, including model loading and viewing, mouse-based interaction, and several configurable options. The framework is built on top of Three.js, so theoretically, it should be easy to extend and customize it with new object types. Example 9-2 shows an excerpt from the Voodoo.js home page that creates a 3D object and inserts it into the page element example2, using just one function call. It doesn't get much easier than this. The result is depicted in the screenshot in Figure 9-3.

*Example 9-2. Inserting a 3D object into a page with Voodoo.js*

```
new VoodooJsonModel({
  elementId: 'example2',
  jsonFile: '3d/tree.json',
  offsetWidthMultiplier: 2.0 / 3.0,
  scale: 50,
  rotationX: Math.PI / 2.0,
  rotationY: Math.PI / 2.0
});
```

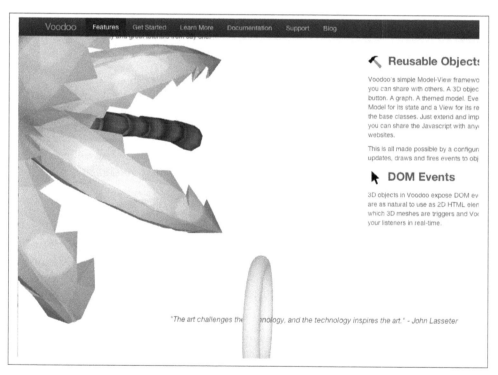

*Figure 9-3. The Voodoo.js home page (http://www.voodoojs.com/), featuring several embedded 3D objects*

## PhiloGL

PhiloGL (*http://www.senchalabs.org/philogl/*) is an experimental package that was created by data visualization scientist Nicolas Garcia Belmonte while working at Sencha Inc.'s labs. The goal of PhiloGL is "to make WebGL programming as fun and easy as developing with any of the mainstream frameworks." Garcia describes his design philosophy in this introductory blog posting (*http://bit.ly/JYTRk7*). Even though this framework is experimental, it merits a look. Sencha, Inc., develops world-class user interface frameworks and knows a thing or two about creating effective user interfaces with HTML5. Example 9-3 shows the code for creating a simple scene using PhiloGL. By defining a few JavaScript objects, we can create a scene with a textured sphere. The PhiloGL website contains several working examples, including a port of the entire set of tutorials from Learning WebGL (*http://www.learningwebgl.com/*).

*Example 9-3. Creating a simple 3D scene with PhiloGL*

```
//Create application
PhiloGL('canvasId', {
    camera: {
        position: {
            x: 0, y: 0, z: -7
        }
    },
    scene: {
        lights: {
            enable: true,
            ambient: { r: 0.5, g: 0.5, b: 0.5 },
            directional: {
                color: { r: 0.7, g: 0.7, b: 0.9 },
                direction: { x: 1, y: 1, z: 1 }
            }
        }
    },
    textures: {
        src: ['moon.gif']
    },
    events: {
        onClick: function(e) {
            /* write event handler here */
        }
    },
    onError: function() {
        alert("There was an error creating the app.");
    },
    onLoad: function(app) {
        //Do things with the application...
        //Add object to the scene
        scene.add(moon)
        //Animate
        setInterval(draw, 1000/60);
        //Draw the scene
```

```
        function draw() {
            //render moon
            scene.render();
        }
    }
});
```

# Vizi: A Component-Based Framework for Visual Web Applications

It's time to take a closer look at the specifics of framework-based 3D development. We want to cover a wide range of possible use cases, so we are going to work with a framework that is designed to be fairly general. While there is no "one size fits all" 3D system, there are many common patterns among applications. It is for this reason that I created Vizi, a WebGL framework of my own design that I used to develop the examples in the following chapters. This section provides an introduction to Vizi by way of exploring framework-based concepts in more detail.

## Background and Design Philosophy

Like the developers of tQuery, Voodoo.js, and PhiloGL, I was frustrated with the state of WebGL development. I count myself among Mr.doob's biggest fans, but in my opinion, Three.js isn't enough by itself to build production-quality applications. Most of the problems we are discussing here have been solved already, years ago, in earlier 3D frameworks and game engines. The underlying platforms have of course evolved in the intervening time, but the problems have, by and large, stayed the same: 1) load scene content, 2) set up the camera, 3) draw some objects, 4) move the objects around based on timers and user input, 5) rinse and repeat.

One thing that *has* changed in recent years is the design of game engines. Over the last two decades, the game industry has become so vital that it has, arguably, spurred some the biggest innovations in computing history. This includes the design of software engines. Most notably, there has been a move away from class- and inheritance-based architectures to component- and aggregation-based ones. (This may seem like a razor-thin technical distinction, but it has huge implications, as we will see presently.) Informed by many previous 3D development projects and, I hoped, armed with a fresh perspective based on current game engine best practices, I decided to embark on a new venture, and Vizi was born.

The goal of Vizi is to make it easy to quickly build *interesting* 3D applications. In terms of feature set, Vizi falls somewhere between a game engine like playcanvas and a presentation framework like Voodoo.js. The product configurator scenario that opened this chapter is a good target for Vizi: a scene with multiple interactive objects, dynamic updates based on user input, models loaded on demand, and sophisticated viewing and camera-based navigation. I believe that this mix of features represents a "sweet spot" for WebGL development, so that is where I have tried to put the design emphasis.

Figure 9-4 shows a prototype Vizi application developed as a concept e-commerce site: a virtual car showroom. High-resolution image panes lazily rotate about the center of the scene, in carousel fashion. The panes cast shadows onto the data cage backdrop, subtly suggested by a wireframe grid. A few seconds after the page loads, a full 3D model of a featured car drives up to the center of the showroom. The highly detailed car shows reflections of the gridded environment behind it. Clicking on a pane zooms it front and center and plays a video ad on the pane. 2D user interface elements frame the borders of the piece, providing access to additional information and other areas of the site. This is only a concept piece, but it illustrates a core idea behind Vizi: bringing together 2D and 3D content to enable new types of interaction for e-commerce and other web applications.

*Figure 9-4. Car showroom concept built with Vizi; car model by be fast (http://www.turbosquid.com/Search/Artists/be-fast), and visual and environment design by TC Chang (http://www.tcchang.com/)*

## The Vizi Architecture

The Vizi architecture is inspired by principles of modern game engine design. Even though 3D games have more intensive requirements than other visual applications, there is a high degree of overlap. Some nongame applications require many of the features of a game engine. For example, an educational simulation might require collision, physics, and avatars, even though nothing is happening at "twitch" speed and nobody is getting blown up.

One of the main features of Vizi architecture is a *component-based object model*. This reflects a modern trend away from classical inheritance-based design and toward aggregation of components. There is a base object type, `Vizi.Object`, which is little more than a container for components. Components implement most of the functionality—for example, a `Visual` component with geometry and materials, a `Picker` component that dispatches mouse events on a per-object basis, and a `Camera` component for viewing. Component-based systems provide a consistent model for accessing capabilities, and allow for a very flexible implementation with a high potential for reuse. They are also a key to supporting extensibility.

Other highlights of the Vizi architecture are:

*Application object*
> A singleton application object takes care of setting up WebGL context creation, DOM event handlers, and Three.js initialization. The application object implements the run loop; objects merely add themselves to the application, and they will be given a chance to update themselves each animation frame.

*Simulation and event model*
> There is one standardized time base used by all objects. Events fire at well-defined times and follow prescribed rules. Objects publish events, to which other objects subscribe. Objects can subscribe to events using listeners, or be directly "connected" to other objects' events in a behavioral chain. This makes for very concise creation of behaviors and interactions.

*Service architecture*
> All subsystems are built as black-box services. During initialization and execution, the application delegates to services such as Time, Events, Graphics, and Input with very little regard for what any of the services actually do. This makes it easy to add new services, such as multiuser networking, that are not in the core build.

*Graphics*
> All graphics are drawn using Three.js. Rather than try to hide Three.js under the covers, Vizi embraces it, wrapping Three.js objects with component-based structure so that other Vizi objects can easily communicate with them.

*Interactions*
> Vizi supports mouse events on a per-object basis, under the covers, using the Three.js `Projector` class to implement hit detection. This results in a much cleaner interface for mouse and touch input. Vizi also provides prebuilt interaction objects that implement various types of dragging (e.g., on a plane or sphere).

*Behaviors*
> Vizi comes with a variety of prebuilt behaviors that automatically rotate, move, bounce, highlight, and otherwise modify objects' states.

*High-level view model*

Vizi allows multiple cameras to be defined, with easy switching between them. Vizi also supplies navigation modes for different uses, such as object viewing, first-person game play, architectural walkthroughs, and more.

*Easy customization*

Custom components can implement new behaviors, interactions, and camera controller scripts—pretty much anything. Components are just JavaScript objects that inherit from `Vizi.Component`; it is simple to create a new component type and add custom functionality by overriding its `realize()` and `update()` methods. Components can be added, nonintrusively, to existing objects to impart new functionality not imagined by the original developer.

*Prefab construction*

Vizi allows the developer to create reusable types consisting of a collection of objects. Because Vizi is based on a component design, types are not created with Java-Script classes, but rather as collections of objects known as *prefabs*. Prefabs typically consist of a hierarchy of game objects and their components, one or more event subscribers or connections, and a controller script to negotiate the interactions among all the constituents.

 The component-based nature of the Vizi architecture is heavily influenced by the work presented in Jason Gregory's seminal textbook, *Game Engine Architecture (http://www.gameenginebook.com/)*. This is a must-read for serious engine and framework designers. The text covers broad ground, but most relevant in this context is Gregory's exploration of object model architectures. He strongly advocates for component-based design over classical class-based inheritance. Component-based design is generally more flexible and extensible, and avoids many known problems that inheritance-based systems encounter, especially as they grow in complexity.

Vizi is also inspired in part by the design of Unity (*http://unity3d.com/*), the most popular commercial game engine in use by indie developers and small studios today. Unity is a highly successful embodiment of Gregory's principles of component-based engine design. As of this writing, Unity does not support WebGL. It was developed long before the ascent of HTML5 and so uses its own scripting language and rendering system. If Unity supported HTML5 and WebGL, I might not have felt the need to create Vizi.

# Getting Started with Vizi

To get started with Vizi, grab the latest version of the repository from GitHub (*https://github.com/tparisi/Vizi*). Under *engine/build/*, you will see several files. Place a copy of *vizi.js* (the unminified, debug version) or *vizi.min.js* (the minified release version) and put it in your project tree.

Now, simply include the Vizi script in your page, and you are ready to start using it:

```
<script src="../<path_to_vizi>/vizi.js"></script>
```

 Vizi comes with a variety of builds; these two files are packaged with all of the libraries they depend on, including Three.js, Tween.js, RequestAnimationFrame.js, and a few supporting Three.js-based objects. If you don't want the build files that include the extra dependences, you can use the "nodeps" versions instead, and include the dependent files yourself elsewhere on the page. Of course, be prepared for version inconsistencies if you are not careful. Please consult the *README* and release notes for additional details, and refer to the Appendix for more information on preparing custom builds of Vizi.

## A Simple Vizi Application

Let's look at a concrete example that illustrates the power of the Vizi framework. Open the example file *Chapter 9/vizicube.html* in your browser. You should see something familiar; the textured cube from Chapters 2 and 3, rewritten once again in Vizi. Compare Example 9-4, which shows the code to create and run the 3D scene using Vizi, to the Three.js-based listing from Example 3-1 in Chapter 3.

*Example 9-4. A simple Vizi application: rotating cube*

```
<script type="text/javascript">

    $(document).ready(function() {

        // Create the Vizi application object
        var container = document.getElementById("container");
        var app = new Vizi.Application({ container : container });

        // Create a Phong-shaded, texture-mapped cube
        var cube = new Vizi.Object;
        var visual = new Vizi.Visual(
                { geometry: new THREE.CubeGeometry(2, 2, 2),
                    material: new THREE.MeshPhongMaterial(
                        {map:THREE.ImageUtils.loadTexture(
                            "../images/webgl-logo-256.jpg")})
                });
        cube.addComponent(visual);

        // Add a rotate behavior to give the cube some life
        var rotator = new Vizi.RotateBehavior({autoStart:true});
        cube.addComponent(rotator);
```

```
        // Rotate the cube toward the viewer to show off the 3D
        cube.transform.rotation.x = Math.PI / 5;

        // Add a light to show shading
        var light = new Vizi.Object;
        light.addComponent(new Vizi.DirectionalLight);

        // Add the cube and light to the scene
        app.addObject(cube);
        app.addObject(light);

        // Run it
        app.run();
    }
);

</script>
```

With Vizi it takes about 40 lines of code to create a rotating, textured cube, instead of the 80 lines of code required when we use just Three.js. But code size is not all there is to the story, as we'll see shortly. Let's walk through the example. First, we create a new application object, of type `Vizi.Application`, passing it the container element. This single act of creation triggers a lot of work under the hood: the creation of a Three.js renderer object and an empty Three.js scene with a default camera, and the addition of event handlers for page resize, mouse, and other DOM events. These are things you would have to add manually via DOM API calls or Three.js functions, but Vizi handles them automatically. Look at the files *core/application.js* and *graphics/graphics ThreeJS.js* under the Vizi source tree to see what is involved in getting all of the details right. There is a lot going on.

Next, we add the objects to the scene. This is where the Vizi component object model comes into play. Any object in a Vizi scene is instantiated as a `Vizi.Object`, and then we add various components to it. For the cube, we create a `Vizi.Visual` object with Three.js cube geometry and a textured Phong material. Note that Vizi does not define its own graphical objects but rather uses Three.js for all graphics. This is a conscious design choice. Rather than try to hide Three.js graphics, we expose its full power so that it's easy to create any type of visual we need.

Once the visual component is created and added to the object, we add a behavior. This is where the Vizi magic really starts to happen. Vizi comes with a predefined set of behaviors that we can apply to an object, simply by adding them as components. In this example, we add a `Vizi.RotateBehavior`, setting its `autoStart` flag to `true` so the object begins rotating as soon as the application runs.

We want to tilt the cube toward the viewer so that we can see it in its full 3D glory. With Vizi, we do that by modifying the rotation property of the object's transform component:

```
// Rotate the cube toward the viewer to show off the 3D
        cube.transform.rotation.x = Math.PI / 5;
```

Note that a transform component is automatically created by default for every Vizi object, for convenience. This covers most use cases. The constructor for `Vizi.Object` has an optional flag, `autoCreateTransform`, which can be set to `false` if a transform component is not needed for a particular object.

To show the Phong shading on the cube, we add a light to the scene as a separate object with a `Vizi.DirectionalLight` component. In later chapters, we will see how we can avoid the need to even explicitly create the lights, by using a prefabricated application template that comes with its own lighting setup. Finally, we are ready to run the application, which we do by calling the application's `run()` method. And that's it. There is no need to write our own `requestAnimationFrame()` function to manually update the cube's rotation every tick. It just works.

### Adding interaction

You may have noticed that the Three.js examples in previous chapters were short on interactivity. This is in part because we just hadn't gotten to it yet. But it is also because this particular aspect of Three.js involves some grunt work. Three.js provides a "projector" object that allows us to figure out which objects the mouse is currently hovering over. But it is not packaged up with an event interface or a model for click-and-drag. The Vizi framework takes care of this problem by implementing mouse picking and dispatching to components automatically.

Let's add a simple interactive behavior to the previous example. Instead of automatically rotating the cube on page load, we will rotate only when the mouse hovers over it. Open the file *Chapter 9/vizicubeinteractive.html* in your browser. The code for this example is shown in Example 9-5. The lines of code highlighted in bold show the changes required. This time, we don't set the `autoRotate` option when we create the behavior, so that it won't start when the application loads. Next, we add a new kind of component, `Vizi.Picker`, to the cube object. The picker defines the usual set of mouse events—over, out, up, down—which it automatically dispatches when the mouse is over the `Visual` within the picker's containing object. All that's left to do is to add the event listeners that start and stop the rotation on mouse over and mouse out, respectively.

*Example 9-5. Adding mouse interaction with a picker component*

```
<script type="text/javascript">

    $(document).ready(function() {

        // Create the Vizi application object
        var container = document.getElementById("container");
        var app = new Vizi.Application({ container : container });

        // Create a Phong-shaded, texture-mapped cube
```

```
            var cube = new Vizi.Object;
            var visual = new Vizi.Visual(
                    { geometry: new THREE.CubeGeometry(2, 2, 2),
                        material: new THREE.MeshPhongMaterial(
                          {map:THREE.ImageUtils.loadTexture(
                              "../images/webgl-logo-256.jpg")})
                    });

        cube.addComponent(visual);

        // Add a rotate behavior to give the cube some life
        var rotator = new Vizi.RotateBehavior;
        cube.addComponent(rotator);

        // Make the cube pickable
        var picker = new Vizi.Picker;
        cube.addComponent(picker);

        // Connect the picker to the rotator, only rotate on hover
        picker.addEventListener("mouseover", function() {
          rotator.start(); });
        picker.addEventListener("mouseout", function() {
          rotator.stop(); });

        // Rotate the cube toward the viewer to show off the 3D
        cube.transform.rotation.x = Math.PI / 5;

        // Add a light to show shading
        var light = new Vizi.Object;
        light.addComponent(new Vizi.DirectionalLight);

        // Add the cube and light to the scene
        app.addObject(cube);
        app.addObject(light);

        // Run it
        app.run();
    }
    );

</script>
```

That was pretty easy. To see what is really happening under the covers, let's look at what is involved in detecting 3D objects under the mouse. Here is how Vizi implements picking using the Three.js class THREE.Projector. It's not trivial. Example 9-6 lists the code for the Vizi graphic subsystem's objectFromMouse() method. This method returns the Vizi object under the mouse cursor, if it can find one. The process involves several steps:

1. First, we transform element-relative mouse coordinates from the event's `ele mentX` and `elementY` properties into viewport-relative values ranging from −0.5 to +0.5 in each dimension, also flipping the *y* coordinate to match the 3D coordinate system. (Note that `elementX` and `elementY` are not DOM-standard mouse event properties; they were calculated in the Vizi DOM event handler before it passed the data into this method.)

2. Once we have viewport-relative coordinates for the mouse, we need to transform those into a 3D position directly beneath the mouse but halfway back into the view volume. This is stored in the variable `vector`.

3. Then, we must transform the viewport-relative position of the mouse pointer from *camera space* into *world space*. Once we have that transformed position, we now know the position of the mouse cursor "inside the world." We do this by calling the `unprojectVector()` of our projector object. (The project was created during initialization of the graphics system. It is of type `THREE.Projector`.)

4. Now that we know the position of the mouse cursor "inside the world," we can create a *ray* from the camera's world space position to the mouse position. Anything that intersects that ray is "under the mouse." (Apologies for the quotes, but we're using the terms "inside" and "under" loosely here.). The ray intersection is performed by the `THREE.Raycaster` method `intersectObjects()`. It takes a list of objects and returns a list of anything that intersects the ray, in front-to-back order.

5. Finally, we grab the first visible element we find in the list, which represents the frontmost picked object.

As I said: not trivial. This is not the kind of code you want to write more than once. Using a framework like Vizi, you don't have to write it at all.

*Example 9-6. Vizi picking implementation using THREE.Projector*

```
Vizi.GraphicsThreeJS.prototype.objectFromMouse = function(event)
{
    var eltx = event.elementX, elty = event.elementY;

    // translate client coords into vp x,y
    var vpx = ( eltx / this.container.offsetWidth ) * 2 - 1;
    var vpy = - ( elty / this.container.offsetHeight ) * 2 + 1;

    var vector = new THREE.Vector3( vpx, vpy, 0.5 );

    this.projector.unprojectVector( vector, this.camera );

    var pos = new THREE.Vector3;
    pos = pos.applyMatrix4(this.camera.matrixWorld);

    var raycaster = new THREE.Raycaster( pos, vector.sub( pos )
      .normalize() );
```

```
        var intersects = raycaster.intersectObjects( this.scene.children,
            true );

    if ( intersects.length > 0 ) {
        var i = 0;
        while(!intersects[i].object.visible)
        {
            i++;
        }

        var intersected = intersects[i];

        if (i >= intersects.length)
        {
            return { object : null, point : null, normal : null };
        }

        return (this.findObjectFromIntersected(intersected.object,
            intersected.point, intersected.face.normal));
    }
    else
    {
        return { object : null, point : null, normal : null };
    }
}
```

## Adding multiple behaviors

Vizi allows us to add multiple behaviors to an object with ease. We are going to adapt the previous example to add behaviors to the cube. When the mouse hovers, it will highlight the cube by turning it light blue. When the mouse is clicked, it will start the object rotating, bouncing up and down, and moving away from the camera. Clicking on the cube again will stop the movement. Launch the file *Chapter 9/vizicubebehav iors.html* and try it out. The relevant code is listed in Example 9-7. The lines in boldface show the changes.

*Example 9-7. Adding multiple behaviors*

```
        // Add several behaviors
        var rotator = new Vizi.RotateBehavior;
        var bouncer = new Vizi.BounceBehavior({loop:true});
        var mover = new Vizi.MoveBehavior({loop:true, duration:2,
            moveVector:new THREE.Vector3(0, 0, -2)});
        cube.addComponent(rotator);
        cube.addComponent(bouncer);
        cube.addComponent(mover);

        // Make the cube pickable
        var picker = new Vizi.Picker;
        cube.addComponent(picker);
```

```
// Add a highlight color for hover
var highlight = new Vizi.HighlightBehavior(
  {highlightColor:0x88eeff});
cube.addComponent(highlight);

// Connect the picker to the rotator.
// Highlight on hover, toggle behaviors on click
picker.addEventListener("mouseover", function() {
  highlight.on(); });
picker.addEventListener("mouseout", function() {
  highlight.off();});
picker.addEventListener("mouseup", function() {
    rotator.toggle();
     bouncer.toggle();
     mover.toggle(); });
```

Adding behaviors to this example is as simple as adding more components. We also add a mouse up handler to the picker, which calls `toggle()` on each of the behaviors to toggle its start/stop state when the mouse is clicked. And that's it. Figure 9-5 shows our old friend, the WebGL textured cube—highlighted, spinning, bobbing, and riding off into the distance, never to be seen again.

*Figure 9-5. Vizi textured cube with behaviors and mouse interaction*

These simple examples illustrate the basics of what a framework like Vizi can do. We will get to know Vizi in more detail in the next several chapters as we look at various 3D application scenarios and techniques.

 Vizi is still very much a work in progress. As of this writing, it is a version 0.6 or 0.7 library: many features are there, but there is still a long way to go. I develop Vizi when I have spare time or when I am fortunate enough to be able to use it on a WebGL development project. By the time this book goes to print, I hope to have released version 1.0.

# Chapter Summary

This chapter looked at engines and frameworks for building 3D applications. While Three.js is powerful, it lacks many constructs required to make our day-to-day development life manageable, such as high-level behaviors and interaction, prebuilt setup and teardown, and many other things that need to be done for nearly all 3D applications.

We also surveyed existing game engines and presentation frameworks designed to solve these problems. The world of WebGL development is new and evolving, and the state of the frameworks reflects that. There is a broad range to choose from and several tradeoffs to be made, including cost of ownership, power, and ease of use.

Finally, we dove into framework-based development by working with Vizi, a new framework I developed to explore framework concepts and build the examples for the book. The simple Vizi examples show how using a framework can free us from common, repetitive development tasks, allowing us to save time, write more reliable code, and focus on the application itself. Vizi may be only one example of a framework; you should feel free to explore the others out there, or even design one for yourself. Whether you choose to buy or build, the reality is that if you are developing a production-quality 3D application, sooner or later you will deal with the issues discussed in this chapter.

# CHAPTER 10

# Developing a Simple 3D Application

Up to now we have been concerned with underpinnings: HTML5 foundation APIs and architecture, JavaScript libraries and frameworks, and content pipeline tools. Now it's time to put this learning into practice. For the remainder of the book, we will shift our focus away from APIs and tools, toward the practical concerns involved in developing working applications.

Let's start by building one of the simpler types of 3D web application: a product viewer/configurator. Such applications typically feature an interactive 3D model of a real-world product as the centerpiece, with a rich user interface for exploring the product's features, mouse interaction for seeing more information, and a way to interactively change one or more aspects of the model. Web-based product configurators have been around for a long time, first in static 2D, then with 2.5 or 3D rendering using Flash, and, most recently, in 3D via the Canvas API and/or WebGL. Product configurators can be high-functioning marketing tools (i.e., a more interactive way to advertise a product's features), or they can be used to actually configure and buy the product online through an integrated e-commerce system.

Figure 10-1 illustrates a concept piece for a "car of the future." Try it out by opening the example file *Chapter 10/futurgo.html*. Use the mouse to rotate the model, and the track-pad or scroll wheel to zoom in and out. As you roll over various parts of the car, information about that part pops up in an overlay. Click on the tabs to the right to expose the car's interior and spin the wheels. You can even change the car's color to suit your personal taste. This "Lifestyle Transportation Device" is the next wave in personal transportation. Part scooter, part golf cart, part smart car, and all high tech—it's the Futurgo!

*Figure 10-1. Futurgo concept car: a 3D product page*

This fun, completely contrived example of a product configurator touches on the key concepts required to deploy a working 3D product page:

*Designing the application*
Developing the visual look of the 3D model and 2D page content, and the defining flow of user interaction.

*Creating the 3D content*
Using a tool like Autodesk Maya to create the models and animations, and converting the art to a web-friendly format for use within the application.

*Previewing and testing the 3D content*
Devising a set of tools for validating that the exported 3D content will work within the application (e.g., looks correct and animates properly).

*Integrating the 3D content into the application*
Integrating the 3D content (once we've verified that it looks and animates correctly) with the 2D page content and other application code.

*Developing 3D behaviors and interaction*
Bringing the 3D content to life by implementing several behaviors and interactive features, including a visual fade effect, a rotating carousel, mouse rollovers, animations triggered by user interaction, and interactively changing the object's colors.

All of the preceding needs to be developed via a repeatable process. As we find bugs and refine the application, changes to the visuals for the application (especially the 3D content) should just "drop in" without our having to recode the application.

To build the Futurgo page and the pipeline tools needed to support it, we will be leaning heavily on the Vizi framework described in Chapter 9. Vizi builds upon Three.js by providing reusable behaviors and packaged objects, making our job simpler and allowing us to do more with less code. We will also be using open source file exporters and converters to get the content out of Maya into a web-friendly format. Let's do it.

# Designing the Application

I designed the Futurgo application in collaboration with 3D artist TC Chang. TC and I wanted the design to lend itself to a product visualization app, but also to be playful and futuristic. The design incorporates elements of personal transportation devices like the well-known Segway, but also has the protective aspects of a car, such as an enclosed body and windshield. We have no idea if this car would ever work, let alone be street legal, but we had a great time putting the concept together!

After kicking around the basic ideas and a few drawings, TC went to work on a full-concept visual treatment. The mockup is depicted in Figure 10-2. Note how close the finished product is to this mockup.[1] We were able to reuse the Photoshop assets, exported to PNG images, and the 3D rendering came straight out of Maya, so it looks remarkably like the version rendered in real time using Three.js. It took a bit of work to ensure that the exported 3D content was faithful to the original rendering, as we will see shortly. But the result was worth the work. This chapter is all about how to achieve this level of visual fidelity, and seamlessly blend the art with the code to create polished, professional applications.

 TC Chang is a veteran art director with a distinguished résumé that includes long tenures at Disney Interactive, Sony, and Electronic Arts, working on franchises such as *The Godfather*, *James Bond*, and *Jet Li* fighting games. TC is also a firm believer in the power of 3D on the Web, having founded Flatland, an early startup in that space. TC's work can be viewed online at *http://www.tcchang.com/*.

---

1. The only noticeable visible difference is the font. TC chose a font called Myriad Pro, which is not a web font. PT Sans, from Google Fonts (*http://www.google.com/fonts/specimen/PT+Sans*) makes for a fair substitute.

*Figure 10-2. Artist's mockup of the Futurgo car concept; design by and image courtesy of TC Chang (http://www.tcchang.com/)*

# Creating the 3D Content

TC used Autodesk Maya version 2013 to create and animate the various parts of the Futurgo model. While the Futurgo is conceptually one object, it is actually made up of several meshes corresponding to different parts of the car: the steel body, the wheels, the interior seating and controls, the windows, and so on. It is important to create the model out of separate parts so that they can be individually animated, and so that we can implement different interactions in the application, such as rolling over the windows or body frame to get more information. Figure 10-3 shows the Futurgo being modeled in Maya. The text in the overlay displays a variety of statistics about the model, including vertex and triangle counts.

During this content creation phase, TC and I carefully planned aspects of the model, such as the scale—that is, what units the Futurgo is modeled in (in this case, meters)— how to set up the lighting, and how to create the animations. Maya is somewhat limited with its animation tools; there is only one animation timeline for the whole file, so all animations within a file must be of the same duration or there will be "dead space" in the shorter ones. We decided to keep the animations short—one second in duration, which is long enough for the windows to zoom away from the body to show the interior, and long enough for a full rotation of the tires.

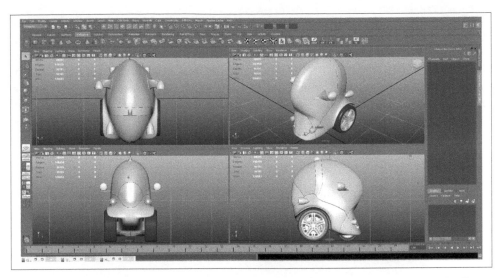

*Figure 10-3. Modeling the Futurgo in Autodesk Maya; image courtesy TC Chang (http://www.tcchang.com/)*

TC and I also put some thought into reasonable polygon counts for performance. The Futurgo weighs in at about 96,000 triangles. This gives us enough triangles for a nice smooth look when rendering in Three.js, while not using so many that it would bog down performance in the browser. Additionally, we needed to keep the polygon counts low to keep the file size small. For a web application, the content needs to download quickly. The final deployed file that was exported from Maya and converted to *glTF* comes in at approximately 6 MB. This seems large, but on a modern consumer-grade Internet connection, streamed from a server configured for server-side compression of *.bin* files, it downloads very quickly (just a couple of seconds).

## Exporting the Maya Scene to COLLADA

Maya files must be converted to a WebGL-friendly format before being displayed in the browser. Because of the small file size and very fast load times, we decided to use *glTF* as the deployed file format. As of this writing, there is no direct way to export glTF from Maya. Instead, we used an export format that is supported in Maya, COLLADA, and then converted to glTF.[2]

The COLLADA exporter that comes with Maya 2013 is buggy and out of date, so we opted to use OpenCOLLADA (*http://opencollada.org/*), a high-performance open source exporter that was independently developed to create quality, spec-compliant

---

2. glTF, the Graphics Library Transmission Format for WebGL, and COLLADA, the XML-based graphics interchange standard, are described in detail in Chapter 8.

COLLADA output. As of this writing, OpenCOLLADA for Maya (there is also a 3ds Max version) is in good working order, and we were able to successfully export the Futurgo to COLLADA using it. The main site contains download links for Maya or 3ds Max, versions 2010 through 2013. (Autodesk tends to upgrade its plugin SDKs on an annual basis, and the exporters must be adapted to match. Make sure to get the exporter version that matches the product release.) Once the exporter is installed, make sure it is turned on in Maya by opening the Plug-in Manager (Window → Settings/Preferences → Plug-in Manager). See Figure 10-4.

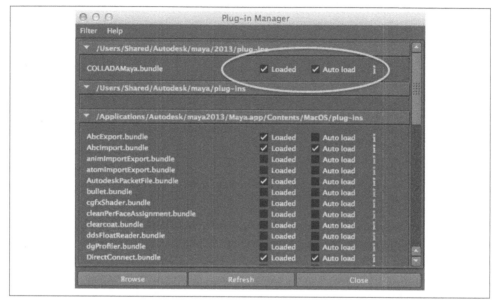

*Figure 10-4. Enabling OpenCOLLADA export in the Autodesk Maya 2013 Plug-in Manager*

The exported COLLADA file for the Futurgo is packaged with the example code in the file *models/futurgo/futurgo.dae*.

 OpenCOLLADA is an open source project, and a bit of a labor of love, so the usual caveats apply. The ongoing care and feeding, especially as Autodesk upgrades its SDKs in future versions of its tools, is not guaranteed. However, recall that COLLADA is just one potential art path out of Maya and 3ds Max. Another potential path would be to convert from FBX to glTF. Autodesk tools will export FBX reliably for some time to come. A few companies, such as Verold (*http://www.verold.com/*), discussed in Chapter 8, are already at work converting FBX to glTF.

## Converting the COLLADA File to glTF

Once the Futurgo model has been extracted from Maya as COLLADA, it can be converted to glTF. Fabrice Robinet, chair of the COLLADA working group and lead designer of glTF, has written a command-line converter that does the job.

On my MacBook Air running Mac OS 10.8, the command for doing that is in an executable called collada2gltf. To convert the Futurgo, I ran the following command. The program's output is shown in italics.

```
$ <path-to-converter>/collada2gltf -f futurgo.dae -d
```

*[option] export pass details*
*converting:futurgo.dae ... as futurgo.json*
*[shader]: futurgo0VS.glsl*
*[shader]: futurgo0FS.glsl*
*[shader]: futurgo2VS.glsl*
*[shader]: futurgo2FS.glsl*
*[shader]: futurgo4VS.glsl*
*[shader]: futurgo4FS.glsl*
*[completed conversion]*

After conversion, you will have the file *futurgo.json* in your folder, along with supporting GLSL shader source files (*.glsl* file extension). Now that the file has been converted to glTF, we can use the glTF loader I wrote for Three.js to load it into the application. We will cover how to do that in the next section. The converted glTF file for the Futurgo is packaged with the example code, in the files *models/futurgo/futurgo.json* for the main JSON file, and *models/futurgo/futurgo.bin* for the associated binary data.

As of this writing, glTF is still in its initial development stages. This has a couple of implications: first, the specification itself is still in flux; therefore, any files you are working with for this book will likely be out of date by the time the specification solidifies, so plan to upgrade/migrate your content as needed. Second, the tools are very young. The collada2gltf converter, for example, must be built from source on the target platform. For information on how to build the converter, go to the glTF repository on GitHub (*https://github.com/KhronosGroup/glTF*) or the main glTF page (*http://gltf.gl/*).

# Previewing and Testing the 3D Content

Now that we have managed to export the content from Maya, we have to deal with our next problem: how to see it in a web page. glTF files don't view themselves—remember, WebGL knows nothing about file formats. We have to load models and scenes using our own code libraries. Before we try building the application, it would be wise to make sure that the 3D content is in good shape—that is, that we can render it in WebGL with all the scene information intact, such as materials, textures, lights, cameras, transformations, and animations. To this end, we are going to create a tool to help us preview and test our 3D content.

## A Vizi-Based Previewer Tool

To create the 3D previewer we turn to Vizi, the framework I created and first introduced back in Chapter 9. Vizi takes a component-based approach to building 3D applications, by automating repetitive tasks such as initialization and cleanup, providing the application's run loop and event handling, and supplying a set of prebuilt behaviors and interactions. The graphics are still Three.js—the de facto library for rendering in WebGL —but Vizi packages it up to make it more reusable and much faster to code.

Figure 10-5 depicts the previewer with the Futurgo glTF file loaded into the scene. The previewer features a main content area for viewing models and scenes, with a gridded ground plane. There is a menu bar containing a single command, Open, and a status label displaying the currently viewed file. To the right is a control panel with several subpanes. The Scene Stats pane shows the current frame rate, the number of meshes and polygons, and the time it took to load the scene. The Cameras, Lights, and Animations panes allow the user to test those parts of the scene by switching between cameras, toggling lights on and off, and running the animations. There is also a Miscellaneous pane that allows us to switch on a *headlight*—that is, an extra light for viewing the object in case the model was not exported with lights—and also a checkbox to show or hide the grid.

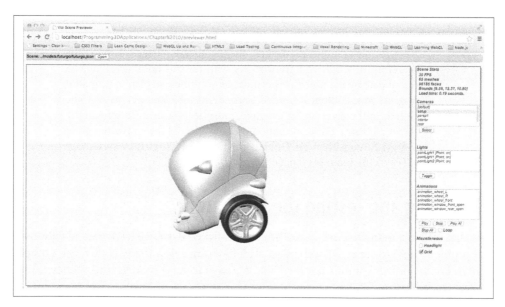

*Figure 10-5. Previewing a glTF model with Vizi*

In addition to letting us visually inspect and test the content, the previewer provides us with vital information about the scene; namely, the ids of the objects to be used when wiring up the interactions in the application. After uploading the exported COLLADA files, TC emailed me a list with the names of the animations; however, that is hardly a reliable method of determining object ids that will be used in code. Using the previewer, we can be sure of the object ids used for the animations in the COLLADA and converted glTF files. (The object ids are the names that appear in the Animations pane in the control panel on the right.)

A previewer like the one featured in this chapter is a simple but invaluable tool. While it is nowhere near a complete development environment, it provides an essential part of the pipeline for validating and testing content before putting it into an application. We will use this kind of previewer in all of the development projects going forward. Let's take a look at how it was built.

## The Vizi Viewer Class

Many 3D applications follow a pattern: initialize the renderer, create an empty scene, load some model content, add an interaction, and run it. This is such a common pattern that I designed a reusable Vizi class to implement it. `Vizi.Viewer` is a subclass of `Vizi.Application`; that is, it is a dedicated type of application for viewing and interacting with models and scenes. You can use it to rotate a model or scene with the mouse; potentially pan it left, right, up and down; and zoom in and out.

`Vizi.Viewer` can be used for many kinds of viewing scenarios: a simple viewer that loads a model and lets the user view and rotate it, with no additional bells and whistles; a previewer such as the one we will look at in this section; and even a full product visualization page, such as the Futurgo (we will see how that's done later in the chapter).

In true framework fashion, `Vizi.Viewer` packages a lot of out-of-the-box functionality into a single class that would otherwise require hundreds of lines of Three.js code. Its features include:

*Model viewing controls*
> `Vizi.Viewer` uses an enhanced version of the `THREE.OrbitControls` object that comes with the Three.js examples. Left mouse rotates the scene; right mouse pans; scroll wheel and trackpad zoom. The viewer also provides options for overriding and remapping those mouse bindings.

*Default camera and lighting*
> For scenes that do not include a camera, `Vizi.Viewer` supplies a default one. For scenes with no lighting, the viewer can optionally create a headlight that automatically lights models, and updates the lighting as the user moves the camera around.

*Utility scene objects*

Vizi.Viewer optionally displays a ground plane with a rectangular grid, and a wireframe bounding box around the model, if desired.

*Scene and rendering statistics*

The viewer can dispatch events to report frame rate, scene statistics such as mesh and polygon counts, bounding box dimensions, and file load times.

*Light, camera, and animation controls*

Vizi.Viewer provides helper methods that allow the programmer to toggle lights on/off, switch between cameras, and start and stop animations. The viewer provides a list of each of these types of objects to the application so that it doesn't have to search for them in code.

*One-button operation*

The THREE.OrbitControls object has been modified to support single-button operation, so that right mouse is either disabled or mapped to the left mouse button, for usability.

To see Vizi.Viewer in action, let's look at how it is used to implement the previewer. To launch the previewer depicted in Figure 10-5, open the example file in *Chapter 10/ previewer.html*. Example 10-1 shows an excerpt from the source, the code to create the Vizi.Viewer object. As always, we pass in a container parameter, the DIV element to which Three.js will add its WebGL renderer (a Canvas with a WebGL drawing context). In addition, we set a few options, telling the viewer to display the grid, and to use a headlight if there are no lights in the scene so that we will be able to see the model. After creating the viewer, we add a couple of event listeners to detect when frame rate and other aspects of the scene change; we will look at those event handlers a little later. We then set up a list of files for selection with the Open command in the menu bar, and finally, call the viewer's run loop to run the application.

*Example 10-1. Creating the Vizi viewer object*

```
    var viewer = null;
$(document).ready(function() {

    var container = document.getElementById("container");
    var renderStats = document.getElementById("render_stats");
    var sceneStats = document.getElementById("scene_stats");

    viewer = new Vizi.Viewer({ container : container,
        showGrid : true, headlight : true,
        showBoundingBox : false });
    viewer.addEventListener("renderstats", function(stats) {
        onRenderStats(stats, renderStats); });
    viewer.addEventListener("scenestats", function(stats) {
        onSceneStats(stats, sceneStats); });
```

```
        buildFileList();

        viewer.run();
    }
);
```

When you launch the previewer, you will see an empty scene window. The orange menu bar at the top provides a user interface for opening one of several 3D files from its file list.

## The Vizi Loader Class

Clicking the Open button at the top will launch a file open dialog and we can select the file. Select the item *../models/futurgo/futurgo.json*. You should see the Futurgo displayed in the scene window, as shown in Figure 10-5. Feel free to interact with it using the mouse and trackpad or scroll wheel.

The previewer loads the model into the Vizi viewer object using another Vizi class, `Vizi.Loader`. See Example 10-2.

*Example 10-2. Loading files with the Vizi.Loader object*

```
function openFile()
{
    var select = document.getElementById("files");
    var index = select.selectedIndex;
    if (index >= 0)
    {
        var url = select.options[index].text;

        var loader = new Vizi.Loader;

        loader.addEventListener("loaded", function(data) {
          onLoadComplete(data, loadStartTime); });
        loader.addEventListener("progress", function(progress) {
          onLoadProgress(progress); });

        var fileViewingName = document.getElementById("fileViewingName");
        fileViewingName.innerHTML=url;

        var loadStartTime = Date.now();
        loader.loadScene(url);

        var loadStatus = document.getElementById("loadStatus");
        loadStatus.style.display = 'block';
    }

    $('#fileOpenDialog').dialog("close");
}
```

`Vizi.Loader` uses the Three.js file loaders for JSON, COLLADA, or glTF to parse the various formats and load them into memory. In addition, it wraps the newly created Three.js scene in Vizi components, resulting in a scene suitable for use in Vizi-based applications. Finally, it dispatches `loaded` and `progress` events to listeners as the file downloads and is parsed. Example 10-3 shows the event listener function, `onLoadCom plete()`, which is used to detect when the file is fully loaded and ready to add to the viewer.

*Example 10-3. Previewer file-loaded event listener*

```
function onLoadComplete(data, loadStartTime)
{
    // Hide the loader bar
    var loadStatus = document.getElementById("loadStatus");
    loadStatus.style.display = 'none';

    viewer.replaceScene(data);

    var loadTime = (Date.now() - loadStartTime) / 1000;
    var loadTimeStats = document.getElementById("load_time_stats");
    loadTimeStats.innerHTML = "Load time: " +
        loadTime.toFixed(2) + " seconds."

    updateCamerasList(viewer);
    updateLightsList(viewer);
    updateAnimationsList(viewer);
    updateMiscControls(viewer);

    if (viewer.cameraNames.length > 1) {
        selectCamera(1);
    }

}
```

The listener does a few things. First, it hides the DIV element that was displayed at the start of scene load with the message "Loading scene..." This indicates to the user that load is complete. Next, it adds the newly loaded content to the viewer by calling the viewer's `replaceScene()` method; this is what allows us to view and manipulate the Futurgo in the scene window. Then the listener updates the load time in the Scene Stats pane. Next, it calls several helpers to update the lists in the user interface (e.g., cameras and lights) based on arrays of those objects being maintained in the viewer. Finally, it calls the function `selectCamera()` to select the first camera in the scene (not counting the default one), if it exists. `selectCamera()` uses the viewer's `useCamera()` method to switch cameras:

```
function selectCamera(index)
{
    var select = document.getElementById("cameras_list");
    if (index === undefined) {
```

```
                index = select.selectedIndex;
            }
            else {
                select.selectedIndex = index;
            }

            if (index >= 0) {
                viewer.useCamera(index);
            }
        }
```

Now, we are ready to use the previewer to examine and test the model. Rotate the model with the mouse. Pan it with the right button. Use the scroll wheel or trackpad to zoom in and out. Play with the various controls on the right to change cameras, toggle lights on and off, and play animations.

The ability to test animations is one of the more important features of the previewer. A lot can go wrong with 3D animation, and a lot of potential problems can crop up in the pipeline. Testing this out in the previewer saves us time that would otherwise be spent troubleshooting problems downstream. Figure 10-6 shows the Futurgo after we have played the animations named `animation_window_front_open` and `animation_win dow_rear_open`. We can see that we have the desired effect: the front and rear windows have been "exploded" out so that we can view the interior of the model.

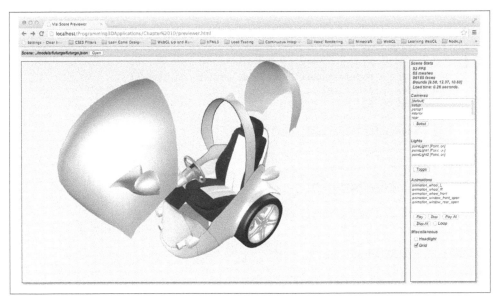

*Figure 10-6. Playing animations in the previewer*

Note that animations aren't part of the Vizi scene graph, per se (or the Three.js scene graph, for that matter). They are stored in a separate array of objects within the viewer.

So we need to use viewer utility methods for playing, stopping, and looping the animations. Example 10-4 shows functions in the HTML that call the various viewer methods to play, stop, and loop animations, including `viewer.playAnimation()`, `viewer.stopAnimation()`, `viewer.playAllAnimations()`, `viewer.stopAllAnimations()`, and `viewer.setLoopAnimations()`.

*Example 10-4. Using Vizi viewer methods to control animation playback*

```
function selectAnimation()
{
    var select = document.getElementById("animations_list");
    var index = select.selectedIndex;
    if (index >= 0)
    {
        viewer.playAnimation(index, viewer.loopAnimations);
    }
}

function playAnimation()
{
    var select = document.getElementById("animations_list");
    var index = select.selectedIndex;
    if (index >= 0)
    {
        viewer.playAnimation(index, viewer.loopAnimations);
    }
}

function stopAnimation()
{
    var select = document.getElementById("animations_list");
    var index = select.selectedIndex;
    if (index >= 0)
    {
        viewer.stopAnimation(index);
    }
}

function playAllAnimations()
{
    viewer.playAllAnimations(viewer.loopAnimations);
}

function stopAllAnimations()
{
    viewer.stopAllAnimations();
}

function onLoopChecked(elt)
{
    viewer.setLoopAnimations(elt.checked);
}
```

# Integrating the 3D into the Application

Now that we have measure of confidence that our 3D content will load, render, and animate as expected, we can proceed to building the application. The first step in doing that is to integrate the 3D into the web page for the app. Once again, launch the file *Chapter 10/futurgo.html* to see the page, depicted in Figure 10-7.

Note how all the elements of the page are smoothly integrated. This is the power of the web browser's compositing engine at work. Each of the page elements is simply a DIV or a few nested DIVs, with proper ordering and *z*-index settings. The 3D view is layered below all the other page elements so that the user interface appears on top. Some of the UI elements are transparent, allowing more of the 3D scene to show through. If you are viewing the image in color, note also the beautiful purple and gray gradient used for the 3D scene background; this is taken directly from TC's design. We are able to use it as the background for the WebGL canvas simply by setting the background property of the container element in the CSS. This is incredibly powerful. As a finishing touch, we decided to keep the gray wireframe grid supplied by Vizi.Viewer. (I will admit that it was originally a copy-and-paste accident, but we liked the look so much we decided to leave it in.)

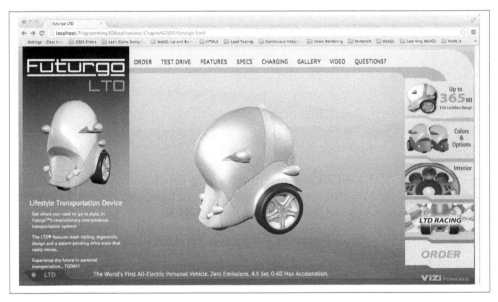

*Figure 10-7. Futurgo model integrated into the HTML page*

The source code for the application resides in the files *Chapter 10/futurgo.html, css/ futurgo.css,* and *Chapter 10/futurgo.js*. We have refactored things slightly in comparison to the previewer. Now, the HTML is just concerned with markup, consisting mostly of

DIVs, and just a few bits of script: the page load code, plus handlers for the rollovers, and UI tabs on the righthand side.

The page load code, shown in Example 10-5, creates a new Futurgo object, passing in the container element and a handful of callbacks for load complete and mouse over/out. It then calls `Futurgo.go()`, which both loads the 3D scene and starts the run loop.

*Example 10-5. Futurgo page loading code*

```
<script>

    var futurgo = null;
    var overlay = null;
    var overlayContents = null;
    var loadStatus = null;
    var part_materials = [];

$(document).ready(function() {

    initControls();
    overlay = document.getElementById("overlay");
    overlayContents = document.getElementById("overlayContents");
    loadStatus = document.getElementById("loadStatus");
    var container = document.getElementById("container");
    futurgo = new Futurgo({ container : container,
            loadCallback : onLoadComplete,
            loadProgressCallback : onLoadProgress,
            mouseOverCallback : onMouseOver,
            mouseOutCallback : onMouseOut,
        });

    loadStatus.style.display = 'block';
    futurgo.go();
}
);
```

The Futurgo object handles most of the gritty loading details; the load callback in the page code merely needs to hide the "Loading scene..." DIV. See Example 10-6. The mouse callbacks, `onMouseOver()` and `onMouseOut()`, will be described in the next section.

*Example 10-6. Hiding the load progress message*

```
function onLoadComplete(loadTime)
{
    // Hide the loader bar
    loadStatus.style.display = 'none';
}
```

Now let's see how the `Futurgo` class initializes the viewer and loads the scene. The setup code is shown in Example 10-7 (source file *Chapter 10/futurgo.js*).

*Example 10-7. Viewer setup and file loading code for the Futurgo application*

```
Futurgo = function(param) {

    this.container = param.container;
    this.loadCallback = param.loadCallback;
    this.loadProgressCallback = param.loadProgressCallback;
    this.mouseOverCallback = param.mouseOverCallback;
    this.mouseOutCallback = param.mouseOutCallback;
    this.part_materials = [];
    this.vehicleOpen = false;
    this.wheelsMoving = false;
}

Futurgo.prototype.go = function() {
    this.viewer = new Vizi.Viewer({ container : this.container,
        showGrid : true,
        allowPan: false, oneButton: true });
    this.loadURL(Futurgo.URL);
    this.viewer.run();
}

Futurgo.prototype.loadURL = function(url) {

    var that = this;

    var loader = new Vizi.Loader;
    loader.addEventListener("loaded", function(data) {
      that.onLoadComplete(data, loadStartTime); });
    loader.addEventListener("progress", function(progress) {
      that.onLoadProgress(progress); });

    var loadStartTime = Date.now();
    loader.loadScene(url);
}
```

By now, much of this code should look familiar. As we did for the previewer, we create Vizi.Viewer and Vizi.Loader objects. We do, however, set a few different options when creating the viewer (see the code in boldface). allowPan controls whether the user can pan the object left, right, up, and down using the right mouse button. We set that to false because we always want the object to be located in the center of the scene. one Button controls whether the right mouse button is also used to rotate the model; by setting it to true, we can use either the left or right mouse buttons to rotate.

The preceding code gets the Futurgo model loaded into the page, looking nice and ready to interact with. In the next section, we will see how to bring it fully to life with 3D behaviors and interactions.

# Developing 3D Behaviors and Interactions

The Futurgo application we have created thus far is already pretty interesting. We can view a 3D model in real time, within a very nicely integrated visual presentation, and even manipulate the model with the mouse. But it gets better. We can make this a truly interactive application that takes full advantage of real-time web graphics by adding 3D behaviors and interactions. These include automatically animating the model on page load using transparency transitions and a carousel-style rotation, implementing mouse rollovers to provide more information on product features, and dynamically changing the 3D object by clicking on 2D elements in the page.

## Vizi Scene Graph API Methods: findNode() and map()

The behaviors described in this section require traversing the scene graph of the 3D content loaded by `Vizi.Loader`, so that we can add behaviors or mouse interaction to certain objects. Sometimes we need to find objects by name or id; other times, we need to go through the scene graph, or a portion of it, to find objects of a certain type. Vizi provides a set of scene graph API methods to do this. These methods can be passed a string identifier, a JavaScript regular expression to match, or a JavaScript object type (compared to using the `instanceof` operator). The methods `findNode()` and `findNodes()` return matching objects; `map()` finds objects and applies a function to the result.

findNode(query)
> This method finds a node (instance of `Vizi.Object` or `Vizi.Component`) given a query. The query can be a string identifier (e.g., "body2"), object type (e.g., `Vizi.Visual`), or a regular expression (e.g., `/windows_front|windows_rear/`). If there are multiple such nodes in the Vizi scene graph, the first is returned.

findNodes(query)
> This method finds *all* nodes (instance of `Vizi.Object` or `Vizi.Component`) given a query. The query can be a string identifier (e.g., "body2"), object type (e.g., `Vizi.Visual`), or a regular expression (e.g., `/windows_front|windows_rear/`).

map(query, callback_function)
> This method uses `findNodes()` to find all nodes that match the search query, and calls the callback function on each.

> You can think of the Vizi scene graph API methods as similar in function to jQuery queries, though they use a completely different query scheme. Vizi has no concept of selectors, relying instead on strings and JavaScript data types. This is a conscious design choice based on the object-and-component nature of the Vizi architecture.

Now, let's walk through the Futurgo load handling code to see how it adds behaviors. See Example 10-8.

First, `onLoadComplete()` adds the loaded Futurgo scene to the viewer by calling `this.viewer.replaceScene(data)`. Under the covers, the viewer not only adds the objects to its scene graph, but it also does the accounting on the lights, cameras, and animations (as described earlier) so that we have a list of those to work with to switch cameras, play animations, and so on, as needed. After that, this function spends its time adding behaviors, even starting some of them. Each of the behaviors set up in this function is described in an upcoming section.

*Example 10-8. Adding behaviors to the Futurgo application after scene load*

```
Futurgo.prototype.onLoadComplete = function(data, loadStartTime)
{
    var scene = data.scene;
    this.viewer.replaceScene(data);

    // Add entry fade behavior to the windows, and pickers
    // for rollover behavior
    var that = this;
    scene.map(/windows_front|windows_rear/, function(o) {
        var fader = new Vizi.FadeBehavior({duration:2, opacity:.8});
        o.addComponent(fader);
        setTimeout(function() {
            fader.start();
        }, 2000);

        var picker = new Vizi.Picker;
        picker.addEventListener("mouseover", function(event) {
            that.onMouseOver("glass", event); });
        picker.addEventListener("mouseout", function(event) {
            that.onMouseOut("glass", event); });
        o.addComponent(picker);
    });

    // Auto-rotate the scene
    var main = scene.findNode("vizi_mobile");
    var carousel = new Vizi.RotateBehavior({autoStart:true,
        duration:20});
    main.addComponent(carousel);

    // Collect the part materials so that we can change colors
    var frame_parts_exp =
/rear_view_arm_L|rear_view_arm_R|rear_view_frame_L|rear_view_frame_R/;

    scene.map(frame_parts_exp, function(o) {
        o.map(Vizi.Visual, function(v) {
            that.part_materials.push(v.material);
        });
    });
```

```
// Add pickers for rollover behavior
scene.map(/body2|rear_view_arm_L|rear_view_arm_R/, function(o) {
    var picker = new Vizi.Picker;
    picker.addEventListener("mouseover", function(event) {
        that.onMouseOver("body", event); });
    picker.addEventListener("mouseout", function(event) {
        that.onMouseOut("body", event); });
    o.addComponent(picker);
});

scene.map("wheels", function(o) {

    var picker = new Vizi.Picker;
    picker.addEventListener("mouseover", function(event) {
        that.onMouseOver("wheels", event); });
    picker.addEventListener("mouseout", function(event) {
        that.onMouseOut("wheels", event); });
    o.addComponent(picker);
});

// Tell the page we're loaded
if (this.loadCallback) {
    var loadTime = (Date.now() - loadStartTime) / 1000;
    this.loadCallback(loadTime);
}
}
```

## Animating Transparency with Vizi.FadeBehavior

We would like to make the windows of the Futurgo model semitransparent so that we can see some of the nice details in the interior. We could just set the transparency as soon as the scene is loaded, but it is much more fun to have a transition effect that fades to the desired value over time. See Example 10-9.

*Example 10-9. Adding a fade effect to the windows*

```
var that = this;
scene.map(/windows_front|windows_rear/, function(o) {
    var fader = new Vizi.FadeBehavior({duration:2, opacity:.8});
    o.addComponent(fader);
    setTimeout(function() {
        fader.start();
    }, 2000);
```

The Vizi.FadeBehavior component fades the materials for any visuals within its containing object. It takes a duration value (in seconds) and a target opacity value. In this example, we fade the opacity to .8 (slightly transparent) over the course of two seconds. We also throw in a two-second delay before starting the fade, using old, reliable setTimeout().

To get an appreciation for what Vizi.FadeBehavior does, let's look under the covers at the implementation. The code excerpt in Example 10-10 is from the Vizi source file located in *src/behaviors/fadeBehavior.js*. When the behavior starts, it iterates through all visuals contained in the object and finds the current opacity value. This will be used as the initial value for a Tween.js tween (see Chapter 5). The tween is then started, and will run for the duration of the behavior. The behavior's evaluate() method, called each time through the run loop if the behavior is active, first checks for a loop condition and restarts the behavior if needed. Then, it goes through all the visuals in the containing object, setting their materials' opacity values to the newly tweened result. This is powerful stuff; by providing a consistent set of interfaces to objects and their components, we can easily create a behavior like FadeBehavior that can be applied to any visual element in the scene.

*Example 10-10. Vizi.FadeBehavior implementation*

```
Vizi.FadeBehavior.prototype.start = function()
{
    if (this.running)
        return;

    if (this._realized && this._object.visuals) {
        var visuals = this._object.visuals;
        var i, len = visuals.length;
        for (i = 0; i < len; i++) {
            this.savedOpacities.push(visuals[i].material.opacity);
            this.savedTransparencies.push(
              visuals[i].material.transparent);
            visuals[i].material.transparent = this.targetOpacity < 1 ?
              true : false;
        }
    }

    this.opacity = { opacity : this.savedOpacities[0] };
    this.opacityTarget = { opacity : this.targetOpacity };
    this.tween = new TWEEN.Tween(this.opacity).to(this.opacityTarget,
      this.duration * 1000)
    .easing(TWEEN.Easing.Quadratic.InOut)
    .repeat(0)
    .start();

    Vizi.Behavior.prototype.start.call(this);
}

Vizi.FadeBehavior.prototype.evaluate = function(t)
{
    if (t >= this.duration)
    {
        this.stop();
        if (this.loop)
            this.start();
```

```
    }

    if (this._object.visuals)
    {
        var visuals = this._object.visuals;
        var i, len = visuals.length;
        for (i = 0; i < len; i++) {
            visuals[i].material.opacity = this.opacity.opacity;
        }
    }

}
```

## Auto-Rotating the Content with Vizi.RotateBehavior

It's great that we can interact with the scene by rotating using the mouse. But it would also be nice to give the scene a little life even when the user isn't directly interacting. So we set up an automatic rotation of the scene on load. Futurgo's load event listener uses findNode() to find the root of the Futurgo scene and add a RotateBehavior component. The rotate behavior is set to start automatically and run on a 20-second loop. See Example 10-11.

*Example 10-11. Adding a Vizi.RotateBehavior to auto-rotate the content*

```
// Auto-rotate the scene
var main = scene.findNode("vizi_mobile");
var carousel = new Vizi.RotateBehavior({autoStart:true,
    duration:20});
main.addComponent(carousel);
```

## Implementing Rollovers Using Vizi.Picker

Mouse rollovers are a great way to provide more information about elements on a page. We can extend that idea to implement rollovers for individual objects within the 3D scene by using the Vizi.Picker component we first saw in Chapter 9. This component provides general-purpose mouse handling that is dispatched when the mouse is over a particular object.

Let's go back to the code where we added the fade behavior to the windows. Note that the code also added picker components. See the lines in bold in Example 10-12. In a similar manner, we add pickers to the body parts and the wheels. Each listener uses a different tag—"glass," "body," and "wheels"—that will be passed to the application to identify the respective part being rolled over.

*Example 10-12. Adding Vizi.Picker components to implement rollovers*

```
// Add entry fade behavior to the windows, and pickers for
// rollover behavior
var that = this;
scene.map(/windows_front|windows_rear/, function(o) {
    var fader = new Vizi.FadeBehavior({duration:2, opacity:.8});
    o.addComponent(fader);
    setTimeout(function() {
        fader.start();
    }, 2000);

    var picker = new Vizi.Picker;
    picker.addEventListener("mouseover", function(event) {
        that.onMouseOver("glass", event); });
    picker.addEventListener("mouseout", function(event) {
        that.onMouseOut("glass", event); });
    o.addComponent(picker);
});
...
// Add pickers for rollover behavior
scene.map(/body2|rear_view_arm_L|rear_view_arm_R/, function(o) {
    var picker = new Vizi.Picker;
    picker.addEventListener("mouseover", function(event) {
        that.onMouseOver("body", event); });
    picker.addEventListener("mouseout", function(event) {
        that.onMouseOut("body", event); });
    o.addComponent(picker);
});

scene.map("wheels", function(o) {

    var picker = new Vizi.Picker;
    picker.addEventListener("mouseover", function(event) {
        that.onMouseOver("wheels", event); });
    picker.addEventListener("mouseout", function(event) {
        that.onMouseOut("wheels", event); });
    o.addComponent(picker);
});
```

The helper methods `Futurgo.onMouseOver()` and `Futurgo.onMouseOut()` simply dispatch to the `onMouseOver` and `onMouseOut` callbacks registered when the `Futurgo` class was instantiated (see Example 10-5).

The rollover behaviors are depicted in Figure 10-8. Whenever the mouse is over one of these objects, a DIV is shown at the approximate *y* location of the mouse cursor, toward the right of the scene window.

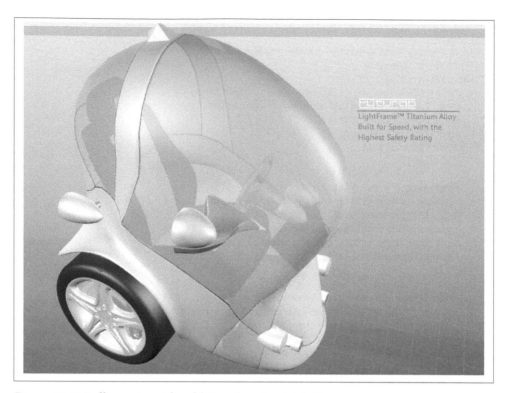

*Figure 10-8. Rollovers provide additional product detail*

## Controlling Animations from the User Interface

We can also use 2D interface elements in the HTML page to control behaviors within the 3D scene. When we click either the Interior or the LTD Racing tab on the righthand side, it triggers animations in the Futurgo. The code in the HTML page sets up on click handlers that call methods of the Futurgo object, as shown in Example 10-13. Those methods call the viewer's playAnimation() and stopAnimation() methods to get the job done. But note that there is one subtlety here: we would like to make the windows explode out when Interior is clicked the first time, and explode back in when it is clicked again. Rather than creating separate animations for the explode-out and explode-in, we simply play the animations *backward* the second time. Have a look at the Futurgo method playCloseAnimations(): it passes additional arguments to the viewer. The second argument, loop, is set to false, but the third argument, reverse, is set to true. Like Tween.js, Vizi's animation engine contains the built-in ability to play animations in either direction.

*Example 10-13. Controlling animations from the user interface*

```
Futurgo.prototype.playOpenAnimations = function() {
    this.playAnimation("animation_window_rear_open");
    this.playAnimation("animation_window_front_open");
}

Futurgo.prototype.playCloseAnimations = function() {
    this.playAnimation("animation_window_rear_open", false, true);
    this.playAnimation("animation_window_front_open", false, true);
}

Futurgo.prototype.toggleInterior = function() {
    this.vehicleOpen = !this.vehicleOpen;
    var that = this;
    if (this.vehicleOpen) {
        this.playOpenAnimations();
    }
    else {
        this.playCloseAnimations();
    }
}

Futurgo.prototype.playWheelAnimations = function() {
    this.playAnimation("animation_wheel_L", true);
    this.playAnimation("animation_wheel_R", true);
    this.playAnimation("animation_wheel_front", true);
}

Futurgo.prototype.stopWheelAnimations = function() {
    this.stopAnimation("animation_wheel_L");
    this.stopAnimation("animation_wheel_R");
    this.stopAnimation("animation_wheel_front");
}

Futurgo.prototype.toggleWheelAnimations = function() {
    this.wheelsMoving = !this.wheelsMoving;
    if (this.wheelsMoving) {
        this.playWheelAnimations();
    }
    else {
        this.stopWheelAnimations();
    }
}
```

## Changing Colors Using the Color Picker

Any self-respecting product page must provide the ability to change colors; Futurgo is
no exception. We have incorporated a jQuery color picker widget to let users select one
of 16 million different shades for their vehicle. Changing the color in the picker widget
updates the color of the Futurgo frame instantly. See Figure 10-9.

*Figure 10-9. Changing colors using the color picker*

Recall the setup code that we used to wire up the frame parts for mouse rollover. Let's look at that code again, from the Futurgo's `onLoadComplete()` method. In Example 10-14, note the recursive call to `map()`: for each node found in the regular expression, we find all of its visuals, and add the Three.js material contained in that visual into the array `part_materials`.

*Example 10-14. Setup code to store the Futurgo body materials*

```
    var frame_parts_exp =
/rear_view_arm_L|rear_view_arm_R|rear_view_frame_L|rear_view_frame_R/;

    scene.map(frame_parts_exp, function(o) {
        o.map(Vizi.Visual, function(v) {
            that.part_materials.push(v.material);
        });
    });
```

Now that we have the materials stored, we can manipulate them from the user interface. `Futurgo` defines two more methods, one each for getting and setting the body color, that are used by the HTML page code's color picker; see Example 10-15.

*Example 10-15. Code to get/set Futurgo body colors*

```
Futurgo.prototype.getBodyColor = function() {
    var color = '#ffffff';
    if (this.part_materials.length) {
        var material = this.part_materials[0];
```

```
        if (material instanceof THREE.MeshFaceMaterial) {
            color = '#' + material.materials[0].color.getHexString();
        }
        else {
            color = '#' + material.color.getHexString();
        }
    }

    return color;
}

Futurgo.prototype.setBodyColor = function(r, g, b) {

    // Convert from hex rgb to float
    r /= 255;
    g /= 255;
    b /= 255;

    var i, len = this.part_materials.length;
    for (i = 0; i < len; i++) {
        var material = this.part_materials[i];
        if (material instanceof THREE.MeshFaceMaterial) {
            var j, mlen = material.materials.length;
            for (j = 0; j < mlen; j++) {
                material.materials[j].color.setRGB(r, g, b);
            }
        }
        else {
            material.color.setRGB(r, g, b);
        }
    }
}
```

getBodyColor() returns the current diffuse color of the body's materials. Even though there are several materials in the list, we actually only need to get the value of the first one, because (in theory) they are all the same. We return the value as a CSS-style hex string. The color picker uses the value to initialize the color swatch and input values before it pops up the dialog.

For setBodyColor(), we must iterate through all of the materials in the array and set their diffuse color. Recall that in Three.js, some objects can have a material of type THREE.MeshFaceMaterial, which is actually an array of per-face materials for a single object. This code takes that into account. The RGB values passed to this function from the color picker are the RGB components of a hex color (i.e., integers in the range 0..255), whereas Three.js requires floats in the range 0..1, so this method does the conversion.

# Chapter Summary

This chapter described the detailed steps required to build a simple but fully working 3D web application. I chose a 3D product page as our example because it thoroughly illustrates the key concepts. After a brief look at the visual design process, we explored how 3D content can be created with Maya, a professional DCC tool, and converted into web-friendly glTF. We then used the Vizi framework to develop a utility for previewing and testing the 3D content. After that, we walked through how to integrate the content into the application's web page. Finally, we added several behaviors and interactions to provide polish, fun, and usability.

The process of developing 3D web applications is quite involved, but, given the proper tools and knowledge, you will also find it tractable. In the next chapter, I will introduce new forms of 3D behavior and interaction, but the overall process and techniques you learned in this chapter will apply to all our development going forward.

# CHAPTER 11

# Developing a 3D Environment

The techniques explored in Chapter 10 cover a lot of use cases. A single 3D model as the centerpiece of interactive content can be used to market, sell, inform, and entertain. But many 3D applications need more. If we want to develop an immersive game, an architectural walkthrough, or an interactive training system, we will need to learn how to create 3D *environments*, with multiple objects and more complex types of interaction.

In this chapter, we will develop a 3D environment with realistic scenery, moving objects, and the ability for the user to navigate within the scene by interactively controlling the camera. Extending the theme we developed in Chapter 10, we are going to create a virtual city and take the Futurgo concept car for a test drive. Figure 11-1 shows the application.

The Futurgo LTD waits parked on a city street, ready for a test drive. The scene spans a few city blocks, with skyscrapers looming in the distance against a dusky sky, reflected in the office buildings nearby. Using the mouse, you can click and drag to look up, down, left, and right. Move forward, back, left, and right using the arrow keys on your keyboard. Walk up to the Futurgo, and click on it to jump inside and take it for a spin. This world may look a little foreboding—but we'll be safe inside our own personal transportation device!

Load the file *Chapter 11/futurgoCity.html* into your browser to try it out. In the course of building this application, we will explore several development topics:

*Creating environment art*
> Assembling a realistic 3D city scene with roads, buildings, and park areas.

*Previewing and testing*
> Adding functionality to the previewer developed in the previous chapter. For this project, we need a previewer that can load multiple files into a single scene, show us the structure of the scene graph, and allow us to inspect the properties of various objects, in preparation for developing the application.

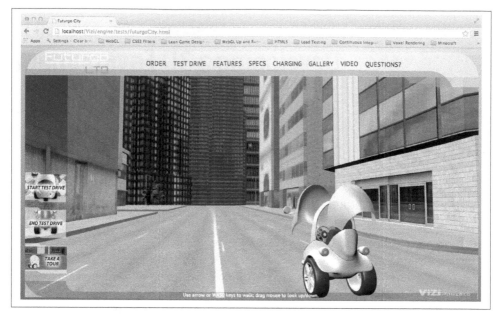

*Figure 11-1. The Futurgo concept car in a 3D environment*

*Creating a 3D background*

Adding a realistic skyline backdrop to the scene using a *skybox*—a textured cube placed infinitely far away in the background. The same skybox texture is also used as a cubic environment map reflecting the skyline on the city buildings and vehicle.

*Integrating the 3D with the application*

Managing the details of loading multiple models into the same application, and adjusting the car model's lighting, position, and other properties to match the surrounding environment.

*Implementing first-person navigation*

Providing ways for the user to look around and move within the scene via the mouse and keyboard, and implementing collision so that the user does not pass through solid objects.

*Working with multiple cameras*

Switching between cameras, allowing the user to see the environment from different views and explore it in multiple ways.

*Creating timed and animated transitions*

Using timers and animation techniques to create a sequence of actions when the user enters and exits the car.

*Scripting object behaviors*
Using the Vizi framework to create custom components to control the behavior and appearance of the Futurgo car.

*Using sound*
Enhancing the environment by adding HTML5 audio elements.

*Rendering dynamic textures*
Providing real-time user feedback by programmatically updating textures of 3D objects using the 2D Canvas API.

The virtual environment we will create in this chapter is quite simple. A typical game or other 3D environment would have many more objects and more sophisticated interactions, but the techniques covered here provide a good starting point for learning how to develop something more complex.

# Creating the Environment Art

To develop the 3D environment, I once again worked with artist TC Chang. Creating the art for a city backdrop is time-consuming, so TC and I decided to look for an existing model. We found an excellent candidate on TurboSquid, depicted in Figure 11-2.

The city model was created with the Lightwave modeler (*https://www.lightwave3d.com/overview/*). The artist had already converted it to a variety of formats, including Autodesk Maya. After we purchased and downloaded the model, TC brought it into Maya to prepare it for use in the application. The model came with fully detailed, textured buildings, but no lights. TC added three light sources, at which point the model was pretty much ready to go. After exporting to COLLADA for use in the previewer (see next section), we found one small issue with transparency on some texture maps; overall, however, it required very little additional art labor to use this model in the application.

# Previewing and Testing the Environment

To test a complex model like the city scene, we need a previewer similar to the one we built in Chapter 10, but with more functionality. The new, improved previewer, shown in Figure 11-3, adds the following features:

*Multiple viewing modes*
The ability to view content as either a single model with the camera pointed at its center, or as a scene with the camera pointed toward the ground plane.

*Scene graph inspection*
A tree-based view of the scene graph showing object names and parent/child relationships.

*Figure 11-2. City model created by ES3DStudios (http://www.turbosquid.com/FullPre view/Index.cfm/ID/652874); image courtesy TurboSquid*

*Object inspection*
> A pop-up property sheet that displays the details of each object, including transform information, mesh statistics, material properties, and camera and light parameters.

*Bounding box display*
> A wireframe box displayed around the selected object, with an option to display wireframe bounding boxes around all the objects in the scene.

*Previewing multiple objects*
> The ability to load multiple additional objects into the same preview so the combined result can be viewed and tested.

Launch the file *Chapter 11/previewer.html*. Click the Open button to see a file open dialog; open the file *../models/futurgo_city/futurgo_city.dae*. Using the Cameras list, select the camera labeled [default] to free-navigate. Using the mouse to rotate and the trackpad/scroll wheel to zoom, you can inspect the city model. (Note that the other cameras do not allow you to free-navigate with the mouse—only [default].)

*Figure 11-3. The city environment displayed in the Vizi previewer*

## Previewing the Scene in First-Person Mode

As you rotate and zoom the city model, you may notice that the camera never quite reaches the ground (street) level of the scene. This is because the previewer is designed by default to treat the model as a single object, with the camera view pointed at the geometric center of the object. The single-object scheme doesn't work so well for environments, so we have added another viewing mode to help.

At the top right of the previewer interface, there is a radio button group allowing you to switch viewing modes. The group is labeled Controller, to distinguish between two different *camera controller* modes, Model and First Person (or FPS). Our city application will be using a first-person controller; that is, one designed for navigating within an environment as opposed to looking at a single model. (First-person navigation will be discussed in some detail later in this chapter.) Click the FPS button; the camera will drop so that the center of rotation is now at street level, and you can zoom directly to the street.

Note that the FPS mode of the previewer does not actually use a first-person navigation mode to view the model. It simply places the camera in a similar position to the camera you would see in real first-person mode, one that is more suitable for previewing a full environment. The previewer is still using a model controller internally, so that we can zoom and rotate around the entire model quickly. In other words, sometimes we want to treat the scene as a single model for easy manipulation, and other times we want to emulate the views we will see when navigating the environment within the application.

The FPS button for the previewer user interface is a simple hack that gives us the best of both.

## Inspecting the Scene Graph

As the scenes we work with become more complex, we need the previewer tool to be able to view them at a finer level of detail. The city scene, for example, consists of over 200 separate meshes, as indicated in the Scene Stats pane in the previewer. To program interactivity into the application, we will need to find the names, sizes, and locations of the individual objects, as well as other properties such as their type (e.g., mesh, camera, or light), and how the objects are grouped into hierarchies. This is especially important when working with models obtained from a third party, where we were not in close communication with the artist when the content was created.

One crude way to inspect the scene graph is to open the COLLADA or glTF file in a text editor and search for specific text strings indicating the type. But it would be a maddening experience for most developers, and it would require detailed technical knowledge of how those file formats are organized. (I personally know both file formats very well; however, I have no patience for poring through huge text files looking for needles in a haystack.) A much better approach is to have the previewer tool present this information for us.

The enhanced previewer contains a new pane, Scene, with a listbox presenting a scrolling tree view of the scene graph hierarchy. Take a moment to scroll through the list, and click on the plus and minus icons to expand/contract the levels of the hierarchy and see how it is organized: at the top level, there are a handful of lights, followed by a group named MidTower_Block_01, and then a few cameras. Notice the plus sign next to the group. If you click on that, the group expands to show the next level of children, with names like Tower_A_01, Roof_Detail_01, and so on. Some of those groups can themselves expand to show additional child objects.

Armed with the ability to see node names and hierarchical relationships within the scene, we can now determine the objects to which we will add interactivity and other details in the running application. For example, after loading the scene into the application, we plan to add environment maps that reflect the skybox background, but only to the buildings, not to the roads or park areas. A scan through the scene hierarchy shows us that the building names all begin with "Tower" or "Office," so we will be able to use the Vizi.Object.map() scene graph API method to find all objects that match a regular expression with this pattern, and change their materials. We will walk through the code to do this a little later in the chapter.

The tree view control used in the previewer was implemented with a jQuery plugin called dynatree (*http://code.google.com/p/dynatree/*). Example 11-1 shows the code to initialize the tree view control with various options, and set up handlers for when items are clicked or double-clicked. The source code for the previewer can be found in the file *Chapter 11/previewer.html*.

*Example 11-1. Initializing the dynatree tree view control*

```
function initSceneTree(viewer) {
    // Initialize the tree inside the <div> element.
    $("#scene_tree").dynatree({
        imagePath: "./images/previewer_skin/",
        title: "Scene Graph",
        minExpandLevel: 2,
        selectMode: 1,
        onDblClick: function(node) {
            openSceneNode(viewer, node);
        },
        onActivate: function(node) {
            selectSceneNode(viewer, node);
            if (infoPopupVisible) {
                openSceneNode(viewer, node);
            }
        },
        onDeactivate: function(node) {
        },
        onFocus: function(node) {
        },
        onBlur: function(node) {
        },
    });
}
```

Now let's talk about how we populate the tree view control based on the contents of the scene graph after a scene file is loaded. First, we have a line in the load callback to call a helper function, updateSceneTree().

```
function onLoadComplete(data, loadStartTime)
{
    // Hide the loader bar
    var loadStatus = document.getElementById("loadStatus");
    loadStatus.style.display = 'none';

    viewer.replaceScene(data);

    var loadTime = (Date.now() - loadStartTime) / 1000;
    var loadTimeStats = document.getElementById("load_time_stats");
    loadTimeStats.innerHTML = "Load time<br>" + loadTime.toFixed(2) + "s"
    // Vizi.System.log("Loaded " + loadTime.toFixed(2) + " seconds.");

    updateSceneTree(viewer);
    updateCamerasList(viewer);
    updateLightsList(viewer);
    updateAnimationsList(viewer);
    updateMiscControls(viewer);
```

```
        if (viewer.cameraNames.length > 1) {
            selectCamera(1);
        }

        addRollovers(viewer, data.scene);
    }
```

updateSceneTree() does a couple of things. First, it reinitializes the tree control widget, in case it was previously populated for viewing another scene, by calling removeChil dren() on the root node of the tree view. Then, it calls another function, buildScene Tree(), to iterate through the scene graph and populate the items in the tree control. Note that the call is wrapped in a setTimeout() to delay it slightly; the delay makes for a friendlier user experience. Building a tree view with dynatree takes a little bit of time, and we don't want that to slow down the initial rendering of the scene. So we put in a placeholder message to start, which we rip out once the timeout fires.

```
    function updateSceneTree(viewer) {

        // Sample: add a hierarchic branch using code.
        // This is how we would add tree nodes programatically
        var rootNode = $("#scene_tree").dynatree("getRoot");
        rootNode.removeChildren();
        var initMessage = rootNode.addChild({
            title: "Initializing...",
            isFolder: false,
        });

        setTimeout(function() {
            rootNode.removeChild(initMessage);
            rootNode.expand(false);
            var i, len = viewer.scenes.length;
            for (i = 0; i < len; i++) {
                buildSceneTree(viewer.scenes[i], rootNode);
            }
        }, 1000);
    }
```

The code to populate the scene tree display is actually fairly simple. The source for function buildSceneTree() is located in the file *Chapter 11/sceneTree.js*. Example 11-2 shows the function in its entirety.

*Example 11-2. Populating the scene tree display*

```
sceneTreeMap = {};

buildSceneTree = function(scene, tree) {

    function build(object, node, level) {

        var noname = level ? "[object]" : "Scene";
```

```
    var childNode = node.addChild({
        title: object.name ? object.name : noname,
        expand: level <= 1,
        activeVisible:true,
        vizi:object,
    });

    sceneTreeMap[object._id] = childNode;

    var i, len = object._children.length;
    for (i = 0; i < len; i++) {
        build(object._children[i], childNode, level+1);
    }
}

build(scene, tree, 0);

}
```

First, we initialize a global object, sceneTreeMap, which will be used to associate Vizi objects in the Vizi scene graph with items in the tree view control. We will use this shortly to support clicking on an object within the scene, and seeing the associated item highlighted in the control.

Inside the body of buildSceneTree(), we define a nested function, build(), that will recursively add items to the tree control. For each object in the Vizi scene graph, the function creates a new tree control node by calling node.addChild(). This method creates a new item with the supplied parameters.

title specifies the label to display for the item. expand indicates whether to initially display the item expanded; we do this only for items at the top level of the scene graph. Setting activeVisible tells the tree view control to scroll to an item and select it if it is "activated" (i.e., selected from within the code, such as when the associated object is clicked within the scene). The last parameter passed in is vizi, the Vizi scene graph object that will be used whenever the user clicks on an item in the tree view control. When clicked, the previewer will highlight the object with a yellow wireframe box, and double-clicking will display a pop up with its properties (see the next section).

Once the tree control item is created, we add it to sceneTreeMap for later use, and call build() recursively to add tree control items for the object's children, if it has any.

 A lot of work goes into building a good HTML-based tree view. Thankfully, the developers of dynatree have saved us that pain. dynatree lets you instantly create a tree view of any hierarchical HTML list. It also has a feature-packed, easy-to-use API for creating/modifying/deleting items, and it supports full visual customization. dynatree is hosted on Google code (*http://code.google.com/p/dynatree/*).

# Inspecting Object Properties

The previewer allows us to inspect each object's properties. Double-click on an object in the scene tree view, and a tabbed jQuery dialog, or *property sheet*, pops up to display the details. See the screenshot in Figure 11-4. The property sheet shows the properties for the object named `Tower_D_01`. It contains three tabs: one for the transform information (position, rotation, and scale); one with details on the geometry, including the number of vertices and faces in the mesh, and its bounding box; and finally, information about the material, including the shading model, colors, and name of the image file for the texture map.

*Figure 11-4. Using the previewer to inspect object properties*

The previewer also allows us to inspect an object's properties by clicking on the object itself in the 3D scene. If you single-click on the object while the property sheet is still displayed, its contents will be replaced with properties for the new object. If the property sheet pop up is not visible, you can double-click on the object to pop up the dialog with the new properties.

Example 11-3 shows the code that adds click handling within the 3D scene (located in the source file *Chapter 11/previewer.html*), so that the user can select individual objects. The function `addRollovers()` uses the Vizi scene graph API method `map()` to find every object in the scene and add mouse handling by creating a new `Vizi.Picker` object. The code adds event handlers for mouse down, up, over, and double-click.

*Example 11-3. Implementing object selection within the scene*

```
function addRollover(viewer, o) {
    var picker = new Vizi.Picker;
    picker.addEventListener("mouseover", function(event) {
        onPickerMouseOver(viewer, o, event); });
    picker.addEventListener("mouseout", function(event) {
        onPickerMouseOut(viewer, o, event); });
    picker.addEventListener("mouseup", function(event) {
        onPickerMouseUp(viewer, o, event); });
    picker.addEventListener("dblclick", function(event) {
        onPickerMouseDoubleClick(viewer, o, event); });
    o.addComponent(picker);
}

function addRollovers(viewer, scene) {
    scene.map(Vizi.Object, function(o) {
        addRollover(viewer, o);
    });
}
```

The event handler code for mouse up, which is used to detect a single click, and the handler for mouse double-click are shown next. They are almost identical. First, we check the button code of the event, because the previewer supports selection only with the left mouse button. If the left mouse button was used, we call `Vizi.Viewer`'s high lightObject() method. This draws a yellow wireframe box around the clicked object. (We will look at the details of implementing bounding box highlighting in the next section.)

Now, we highlight the associated item in the tree view, using the Vizi object's _id property—a property that is automatically generated by the Vizi engine when the object is created—as the index to look up which tree item to highlight. Finally, if it is a single click and the property sheet is already visible (flagged in the Boolean variable infoPo pupVisible), we call openSceneNode(), a helper function that repopulates the property sheet's contents with the newly selected node. For the double-click case, we call open SceneNode() regardless, and the dialog will be popped up if it was not already visible.

```
function onPickerMouseUp(viewer, o, event) {
    if (event.button == 0) {
        viewer.highlightObject(o);
        node = selectSceneNodeFromId(viewer, o._id);
        if (node && infoPopupVisible) {
            openSceneNode(viewer, node);
        }
    }
}

function onPickerMouseDoubleClick(viewer, o, event) {
    if (event.button == 0) {
        viewer.highlightObject(o);
```

```
            node = selectSceneNodeFromId(viewer, o._id);
            openSceneNode(viewer, node);
        }
    }
```

# Displaying Bounding Boxes

The previewer uses bounding box display for a couple of purposes: to highlight the selected object, and to show the bounding boxes for all objects if you choose that option in the user interface.

To highlight the selected object, `Vizi.Viewer` provides a method called `highlightOb ject()`. Example 11-4 shows the implementation. First, the viewer removes the highlight on the current object, if one exists. Then, it computes the bounding box of the new object, using that to create a yellow wireframe box that it will place around the object.

There are a few subtleties to this; see the lines of code highlighted in bold. We create a `Vizi.Decoration` object to contain the bounding box cube geometry. This class is a special subclass of `Vizi.Visual` that the framework uses to render content that you can see, but not interact with; it will not interfere with picking or collision. After that, we add the decoration to the *parent* of the object, not the object itself. The bounding box for any object is computed in the coordinate system of the parent, so we need to add it to the scene graph as a child of the parent in order for the box to be transformed correctly.

*Example 11-4. Creating the highlight box for the selected object*

```
Vizi.Viewer.prototype.highlightObject = function(object) {

    if (this.highlightedObject) {
        this.highlightedObject._parent.removeComponent(
            this.highlightDecoration);
    }

    if (object) {
        var bbox = Vizi.SceneUtils.computeBoundingBox(object);

        var geo = new THREE.CubeGeometry(bbox.max.x - bbox.min.x,
                bbox.max.y - bbox.min.y,
                bbox.max.z - bbox.min.z);

        var mat = new THREE.MeshBasicMaterial({color:0xaaaa00,
            transparent:false,
            wireframe:true, opacity:1})

        var mesh = new THREE.Mesh(geo, mat);
        this.highlightDecoration = new Vizi.Decoration({object:mesh});
        object._parent.addComponent(this.highlightDecoration);

        var center = bbox.max.clone().add(bbox.min)
                .multiplyScalar(0.5);
```

```
        this.highlightDecoration.position.add(center);
    }

    this.highlightedObject = object;
}
```

The previewer allows you to see the bounding boxes for all objects. In the Miscellaneous pane on the bottom right, there is a checkbox labeled Boxes. Click that to turn on bounding box display. You should see green wireframe objects similar to those depicted in Figure 11-5.

*Figure 11-5. The previewer displaying bounding boxes for all objects in the scene*

The code to display bounding boxes for each object is similar to creating the highlight box, only this time we apply it to every object in the scene graph using the Vizi scene graph map() API method. See Example 11-5.

*Example 11-5. Creating rendered bounding boxes for all objects in the scene*

```
this.sceneRoot.map(Vizi.Object, function(o) {
    if (o._parent) {
        var bbox = Vizi.SceneUtils.computeBoundingBox(o);

        var geo = new THREE.CubeGeometry(bbox.max.x - bbox.min.x,
                bbox.max.y - bbox.min.y,
                bbox.max.z - bbox.min.z);
        var mat = new THREE.MeshBasicMaterial(
```

```
                {color:0x00ff00, transparent:true,
                     wireframe:true, opacity:.2})
          var mesh = new THREE.Mesh(geo, mat);
          var decoration = new Vizi.Decoration({object:mesh});
          o._parent.addComponent(decoration);

          var center = bbox.max.clone().add(bbox.min)
                 .multiplyScalar(0.5);
          decoration.position.add(center);
          decoration.object.visible = this.showBoundingBoxes;
      }
});
```

Now, when the user clicks the Boxes option to toggle that feature, the previewer calls the viewer's `setBoundingBoxesOn()` method. The function uses `map()` to find each object of type `Vizi.Decoration` and toggle its visibility by setting its `visible` property.

```
Vizi.Viewer.prototype.setBoundingBoxesOn = function(on)
{
    this.showBoundingBoxes = !this.showBoundingBoxes;
    var that = this;
    this.sceneRoot.map(Vizi.Decoration, function(o) {
        if (!that.highlightedObject || (o != that.highlightDecoration)) {
            o.visible = that.showBoundingBoxes;
        }
    });
}
```

## Previewing Multiple Objects

When you are building an environment using multiple objects, it is critical to be able to preview and test them together. We need to make sure objects are modeled to the same scale, positioned properly relative to each other, lit compatibly, and so on. This is especially true if the objects are coming from multiple sources, created by different artists, or hosted at different model-sharing sites.

Let's bring the Futurgo car model into the city scene to test these properties. Click Add on the menu bar at the top. In the file selection dialog, choose *../models/futurgo_mobile/futurgo_mobile.json*. (Make sure you are using the default camera and are looking at the main road in the center of the scene; this is where the model will appear.) The model should appear in the center of the scene. Zoom up to it for a closer look, as depicted in Figure 11-6.

The code to add more models into the existing scene is nearly identical to that for loading the original model: create a `Vizi.Loader` object, add an event listener for when the model is loaded, and in the event listener, add new scene objects to the viewer. The only difference is that we will *add* the objects to the viewer, not replace them. Example 11-6 shows the code (from source file *Chapter 11/previewer.html*). We call `viewer.addTo`

Scene(), which adds the objects to the running scene graph (in this case, the Futurgo car model), and updates the viewer's data structures. Then we update the user interface elements as before: the tree view, and the lists of lights, cameras, and animations.

*Figure 11-6. The Futurgo model added to the city scene*

*Example 11-6. Inserting additional models into the scene*

```
function onAddComplete(data, loadStartTime)
{
    // Hide the loader bar
    var loadStatus = document.getElementById("loadStatus");
    loadStatus.style.display = 'none';

    viewer.addToScene(data);

    var loadTime = (Date.now() - loadStartTime) / 1000;
    var loadTimeStats = document.getElementById("load_time_stats");
    loadTimeStats.innerHTML = "Load time<br>" + loadTime.toFixed(2) + "s"
    // Vizi.System.log("Loaded " + loadTime.toFixed(2) + " seconds.");

    updateSceneTree(viewer);
    updateCamerasList(viewer);
    updateLightsList(viewer);
    updateAnimationsList(viewer);
    updateMiscControls(viewer);

    addRollovers(viewer, data.scene);
}
```

You may have noticed how overly bright the Futurgo looked when it was added to the scene. This is because the Futurgo model contains its own lights, which we used in the application we built in Chapter 10. I could have asked TC to make a special version of the car without lights for use in this application, but there is no need. Using the previewer, we can figure out which lights are causing the problem and turn them off, then note the names of the lights for when we want to do the same in the application.

Using the previewer's Lights list, we turn off the offending lights. I had a notion (correctly so) that they would be lights added to the end of the list, since the Futurgo model was added to the scene last. So I turned off the three point lights at the end of the list. The car still looked a little washed-out, so I turned off the ambient light as well. This did the trick. Figure 11-7 shows the result with those four lights turned off. See the oval highlighting the changed values in the user interface.

*Figure 11-7. The Futurgo model in the city scene, after the lighting has been adjusted*

## Using the Previewer to Find Other Scene Issues

Using the previewer turned up an additional technical issue with this scene: the trees. The creator of this scene used a time-tested hack to render trees cheaply: a set of overlapping flat polygons with texture maps of the tree from different angles. Typically, there are two vertical polygons arranged in an X pattern, and one or more horizontal polygons crisscrossing the X shape. This is one of those cheap tricks modelers have used for years to save polygons; imagine the number of triangles required to make the leaves of a tree look realistic otherwise.

The only problem with using the author's tree setup in WebGL is the choice of image file format: the textures for each polygon were created as a pair of Microsoft BMP files, one with the color information, and the second with an alpha mask. We don't know how to deal with that easily in Vizi/Three.js. It is technically possible, but the engine does not currently support it. So I asked TC to convert the tree BMP image file pairs to a single PNG with alpha channel. He did so, updated the Maya file, and re-exported. The before-and-after comparison is shown in Figure 11-8.

 While the image on the right hardly seems better, it actually renders properly in the live application. The artifact you see here is due to a limitation of the current previewer implementation. Even though there is transparency information in the PNG file, neither Vizi nor Three.js know this fact without the author setting a transparency value on the material itself. Since those values were not specified in the content, we will have to set them manually in the application after the scene is loaded.

*Figure 11-8. This side-by-side comparison of trees using overlapping rectangular geometry depicts the texture maps in the previewer, before and after conversion from two BMP files with alpha mask (left) to a single PNG (right); the white areas surrounding the trees on the right are artifacts of the previewer, and will disappear in the application code when we explicitly tell Three.js to use transparency*

# Creating a 3D Background Using a Skybox

Now that we've previewed and debugged the city art, and seen how the Futurgo will integrate with it, it's time to start building the application. But first, we need to deal with another topic. The art for this city model is nice, but it is confined to the four city blocks it spans. If we want a compelling, realistic scene through which to drive the car, we need to create the illusion of a much bigger city. We can do that by rendering a skybox background.

# 3D Skyboxes

Unlike a typical background image for a web page, we need the background for our scene to be 3D: as the camera moves around, we expect to see the backdrop change. A *skybox* is a panoramic image consisting of six texture maps wrapped on the inside of a cube. The cube is rendered from a stationary camera that rotates along with the camera, exposing different parts of the background. Skyboxes are a dead simple way to provide a realistic 3D painted background.

The Three.js example set features a few demonstrations of skybox functionality. Open the file *webgl_materials_cubemap_balls_reflection.html* in the Three.js examples to see one in action. This looks great in this example. However, it is based on a crude implementation of skyboxes that has a serious limitation. In these examples, the authors simply create a really big cube at the outer edges of the scene. It looks far away, but if you were able to navigate around the scene, you would actually be able to get closer to one of the edges of the box, and eventually even reach it, destroying the illusion.

 Illusion is everything in 3D graphics. Skyboxes create a convincing illusion of an infinite background landscape—but only if you never get closer to it as you move. If you have ever seen Peter Weir's genius film *The Truman Show*, recall the scene in which Truman slams into a solid wall, painted with the backdrop of the artificial world created for him by the show's director. Once he ran into that wall... the jig was up.

## The Vizi Skybox Object

To create a convincing city scene, we need to use a proper skybox. Happily, the Vizi framework comes with one. Before we put a skybox into the city application, let's create a simple example to show how it's done. Open the sample in *Chapter 11/skybox.html*, depicted in Figure 11-9. Using the mouse, rotate around to see the whole background. Using the trackpad or scroll wheel, zoom in and out. The cube gets closer and farther away, but the box stays infinitely far away. Note how the skybox background is also reflected on the surface of the foreground cube; this effect is accomplished through a cubic environment map created with the same texture.

The panoramic image of the skybox consists of six bitmaps laid out as depicted in Figure 11-10. The bitmaps have been created so that they stitch together perfectly when mapped onto the inside faces of a cube.

Figure 11-9. A skybox background, with a cube in the foreground—as the user moves forward and back, the cube gets closer or farther away, but the background remains at an infinite distance; the cube reflects the background art using a cubic environment map with the same texture

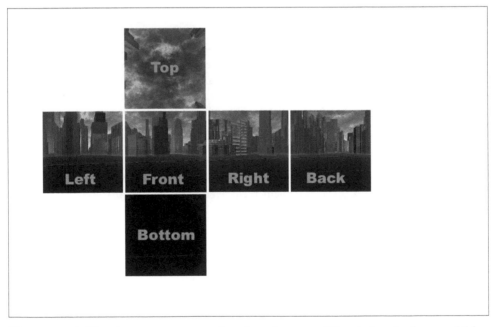

Figure 11-10. The six textures composing the cube map of the skybox background (skybox textures from http://www.3delyvisions.com/skf1.htm)

Example 11-7 shows the code to create the skybox and add it to the scene. First, we use the Three.js utility to create a cubic texture map, `THREE.ImageUtils.loadTexture Cube()`. Then, we call a Vizi function to create the skybox prefab (or prebuilt object), `Vizi.Prefabs.Skybox()`. We then set the skybox's `texture` property to the cube texture, and add it to the application.

*Example 11-7. Creating the skybox background*

```
var app = new Vizi.Application({ container : container });

// Skybox from http://www.3delyvisions.com/
// http://www.3delyvisions.com/skf1.htm
var path = "../images/sky35/";

var urls = [ path + "rightcity.jpg", path + "leftcity.jpg",
             path + "topcity.jpg", path + "botcity.jpg",
             path + "frontcity.jpg", path + "backcity.jpg" ];

var cubeTexture = THREE.ImageUtils.loadTextureCube( urls );

var skybox = Vizi.Prefabs.Skybox();
var skyboxScript = skybox.getComponent(Vizi.SkyboxScript);
skyboxScript.texture = cubeTexture;

app.addObject(skybox);
```

 So…what's with this "prefab" business?

In Vizi, a *prefab* is a prebuilt set of objects and components that can be created and dropped right into a scene. The prefab design pattern occurs frequently in game engines such as Unity. Recall that in modern game engine design, the trend has moved away from creating classes to extend functionality, and toward aggregating simple components into richer structures.

In the case of the Vizi skybox, it is a cube set up to draw in the background and track the movements of the main camera so that it keeps the cube properly oriented. If you are curious about how the Vizi skybox prefab is implemented, refer to the file *objects/skybox.js* in the Vizi source tree.

The cube in this example appears to reflect the background skybox image. We did this easily, by using the same cubic texture map as an environment map on the cube's material. The code to do this is shown in Example 11-8.

*Example 11-8. Adding the cube map to a foreground object*

```
var cube = new Vizi.Object;

var visual = new Vizi.Visual(
        { geometry: new THREE.CubeGeometry(2, 2, 2),
            material: new THREE.MeshPhongMaterial({
                color:0xffffff,
                envMap:cubeTexture,
                reflectivity:0.8,
                refractionRatio:0.1
                })
        });


cube.addComponent(visual);
app.addObject(cube);
```

# Integrating the 3D Content into the Application

Using the previewer, we have browsed through the scene graph to find the names and properties of objects and gotten a look at lighting and other visual aspects of the content, taking note of things that need to be done with the models once loaded into the app. We also studied how to build a skybox background and reflect it onto objects in this scene. We are finally ready to assemble our 3D environment into an application.

## Loading and Initializing the Environment

The Futurgo test drive application is located in the HTML file *Chapter 11/futur goCity.html*. The jQuery-ready code for this file is very simple; it just creates an instance of the class FuturgoCity, which loads the models, assembles the scene, and runs the application. The source code for FuturgoCity can be found in the file *Chapter 11/ futurgoCity.js*.

The application's setup begins by loading the city model. The file load callback, onLoad Complete(), assembles the environment from there. Refer to Example 11-9. After calling the viewer's replaceScene() method to add the newly loaded content to the scene, we ask the viewer to use first-person navigation by calling setController("FPS"). (We will discuss camera controllers and first-person navigation in detail later in the chapter.) We then save the information about the viewer's camera controller and current camera; we'll need those later. After that, we call several helper methods to add the skybox and environment maps, and do other important setup tasks.

*Example 11-9. Callback code called after environment load*

```
FuturgoCity.prototype.onLoadComplete = function(data, loadStartTime)
{
    var scene = data.scene;
    this.scene = data.scene;
    this.viewer.replaceScene(data);

    if (this.loadCallback) {
        var loadTime = (Date.now() - loadStartTime) / 1000;
        this.loadCallback(loadTime);
    }

    this.viewer.setController("FPS");
    this.cameraController = this.viewer.controllerScript;
    this.walkCamera = this.viewer.defaultCamera;

    this.addBackground();
    this.addCollisionBox();
    this.fixTrees();
    this.setupCamera();
    this.loadFuturgo();
}
```

addBackground() creates the skybox, as in the example from the previous section. Then, it adds the environment maps to the buildings. Recall that we used the previewer to find the names of the big buildings. All of them began with the string "Tower" or "Office." Note the line in bold with the regular expression. We use the Vizi scene graph map() method to find the matching objects, and set the environment map on the Three.js material for each object.

```
this.scene.map(/Tower.*|Office.*/, function(o) {

    var visuals = o.visuals;
    if (visuals) {
        for (var vi = 0; vi < visuals.length; vi++) {
            var v = visuals[vi];
            var material = v.material;
            if (material) {
                if (material instanceof THREE.MeshFaceMaterial) {
                    var materials = material.materials;
                    var mi, len = materials.length;
                    for (mi = 0; mi < len; mi++) {
                        addEnvMap(materials[mi]);
                    }
                }
                else {
                    addEnvMap(material);
                }
            }
        }
```

```
        }
    });
```

Next, we are going to add a collision box. Later in this chapter, we will see how to implement collision to go with navigating the scene in first-person mode. For now, here is the code to set up an invisible box at the boundaries of the city, so that we can't walk or drive outside of those limits. It is pretty simple: create a new `Vizi.Visual` that contains a cube with dimensions matching the bounding box of the scene, and make sure it is transparent by setting its material's `opacity` to 0. Additionally, we want to make sure that we collide against the *inside* of the cube, by asking Three.js to render the backfaces of the cube's geometry via setting its `side` property to the enumerated value `THREE.DoubleSide` (i.e., render both sides of the cube). The code is listed in Example 11-10.

*Example 11-10. Adding a collision box to the scene*

```
FuturgoCity.prototype.addCollisionBox = function() {

    var bbox = Vizi.SceneUtils.computeBoundingBox(this.scene);

    var box = new Vizi.Object;
    box.name = "_futurgoCollisionBox";

    var geometry = new THREE.CubeGeometry(bbox.max.x - bbox.min.x,
            bbox.max.y - bbox.min.y,
            bbox.max.z - bbox.min.z);

    var material = new THREE.MeshBasicMaterial({
        transparent:true,
        opacity:0,
        side:THREE.DoubleSide
        });

    var visual = new Vizi.Visual({
        geometry : geometry,
        material : material});

    box.addComponent(visual);

    this.viewer.addObject(box);
}
```

We also need to fix that transparency issue with the trees. In the method `fixTrees()`, we again use `map()` to find all nodes whose names begin with "Tree," find any visuals those nodes contain, and set the `transparent` property of their materials to `true`. This flag tells the Three.js rendering system to turn on alpha blending; without it, the trees would be drawn opaquely, as we saw in the previewer in Figure 11-8.

```
this.scene.map(/^Tree.*/, function(o) {

    o.map(Vizi.Visual, function(v){
        var material = v.material;
        if (material instanceof THREE.MeshFaceMaterial) {
            var materials = material.materials;
            var i, len = materials.length;
            for (i = 0; i < len; i++) {
                material = materials[i];
                material.transparent = true;
            }
        }
        else {
            material.transparent = true;
        }

    });
});
```

After placing the camera's position at a good spot for initial viewing, we are ready for the last big step in setting up the application: loading the car model.

## Loading and Initializing the Car Model

Loading and preparing the car model involves several activities: add the loaded model to the scene, add behaviors to fade the windows to various transparency levels, add environment maps to the windows and body to reflect the skybox, take out the extra lights we saw in the previewer, and finally, place the car. After all that, we will still need to set up the interactive objects for driving and animating the car, both of which we will discuss in upcoming sections.

Our file-loaded callback function begins as follows. Call `this.viewer.addToScene()` to add the object to the scene. Then, as with the application from the previous chapter, we add fade behaviors to the windows and start them off automatically, resulting in the two-second fade to semi-opaque. In addition, we save away the fader objects into the application object's property `faders`, an array that will be used later to fade the windows to even more transparent when we go inside the car, and back to semi-opaque when we exit the car. While we are iterating through the window materials, we also add the same environment map that is used on the buildings—namely, the cube map texture of the skyscrapers in the skybox background. Example 11-11 shows this sequence of calls.

*Example 11-11. Callback code to handle loading of the Futurgo car*

```
FuturgoCity.prototype.onFuturgoLoadComplete = function(data) {

    // Add the Futurgo to the scene
    this.viewer.addToScene(data);
    var futurgoScene = data.scene;
```

```
// Add some interaction and behaviors
var that = this;

// Add environment map and faders to the windows;
// fade the windows on start
this.faders = [];
futurgoScene.map(/windows_front|windows_rear/, function(o) {

    var fader = new Vizi.FadeBehavior({duration:2,
        opacity:FuturgoCity.OPACITY_SEMI_OPAQUE});
    o.addComponent(fader);
    fader.start();
    that.faders.push(fader);

    var visuals = o.visuals;
    var i, len = visuals.length;
    for (i = 0; i < len; i++) {
        visuals[i].material.envMap = that.envMap;
        visuals[i].material.reflectivity = 0.1;
        visuals[i].material.refractionRatio = 0.1;
    }

});
```

We then add the environment map to the body of the car (metal frame and rearview mirrors).

```
// Add environment map to the body
futurgoScene.map(/body2/, function(o) {
    var visuals = o.visuals;
    var i, len = visuals.length;
    for (i = 0; i < len; i++) {
        visuals[i].material.envMap = that.envMap;
        visuals[i].material.reflectivity = 0.1;
        visuals[i].material.refractionRatio = 0.1;
    }

});
```

Next, we iterate through all the parts of the body in order to add Vizi.Picker objects. These will allow us to click anywhere on the Futurgo to start the test drive. We save these away into the object's pickers array, because we are going to disable and re-enable each picker when entering and exiting the car, respectively.

Next, we deal with the lighting issues we saw when previewing the Futurgo imported into the scene using the previewer. The presence of the extra lights in the Futurgo model was causing it to look washed-out when combined with the lights that already existed in the scene. So we need to turn off all lights that came in with the Futurgo model; in addition, we need to turn off the ambient light supplied with the city model.

```
// The combined lighting from the two scenes
// makes the car look too washed-out;
// Turn off any lights that came with the car model
futurgoScene.map(Vizi.PointLight, function(light) {
    light.intensity = 0;
});

// Also turn off the ambient light that came with
// the city model
this.scene.map(/ambient/, function(o) {
    o.light.color.set(0, 0, 0);
});
```

Finally, we place the car in a good initial spot for viewing when we enter the scene. Since the camera's *x* and *z* position values are both zero, we place the car a few units to the right and back from that.

```
// Drop the Futurgo at a good initial position
var futurgo = futurgoScene.findNode("vizi_mobile");
futurgo.transform.position.set(2.33, 0, -6);
```

We still need to add some behaviors and interaction to drive the car, which we will cover in later sections—but at this point, the scene is fully assembled. You can see the skybox background and environment map reflections; the car is in place, with the windows faded and environment maps of the background reflecting on the car body. The result is depicted in Figure 11-11, a screenshot of the entry view when the page is loaded.

*Figure 11-11. Entry view of the Futurgo city application*

Let's take a moment to take this all in. Drag the mouse to look around; use the arrow keys to walk through the scene; see the buildings towering overhead, reflecting the twilight sky. We built this—with just a few days' work. That's a pretty impressive accomplishment.

OK, that's enough dawdling; time to get back to work.

# Implementing First-Person Navigation

Now that we have an environment loaded, we need to move around in it. We want to allow the user to explore the city on foot, or take a test drive in the Futurgo. In this section, we will discuss how to implement game-style walking navigation, also known as *first-person navigation*.

The term *first-person*, or *first-person perspective*, refers to rendering a 3D scene from the point of view of the user. Essentially, the camera is placed as if it were between the user's eyes. First-person *navigation* is a mode of moving the camera in response to mouse, keyboard, joystick, and/or game controller input. First-person navigation is very popular in video games, especially combat games known as *first-person shooters* (FPS).

On a desktop computer, first-person navigation is usually operated by the mouse and keyboard, with the mouse controlling the direction the camera points in, and the keyboard moving, sliding, or turning the user. Table 11-1 shows the typical keyboard and mouse bindings used in first-person navigation. The arrow keys are used to move the view forward, back, left, and right, with the *W*, *A*, *S*, and *D* keys (known collectively as "WASD" or "wazz-dee" keys) mirroring that functionality, which affords the use of the left hand to move while the mouse turns the camera (or shoots at enemies, in the case of a shooter game).

*Table 11-1. Typical keyboard and mouse bindings for first-person mode*

| Key/mouse action | Action |
| --- | --- |
| W, up arrow | Move forward |
| A, left arrow | Slide left |
| S, down arrow | Move back |
| D, right arrow | Slide right |
| Mouse drag up | Tilt camera up |
| Mouse drag down | Tilt camera down |
| Mouse drag left | Turn camera left |
| Mouse drag right | Turn camera right |

Take a walk around the city scene using the arrows or WASD keys; look up, down, left, and right by clicking and dragging the left mouse button. See Figure 11-12.

*Figure 11-12. Exploring the city in first-person mode*

# Camera Controllers

To implement first-person navigation, we are going to use an object known as a *camera controller*. Camera controllers, as the name suggests, control movement of the camera based on user input. `Vizi.Viewer` supports different camera controller modes: model and first-person. It automatically creates camera controller objects for each mode. Simply call the viewer's `setController()`, which takes a string indicating which controller to use; valid values are `"model"` and `"FPS"`.

The Futurgo application in Chapter 10 used the model controller, a camera controller designed to orbit the camera around the object, always facing at its center. The net effect is that the model appears to rotate as you drag the mouse, or get closer or farther away as you use the trackpad or scroll wheel (when in fact, the camera is being moved). This type of camera controller is perfect for an application that uses a single model. For the city application, however, we are going to use the first-person controller.

# First-Person Controller: The Math

The key to implementing a first-person controller is to translate changes in mouse position to rotations of the camera: dragging to the left or right rotates the camera about its current y-axis, for example, and dragging up or down rotates it about its x-axis. Movement based on the keyboard typically follows the direction the camera is facing: press the up arrow key, and the camera moves forward along the line of sight.

To get a feel for the math involved in programming a first-person controller, let's look at a few excerpts from the Vizi implementation. The update() method of Vizi.First PersonControls, called each time through the run loop, calculates the amount to rotate about the x- and y-axes. See the code listing in Example 11-12.

*Example 11-12. Vizi.FirstPersonControls code*

```
if (this.mouseDragOn || this.mouseLook) {

    var deltax = this.lastMouseX - this.mouseX;
    var dlon = deltax / this.viewHalfX * 900;
    this.lon += dlon * this.lookSpeed;

    var deltay = this.lastMouseY - this.mouseY;
    var dlat = deltay / this.viewHalfY * 900;
    this.lat += dlat * this.lookSpeed;

    this.theta = THREE.Math.degToRad( this.lon );

    this.lat = Math.max( - 85, Math.min( 85, this.lat ) );
    this.phi = THREE.Math.degToRad( this.lat );

    var targetPosition = this.target,
        position = this.object.position;

    targetPosition.x = position.x - Math.sin( this.theta );
    targetPosition.y = position.y + Math.sin( this.phi );
    targetPosition.z = position.z - Math.cos( this.theta );

    this.object.lookAt( targetPosition );

    this.lastMouseX = this.mouseX;
    this.lastMouseY = this.mouseY;
}
```

First, we compute the change in mouse *x* and *y* positions relative to the previous ones. We then convert that to a rotational delta as degrees of longitude and latitude. The local variable dlon represents the change in longitude in degrees. We compute that via the following formula:

```
var dlon = deltax / this.viewHalfX * 900;
```

We are using the change in mouse *x* position divided by half the width of the screen to calculate a percentage of the screen size that the mouse has moved. Each 10% of the screen width equates to 90 degrees of rotation (hence the multiply by 900). Then, we add this delta to the current longitudinal (horizontal) rotation:

```
this.lon += dlon * this.lookSpeed;
```

The longitudinal rotational in degrees is then converted to radians for use with Three.js, and saved in the property this.theta:

```
this.theta = THREE.Math.degToRad( this.lon );
```

In a similar manner, we calculate a new rotation for the latitude (vertical rotation) using changes in the mouse's *y* position and save that into this.phi. Now that we have new values for the latitude and longitude, we can rotate the view. We do this by calculating a "look at" position on a unit sphere centered at the camera position, and ask Three.js to have the camera look there using the camera's lookAt() method. Now, the camera is pointing in the new direction.

```
targetPosition.x = position.x - Math.sin( this.theta );
targetPosition.y = position.y + Math.sin( this.phi );
targetPosition.z = position.z - Math.cos( this.theta );
this.object.lookAt( targetPosition );
```

Camera movement follows the line of sight. If the user has pressed any of the navigation keys, we set the accompanying Boolean properties moveForward, moveBackward, moveLeft, and moveRight to flag that fact, and test those in update().

```
this.update = function( delta ) {

    this.startY = this.object.position.y;

    var actualMoveSpeed = delta * this.movementSpeed;

    if ( this.moveForward  )
        this.object.translateZ( - actualMoveSpeed );
    if ( this.moveBackward )
        this.object.translateZ( actualMoveSpeed );

    if ( this.moveLeft )
        this.object.translateX( - actualMoveSpeed );
    if ( this.moveRight )
        this.object.translateX( actualMoveSpeed );

    this.object.position.y = this.startY;
```

We use Three.js to help us calculate the camera's new position. The methods translateZ() and translateX() move the camera along those axes, respectively. Because the camera may be pointing up or down from the horizontal, this could result in movement upward in the *y* dimension. We don't want that to happen; we want to stay on the ground at all times. So we override any changes to the *y* position by setting it back to the previously saved value.

## Mouse Look

In this application, the user must click and drag the mouse to rotate the camera view. Camera controllers in many first-person games rotate the view when the mouse is moved, *without* having to click. This mode is often known as *mouse look*. It's very handy for full-screen first-person gaming, as it is faster and requires less effort; it also frees up the mouse up/down action for other things such as shooting or opening an inventory page.

For windowed web navigation, however, mouse look can be a disaster. The user might want to move the mouse in order to click on the browser's address bar or tabs, or to pick an action from the page's 2D interface. But any attempt to do that will also rotate the camera view within the 3D window, resulting in the camera "flying around" any time the user tries to do something. It's not fun. If you want to find out for yourself, try setting the controller's mouseLook property to true in this application, and see how frustrating it is. In my opinion, mouse look is really only for full-screen use.

 Mouse look can also go hand in glove with hiding the pointer, as is done in many first-person games. Newer browsers also support this feature, known variously as the *pointer lock* and *mouse lock* API. The official W3C recommendation on the feature can be found online (*https://dvcs.w3.org/hg/pointerlock/raw-file/tip/index.html*). There is also an excellent article on the topic by John McCutcheon of Google (*http://www.html5rocks.com/en/tutorials/pointerlock/intro/*).

## Simple Collision Detection

An important aspect in maintaining the illusion of a realistic environment is the use of *collision detection*: determining when the user's view (or any other object) collides with geometry in the scene, and preventing the object from passing through that geometry. It wouldn't be a convincing virtual cityscape if the user could just walk through walls.

In this section, we will look at implementing a very simple version of collision detection for use with the Futurgo city environment. It uses the Three.js math objects to cast a ray from the eye point, finding any objects lying along the line of sight. If any objects are found that are within a certain distance, this is considered a collision and we are not allowed to move in that direction.

The class Vizi.FirstPersonControllerScript is a component of the prefab that implements Vizi's first-person navigation system. Example 11-13 shows an excerpt from the code. First, we save the original camera position. Then, we let Vizi.FirstPerson Controls update the camera position based on the mouse and keyboard input, potentially resulting in a new camera position. We then call the helper method testColli sion() to determine if moving between the saved position and the new position would result in a collision; if so, we restore the camera back to its original position and dispatch a "collide" event in case someone is listening. (Which—trust me—someone will be. More on this later.)

*Example 11-13. Collision code from the first-person controller script*

```
Vizi.FirstPersonControllerScript.prototype.update = function()
{
    this.saveCamera();
    this.controls.update(this.clock.getDelta());
    var collide = this.testCollision();
    if (collide && collide.object) {
        this.restoreCamera();
        this.dispatchEvent("collide", collide);
    }
```

Now let's look at the method `testCollision()`. Recall the picking code from the discussion of `Vizi.Picker` in Chapter 9. The Vizi graphics system uses Three.js ray casting to find the intersection between a ray from the eye point through the geometry. If there is a ray segment that falls between the minimum distance, 1, and the maximum distance, 2, that intersects any geometry, an object will be returned and saved in the variable `collide`.

```
Vizi.FirstPersonControllerScript.prototype.testCollision = function() {

    this.movementVector.copy(this._camera.position).sub(this.savedCameraPos);
    if (this.movementVector.length()) {

        var collide = Vizi.Graphics.instance.objectFromRay(null,
                this.savedCameraPos,
                this.movementVector, 1, 2);

        if (collide && collide.object) {
            var dist = this.savedCameraPos.distanceTo(collide.hitPointWorld);
        }

        return collide;
    }

    return null;
}
```

 The preceding algorithm is about the simplest version of collision detection possible. We are using the camera position to cast a ray in the direction of viewing. Because it is a ray, it has no volume; it is infinitely thin. That is not very realistic. Real avatars have curves, or at least, volume. A more rigorous implementation would try to collide a sphere, cylinder, or other geometry against geometry in front of it. That's exactly what most game engines do. But for our purposes here, ray-based collision is enough to keep us from passing through walls.

# Working with Multiple Cameras

One of the great things about 3D is the ability to use different cameras so that we can render a scene from various points of view, using different viewing angles and aspect ratios. We could always use a single camera to achieve this, and dynamically change its properties as needed. However, Three.js makes it easy to create multiple cameras, and keep each one lying around for when it's needed. The Vizi framework wraps Three.js cameras into components, and also manages switching between them and doing other bookkeeping tasks under the covers such as updating their aspect ratios automatically when the rendering window is resized. We are going to take advantage of these features in the Futurgo city experience by creating a second camera placed inside the car. Figure 11-13 shows the view from inside the Futurgo using this additional camera.

*Figure 11-13. View from a camera placed inside the Futurgo vehicle*

Example 11-14 shows the code to create the second camera. First, we create a new Vizi.Object, driveCam, to hold the camera component. driveCam will be added as a child of the Futurgo car. Why? So that when the car moves—we'll get to this in a few pages— the camera will move along with it. Remember the discussion of the *transformation hierarchy* in earlier chapters: the transform properties of an object (position, rotation, scale) affect the transforms of its children. Whenever the car moves or turns, the camera comes along for the ride.

Next, we position the camera within the vehicle. Adding it as a child of the Futurgo places it at the car's origin by default; in this case, that means the camera would end up on the ground. So we place it appropriately. However, we have to do something a little gross to position it: when TC modeled the Futurgo, he left a scale value in there. (I verified this by loading the model into the previewer and checking the scale values of the top-level group.) Rather than ask TC to labor through rescaling the model, I simply adjusted the positional values of the camera to compensate for it by dividing the desired values by the scale of each dimension. The result is a camera positioned at eye level for a seated driver who is approximately six feet tall, as depicted in Figure 11-13.

*Example 11-14. Creating the drive camera*

```
// Drop a camera inside the vehicle
var driveCam = new Vizi.Object;
var camera = new Vizi.PerspectiveCamera;
camera.near = 0.01;
driveCam.addComponent(camera);
futurgo.addChild(driveCam);
// Account for scale in model so that
//   we can position the camera properly
var scaley = futurgo.transform.scale.y;
var scalez = futurgo.transform.scale.z;
var camy = FuturgoCity.AVATAR_HEIGHT_SEATED / scaley;
var camz = 0 / scalez;
driveCam.transform.position.set(0, camy, camz);
this.driveCamera = camera;
```

In the next section, I will show you how to switch to this camera, as part of a sequence of transitions to get in and out of the car to start and stop test-drive mode.

# Creating Timed and Animated Transitions

We're getting close to being able to take our test drive. Clicking on the Futurgo with the mouse, or clicking the Start Test Drive tab on the left, pops us inside the car so that we can drive. In order to make this fun and a somewhat real-feeling experience, we will program a series of transitions and animations using a combination of Vizi components and simple timers based on `setTimeout()`.

The sequence, implemented in the code listed in Example 11-15 and subsequent code fragments, is as follows:

1. Disable picking from inside the car. We don't want stray mouse clicks to trigger unwanted animations.

2. Open the car by animating the windows out.

3. After the window open animation finishes, jump inside the car.

4. Once inside the car, close the windows and fade them to fully transparent so that we can see outside. Also turn down the volume of the city background sound. Finally, enable the scripts that drive the car.

After performing the preceding sequence, we will be inside the car and ready to drive. Let's look at the code step by step.

First, we turn off the pickers and start the open animations.

*Example 11-15. Animating transitions to enter the car and start test drive*

```
FuturgoCity.prototype.startTestDrive = function(event) {

    if (this.testDriveRunning)
        return;

    this.testDriveRunning = true;

    // Disable the pickers while inside the car body
    var i, len = this.pickers.length;
    for (i = 0; i < len; i++) {
        this.pickers[i].enabled = false;
    }

    // Open the car windows
    this.playOpenAnimations();
```

After a one-second delay we do the next step: jump to the `driveCamera` view. We do this by setting the camera's `active` property to `true` (which, under the covers, tells Vizi to render using this new camera). We also disable the first-person camera controller's ability to move by setting its `move` property to `false`. We still want to be able to look around, so we continue to use the first-person controller for that: while inside the car, we will be able to use the mouse to tilt and turn the camera orientation.

```
    // After opening the car, move to the inside camera
    // and activate the controller for test drive - on a
    // delay
    var that = this;
    setTimeout(function() {

        // Switch to the car interior camera
        that.cameraController.camera = that.driveCamera;
        // Don't allow camera move, we want to
        // stay in the car
        that.cameraController.move = false;
        that.driveCamera.rotation.set(0, 0, 0);
        that.driveCamera.active = true;

    }, 1000);
```

Now we are settled in the car, looking out from the seat. Let's trigger another sequence to close it, a second later. We play the animations to close the windows. We also lower the volume of the exterior sounds (later in the chapter, we will discuss adding sound to the application). We fade the windows to almost completely transparent, so that we can see out. Finally, we enable the scripts that drive the car and animate the dashboard. Now we are ready to roll.

```
// Now that we're inside, enable the car controller
// Also shut the windows and fade them
// to nearly transparent so we can see the city
setTimeout(function() {

    // Close the car windows
    that.playCloseAnimations();

    // Dampen city background sounds
    that.sound.interior();

    // Fade the windows
    var i, len = that.faders.length;
    for (i = 0; i < len; i++) {
        var fader = that.faders[i];
        fader.opacity = FuturgoCity.OPACITY_MOSTLY_TRANSPARENT;
        fader.start();
    }

    // Enable the car scripts - controller and dashboard animations
    that.carController.enabled = true;
    that.dashboardScript.enabled = true;


}, 2000);
```

The code to exit test-drive mode, in method `endTestDrive()`, not shown here, essentially reverses the previous steps:

1. Disable the car scripts.

2. Open the windows.

3. Re-enable the pickers; jump the camera back to outside view; re-enable move mode in the camera controller; restore the outside sound to full volume; fade the windows back to semi-opaque.

4. Close the windows.

# Scripting Object Behaviors

Now it is time to make the car move. To do that, we will write a controller similar in style to the first-person controller used for walking around in the scene. In this case, the keyboard moves and turns the car instead of the camera. (We still want to have the mouse tilt and turn the view, so we will continue to use the existing camera controller for that, but we will connect the interior camera `driveCamera` to it, as described in the previous section.) To create the controller, we are going to build a custom component using the Vizi framework.

## Implementing Custom Components Based on Vizi.Script

Ultimately, Vizi derives its power from the combination of two simple ideas: 1) a set of code created to handle common 3D design patterns (e.g., start/stop an action, find an object under the mouse, switch a camera), and 2) the ability to plug things together and have the parts interoperate. Vizi components can work with virtually any object because objects are organized consistently and follow a few simple rules. For example, each `Vizi.Object` instance contains a transform component with `position`, `rotation`, and `scale` properties that the other components of the object can manipulate.

The prefabs discussed earlier in this chapter, such as `Vizi.Prefabs.Skybox()` and `Vizi.Prefabs.FirstPersonController()`, are functions that create a hierarchy of pre-built objects and return a `Vizi.Object` as the root of the newly created hierarchy. The object could be a single, simple thing that just contains, say, a cube; on the other hand, it could be a complex hierarchy consisting of several objects and components. Prefabs that contain anything other than dumb geometry will likely also have one or more *scripts* that implement the logic for the prefab. For example, the Vizi skybox prefab contains cube geometry, as well as a script responsible for matching the orientation of the skybox to the orientation of the main camera in the scene.

For the Futurgo city application, we need to create a script that drives the car. If we make this script a Vizi component and simply add it to the Futurgo car object, the Vizi framework will make sure its `update()` method is called each time through the run loop, giving it a chance to respond to user input and move the car accordingly. Let's look at how to build it.

## A Controller Script to Drive the Car

Recall the code that handled initializing the car after the model was loaded. It added picker components, faders, and so on, and added environment maps. It also did this:

```
// Add the car controller
this.carController = new FuturgoController({enabled:false,
    scene: this.scene});
futurgo.addComponent(this.carController);
```

`FuturgoController` is a component created to do one job: drive the car using the arrow keys. The up arrow accelerates the car forward; the down arrow applies the brakes; the left and right arrows turn it. The controller also tests for collision to keep the car from driving through walls, and it follows the terrain so that the car drives up and onto curbs or other elevated features, rather than "plowing" through them. And because we placed the `driveCamera` camera inside the car, thanks to the magic of the transform hierarchy, the camera will move as the car moves, so we can enjoy the ride.

Let's look at the code that implements this controller (Example 11-16). The source file is located in *Chapter 11/futurgoController.js*. The constructor function first subclasses `Vizi.Script`, the base type for any script components used by the framework. It then initializes several properties: the state of movement keys, the current speed and acceleration, a few bookkeeping variables that will help support the collision and terrain-following algorithms, and several timestamps to help implement the pseudophysics algorithms we will use to control the speed of the car.

*Example 11-16. Constructor for the FuturgoController component*

```
FuturgoController = function(param)
{
    param = param || {};

    Vizi.Script.call(this, param);

    this.enabled = (param.enabled !== undefined) ? param.enabled : true;
    this.scene = param.scene || null;

    this.turnSpeed = Math.PI / 2; // 90 degs/sec

    this.moveForward = false;
    this.moveBackward = false;
    this.turnLeft = false;
    this.turnRight = false;

    this.accelerate = false;
    this.brake = false;
    this.acceleration = 0;
    this.braking = 0;
    this.speed = 0;
    this.rpm = 0;

    this.eyePosition = new THREE.Vector3;
    this.downVector = new THREE.Vector3(0, -1, 0);
    this.groundY = 0;
    this.avatarHeight = FuturgoCity.AVATAR_HEIGHT_SEATED;

    this.savedPos = new THREE.Vector3;
    this.movementVector = new THREE.Vector3;

    this.lastUpdateTime = Date.now();
```

```
    this.accelerateStartTime = this.brakeStartTime =
        this.accelerateEndTime = this.brakeEndTime =
        this.lastUpdateTime;
}
```

Vizi components usually implement two methods: `realize()` and `update()`. `real ize()` is called by the framework when it's time to create the data structures required for rendering, input, networking, or other browser-supplied services. For the car controller, `realize()` does two things: save the initial position of the car, and create a bounce behavior that will be triggered when the car collides with something. The car is accessed via the property `this._object`, which Vizi automatically sets on a component when it is added to an object.

```
FuturgoController.prototype.realize = function()
{
    this.lastUpdateTime = Date.now();

    // Save ground position
    this.groundY = this._object.transform.position.y;

    // Add a bounce behavior to run on collide
    this.bouncer = new Vizi.BounceBehavior(
            { duration : FuturgoController.BOUNCE_DURATION }
            );
    this._object.addComponent(this.bouncer);
}
```

Now for `update()`: this method is called for every component of every object in the Vizi scene graph, each time through the application's run loop. For the car controller, `up date()` has to do several things. First, it saves the current position of the car, which will be used to restore it if there is a collision or if we need to move up or down to follow the terrain. Then, it updates the speed based on its internal physics algorithm. After that, it uses the speed property to calculate a new position. Finally, it tests for collision and terrain following.

```
FuturgoController.prototype.update = function()
{
    if (!this.enabled)
        return;

    var now = Date.now();
    var deltat = now - this.lastUpdateTime;

    this.savePosition();
    this.updateSpeed(now, deltat);
    this.updatePosition(now, deltat);
    this.testCollision();
    this.testTerrain();
```

```
        this.lastUpdateTime = now;
    }
```

Updating the speed involves using a simple pseudophysics algorithm that fakes acceleration and momentum; see Example 11-17. The longer the up arrow key is pressed, the more acceleration increases; the longer the down arrow key is pressed, the more the brakes are applied and the car slows down. If no keys are pressed, there will still be a certain amount of momentum applied if the car was already traveling forward. After these computations, if either the speed or acceleration changes, we also dispatch events to tell listeners that the speed has changed. The dashboard controller (covered later in the chapter) will use that information to change the speed and RPM represented on its dials.

*Example 11-17. Updating the car speed*

```
FuturgoController.prototype.updateSpeed = function(now, deltat) {

    var speed = this.speed, rpm = this.rpm;

    // Accelerate if the pedal is down
    if (this.accelerate) {
        var deltaA = now - this.accelerateStartTime;
        this.acceleration = deltaA / 1000 * FuturgoController.ACCELERATION;
    }
    else {
        // Apply momentum
        var deltaA = now - this.accelerateEndTime;
        this.acceleration -= deltaA / 1000 * FuturgoController.INERTIA;
        this.acceleration = Math.max( 0, Math.min( FuturgoController.MAX_ACCELERATION,
            this.acceleration) );
    }

    speed += this.acceleration;

    // Slow down if the brake is down
    if (this.brake) {
        var deltaB = now - this.brakeStartTime;
        var braking = deltaB / 1000 * FuturgoController.BRAKING;

        speed -= braking;
    }
    else {
        // Apply inertia
        var inertia = deltat / 1000 * FuturgoController.INERTIA;
        speed -= inertia;
    }

    speed = Math.max( 0, Math.min( FuturgoController.MAX_SPEED, speed ) );
    rpm = Math.max( 0, Math.min( FuturgoController.MAX_ACCELERATION,
        this.acceleration ) );
```

```
    if (this.speed != speed) {
        this.speed = speed;
        this.dispatchEvent("speed", speed);
    }

    if (this.rpm != rpm) {
        this.rpm = rpm;
        this.dispatchEvent("rpm", rpm);
    }
}
```

To update the position of the car, we use the current speed to move along the line of sight (negative z-axis). We also turn the car by rotating the object around its y-axis.

```
FuturgoController.prototype.updatePosition = function(now, deltat) {

        var actualMoveSpeed = deltat / 1000 * this.speed;
        var actualTurnSpeed = deltat / 1000 * this.turnSpeed;

        // Translate in Z...
        this._object.transform.object.translateZ( -actualMoveSpeed );

        // ...but keep the vehicle on the ground
        this._object.transform.position.y = this.groundY;

        // Turn
        if ( this.turnLeft ) {
            this._object.transform.object.rotateY( actualTurnSpeed );
        }

        if ( this.turnRight ) {
            this._object.transform.object.rotateY( -actualTurnSpeed );
        }

    }
```

### Detecting collisions between the car and scene

The code to detect collisions between the car and buildings is similar to the code used in Vizi.FirstPersonController. It calls the graphics system's objectFromRay() method to calculate the intersection of the ray from the current camera position to the desired one, and any geometry in the scene. Note the first argument passed to objectFrom Ray(): this.scene contains all the geometry in the city scene, but it does not include the car itself. If we included the car's geometry in the collision test, well, it would always return true.

```
FuturgoController.prototype.testCollision = function() {

        this.movementVector.copy(this._object.transform.position)
            .sub(this.savedPos);
        this.eyePosition.copy(this.savedPos);
```

```
        this.eyePosition.y = this.groundY + this.avatarHeight;

    var collide = null;
    if (this.movementVector.length()) {

        collide = Vizi.Graphics.instance.objectFromRay(this.scene,
            this.eyePosition,
                this.movementVector,
                FuturgoController.COLLISION_MIN,
                FuturgoController.COLLISION_MAX);

        if (collide && collide.object) {
            var dist = this.eyePosition.distanceTo(collide.hitPointWorld);
        }
    }

    if (collide && collide.object) {
        this.handleCollision(collide);
    }


}
```

### Implementing collision response

In our walk through the city, the first-person controller kept us from passing through solid buildings. Whenever a collision happened, we stopped dead. For the car, we would like to do something a little subtler. In the real world, when a car hits a building, it's going to bounce, if not crash. In our easygoing simulation, we want to have the Futurgo bounce softly when it collides with something in the scene. The concept of how a 3D application behaves when objects collide is known as *collision response.*

Example 11-18 shows how the bounce collision response is implemented in the car controller. First, we dispatch a "collide" event to any listeners. The application will be listening for this to trigger a sound when the car collides. Then, we reset the car's position to its original value so that it doesn't pass through the geometry, by calling `restorePo sition()`. Next, recall that the `realize()` method added a `Vizi.BounceBehavior` component to the car. We trigger that bounce behavior, which makes the car bounce backward a bit. *Backward* here means in the opposite direction of movement; see how we set the bounder's `bounceVector` property to the negative of the movement vector, and scale it down to a third to simulate that some of the force of movement was absorbed on "impact." Finally, we kill the motor.

*Example 11-18. Handling collision with a collision response*

```
FuturgoController.prototype.handleCollision = function(collide) {

    // Tell any listeners
    this.dispatchEvent("collide", collide);

    // Move back to previously saved position
```

```
this.restorePosition();

// Run the bounce response
this.bouncer.bounceVector
    .copy(this.movementVector)
    .negate()
    .multiplyScalar(.333);
this.bouncer.start();

// Kill the motor
this.speed = 0;
this.rpm = 0;
}
```

## Implementing terrain following

The city environment is pretty flat, but there are a couple of bits of elevation. The curb
rests above street level. We need to decide what to do when the Futurgo drives up to it.
It could either stop, or climb up onto the curb. What we don't want to happen is for the
car to "plow" through the curb, driving through it like it wasn't there. Stopping at the
point it hits the pavement would be easy, but not much fun. Instead, we are going to
have the car drive up and onto the curb. To do that, we need to implement terrain
following.

*Terrain following* refers to algorithms that keep the camera or avatar at a constant distance above the ground. As the camera moves within the scene, a ray is cast downward.
If it collides with any geometry, the distance is checked against the desired height of the
camera. If the distance is less than the desired value, the camera is moved upward,
seemingly "stepping" up; if the distance is greater than the desire value, the camera is
moved down.

The Futurgo car controller performs a terrain following check each time through its
update method. Once again, we'll use the Vizi methods to test collision against the scene
geometry, but this time with a ray pointing downward (downVector = [0, -1, 0]). Try
it out for yourself. Drive toward a building, and the car will climb up onto the curb.
Drive back toward the street, and it will climb back down to the pavement. See the code
in Example 11-19, and the illustration of collision and terrain following in Figure 11-14.

*Example 11-19. Terrain following in the Futurgo*

```
FuturgoController.prototype.testTerrain = function() {

    var EPSILON = 0.00001;

    var terrainHit = Vizi.Graphics.instance.objectFromRay(this.scene,
                this.eyePosition,
                this.downVector);

    if (terrainHit && terrainHit.object) {
```

```
        var dist = this.eyePosition.distanceTo(terrainHit.hitPointWorld);
        var diff = this.avatarHeight - dist;
        if (Math.abs(diff) > EPSILON) {
            console.log("distance", dist);


            this.eyePosition.y += diff;
            this._object.transform.position.y += diff;
            this.groundY = this._object.transform.position.y;
        }
    }
}
```

*Figure 11-14. Collision and terrain following: the car stops at walls and drives up onto sidewalk using ray casting*

# Adding Sound to the Environment

This is getting pretty fun—blazing through city streets in our Car of the Future—but something is missing: sound. Sound might be a luxury in page-based web applications, but in a realistic 3D environment, its absence is all too conspicuous. Thankfully, it is easy to add basic sounds using standard HTML5 audio.

For this application, we need only two sounds: a looped ambient sound for the city background, and a short sound to make a "bump" noise when the car collides with something. First, we add <audio> and <sound> elements to the HTML page (file *Chapter 11/futurgoCity.html*):

```
<audio volume="0.0" id="city_sound">
<!-- http://www.freesound.org/people/synthetic-oz/sounds/162704/  -->
  <source src="../sounds/162704__synthetic-oz__city-trimmed-looped.wav"
    type="audio/wav" />
  Your browser does not support WAV files in the audio element.
</audio>
<audio volume="0.0" id="bump_sound">
<!-- http://www.freesound.org/people/Calethos/sounds/31126/  -->
  <source src="../sounds/31126__calethos__bump.wav" type="audio/wav" />
  Your browser does not support WAV files in the audio element.
</audio>
```

Now we just need to write a little code to change volumes and trigger sound playback. When we go inside the Futurgo for the test drive, the city sound volume should be lowered; when we step out, we should hear the city at full volume again. When we collide, the bump sound should play once.

Sound is implemented in the source file *Chapter 11/futurgoSound.js*. It is quite simple, using standard HTML5 DOM audio methods. Example 11-20 shows the code in its entirety. The methods interior() and exterior() raise and lower the ambient background sound, respectively. The method bump() plays the bump sound once.

*Example 11-20. Managing sounds in the Futurgo city scene*

```
FuturgoSound = function(param) {

    this.citySound = document.getElementById("city_sound");
    this.citySound.volume = FuturgoSound.CITY_VOLUME;
    this.citySound.loop = true;

    this.bumpSound = document.getElementById("bump_sound");
    this.bumpSound.volume = FuturgoSound.BUMP_VOLUME;
}

FuturgoSound.prototype.start = function() {

    this.citySound.play();

}

FuturgoSound.prototype.bump = function() {

    this.bumpSound.play();

}
```

```
FuturgoSound.prototype.interior = function() {

    $(this.citySound).animate(
            {volume: FuturgoSound.CITY_VOLUME_INTERIOR},
            FuturgoSound.FADE_TIME);
}

FuturgoSound.prototype.exterior = function() {

    $(this.citySound).animate(
            {volume: FuturgoSound.CITY_VOLUME},
            FuturgoSound.FADE_TIME);
}

FuturgoSound.prototype.bump = function() {

    this.bumpSound.play();

}

FuturgoSound.CITY_VOLUME = 0.3;
FuturgoSound.CITY_VOLUME_INTERIOR = 0.15;
FuturgoSound.BUMP_VOLUME = 0.3;
FuturgoSound.FADE_TIME = 1000;
```

The only thing left to do is to wire these methods into the application. Recall the action sequence from `startTestDrive()` (file *Chapter 11/futurgoCity.js*):

```
// Dampen city background sounds
that.sound.interior();
```

Exiting the car calls `exterior()` to restore the sound to its original volume.

The `FuturgoCity` class also handles the collision sound, by adding an event listener to the car controller:

```
this.carController.addEventListener("collide", function(collide) {
        that.sound.bump();
    });
```

# Rendering Dynamic Textures

We have reached the final leg of our tour through creating a realistic environment. The car is now ready to roll. After implementing the sound, I thought I was all done writing code. But when I jumped in to take the car for a drive, it felt lifeless. I quickly realized that's because the dials on the control panel were dead—the dials on the speedometer and tachometer gauges didn't move when the car did. As was the case with sound, the realism of the environment created elevated expectations on my part. If the car is moving, the dials have to spin, too. So, we needed to animate the dashboard—or at least, its texture map.

In this section, we are going to create a *procedural texture*; that is, a texture map drawn dynamically from program code (versus a static image loaded from a file). To do that, we turn to an old standby: 2D canvas rendering. The dashboard uses the 2D Canvas API to generate a procedural texture representing the current speed and RPM values on the gauges.

The original dashboard texture map on the Futurgo came with dials in fixed positions. I asked TC to split the dial out from the rest of the dashboard as a separate image. He did that and gave me the sliced images. TC didn't need to change the 3D art, just the textures. The two bitmap files are depicted in Figures 11-15 and 11-16.

To do the dashboard animation, we are going to create another Vizi custom component, `FuturgoDashboard`. It is a script that creates an HTML Canvas element, loads the two bitmaps during `realize()`, and updates the dials during `update()` based on the current speed and RPM. We will track the speed and RPM by adding event listeners to the `FuturgoController`.

*Figure 11-15. Texture map for the dashboard gauges*

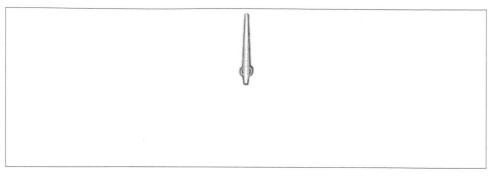

*Figure 11-16. Texture map for the rotatable dial*

Example 11-21 shows how we set this up. `realize()` creates a new Canvas element, and a Three.js texture object to hold it. We then set that new texture as the `map` property of the dashboard's material. Later, we can use standard Canvas 2D drawing API calls to update the contents of the canvas, and those changes will be reflected in the texture map on the object.

*Example 11-21. Creating a canvas texture for the dashboard*

```
FuturgoDashboardScript.prototype.realize = function()
{
    // Set up the gauges
    var gauge = this._object.findNode("head_light_L1");
    var visual = gauge.visuals[0];

    // Create a new canvas element for drawing
    var canvas = document.createElement("canvas");
    canvas.width = 512;
    canvas.height = 512;

    // Create a new Three.js texture with the canvas
    var texture = new THREE.Texture(canvas);
    texture.wrapS = texture.wrapT = THREE.RepeatWrapping;
    visual.material.map = texture;

    this.texture = texture;
    this.canvas = canvas;
    this.context = canvas.getContext("2d");
```

Continuing with `realize()`, here is the code to load the textures. We use DOM properties to do this: first, set an `onload` hander, which will tell us when the image is loaded and ready. Then, we set the `src` property to load the image.

```
    // Load the textures for the dashboard and dial
    this.dashboardImage = null;
    this.dialImage = null;

    var that = this;
```

```
var image1 = new Image();
image1.onload = function () {
    that.dashboardImage = image1;
    that.needsUpdate = true;
}
image1.src = FuturgoDashboardScript.dashboardURL;

var image2 = new Image();
image2.onload = function () {
    that.dialImage = image2;
    that.needsUpdate = true;
}
image2.src = FuturgoDashboardScript.dialURL;

// Force an initial update
this.needsUpdate = true;
}
```

It's time to draw; see Example 11-22. Each time through the dashboard script's up
date() method, we will test whether we need to redraw the texture, based on whether
the speed or RPM value of the car controller has changed. If it has, we call draw() to
apply the Canvas API drawing to the texture. draw() begins by clearing the contents of
the canvas with the current text color. Then, if the dashboard bitmap has been loaded,
it draws that to the canvas using the context's drawImage() method, covering the entire
canvas with the pixels from the image.

*Example 11-22. Drawing the background dashboard image*

```
FuturgoDashboardScript.prototype.draw = function()
{
    var context = this.context;
    var canvas = this.canvas;

    context.clearRect(0, 0, canvas.width, canvas.height);
    context.fillStyle = this.backgroundColor;
    context.fillRect(0, 0, canvas.width, canvas.height);

    context.fillStyle = this.textColor;

    if (this.dashboardImage) {
        context.drawImage(this.dashboardImage, 0, 0);
    }
}
```

 If you are rusty on the Canvas API, Chapter 7 covers the basics of
Canvas drawing.

Now, we need to draw the dial on top. We have been keeping track of the car's speed and tachometer (more on this in a bit); we use those values to calculate an angle of rotation for the dial bitmap. Recall that the 2D Canvas API provides methods, `save()` and `restore()`, for saving the current state of the context before a set of drawing calls, and restoring to that state after doing the drawing. We'll bracket the drawing of each dial with those calls. After saving state, we perform 2D transforms on the context, translating the dial bitmap we are about to draw to the correct position on the gauge, and rotating it by the right amount to match the current speed and RPM values. Then, we draw the image and restore the context. We do this for each gauge. (I figured out the translation values used here based on the size of the dial bitmap, and a location I was able to determine by messing around in an image editing program.)

```
var speeddeg = this._speed * 10 - 120;
var speedtheta = THREE.Math.degToRad(speeddeg);
var rpmdeg = this._rpm * 20 - 90;
var rpmtheta = THREE.Math.degToRad(rpmdeg);

if (this.dialImage) {
    context.save();

    context.translate(FuturgoDashboardScript.speedDialLeftOffset,
            FuturgoDashboardScript.speedDialTopOffset);
    context.rotate(speedtheta);
    context.translate(-FuturgoDashboardScript.dialCenterLeftOffset,
            -FuturgoDashboardScript.dialCenterTopOffset);
    context.drawImage(this.dialImage, 0, 0);
    context.restore();

    context.save();

    context.translate(FuturgoDashboardScript.rpmDialLeftOffset,
            FuturgoDashboardScript.rpmDialTopOffset);
    context.rotate(rpmtheta);
    context.translate(-FuturgoDashboardScript.dialCenterLeftOffset,
            -FuturgoDashboardScript.dialCenterTopOffset);
    context.drawImage(this.dialImage, 0, 0); // 198, 25, 115);
    context.restore();
}
}
```

The only thing remaining to do is to wire up the car controller to the dashboard, so that it can listen to those speed and RPM changes.

The city app sets the `carController` property of the dashboard after it is created:

```
this.dashboardScript.carController = this.carController;
```

`carController`, shown in Example 11-23, is a JavaScript property that we created using `Object.defineProperties`. Under the covers, setting the property results in calling the `setCarController()` accessor method of the object. This method saves the controller in a private property, `this_carController`, and adds event listeners for the car controller's "speed" and "rpm" events. Those listeners save the new values, and flag that the dashboard needs to be redrawn by setting its `needsUpdate` property. Now, whenever the car speeds up or slows down, the dashboard display will redraw to reflect it.

*Example 11-23. Dashboard controller script setting up listeners for car speed and RPM changes*

```
FuturgoDashboardScript.prototype.setCarController =
  function(controller) {

    this._carController = controller;

    var that = this;
    controller.addEventListener("speed", function(speed) {
      that.setSpeed(speed); });
    controller.addEventListener("rpm", function(rpm) {
      that.setRPM(rpm); });
}
```

 The power of using a Canvas element as a WebGL texture cannot be overestimated. It allows developers to use a familiar, easy API to dynamically draw textures in JavaScript, opening up possibilities for mind-blowing effects. The designers of WebGL got it right with that one. WebGL also supports HTML video element textures, making for even more potentially powerful combinations.

# Chapter Summary

This was a long chapter, but it covered huge ground.

You learned how to deliver a working, realistic-looking 3D environment in a web page, with a panoramic background, environment map reflections, user-controlled navigation, sound design, and a moving object with interactive behaviors. We fortified our tool set, adding features to the previewer that allowed us to see the structure of the scene graph and detailed properties of each object. You learned to develop simplified versions of several classic 3D game algorithms and effects, such as first-person navigation, collision and terrain following, skybox rendering, and procedural textures.

Creating 3D environments in a browser is hard work, but it can be done on web time with a web budget. And now, you have a sense of what it takes to get the job done.

# CHAPTER 12

# Developing Mobile 3D Applications

As HTML5 evolved over the past decade, an even more revolutionary set of developments was taking place in mobile phones and tablets. The designs first popularized by Apple's iPhone and iPad have blurred the lines between mobile devices and traditional computers. Mobile devices now outpace traditional computers in terms of units shipped annually, as consumers look to simpler, smaller, and more portable devices for playing games, watching videos, listening to music, emailing, surfing the Internet, and, yes, even making phone calls. These new handheld computers have also unleashed an explosion of features, including location-based services, touchscreen interfaces, and device orientation input.

To access the new capabilities of smartphones and tablets, developers have typically had to learn new programming languages and operating systems. For example, building applications for Apple's devices requires using the APIs of the iOS operating system and programming in the Objective-C language (or bridging to it from other native languages such as C++); programming for the Android operating system requires learning a different set of APIs and building applications in Java; and so on. For some time now, mobile platforms have provided a limited ability to develop with HTML5, via use of WebKit-based controls that can be included in an application. This allowed programmers to develop the presentation and some application logic using markup, CSS, and JavaScript, but they still wrote much of the application using native code in order to access platform features—including OpenGL-based 3D graphics—not present in the mobile web browsers at the time.

Over the past few years, the browser has caught up. Most of the features innovated initially in mobile platforms have found their way into the HTML5 specifications. The once separate worlds of native, device-specific mobile programming and web development look like they are about to converge. For many web and mobile application developers, this represents a boon: HTML5 and JavaScript for ease of development, plus the potential to create true cross-platform code. 3D is one of the more recent additions to this set of tools. CSS3 mobile support is ubiquitous, and WebGL is now nearly universally adopted in mobile platforms. In this chapter, we look at the issues surrounding developing mobile HTML5-based 3D applications.

# Mobile 3D Platforms

While native mobile APIs are still ahead of HTML5 in terms of features, the gap is rapidly closing. 3D has arrived in most mobile browsers, though there are limitations. Most browsers have WebGL, but some—like Mobile Safari—do not. At the time of this writing, here's what the landscape looks like for developing HTML5-based 3D applications on mobile devices:

- WebGL is supported in many, but not all, mobile browsers. Table 12-1 summarizes the mobile browsers that support WebGL.

- CSS 3D Transforms, Transitions, and Animations are supported in all mobile browsers. The examples developed in Chapter 6 should work in any modern mobile environment. If your application's 3D needs are simple, consisting of primarily 3D effects on 2D page elements, then you should seriously consider using CSS3 over WebGL, due to WebGL's lack of complete coverage on mobile devices.

- The 2D Canvas API is supported in all mobile browsers. This can be used as a potential fallback for mobile platforms that do not support WebGL, albeit with a performance penalty, since the 2D Canvas element is not hardware-accelerated.

*Table 12-1. WebGL support on mobile devices and operating systems*

| Platform/device | Supported browsers |
| --- | --- |
| Amazon Fire OS (Android-based) | Amazon Silk (Kindle Fire HDX only) |
| Android | Mobile Chrome, Mobile Firefox |
| Apple iOS | Not supported in Mobile Safari or Chrome; supported in iAds framework for creating HTML5-based ads for use within applications |
| BlackBerry 10 | BlackBerry Browser |
| Firefox OS | Mobile Firefox |
| Intel Tizen | Tizen Browser |
| Windows RT | Internet Explorer (requires Windows RT 8.1 or higher) |

The most obvious gap in the preceding table is the lack of support for WebGL in Mobile Safari and Mobile Chrome on iOS. Though Android has made major strides in mobile market share, and the other systems are gaining in popularity, iOS is a still a very popular mobile platform and commands significant developer attention. The situation with iOS may change in the future, but the reality today is that WebGL does not run in web browsers on iOS.

On platforms for which WebGL is not enabled in the browser, there are adapter technologies, so-called "hybrid" solutions that provide the WebGL API to applications. Developers can write their applications using JavaScript code that talks to a set of native code responsible for implementing the API. The result won't be a browser-based application, but it can perform at native speeds and still reap the benefits of rapid, easy JavaScript development. We will explore one such technology, Ludei's CocoonJS, later in the chapter.

For the mobile platforms that do support WebGL, there are often two avenues of deployment: browser-based applications, and packaged applications usually referred to as *web apps*. For browser-based mobile WebGL, you simply develop your application as you would for the desktop, and deliver it as a set of files from your servers. For web apps, you use the platform's tools to package the files—usually the same files as you would deploy from your server, perhaps with the addition of an icon and some metadata information—which are then distributed through the platform's app store or similar service.

Regardless of how you deploy your application, there are going to be special concerns when you are developing 3D for mobile. First, you will want to add support for device capabilities such as touch input, location, and device orientation. You also have to be much more mindful about performance, given the smaller memory footprint and (generally) less capable CPU and GPU processors present on the devices. These topics will be covered later in the chapter.

 HTML5 mobile platforms are a moving target; new platforms seem to be hitting the scene on a daily basis. There is a good overview and other background information in the Wikipedia entry (*http://en.wiki pedia.org/wiki/HTML5_in_mobile_devices*).

# Developing for Mobile Browsers

If you already have experience creating a WebGL application for desktop browsers, getting started with mobile development can be as easy as pointing the browser at the URL. If your mobile platform claims support for WebGL, it should just work. Performance can vary. The devices and operating system platforms support many different hardware configurations: some are quite low end, such as the Firefox OS phones from GeeksPhone; others, such as the newer Samsung Galaxy and Google Nexus tablets, have very fast performance. But they all should at least render something on the screen to get you started.

One of the most impressive devices I tested was the Amazon Kindle Fire HDX. Released in October 2013, this upgrade to the Kindle Fire line features solid hardware specs—a quad-core Snapdragon processor and Adreno 330 GPU from Qualcomm—plus first-class HTML5 support. The seven-inch version worked very well with the book examples. See Figure 12-1 for a screenshot of the Futurgo concept car site (see Chapter 10) running on the Kindle Fire HDX in the Amazon Silk browser. Note how it looks exactly like the desktop example from Chapter 10. Swipe a finger in the canvas area to rotate the Futurgo. Pinch the screen with two fingers in the canvas area to zoom the model in/out. Tap on the Interior and LTD Racing tabs to start the animations. Tap on a part of the Futurgo body to bring up the overlay. The performance is great, beyond anything you would expect from a super-lightweight, seven-inch handheld device.

Figure 12-1. Futurgo application on the Kindle Fire HDX

It is worth nothing that I did *no* additional work initially to get this example running on the Kindle device. I simply typed a URL into the browser, and within a few seconds, the page was fully rendered and animating. A mobile device like this has no mouse, so in order to implement interaction, I needed to add touch input support.

## Adding Touch Support

Mobile HTML5 browsers automatically handle touch input for page elements, generating the appropriate `mouseclick` events. The tabs on the righthand side of the Futurgo page just worked, triggering the animations to open the car and rotate the wheels. However, the browsers do not automatically generate mouse events for Canvas elements. We need to add the support ourselves, by handling browser *touch events*.

Touch events were added to web browsers as touch interfaces became popular on mobile devices. They are somewhat similar to mouse events, in that they supply client-, page- and screen-relative $x$ and $y$ coordinates. However, they also include some different information; in particular, because most devices support more than one source of touch input simultaneously (for example, one per finger touching the screen), touch events include separate information for each source.

The browser also defines new event types, as summarized in Table 12-2.

*Table 12-2. Browser touch events*

| Event | Description |
| --- | --- |
| touchstart | Triggered when a touch is detected (e.g., when a finger first touches the screen) |
| touchmove | Triggered when a touch position changes (e.g., when a finger moves across the screen) |
| touchend | Triggered when the touch ends (e.g., the finger is removed from the screen) |
| touchcancel | Triggered when a touch moves outside the touch-sensitive area of the screen, or the touch has been interrupted in some other implementation-specific manner (e.g., too many touch points) |

The complete browser touch events specification can be found on the W3C recommendations pages (*http://bit.ly/w3-touch-events*).

Note that touch events support is still a work in progress in some browsers, and you may encounter browser-specific issues. Desktop Internet Explorer, for example, supports touch events for touch-enabled PCs; however, there are differences in the DOM event types, and browser-specific CSS properties (-ms- prefix) are required for proper functioning. Consult the developer documentation for your target browsers.

To add touch support to the Futurgo application, we will need to implement event handlers for the aforementioned events. We want to add them to the model controller used by the Vizi viewer, to support rotating and zooming the model. We also want to implement touch on the Futurgo application itself to handle when the user touches a part of the car.

### Implementing touch-based model rotation in the viewer

One of the neat features of the desktop Futurgo application is the ability to rotate the model with the mouse, and zoom in and out using the mouse wheel and trackpad. Since neither of these input sources is available on a mobile device, we will use touch instead.

Recall from Chapter 10 that the Futurgo application uses the Vizi.Viewer object, and its built-in *model controller*, to manipulate the model with the mouse. We will modify the model controller to use touch input. The source code for this class can be found in the Vizi sources in the file *src/controllers/orbitControls.js*.

First, we add an event listener for `touchstart`, which will call the method onTouch
Start().

```
this.domElement.addEventListener( 'touchstart', onTouchStart,
    false );
```

The other touch event listeners are added in the body of onTouchStart() as follows.
(Note that the variable `scope` is a JavaScript closure scope variable, the saved value of
`this` for the orbit control object.)

```
scope.domElement.addEventListener( 'touchmove', onTouchMove,
    false );
scope.domElement.addEventListener( 'touchend', onTouchEnd,
    false );
```

Now we are ready to handle touch events. Example 12-1 shows the code for the handler
onTouchStart(); we basically fake a mouse down event and call the event handler,
onMouseDown(), used by the mouse event handling code. The detail for each touch input
source is stored in the event's `touches` lists, an array of Touch objects. We assume a single
touch here, ignoring anything but the 0th object in the list. Values from the object are
copied into our fake mouse event and passed to onMouseDown(), and the event is then
handled like a regular mouse down event.

In the immortal words of Mr. Spock: "Crude methods—but effective."

*Example 12-1. Handling touch start by synthesizing a mouse down event*

```
// synthesize a left mouse button event
var mouseEvent = {
    'type': 'mousedown',
    'view': event.view,
    'bubbles': event.bubbles,
    'cancelable': event.cancelable,
    'detail': event.detail,
    'screenX': event.touches[0].screenX,
    'screenY': event.touches[0].screenY,
    'clientX': event.touches[0].clientX,
    'clientY': event.touches[0].clientY,
    'pageX': event.touches[0].pageX,
    'pageY': event.touches[0].pageY,
    'button': 0,
    'preventDefault' : function() {}
    };

onMouseDown(mouseEvent);
```

We implement similar cheap hacks for `touchmove` and `touchend`, except that we use the
`event.changedTouches` array instead. `changedTouches` contains new values for any
touch input source that has moved. Again, this all assumes single-touch operation.
That's OK; we have other plans for multitouch. See the code for the onTouchMove() and
onTouchEnd() methods for the details.

## Implementing multitouch-based model zoom

Most devices support more than one touch input, or *multitouch* operation. A common multitouch interface paradigm is to use two fingers to "pinch" the screen, moving the fingers either closer together or farther apart to zoom the view in or out. For the Vizi model controller, we are going to do just that.

Programming multitouch is a little more involved than simple single-touch, because we have to track the separate movements of more than one touch input. Each Touch object in the event's touches or changedTouches list contains an identifier property, a unique id for the touch that is guaranteed to stay the same for its duration (from touch start through touchmove, until touchend or touchcancel).

Let's look at the code. In the beginning of onTouchStart(), we check to see if we have more than one touch. If so, we are treating this as a pinch-to-zoom gesture, not a model rotation. We use the first two items of the touches array to calculate the distance between the touches, saving them into the property touchDistance. This will be used later to determine whether we have pinched inward or outward.

```
if ( event.touches.length > 1 ) {
        scope.touchDistance = calcDistance(event.touches[0],
            event.touches[1]);
        scope.touchId0 = event.touches[0].identifier;
        scope.touchId1 = event.touches[1].identifier;
}
```

We also have to save the string identifiers for the two touch objects in the properties touchId0 and touchId1. We do this because, as we receive subsequent touchmove events, we must determine which touches have moved; there is no guarantee that the individual touch objects will be stored in the same order in the new events' changedTouches lists as they were during the original touchstart event. The only information that uniquely identifies each Touch object is its identifier property. So we save these for later.

Now it's time to handle touchmove. See Example 12-2. In the method onTouchMove(), we first figure out if we have a multitouch event. If so, we search changedTouches for the two identifiers we saved previously, touchId0 and touchId1. Touch objects with those identifiers are the ones we are interested in. Once we have those, we can calculate the new distance using the helper function calcDistance(). We compare that to the previous distance. If the difference is positive, that means our fingers are moving farther apart and we zoom the camera in so the model appears closer; if the difference is negative, that means we are moving our fingers closer together, and we zoom out.

*Example 12-2. Handling a pinch with multiple touch events*

```
if ( event.changedTouches.length > 1 ) {
    var touch0 = null;
    var touch1 = null;
    for (var i = 0; i < event.changedTouches.length; i++) {
        if (event.changedTouches[i].identifier ==
```

```
            scope.touchId0)
                touch0 = event.changedTouches[i];
            else if (event.changedTouches[i].identifier ==
                scope.touchId1)
                touch1 = event.changedTouches[i];

        }
        if (touch0 && touch1) {
            var touchDistance = calcDistance(touch0, touch1);
            var deltaDistance = touchDistance -
                scope.touchDistance;
            if (deltaDistance > 0) {
                scope.zoomIn();
            }
            else if (deltaDistance < 0) {
                scope.zoomOut();
            }
            scope.touchDistance = touchDistance;
        }
    }
}
```

Let's look at how distance is calculated. Example 12-3 shows `calcDistance()` in its entirety. The calculation is simple, using the classic Pythagorean distance formula.

*Example 12-3. Calculating pinch distance*

```
    function calcDistance( touch0, touch1 ) {
        var dx = touch1.clientX - touch0.clientX;
        var dy = touch1.clientY - touch0.clientY;
        return Math.sqrt(dx * dx + dy * dy);
    }
```

### Turning off user scaling in the web page

There is one small but very important detail remaining to get our touch implementation right. By default, mobile web browsers allow the user to scale the page content using touch. However, that will interfere with our ability to pinch to scale the 3D content. The good news is that there is a way to turn this feature off from within the markup. By including the following HTML5 `meta` tag, we can prevent user scaling of the page (see *Chapter 12/futurgo.html*):

```
    <meta name="viewport"
        content="width=device-width, initial-scale=1.0, user-scalable=no">
```

### Adding Vizi.Picker touch events to the Futurgo model

The desktop version of Futurgo contained a really nice feature: informational callouts for different parts of the car model. Rolling the mouse over a part of the car (windshield, body, tires) pops up a DIV with additional information on that part. However, mobile devices don't have mice, so rollover-based callouts don't work. Instead, we would like to be able to launch the callouts when different parts of the model are touched. `Vizi.Picker` includes support for touch events. See *Chapter 12/futurgo.js*, line 44, for the code we added to Futurgo to trigger callouts based on touch. Note the lines in bold in Example 12-4.

*Example 12-4. Adding Vizi.Picker touch events to the Futurgo model*

```
// Add entry fade behavior to the windows
var that = this;
scene.map(/windows_front|windows_rear/, function(o) {
    var fader = new Vizi.FadeBehavior({duration:2, opacity:.8});
    o.addComponent(fader);
    setTimeout(function() {
        fader.start();
    }, 2000);

    var picker = new Vizi.Picker;
    picker.addEventListener("mouseover", function(event) {
        that.onMouseOver("glass", event); });
    picker.addEventListener("mouseout", function(event) {
        that.onMouseOut("glass", event); });
    picker.addEventListener("touchstart", function(event) {
        that.onTouchStart("glass", event); });
    picker.addEventListener("touchend", function(event) {
        that.onTouchEnd("glass", event); });
    o.addComponent(picker);
});
```

The touch event handlers are simple: again, we pull the cheap trick of just dispatching to an existing mouse handler.

```
Futurgo.prototype.onTouchEnd = function(what, event) {
    console.log("touch end", what, event);
    this.onMouseOver(what, event);
}
```

 Thankfully, there is nothing in `onMouseOver()` that expects an actual DOM `MouseEvent`, or this code would break. We got off easy here —try to *not* do this kind of thing in your production code, or you might find bugs much later on, when you least expect them.

# Debugging Mobile Functionality in Desktop Chrome

Once we learned how to handle touch events, it was pretty easy to add the support to the Vizi core and the Futurgo application. Even the multitouch handling for pinch-to-zoom, while a bit detailed, was not rocket science. Though this kind of thing comes easy, we are still human and make mistakes, so we need to be able to debug and test the new features as we add them.

Each mobile HTML5 platform listed in Table 12-1 provides a different way of connecting debuggers to debug the application on the device. Some of these systems work well; others are, in my experience, pretty painful to deal with. Be that as it may, at some point you will find yourself needing to get into that process. We are not going to cover the specifics of any of the tools here. Consult the documentation for your target platform for more information.

In the meantime, it would be great if we could use the desktop version to do some debugging before moving the application to the device. Thankfully, the debugger tools in desktop Chrome provide a way to do this by allowing you to emulate certain mobile features, such as touch events. When touch event emulation is turned on, you can use the mouse to trigger the touch events. Here is a quick walkthrough:

1. Launch your application in the Chrome browser.

2. Open the Chrome debugger.

3. Click on the settings (cog) icon on the bottom right. You should see a user interface pane come up over the debugging area. See Figure 12-2. The relevant input fields are circled.

4. Select the Overrides tab in the Settings section (leftmost column).

5. Check the Enable checkbox in the column labeled Overrides.

6. Scroll down until you see "Emulate touch events" in the detail area on the right. Select that checkbox.

7. Now you can click the close box on the top left to dismiss this pane. However, make sure to keep the debugger open.

*Figure 12-2. Enabling touch event emulation in desktop Chrome*

Note that Chrome touch event emulation works only when the debugger is open. When you close the debugger, you lose touch overrides.

At this point, browser touch event emulation is enabled in Chrome. Mouse events will be converted to touch events and sent to your application. See Figure 12-3. Note the black rectangle with red text at the top right of the window (circled in the figure). This tells us what event overrides have been turned on. Now use the mouse to click on the Futurgo; we can see the messages written to the console when touchstart and tou chend events are triggered, circled within the console window. This simple capability is a great way to debug your touch code before trying out the application on the device. Unfortunately, only single-touch emulation is supported.

Figure 12-3. Debugging touch events for the Futurgo in desktop Chrome

# Creating Web Apps

Sometimes, you would like to package your creation as a finished application to deploy to the device. Perhaps you want to use in-app purchase, or other platform features provided for applications but not available to code running in the browser. Or you may simply wish to install an icon onto the user's device so that he or she can directly launch your application. Most of the new mobile device platforms support developing in Java-Script and HTML5, and then packaging the result as a finished application, or *web app*.

## Web App Development and Testing Tools

The developer tools to create web apps in HTML5 differ from platform to platform; each has its own way to test-launch, debug, and then package the app for distribution.

Amazon provides a Web App Tester for Amazon Fire OS on Kindle devices. Fire OS is an Android-based operating system developed at Amazon for use with Kindle Fire devices. The Web App Tester is a Kindle Fire application available on the Amazon store. For details, go to *https://developer.amazon.com/sdk/webapps/tester.html*. The Web App Tester is depicted in Figure 12-4.

This utility couldn't be simpler: just type a URL to your page, and it will launch the page in a full-screen view. After you have typed it once, the Tester stores the URL in its history so that you can easily launch it again.

 As mentioned, the developer tools for creating web apps differ from platform to platform. This is true even for different vendor-specific versions of Android: though Kindle Fire OS is Android-based, Amazon has added a lot of value with a custom set of tools for developing, testing, and packaging. For other Android-based systems, check the vendor documentation or have a look at the Android developer web app pages (*http://bit.ly/dev-android-webapps*).

## Packaging Web Apps for Distribution

Once you have debugged and tested your apps, it's time to deploy. This is another area where each platform differs greatly. Amazon provides the Amazon Mobile App Distribution Portal, which allows registered Amazon developers to create Kindle Fire and Android apps published by the company. Publishing your apps through this portal requires going through several steps. One of the first steps is to create a *manifest file* for the application; that is, a file that contains data about the contents and features of the application. Here is a sample from a very simple Amazon web app manifest file. The only required field is `verification_key`, a value generated by Amazon as part of the publishing process. Other metadata about the application, such as icons and a description, is supplied online as part of app submission, not in the manifest file itself.

---

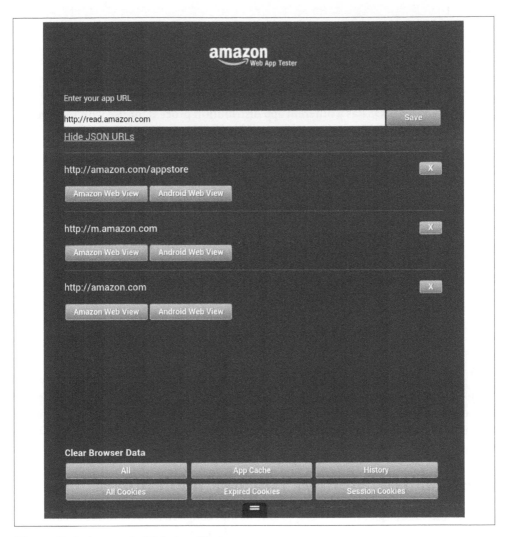

*Figure 12-4. Amazon's Web App Tester*

Complete information on Amazon manifest files can be found at *https://develop er.amazon.com/sdk/webapps/manifest.html.*

```
{
    "verification_key":
      "insert your verification key from the App File(s) tab",
    "launch_path": "index.html",
    "permissions": [
        "iap",
        "geolocation",
        "auth"
```

```
    ],
    "type": "web",
    "version": "0.1a",
    "last_update": "2013-04-08 13:30:00-0800",
    "created_by": "webappdev"
}
```

By contrast, Firefox OS has a different app distribution process for use with the Firefox Marketplace, and a different syntax for manifest files. Here is a simple example:

```
{
  "name": "Your_Application_Name_Here",
  "description": "Your Application Description Here",
  "version": 1,
  "installs_allowed_from": ["*"],
  "default_locale": "en",
  "launch_path": "/index.html",
  "fullscreen": "true",
  "orientation": ["landscape"],
  "icons": {
    "128": "/images/icon-128.png"
  },
  "developer": {
    "name": "Your Name Here",
    "url": "http://your.company.url.com"
  }
}
```

In Firefox manifest files, we specify the files contained in the package, an icon for the app, an app name and description, and some developer information. Find more information on Firefox OS app creation at *https://developer.mozilla.org/en-US/Apps/Devel oping/Packaged_apps*.

# Developing Native/HTML5 "Hybrid" Applications

HTML5 and mobile platform APIs appear to be on a collision course. You could imagine a very near future where any application could be developed once in HTML5, and simply deployed on the various mobile platforms using those vendors' packaging technologies. However, that future is not here yet. There are still several differences among the platforms, and 3D in particular is still shaking out. As discussed, WebGL is enabled in nearly all the mobile browsers already, but it is not ubiquitous.

For this reason and others, you may want to consider using one of a handful of technologies that enable WebGL on the target device by providing a native library, or *adapter*, that makes a version of the WebGL API accessible to JavaScript. Using an adapter technology, you can combine JavaScript and HTML with native code into a packaged application—a "hybrid," if you will—that has the best of both worlds in one application.

Developers may turn to the hybrid approach for any of the following reasons:

*Lack of browser support*
> Even though iOS is the remaining holdout on implementing WebGL, it's a big one. For platforms like iOS, or other mobile platforms (such as earlier versions of Android) that may or may not support WebGL, a hybrid solution provides a path that allows the developer to build a 3D application on the WebGL API using JavaScript, and deploy on the target platform.

*Performance*
> The adapter libraries tend to offer slightly higher performance than the equivalent browser-based WebGL application for a couple of reasons. First, they can provide an optimized, better-tuned JavaScript virtual machine. Second, they can circumvent the additional layers of WebGL security that are required per the browser's security mode—essential for a web-based application, but unnecessary in a native application.

*Deployment as an application*
> If the intent is to deliver the finished product as a mobile application instead of a browser-based website, then it's OK, maybe even desirable, to use a hybrid solution. Some of these even offer value-added JavaScript access to features that would otherwise be unavailable in a pure browser-based application, such as in-app purchase, native ad SDKs, and push notifications.

Over the years, several adapter technologies have emerged that support this hybrid approach. While many of them provide hardware-accelerated Canvas and other special features—the most well known being Adobe's PhoneGap (*http://phonegap.com/*)—only a few hybrid frameworks include support for WebGL. The two most notable are CocoonJS and Ejecta. While the two tools attempt to solve the same problem, they approach it quite differently. Here is a quick comparison:

*CocoonJS (http://www.ludei.com/tech/cocoonjs)*
> CocoonJS runs on Android and iOS. It hides the details of the underlying system, in an easy-to-use application container for HTML5 and JavaScript code. It provides implementations of Canvas, WebGL, Web Audio, Web Sockets, and more. CocoonJS also comes with a system for building projects in the cloud, so all you have to do is sign your project and build it; developers do not need to understand the intricacies of creating applications using native platform tools such as Xcode for iOS. CocoonJS is a closed source project tightly controlled by its developer, San Francisco–based Ludei.

*Ejecta (http://impactjs.com/ejecta)*
> Ejecta is an open source library that supplies many of the same features as CocoonJS, but for iOS only. Ejecta was born out of ImpactJS, a project to create a game engine for HTML5. Ejecta is a bit more DIY, requiring the developer to have a fair amount of knowledge about Xcode and native platform APIs.

Even though Ejecta is open source, its reliance on iOS-specific features and Xcode make it inappropriate for this book. We will instead use CocoonJS for our tour of developing a hybrid application.

## CocoonJS: A Technology to Make HTML Games and Applications for Mobile Devices

CocoonJS is an adapter technology to make hybrid HTML5 applications that run on mobile devices. It acts as an HTML5 native wrapper: the application or game is executed as a native application, while executing JavaScript and HTML inside. CocoonJS runs on both iOS and Android, providing an identical environment for execution across these platforms and a variety of devices.

CocoonJS allows the developer to supply an HTML file and associated JavaScript code that will be rendered in a full-screen 2D or 3D Canvas using the standard 2D and WebGL APIs, plus Web Audio, image loading, `XMLHttpRequest` for Ajax development, and WebSockets support. CocoonJS implements native, hardware-accelerated versions of these APIs and provides a customized JavaScript *virtual machine* (VM) specially tuned by Ludei to provide better performance. Figure 12-5 shows a screenshot of the Futurgo running as a full-screen native iOS application on the Apple iPad 4.

To make development and testing easier, CocoonJS comes with a Launcher application that allows the developer to load a URL and preview the result, or to drop a ZIP archive containing all the content into the Launcher app on the device. The CocoonJS Launcher, depicted in Figure 12-6, can be downloaded from the Apple and Android app stores. To test your application, click the Your App button and either type URLs to your test files in the text window, or open ZIP files that have been dropped into the Launcher using iTunes or Android SDK tools. Consult the CocoonJS documentation for all the details.

Once you've previewed and tested the application with the Launcher, you can build it as a native app using Ludei's cloud-hosted service: upload the application files, and a few minutes later you will be ready to download a final bundle suitable for distribution through iOS, Amazon, GooglePlay, and other app stores.

*Figure 12-5. The Futurgo running as a native iPad application, built with Ludei CocoonJS*

*Figure 12-6. CocoonJS Launcher home screen*

# Assembling an Application with CocoonJS

Though the makers of CocoonJS contend that it can be used to build any kind of native/HTML5 application, their main focus so far has been to enable the creation of high-performance games. To that end, let's put together a very simple game to show off how to build an application. This is really more of a game demo than a whole game, designed to show off the process. Before we get into the CocoonJS particulars, let's look at a version of the game that runs on the desktop. Then we will adapt it for use with CocoonJS.

Launch the file *Chapter 12/omegacity/omegacity.html* in your browser. You will see the start screen depicted in Figure 12-7. The model should look familiar; it is the "virtual city" sample scene loaded from a glTF file using the example program from Chapter 8 (*Chapter 8/pipelinethreejsgltfscene.html*).

*Figure 12-7. Omega City game start screen: 2D art and design by GameSalad (http://www.gamesalad.com/), virtual city scene courtesy of 3DRT (http://bit.ly/1hTUdXJ), and sounds from FreeSound (http://www.freesound.org/); all rights reserved*

This awesome model was purchased from 3DRT (*http://www.3drt.com/*). The demo shown here was developed in collaboration with Austin-based GameSalad (*http://www.gamesalad.com/*), the makers of an easy-to-use 2D game creation tool for HTML and mobile games. Remember that this model, like the others distributed with the book, is subject to copyright and therefore you cannot use it in your own applications, or outside of the purpose of learning with this book, without purchasing your own copy of the model.

Welcome to Omega City, the frontier outpost of the galaxy. You and your squad are humanity's last best hope as aliens attack. To save the city…you may have to destroy it! Click the blinking START label to enter the game. This will take you to the main screen shown in Figure 12-8. The ship is on autopilot; you can only fire weapons. Hit the up arrow on the keypad to shoot lasers; you will see blue laser fire converging in the center of the view. Hit the space bar to launch a missile; after a power-up sound, the missile will fire from the heart of the ship and, once it hits its target, explode in a green flash. This is simple stuff, designed only to show off how to build something game-like so that we can get a taste of hybrid iOS development using CocoonJS.

Figure 12-8. Omega City game demo running on the desktop

## Creating the main and overlay views

You may have noticed a subtle difference between the Futurgo running on Kindle Fire HDX using pure HTML5, shown in Figure 12-1, and the native version running in iOS with CocoonJS (Figure 12-5). The Kindle Fire version looks exactly like the desktop web version, with a purple image gradient showing through behind the 3D model and wireframe grid, whereas the CocoonJS iOS version has a black background showing through behind the grid. This is because CocoonJS is not a full HTML5 browser and compositing engine, but rather a native implementation of the Canvas element, intended to make native 2D and 3D graphics development accessible to JavaScript programmers. CocoonJS can read and parse HTML tags, but it ignores most of the tags and style information.

CocoonJS interprets the HTML tag for the main canvas, plus any associated JavaScript files, but that's about it. You should not expect random CSS styling to work. The background image for the Futurgo is specified in the CSS for the `container` DIV element, which CocoonJS ignores when it processes the HTML file. If we want this kind of background imagery to work in CocoonJS, we have to draw it ourselves on the canvas. For example, we could add a Three.js object in the far background, or perhaps a Vizi skybox (see Chapter 11). This is hardly worth the bother for the quick-and-dirty exercise we have here, but you will have to deal with this issue in your own applications if you require the feature.

Even though CocoonJS is weak on styling background elements, Ludei realizes that as a practical matter, many web developers will want to use HTML to lay out and program game user interfaces. So it provides a way to layer a second HTML file, rendered in a WebView window, on top of the main canvas. The key to making this work is to split the canvas and overlay HTML elements into two separate files, or views. Figure 12-9 shows the contents of the two views side by side.

*Figure 12-9. Left to right: canvas and overlay views for the CocoonJS version of Omega City*

To adapt *Omega City* for use with CocoonJS, we first have to split up the original file, *omegacity.html*, into two separate files. The new files are *index.html* and *wv.html. index.html* contains the code for the main canvas. *wv.html* contains the code for the overlay view. Once the files have been broken up, we add CocoonJS-specific helper code from JavaScript files supplied by Ludei. Those files will manage adding the overlay view using a WebView control, and provide facilities so that the two views can communicate with each other—more on this in a moment. The CocoonJS JavaScript libraries have been designed to also work with desktop browsers, so we can preview the result in desktop Chrome before testing it in Cocoon's app launcher.

The code for the main canvas view can be found in *Chapter 12/omegacity-iOS/index.html*, listed in Example 12-5. First, we include some CocoonJS-specific files. Then, on page load, we build the game object, which is the object that will render to the main WebGL canvas. The source for the game object can be found in *Chapter 12/omegacity-iOS/omegacity.js*. We then create an object to manage the overlay view, or *heads-up display* (HUD), and an object to manage the sounds in the game. (Note the use of the prefix *proxy* for the HUD class; we will be looking at this momentarily.)

*Example 12-5. Main view code for CocoonJS application*

```
<script src="./libs/cocoon_cocoonjsextensions/CocoonJS.js">
</script>
<script src="./libs/cocoon_cocoonjsextensions/CocoonJS_App.js">
</script>
<script
src="./libs/cocoon_cocoonjsextensions/CocoonJS_App_ForCocoonJS.js">
</script>
<script src="./libs/vizi/vizi.js"></script>
<script src="omegacity.js"></script>
<script src="omegacityProxyHUD.js"></script>
<script src="omegacitySound.js"></script>
<script>

    var game = null;
    var hud = null;
    var sound = null;
    var gameLoadComplete = false;
    var wvLoadComplete = false;

var handleLoad = function() {

    var container = document.getElementById("container");

    game = new OmegaCity({ container : container,
            loadCallback : onLoadComplete,
            loadProgressCallback : onLoadProgress,
        });

    hud = new ProxyHUD({game : game});

    sound = new OmegaCitySound({game : game});
```

After creating the game objects, we then load the overlay view in file *wv.html*, by calling the CocoonJS application method `loadInTheWebView()`:

```
        setTimeout(function() {

            CocoonJS.App.onLoadInTheWebViewSucceed.addEventListener(
                function(url) {
                    CocoonJS.App.showTheWebView();
                    Vizi.System.log("load web view succeeded.");
                    wvLoadComplete = true;

                    if (gameLoadComplete) {
                        gameReady();
                    }
                }
            );
            CocoonJS.App.onLoadInTheWebViewFailed.addEventListener(
                function(url) {
                    Vizi.System.log("load web view failed.", url);
                }
            );
            CocoonJS.App.loadInTheWebView("wv.html");
        }, 10);

        sound.enterState("load");
        game.load();

    }
```

The overlay view contains all the markup and JavaScript code to implement the HTML elements the overlay comprises (Example 12-6). Open the file *Chapter 12/omegacity-iOS/wv.html* to see an excerpt. After the markup for the HUD objects, we include CocoonJS-specific files to help manage the view, and then we create some objects of our own, but these are only for use in the user interface. (Again, there are proxy objects, this time for the game and sound classes. We will go through this shortly.)

*Example 12-6. Overlay view code for CocoonJS application*

```
<!-- Loading message -->
<div id="loadStatus" style="display:none">
Loading...
</div>
<!-- Click-to-start screen -->
<div id="startScreen" style="display:none">
<!-- Logo -->
<div id="logowtext"></div>
<div id="startScreenText">
Welcome to Omega City, the frontier outpost of the galaxy.
You and your squad are humanity's
last best hope as aliens attack.<br></br>
To save the city... you may have to destroy it!
</div>

... <!-- more markup here -->
```

```
<script src="./libs/cocoon_cocoonjsextensions/CocoonJS.js">
</script>
<script src="./libs/cocoon_cocoonjsextensions/CocoonJS_App.js">
</script>
<script
src="./libs/cocoon_cocoonjsextensions/CocoonJS_App_ForWebView.js">
</script>
<script src="omegacityGameProxy.js"></script>
<script src="omegacityProxySound.js"></script>
<script src="omegacityHUD.js"></script>
<script>

    var hud = null;
    var game = null;
    var sound = null;

var onload = function() {

    hud = new OmegaCityHUD();
    sound = new ProxySound();
    game = new OmegaCityGameProxy();
}
```

We need to do one more thing to bring these two views together: make sure that we can see through the overlay view. So we modify the CSS for the overlay view by setting the background color of all body elements to transparent. See the file *Chapter 12/omegacity-iOS/css/omegacity.css*. Here is the CSS:

```
body {
    background-color:rgba(0, 0, 0, 0);
    color:#11F4F7;
    padding:0;
    margin-left:0;
    margin-right:0;
    overflow:hidden;
}
```

### Managing communication between the canvas and overlay views

The overlay web view provided by CocoonJS is implemented as a WebView control that is layered on top of the main CocoonJS canvas view. This architecture has a major implication: the JavaScript virtual machine driving the canvas view is actually completely separate from the JavaScript virtual machine running scripts in the WebView. In other words, the two scripting engines are executing in different contexts, most likely even using two completely different JavaScript virtual machines! The VM for the main view is using the CocoonJS VM, while the WebView control on top is using whatever scripting engine comes native with the platform. If you write code in the main view that tries to call functions in the overlay view, your code will fail because those functions are not implemented, and vice versa. However, CocoonJS provides a way for the two views to talk to each other, by sending messages. Happily, it does this without our having to understand the details.

CocoonJS provides an application method, `forwardAsync()`, which allows us to pass strings between the two contexts. The strings will be evaluated via JavaScript `eval()`. So, to call a function in the other context, just create a string that, when evaluated, calls the function.

To make this kind of code more readable, we'll wrap each `forwardAsync()` call into a straightforward method call on a "proxy" object: calling the method of the proxy object, under the hood, calls `forwardAsync()`, which in turn sends the message to the other ("remote") context. When the message is evaluated, the function in the other context is called, and it can finally call the method of the remote object.

To illustrate, let's look at the code that starts the game when the START label is clicked. This code, in *Chapter 12/omegacity-iOS/omegacityProxyHUD*, shows a method from the `OmegaCityGameProxy` class that forwards a message from the overlay view to the main view:

```
OmegaCityGameProxy.prototype.play = function() {
    CocoonJS.App.forwardAsync("playGame();");

}
```

The code in the main view that handles receiving the `playGame()` message tells the sound engine to play the main game sounds, and then tells the real game object to start playing.

```
function playGame() {
    sound.enterState("play");
    game.play();
}
```

In the other direction, there are events occurring within the game that can update the display, such as decrementing the missile counter when a missile is fired. And when the alien ship gets close, we set a proximity alert, which updates the message area at the top with new blinking red text. We implement these methods of the HUD using a proxy object for the HUD that sends messages in the other direction—that is, from the main view to the overlay view.

```
ProxyHUD.prototype.enterState = function(state, data) {

    CocoonJS.App.forwardAsync("hudEnterState('" + state + "','" +
      data + "');");

}
```

The overlay view code then handles the `hudEnterState()` message by calling the real HUD object's `enterState()` method:

```
function hudEnterState(state, data) {
    console.log("HUD state: " + state + " " + data);
    hud.enterState(state, data);
}
```

The design patterns just shown may seem strange, but they are actually fairly common in systems that feature *interprocess communication* (IPC) using techniques such as *remote procedure calls* (RPC), where two separate computer processes communicate with each other via messages that are wrapped in function calls.

The CocoonJS two-view architecture essentially requires use of RPC if we want to build an HTML5-based overlay on our hybrid application. The process of writing proxy code in both directions is a bit tedious, and could be made easier with automated tools; in my discussions with Ludei's developers, they have hinted that this is in the works.

## Hybrid WebGL Development: The Bottom Line

In this section, we explored developing a mobile 3D application with HTML5, using a hybrid approach: a native app that uses a WebView for the HTML, plus a native library to emulate the WebGL API. This approach is something we need to consider for environments such as iOS, where WebGL is not enabled in the Mobile Safari and Mobile Chrome browsers.

We took a look at Ludei's CocoonJS as one possible hybrid solution. CocoonJS allowed us to easily assemble the application without requiring us to learn native APIs like Cocoa for iOS. We did, however, need to go through an extra step to enable an HTML5 overlay view. Because CocoonJS is not a full web browser, just a canvas renderer, we needed to separate all HTML5 UI elements into a second WebView control, and mediate communication between that view and the canvas using special JavaScript APIs. While that solution isn't without its limitations, it is good enough for many uses. CocoonJS, however, is not open source, and the company is actively exploring options for licensing the tool to developers. An open source alternative is Impact Ejecta, but using that library requires extensive iOS development knowledge. It is also a little less polished, a work in progress.

The bottom line with 3D hybrid development is that there is no one ideal solution. But there are viable development options, depending on your needs and budget.

# Mobile 3D Performance

Mobile platforms are more resource-challenged than their desktop counterparts, typically having less physical memory, and less powerful CPUs and GPUs. Depending on the network setup and/or data plan for the device, mobile platforms can also be bandwidth-challenged. Whether you are building a browser-based web application, a pure HTML5 packaged web app, or a native/HTML5 hybrid using CocoonJS or Ejecta, you will need to pay special attention to performance when developing your mobile 3D applications.

While a full treatment of performance issues is out of scope for this book, we can take a quick look at some of the more prominent concerns and cover a few techniques to keep in our back pocket. In no particular order, here are some performance topics to bear in mind:

*JavaScript memory management*
JavaScript is an automatically garbage-collected language. What this means in plain English is that programmers do not explicitly allocate memory, the virtual machine does it; it also frees memory when it is no longer used and reclaims it for later use, in a process known as *garbage collection*. By design, garbage collection happens whenever the VM decides it's a good time. As a consequence, applications can suffer from palpable delays when the VM needs to spend time garbage collecting. There are many techniques for reducing the amount of time the VM spends in garbage collection, including:

- Preallocating all memory at application startup
- Creating reusable "pools" of objects that can be recycled at the behest of the developer
- Returning complex function values in place by passing in objects, instead of by returning newly created JavaScript objects
- Avoiding closures (i.e., objects that hang on to other objects outside the scope of a function that uses them)
- In general, avoiding using the new operator except when necessary

Mobile platforms in particular can really feel the pain of garbage collection, given that they have less memory to work with in the first place.

*Less powerful CPUs and GPUs*
One way that manufacturers are able to make mobile devices lighter and less expensive is to use less powerful, less expensive parts, including the central processing unit (CPU) and the graphics processing unit (GPU). While mobile platforms are becoming surprisingly powerful, they are still not as fierce as desktops. To go easy on smaller CPUs and GPUs, providing a better user experience and potentially saving battery life, consider the following strategies:

- *Delivering lower-resolution 3D content.* 3D content can tax both the CPU and the GPU of a mobile device. For phones especially, there may not be a reason to deliver very high resolution, since there aren't that many pixels on the display.

Why waste the extra resolution? This technique will also help alleviate the data payload for less powerful data networks, via smaller download sizes. On the flipside, the newer tablets are providing very high resolution for their size. So a careful balance must be struck.

- *Watching your algorithms.* A really fast machine might mask bad code; however, a mobile device will likely cast a sharp spotlight on it. As an example, try tapping on the metal body of the Futurgo on the Kindle Fire HDX version. Sometimes you will see a pregnant pause as the code tries to figure out which object was hit. This is a side effect of the picking implementation inside Three.js; the code uses algorithms that were never optimized, and it shows on a small device. Someday this code will either get fixed in Three.js or implemented differently and better in a framework like Vizi, but for now, keep an eye on potential performance gotchas like this, and if need be, work around them to give the processors a break.

- *Simplifying shaders.* GLSL-based shaders can get complex—so complex that in fact the compiled code on the machine can blow out hardware limits on the more limited chips in some mobile devices. Take care to simplify your shaders when deploying on those platforms.

### Limited network resources

For devices on mobile data networks or using restricted data plans, it is good to try to economize on data transfer. 3D content is rich, and presents the possibility of pushing more bits down the wire. Think about the following ideas when designing your applications:

- *Prepackaging assets.* If you are able to deliver a packaged web app, this is ideal. The content is delivered exactly once, when the app is installed.

- *Using the browser cache.* If possible, design your assets to take advantage of the browser cache to avoid downloading them more than necessary.

- *Batching assets.* This now-classic web performance technique can save on the number of network requests and server roundtrips. If delivering multiple bitmaps, for example to implement a progress bar, consider packing the bitmaps into CSS image sprites (i.e., all images are stored in one file, with offsets into the file specified in CSS).

- *Using binary formats and data compression.* A big motivation for the glTF file format described in Chapter 8 is to reduce file sizes, and therefore download times, by using a binary representation. This technique can be combined with server-side compression and even domain-specific compression algorithms, such as 3D geometry compression, to further reduce download times and the burden on the data network.

# Chapter Summary

This chapter surveyed the brave new world of developing mobile 3D applications using HTML5 and WebGL. Mobile platforms are reaching parity with desktop platforms in terms of power; at the same time, HTML5 has been infused with new features directly influenced by the great new capabilities of today's mobile devices. Most mobile platforms now support 3D: CSS3 is everywhere, and WebGL works in all mobile browsers except for Mobile Safari and Mobile Chrome on iOS.

The process of developing WebGL for mobile browsers is remarkably simple. Existing applications generally just work with no modification. However, mouse-based input must be replaced with touch input. We looked at how touch events were added to the Vizi viewer to implement swiping to rotate and pinching to zoom. We also added tap handling to the Futurgo model so that touching various parts of the car brings up overlays. To facilitate developing and testing touch features on the desktop, we can set up desktop Chrome to emulate touch events. We can also use WebGL code to create packaged 3D applications, "web apps" for the platform, using packaging and distribution technologies provided by the platform vendor, such as Amazon's Mobile App Distribution Portal.

For browser platforms that do not support WebGL, we can use adapter technologies such as CocoonJS and Ejecta to create "hybrid" applications combining HTML5 with native code. This allows us to build in JavaScript and deploy a fast, platform-compliant native application, and potentially access features only available on the native platform, such as in-app purchases and push notifications.

Finally, we took a quick look at mobile performance issues. While mobile platforms have progressed by leaps and bounds in the last few years, they still tend to be less powerful than desktop systems. We need to be mindful about performance—in particular, memory management, CPU and GPU usage, and bandwidth—and design accordingly.

# Resources

This appendix lists 3D web development resources by category. I frequent many of the following sites to find the latest technical information, libraries, tools, cutting-edge demos, and thought pieces by leaders in the 3D development community.

## WebGL Resources

### The WebGL Specification

The WebGL standard is developed and maintained by the Khronos Group, the industry body that also governs OpenGL, COLLADA, and other specifications you may have heard of. You can find the latest version of the official WebGL specification on the Khronos website (*http://www.khronos.org/registry/webgl/specs/latest/1.0/*).

### WebGL Mailing Lists and Forums

Khronos maintains a public mailing list to discuss drafts of the WebGL specification. You can subscribe to the list *public_webgl@khronos.org* by following the instructions at *http://www.khronos.org/webgl/public-mailing-list/*.

There is also a Google group for discussing more general WebGL development topics outside of the core specification. You can sign up for this list at *http://goo.gl/CJIvC4*.

## WebGL Blogs and Demo Sites

There are many fantastic blog sites devoted to WebGL development. Here are some that I visit on a regular basis:

*Learning WebGL (http://learningwebgl.com/blog/)*
> The granddaddy of WebGL sites, created by Giles Thomas and currently maintained by me. This should be your very first stop to learn the basics of low-level WebGL programming and use of the API. It also features a weekly roundup of the latest WebGL demos and development projects.

*Learning Three.js (http://learningthreejs.com/)*
> The blog site of Jerome Etienne, focused on Three.js techniques and hands-on development.

*TojiCode (http://blog.tojicode.com/)*
> Google engineer Brandon Jones's blog, featuring a wealth of in-depth technical information on the WebGL API and expert development topics.

*Three.js on Reddit (http://www.reddit.com/r/threejs)*
> A Reddit for Three.js, maintained by Theo Armour and updated frequently. This Reddit is a grab bag of demos, techniques, news, and articles.

*WebGL.com*
> Curated by New York–based Darien Acosta, this is a site for discovering new WebGL games, demos, and applications.

*WebGL Mozilla Labs Demos (https://developer.mozilla.org/en-US/demos/tag/tech:webgl/)*
> Demos created by Mozilla Labs and partners.

*WebGL Chrome Experiments (http://www.chromeexperiments.com/webgl)*
> Demos created by Google and partners.

## WebGL Community Sites

I host a WebGL Meetup group for the Bay Area (*http://www.meetup.com/WebGL-Developers-Meetup/*). There are also WebGL Meetups in Los Angeles, New York, Boston, London, and elsewhere. Meetups are a good way to get together with like-minded individuals. If you don't live around San Francisco, search Meetups.com for a WebGL group in your area, or start one yourself!

There is also a LinkedIn group (*http://www.linkedin.com/groups?gid=2426944*) and a Facebook page (*https://www.facebook.com/groups/webgl/*).

# CSS3 Resources

## CSS3 Specifications

The World Wide Web Consortium (W3C) maintains the core CSS3 specifications covering 3D transforms, transitions, animations, and filter effects:

*http://www.w3.org/TR/css3-transforms/*
*http://www.w3.org/TR/css3-transitions/*
*http://www.w3.org/TR/css3-animations/*
*http://www.w3.org/TR/filter-effects/*

CSS Custom Filters, covered in Chapter 6, is primarily championed by Adobe. It is not yet widely supported in browsers—at the moment it is only in Chrome—so you should take care when developing with it. The latest information can be found at *http://adobe.github.io/web-platform/samples/css-customfilters/*.

## CSS3 Blogs and Demo Sites

David DeSandro, currently working at Twitter, has created the best resource for understanding how to use CSS 3D transforms (*http://24ways.org/2010/intro-to-css-3d-transforms/*).

Codrops (*http://tympanus.net/codrops/*), a web design and development blog, has several great demos of CSS 3D effects, including the 3D Book Showcase (*http://tympanus.net/codrops/2013/01/08/3d-book-showcase/*) highlighted in Chapter 6.

Dirk Weber's HTML5 development site, *http://www.eleqtriq.com*, features several compelling CSS 3D demonstrations.

Keith Clark has pushed the CSS envelope, creating a mind-blowing first-person shooter demo entirely in CSS 3D (*http://blog.keithclark.co.uk/creating-3d-worlds-with-html-and-css/*).

Microsoft's Kirupa Chinnathambi provides deep information about CSS Transitions and Animations. In particular, see the articles at *http://bit.ly/kirupa-transitions* and *http://bit.ly/kirupa-animations*.

Bradshaw Enterprises (*http://css3.bradshawenterprises.com/*) has several worthwhile articles, how-tos, and resources for learning about CSS3 transitions, transforms, animations, and filter effects.

# Canvas Resources

## Canvas 2D Context Specification

The 2D Canvas API specification is maintained by W3C. You can find the latest specification at *http://www.w3.org/TR/2dcontext2/*.

## Canvas 2D Tutorials

As discussed in Chapter 7, developers can create 3D applications that are rendered with the 2D Canvas API using Three.js or K3D/Phoria (described shortly). These libraries hide the details of 2D Canvas rendering, providing high-level 3D constructs to program with. However, if you want to learn about what is under the hood in the 2D Canvas API, there are a host of resources online. Here are a few links that I found quite helpful in doing research for the book:

> *http://bit.ly/canvas-tutorial*
> *http://bit.ly/draw-graphics-w-canvas*
> *http://www.w3schools.com/html/html5_canvas.asp*
> *http://diveintohtml5.info/canvas.html*

# Frameworks, Libraries, and Tools

## 3D Development Libraries

The last few years have seen the emergence of several open source 3D JavaScript libraries. Here is a list of some good ones, in no particular order:

*Three.js (http://threejs.org/)*
> By far the most popular scene graph library for developing WebGL applications, Three.js has been used to develop many of the well-known flagship WebGL demos. It provides an easy, intuitive set of objects that are commonly found in 3D graphics. It is fast, using many best-practice graphics engine techniques. It is powerful, with several built-in object types and handy utilities. Three.js also features a plug-in rendering system, allowing 3D content to be rendered (with some restrictions) to the 2D Canvas API, SVG, and CSS3 with 3D transforms. Three.js is well maintained, with several authors contributing to it.

*SceneJS (http://www.scenejs.org/)*
> An open source 3D engine for JavaScript that provides a JSON-based scene graph API on WebGL, SceneJS specializes in efficient rendering of large numbers of individually pickable and articulated objects as required by high-detail model-viewing applications in engineering and medicine. SceneJS also supports physics

and provides some higher-level constructs than Three.js, such as an event model and jQuery-style scene graph API.

*GLGE (http://www.glge.org/)*
GLGE is a JavaScript library intended to ease the use and minimize the setup time of WebGL, so that developers can then spend their time creating richer content for the Web. GLGE has good support for the basics but is not as feature-rich as either Three.js or SceneJS.

*K3D and Phoria (http://www.kevs3d.co.uk/dev/phoria/)*
K3D, and its successor Phoria, render 3D graphics using only the 2D Canvas API. Phoria is the creation of UK-based Kevin Roast (*http://www.kevs3d.co.uk/dev/*; @kevinroast on Twitter). Kevin is a UI developer and graphics enthusiast. While Phoria is early in its development and not as feature-rich as Three.js, it is very impressive. In particular, it is fast and does a great job with shading and textures. However, given that Phoria is built with a software renderer, it is limited in its 3D capabilities. Certain 3D features are nearly impossible to implement (or implement well) in software only.

## 3D Game Engines

We are now seeing many WebGL game engines hit the market. These libraries are a good choice for building games and complex 3D applications, but perhaps are overkill for simple 3D development projects. (For more on this, see the next section on frameworks.) Unless otherwise stated, the game engines listed here are open source:

*playcanvas (http://www.playcanvas.com/)*
London-based playcanvas has developed a rich engine and cloud-based authoring tool. The authoring tool features real-time collaborative scene editing to support team development; GitHub and Bitbucket integration; and one-button publishing to social media networks. As of this writing, playcanvas distributes the source code to the client engine; however, it has not published licensing terms.

*Turbulenz (http://biz.turbulenz.com/developers/)*
Turbulenz is an extremely powerful, open source, royalty-free game engine, packaged as a downloadable SDK. The company charges royalties if developers want to publish through its network (*https://turbulenz.com/#*). Turbulenz is the most intense of the APIs, with a huge class set and steep learning curve. It is definitely for experienced game developers. Turbulenz offers its client-side library in open source, reserving other parts of the system (server, virtual economy, etc.) for revenue generation.

*Goo Engine (http://www.gootechnologies.com/)*
> Goo recently released an invite-only beta of its engine and content creation tool. In addition to its engine, the company offers an easy-to-use content creation frontend targeting mainstream web developers. As of this writing, Goo is not open source.

*Verold (http://www.verold.com/)*
> A lightweight publishing platform for 3D interactive content developed by Toronto-based Verold, Inc., which describes it as "a no-plugin, extensible system with simple JavaScript so that hobbyists, students, educators, visual communication specialists and web marketers can integrate 3D animated content easily into their web properties." Like Goo, Verold is targeting general web graphics development with a simplified frontend to a complex game engine. As of this writing, Verold is not open source.

*Babylon.js (http://www.babylonjs.com/)*
> Babylon.js, developed by Microsoft employee David Catuhe as a personal project, is an easy-to-use engine that lies somewhere on the spectrum between Three.js and a hardcore game engine, in terms of feature set and ease of use. The demo site shows a range of applications, from space shooters to architectural walkthroughs.

*KickJS (http://www.kickjs.org/)*
> An open source game engine and rendering library created by Morten Nobel-Jørgensen, this project grew out of his academic work. KickJS appears to have less development and support behind it than the other game engines listed here. It is included in the study primarily because, of any of the game engines covered, KickJS most closely follows established best practices in modern game engine design.

## 3D Presentation Frameworks

The need to rapidly accelerate 3D development has led to the creation of several experimental presentation frameworks. Unlike a full game engine, the emphasis of these frameworks is fast and easy embedding of graphics on a page, for data visualization, product viewing, simple animations, and so on.

*Voodoo.js (http://www.voodoojs.com/)*
> The goals of Voodoo.js are to make it easy to create 3D content, and easy to integrate it into web pages. Voodoo.js features an extremely simple API for adding 3D models to web pages: just supply the model URL, the id of a DIV element, and a few configuration parameters, and you have 3D on a page. Voodoo.js does little beyond simple model viewing on a page, but for that use alone it is good.

*tQuery (http://jeromeetienne.github.io/tquery/)*
> tQuery is the creation of Jerome Etienne, who operates the popular blog site Learning Three.js (*http://learningthreejs.com/*). Modeled after the jQuery library, tQuery aims to provide "Three.js Power + jQuery API Usability"—that is, a very simple

API to the Three.js scene graph. It uses a chained-function programming style and supports high-level interactive behaviors via callbacks. Using tQuery can save many lines of Three.js handcoding. It is probably not accurate to call tQuery a framework, since it is more of a nonintrusive library in the spirit of jQuery. tQuery can be a timesaving boon for Three.js developers looking to save a few keystrokes.

*PhiloGL (http://www.senchalabs.org/philogl/)*
PhiloGL is an experimental package that was created by data visualization scientist Nicolas Garcia Belmonte while working at Sencha, Inc.'s labs. The goal of PhiloGL is "to make WebGL programming as fun and easy as developing with any of the mainstream frameworks." Garcia describes his design philosophy in this introductory blog posting (*http://bit.ly/sencha-philoGL*). Even though this framework is experimental, it merits a look. Sencha, Inc., develops world-class user interface frameworks and knows a thing or two about creating effective user interfaces with HTML5. The PhiloGL website contains several working examples, including a port of the entire set of tutorials from Learning WebGL (*http://www.learning webgl.com/*).

*Vizi (https://github.com/tparisi/Vizi)*
A presentation framework of my own design, Vizi embodies several years of experience developing earlier 3D frameworks and engines (such as VRML and X3D). Vizi incorporates current game engine best practices, most notably its use of components and aggregation to build higher levels of functionality, versus class-based inheritance. The goal of Vizi is to make it easy to quickly build interesting 3D applications. Like Voodoo.js, Vizi allows the developer to drop a model into a page with a few lines of code; however, it also provides a complete high-level API for adding interaction, animations, and behaviors to any element in a scene.

# 3D Authoring Tools

## Traditional modeling and animation packages

Autodesk (*http://www.autodesk.com/*) supplies a range of 3D modeling and animation software packages. Prices tend to be on the higher side, though the company is beginning to offer learning and trial editions that merit a try.

In addition to the Autodesk professional suites, there are several free or very affordable packaged software options for creating 3D content, including:

*Blender (http://www.blender.org/)*
A free, open source, cross-platform suite of tools for 3D creation, Blender runs on all major operating systems and is licensed under the GNU General Public License (GPL). Blender was created by Dutch software developer Ton Roosendaal, and is maintained by the Blender Foundation, a Netherlands-based nonprofit organiza-

tion. Blender is extremely popular, with the foundation estimating two million users. It is used by artists and engineers from hobbyist/student level to professional.

*SketchUp (http://www.sketchup.com/)*
SketchUp is an easy-to-use 3D modeling program used in architecture, engineering, and to a lesser degree, game development. You can find free and low-cost professional SketchUp downloads at their site.

*Poser (http://poser.smithmicro.com/)*
An intermediate 3D tool for character animation, Poser, like SketchUp, is priced attractively and targets a casual content creation audience. It has an intuitive user interface for posing and animating characters. Poser comes with a large library of modeled, rigged, and fully textured human and animal characters as well as set background scenes and props, vehicles, cameras, and lighting setups. Poser is used to create both photorealistic still renderings and real-time animations.

### Browser-based integrated environments

With cloud computing and the ability to render in WebGL, we are seeing a new kind of authoring tool: the in-browser 3D integrated development environment. The following tools are still early in development but very promising.

*Goo Create (http://www.gootechnologies.com/)*
The Goo engine, described earlier, comes with an easy-to-use content creation frontend targeting mainstream web developers. Goo Create also features several prebuilt models and animations to get developers started.

*Verold Studio (http://www.verold.com/)*
Verold Studio is a browser-hosted 3D content creation tool and programming environment that comes with the Verold game engine, described previously.

*Sketchfab (http://sketchfab.com/)*
Sketchfab is a web service to publish and share interactive 3D models online in real time without a plugin. With a few clicks, the artist can upload a 3D model to the website in any of several formats, and get the HTML code for sharing an embedded view of the model, hosted on the Sketchfab website.

*SculptGL (https://github.com/stephomi/sculptgl)*
A free and open source web-based solid modeling tool with a very easy-to-use interface for creating simple sculptured models, SculptGL features export to various formats, and direct publishing to both Verold and Sketchfab.

# Animation Frameworks

Today's applications should use `requestAnimationFrame()` to animate content. To ensure cross-browser support for this feature, use Paul Irish's great polyfill (*http://paulir ish.com/2011/requestanimationframe-for-smart-animating/*).

---

For simple tween-based animations, Tween.js (*https://github.com/sole/tween.js*) is a popular open source tweening utility created by Soledad Penadés.

For key frame animation, there are some built-in classes that come with Three.js, and a few more in the examples shipped with the project. This is an area that will evolve as more tools come online and web-friendly content formats like glTF mature.

## Debugging and Profiling WebGL Applications

New versions of browsers come with a variety of WebGL debugging and profiling tools. Patrick Cozzi, graphics architect at AGI (developer of Cesium, a WebGL-based virtual globe and map engine), has compiled an excellent roundup of browser built-in WebGL tools (*http://www.realtimerendering.com/blog/webgl-debugging-and-profiling-tools/*).

## Mobile 3D Development Resources

Adding touch support is key to creating compelling mobile 3D applications. The browser touch events specification can be found on the W3C recommendations pages (*http://www.w3.org/TR/2013/REC-touch-events-20131010/*).

Android's developer pages (*http://developer.android.com/guide/webapps/index.html*) contain thorough information on developing HTML5-based web apps.

Amazon has an extensive system for publishing web apps, including a Web App Tester application for the Android-based Kindle Fire OS (*https://developer.amazon.com/sdk/webapps/tester.html*), and an app distribution portal for packaging and distributing the final app (*https://developer.amazon.com/sdk/webapps/manifest.html*).

On environments that do not natively support WebGL, such as iOS, there are "hybrid" technologies for building applications that combine HTML5 and JavaScript with native code. While Adobe's PhoneGap (*http://phonegap.com/*) is the kingpin of mobile hybrid libraries, it does not currently support WebGL. For WebGL support on iOS, use one of the following hybrid frameworks:

CocoonJS (*http://www.ludei.com/tech/cocoonjs*)
> CocoonJS runs on Android and iOS. It hides the details of the underlying system in an easy-to-use application container for HTML5 and JavaScript code. It provides implementations of Canvas, WebGL, Web Audio, Web Sockets, and more. CocoonJS also comes with a system for building projects in the cloud, so all you have to do is sign your project and build it; developers do not need to understand the intricacies of creating applications using native platform tools such as Xcode for iOS. CocoonJS is a closed source project tightly controlled by its developer, San Francisco–based Ludei.

*Ejecta (http://impactjs.com/ejecta)*

An open source library that supplies many of the same features as CocoonJS, but for iOS only, Ejecta was born out of ImpactJS, a project to create a game engine for HTML5. Ejecta is a bit more DIY, requiring the developer to have a fair amount of knowledge about Xcode and native platform APIs. Ejecta is open source.

# 3D File Format Specifications

3D file formats fall into three general categories: model formats, used to represent single objects; animation formats for animating key frames and characters; and full-featured formats that support entire scenes, including multiple models, transform hierarchy, cameras, lights, and animations. There are many 3D file formats, too numerous to list here.

The following 3D formats are best suited for developing web applications.

## Model Formats

- Wavefront OBJ (*http://en.wikipedia.org/wiki/Wavefront_.obj_file*)
- STL—text-based 3D printing file format (*http://en.wikipedia.org/wiki/STL_%28file_format%29*)

## Animation Formats

- id Software MD2 (*http://tfc.duke.free.fr/coding/md2-specs-en.html*) and MD5—character animation formats (*http://tfc.duke.free.fr/coding/md5-specs-en.html*)
- BioVision BVH animation format for motion capture (*http://research.cs.wisc.edu/graphics/Courses/cs-838-1999/Jeff/BVH.html*)

## Full-Scene Formats

- VRML (*http://bit.ly/web3d-vrml*) and X3D (*http://bit.ly/web3d-x3d*)—the original web 3D formats
- COLLADA—digital asset exchange schema (*http://www.khronos.org/files/collada_spec_1_4.pdf*)
- glTF—Graphics Library Transmission Format (*http://gltf.gl/*)

# Related Technologies

3D development doesn't happen in a vacuum. There are other interesting web technologies that you may want to consider incorporating into your 3D projects. Here are a few.

## Pointer Lock API

For full-screen 3D applications such as games, you might want to have finer control over mouse input than the traditional DOM windowed events provide. To that end, browsers recently introduced the Pointer Lock API, which allows developers to hide the mouse cursor and get low-level mouse motion events in the style required for game development.

John McCutchan of Google has written a nice introduction to using the Pointer Lock API (*http://www.html5rocks.com/en/tutorials/pointerlock/intro/*).

You can find the current W3C specification for the Pointer Lock API at *http://www.w3.org/TR/pointerlock/*.

## Page Visibility API

Sixty-frame-per-second 3D applications can consume machine cycles. If the tab or window for an application is not currently visible, then there is no need to render the scene. Also, the application might still want to compute results when it is in the background, but just not as frequently. Recent browsers support a new feature, the Page Visibility API, that allows developers to know when pages or tabs aren't visible, and adjust execution accordingly to conserve machine resources.

There is a good overview of the Page Visibility API on Google's developer site (*https://developers.google.com/chrome/whitepapers/pagevisibility*).

You can find the current W3C specification for the Page Visibility API at *http://www.w3.org/TR/page-visibility/*.

## WebSockets and WebRTC

If you are developing a multiplayer 3D game, virtual world, or real-time collaborative application, you will need to implement communication between web clients and servers. Two technologies for doing this are WebSockets and WebRTC.

WebSockets (more formally, the WebSocket specification) is a standardized browser implementation of the TCP/IP protocol. It can be used for two-way communication between clients and servers. TCP/IP was not originally designed for real-time communication, so WebRTC (described next) may be more appropriate, depending on the needs of your applications. There is a tutorial on WebSockets (*http://net.tutsplus.com/*

*tutorials/javascript-ajax/start-using-html5-websockets-today/*), and you can visit the main WebSockets project page (*http://www.websocket.org/*).

WebRTC is a standard for sending real-time messages between web clients and servers. It may be more suitable for multiuser messaging than the WebSocket protocol, as it was designed from the ground up for real-time messaging. For a tutorial, refer to *http://www.html5rocks.com/en/tutorials/webrtc/basics/*. The main project page, maintained by Google, is at *http://www.webrtc.org/*, and the current W3C recommendation is located at *http://www.w3.org/TR/webrtc/*.

## Web Workers

Web Workers (*http://www.w3.org/TR/workers/*) support multithreaded programming in JavaScript. 3D applications can benefit from doing certain tasks in background threads, such as loading models or running physics simulations. By performing those tasks in the background, the application can ensure that the user interface is always responsive, even when the application is handling computationally intensive operations.

There are subtleties to using Web Workers, such as passing memory objects between threads. There is a great article on *HTML5 Rocks* that goes into the details (*http://updates.html5rocks.com/2011/12/Transferable-Objects-Lightning-Fast*).

## IndexedDB and Filesystem APIs

3D files can get big. For your projects, you may want to consider using new HTML5 technologies that can help save download overhead by storing your data locally on the user's hard drive. Browser caches can't be relied on, because they aren't that big, and they are not under application control—the user can clear the cache at any time, or other web data may push your application's content out of the cache.

Ray Camden, a developer evangelist at Adobe and one of the technical reviewers for this book, mentioned the idea of using IndexedDB, the browser database API, to store local data. He wrote an article on the topic in the context of developing rich SVG applications (*http://bit.ly/camden-richSVG*). You can find the IndexedDB specification at *http://www.w3.org/TR/IndexedDB/*.

IndexedDB is not a filesystem, however. It is a database API. If you want to store and retrieve content on the user's computer using a filesystem-style API, you are in luck. There is an experimental API called the FileSystem API (*http://www.w3.org/TR/filesystem-api/*). With this API, web applications can read and write files and hierarchical folders on the user's hard drive. There is an excellent tutorial located on *HTML5 Rocks* (*http://www.html5rocks.com/en/tutorials/file/filesystem/*). Note that the FileSystem API is currently supported only in desktop Chrome and Opera. Also note that this API is not to be confused with the File API (*http://www.w3.org/TR/FileAPI/*), which allows only for read access to the local filesystem.

# Index

## Symbols

% mod operator, 103
100,000 Stars project, 3–4
2D Canvas API
    3D rendering libraries and, 174–182
    additional resources, 364
    background, 164
    drawing features, 166–171
    programmable shaders and, 16
    rendering 3D, 172–174
    Three.js rendering, 176–182
    WebGL and, 163
3D environments, 157
    (see also developing 3D environments)
    browser-based integrated, 196–200
    rendering, 157–159
    WebGL framework and, 232
3D geometry
    creating, 29–33
    CSS3 support, 158
    prebuilt geometry classes, 60–65
    prebuilt geometry types, 59–60
3D graphics
    background, 3–4
    browser support, 7
    cameras, 13, 52
    coordinate systems, 9
    defined, 8
    geometry in, 29–33, 59–65

    lights, 11, 55–57, 79–81
    materials, 11, 53, 72–78
    matrices, 13, 24
    meshes, 10, 53, 65–67
    perspective, 13
    polygons, 10
    projections, 13, 24
    rendering with Canvas API, 172–174
    scene graphs, 67–72
    shaders, 14–16, 25–27, 32, 86
    shadows, 81–86
    textures, 11, 34–41, 53
    transform hierarchy, 68–72, 139–141
    transforms, 12–13
    vertices, 10, 23
    viewports, 13, 23
    Vizi framework, 242
    WebGL framework, 232
3D libraries, 174–182
3D modeling, 188
3D objects, 283
    (see also developing 3D applications)
    animating, 33
    depth-sorted, 33
    rendering, 133, 155–157, 160, 172, 283
    scene graphs and, 67
    shaders for, 25
    texture mapping and, 189
    transforming, 61, 141

*We'd like to hear your suggestions for improving our indexes. Send email to index@oreilly.com.*

inspecting
    object properties, 284, 290–291
    scene graphs, 283–289
integration
    browser-based environments and, 196–200
    content into applications, 254, 267–269,
        301–307
    environment with applications, 282
interactions
    developing, 254, 270–279
    Vizi framework, 242, 246–249
    WebGL framework and, 232
interpolation technique
    described, 105
    key frames and, 110
    morphing and, 119
    tweening and, 105
Interpolator class, 111
Irish, Paul, 100

## J

JavaScript Virtual Machine, 6
Jones, Brandon, 24
Jones, Norah, 43
JSFiddle tool, 199
JSON file format, 120
JSONLoader class, 122, 218

## K

K3D library, 175
key frames
    in animation, 98, 110–115, 189
    articulated animation, 113–115
    curves and paths, 116–118
    defined, 98, 110
    interpolation and, 110
    Keyframe.js utility, 110–113
Keyframe.js utility, 110–113
KeyFrameAnimation class, 115
KeyFrameAnimator class, 111
Khronos Group, 18, 195, 207, 213
KickJS game engine, 236
Kindle Fire HDX, 335
Klas (OutsideOfSociety), 121, 204
Klumpp, Uli, 196

## L

Lambertian reflectance, 73
@Last Software, 194
lava effect animation, 125
Learning WebGL site, 22
lights
    ambient, 79
    common properties, 79
    CSS3 support, 158
    defined, 11
    directional, 56, 79
    glTF format support, 213
    lighting scenes, 55–57, 79–81
    point, 79
    spotlights, 79
    Vizi framework, 261
Lightwave modeler, 283
linear interpolation, 105
Luppi, Daniele, 43

## M

manifest file, 344
materials
    adding realism with multitexturing, 74–78
    defined, 11, 53, 72
    glTF format support, 213
    material types, 57, 73
    standard mesh, 73–74
matrices
    defined, 13
    WebGL example, 24
Maya package (Autodesk)
    described, 192
    exporting scene to COLLADA, 257–259
    pricing, 192
    timeline controls, 189
McCutcheon, John, 311
McKegney, Ross, 197
MD2 file format, 120, 204
MD5 file format, 204
memory management, 233, 358
Mesh class, 66, 219
MeshBasicMaterial class, 73
meshes
    adding to scenes, 53
    defined, 10
    glTF format support, 213
    importing from modeling packages, 66–67

## About the Author

**Tony Parisi** is an entrepreneur and career CTO/architect. He has developed international standards and protocols, created noteworthy software products, and started and sold technology companies. Tony's passion for innovating is exceeded only by his desire to bring coolness and fun to the broadest possible audience.

Tony is perhaps best known for his work as a pioneer of 3D standards for the Web. He is the co-creator of VRML and X3D, ISO standards for networked 3D graphics. He also co-developed SWMP, a real-time messaging protocol for multiuser virtual worlds. Tony continues to build community around innovations in 3D as the co-chair of the WebGL Meetup and a founder of the Rest3D working group.

Tony is currently a partner in a stealth online gaming startup and has a consulting practice developing social games, virtual worlds, and location-based services for San Francisco Bay Area clients.

## Colophon

The animal on the cover of *Programming 3D Applications with HTML5 and WebGL* is a MacQueen's bustard (*Chlamydotis macqueenii*), a large bird that ranges through the Middle East and southwestern Asia. It is named after General Thomas MacQueen, a 19th century British soldier who was stationed in India. MacQueen was a collector of natural history specimens and donated a bustard he had shot to the British Museum; the bird was named after him in 1832.

MacQueen's bustards live and breed in arid sandy areas, with a diet made up of seeds, plant shoots, and insects. While females are slightly smaller, the birds are generally about 2 feet in length, with an average wingspan of 55 inches. They have light brown plumage, black stripes on their necks, and white underbellies. The fluffy feathers on their head and neck are fanned out in mating displays—this species does not often vocalize. They nest in holes scraped in the ground, laying 2–4 eggs at a time.

This species (and a close relative, the Houbara bustard) are becoming rare, as they are a popular target for falconers and have been overhunted. Some Middle Eastern leaders, including the royal families of Saudi Arabia and the United Arab Emirates, have made conservation efforts in recent years, but the birds' status is still vulnerable.

The cover image is from Johnson's *Natural History*. The cover fonts are URW Typewriter and Guardian Sans. The text font is Adobe Minion Pro; the heading font is Adobe Myriad Condensed; and the code font is Dalton Maag's Ubuntu Mono.

# Have it your way.

# Get even more for your money.

## Join the O'Reilly Community, and register the O'Reilly books you own. It's free, and you'll get:

- $4.99 ebook upgrade offer
- 40% upgrade offer on O'Reilly print books
- Membership discounts on books and events
- Free lifetime updates to ebooks and videos
- Multiple ebook formats, DRM FREE
- Participation in the O'Reilly community
- Newsletters
- Account management
- 100% Satisfaction Guarantee

### Signing up is easy:

1. **Go to: oreilly.com/go/register**
2. **Create an O'Reilly login.**
3. **Provide your address.**
4. **Register your books.**

Note: English-language books only

**To order books online:**
oreilly.com/store

**For questions about products or an order:**
orders@oreilly.com

**To sign up to get topic-specific email announcements and/or news about upcoming books, conferences, special offers, and new technologies:**
elists@oreilly.com

**For technical questions about book content:**
booktech@oreilly.com

**To submit new book proposals to our editors:**
proposals@oreilly.com

**O'Reilly books are available in multiple DRM-free ebook formats. For more information:**
oreilly.com/ebooks

**O'REILLY®**

Spreading the knowledge of innovators      **oreilly.com**

9 781449 362966